Political Communication in America

Recent Titles in the
Praeger Series in Political Communication
Robert E. Denton, Jr., *General Editor*

Campaign Craft: The Strategies, Tactics, and Art of Political Campaign Management
Daniel M. Shea

Inside Political Campaigns: Theory and Practice
Karen S. Johnson-Cartee and Gary A. Copeland

Rhetorical Studies of National Political Debates—1996
Robert V. Friedenberg, editor

Communication Consultants in Political Campaigns: Ballot Box Warriors
Robert V. Friedenberg

Manipulation of the American Voter: Political Campaign Commercials
Karen S. Johnson-Cartee and Gary A. Copeland

Presidential Crisis Rhetoric and the Press in the Post–Cold War World
Jim A. Kuypers

The 1996 Presidential Campaign: A Communication Perspective
Robert E. Denton, Jr., editor

Reconciling Free Trade, Fair Trade and Interdependence: The Rhetoric of Presidential Economic Leadership
Delia B. Conti

Politics and Politicians in American Film
Phillip L. Gianos

Electronic Whistle-Stops: The Impact of the Internet on American Politics
Gary W. Selnow

Newspapers of Record in a Digital Age: From Hot Type to Hot Link
Shannon E. Martin and Kathleen A. Hansen

Campaign '96: A Functional Analysis of Acclaiming, Attacking, and Defending
William L. Benoit, Joseph R. Blaney, and P. M. Pier

Political Communication in America

THIRD EDITION

Robert E. Denton, Jr.
and Gary C. Woodward

Praeger Series in Political Communication

PRAEGER

Westport, Connecticut
London

Library of Congress Cataloging-in-Publication Data

Denton, Robert E., Jr.
Political communication in America / Robert E. Denton, Jr. and Gary C. Woodward. — 3rd ed.
p. cm. — (Praeger series in political communication, ISSN 1062–5623)
Includes bibliographical references and index.
ISBN 0–275–95782–9 (alk. paper). — ISBN 0–275–95783–7 (pbk. : alk. paper)
1. Communication in politics—United States. 2. United States—Politics and government. I. Woodward, Gary C. II. Title.
JA85.2.U6D46 1998
306.2'0973—DC21 98–24557

British Library Cataloguing in Publication Data is available.

Library of Congress Catalog Card Number: 98–24557
ISBN: 0–275–95782–9
ISBN: 0–275–95783–7 (pbk.)

First published in 1998

Praeger Publishers, 88 Post Road West, Westport, CT 06881
An imprint of Greenwood Publishing Group, Inc.

Printed in the United States of America

The paper used in this book complies with the Permanent Paper Standard issued by the National Information Standards Organization (Z39.48–1984).

10 9 8 7 6 5 4 3 2 1

We dedicate this book to our children:
Bobby and Chris,
Hilary and Trevor

Contents

Series Foreword

Those of us from the discipline of communication studies have long believed that communication is prior to all other fields of inquiry. In several other forums I have argued that the essence of politics is "talk" or human interaction.[1] Such interaction may be formal or informal, verbal or nonverbal, public or private, but it is always persuasive, forcing us consciously or subconsciously to interpret, to evaluate, and to act. Communication is the vehicle for human action.

From this perspective, it is not surprising that Aristotle recognized the natural kinship of politics and communication in his writings *Politics* and *Rhetoric*. In the former, he established that humans are "political beings [who] alone of the animals [are] furnished with the faculty of language."[2] In the latter, he began his systematic analysis of discourse by proclaiming that "rhetorical study, in its strict sense, is concerned with the modes of persuasion."[3] Thus, it was recognized over twenty-three hundred years ago that politics and communication go hand in hand because they are essential parts of human nature.

In 1981, Dan Nimmo and Keith Sanders proclaimed that political communication was an emerging field.[4] Although its origin, as noted, dates back centuries, a "self-consciously cross-disciplinary" focus began in the late 1950s. Thousands of books and articles later, colleges and universities offer a variety of graduate and undergraduate coursework in the area in such diverse departments as communication, mass communication, journalism, political science, and sociology.[5] In Nimmo and Sanders's early assessment, the "key areas of inquiry" included rhetorical analysis, propaganda analysis, attitude change studies, voting studies, government and the news media, functional and systems analyses, technological changes, media technologies, campaign techniques, and research techniques.[6] In a survey of the state of the field in 1983, the same authors and Lynda Kaid found additional, more specific areas of concerns such as the presidency, political polls, public opinion, debates, and advertising.[7] Since the first study, they have also noted a shift away from the rather strict behavioral approach.

A decade later, Dan Nimmo and David Swanson argued that "political communication has developed some identity as a more or less distinct domain of scholarly work."[8] The scope and concerns of the area have further expanded to include critical theories and cultural studies. Although there is no precise definition, method, or disciplinary home of the area of inquiry, its primary domain comprises the role, processes, and effects of communication within the context of politics broadly defined.

In 1985, the editors of *Political Communication Yearbook: 1984* noted that "more things are happening in the study, teaching, and practice of political communication than can be captured within the space limitations of the relatively few publications available."[9] In addition, they argued that the backgrounds of "those involved in the field [are] so varied and pluralist in outlook and approach, . . . it [is] a mistake to adhere slavishly to any set format in shaping the content."[10] More recently, Swanson and Nimmo have called for "ways of overcoming the unhappy consequences of fragmentation within a framework that respects, encourages, and benefits from diverse scholarly commitments, agendas, and approaches."[11]

In agreement with these assessments of the area and with gentle encouragement, in 1988 Praeger established the series entitled "Praeger Series in Political Communication." The series is open to all qualitative and quantitative methodologies as well as contemporary and historical studies. The key to characterizing the studies in the series is the focus on communication variables or activities within a political context or dimension. As of this writing, over 70 volumes have been published and numerous impressive works are forthcoming. Scholars from the disciplines of communication, history, journalism, political science, and sociology have participated in the series.

I am, without shame or modesty, a fan of the series. The joy of serving as its editor is in participating in the dialogue of the field of political communication and in reading the contributors' works. I invite you to join me.

Robert E. Denton, Jr.

NOTES

1. See Robert E. Denton, Jr., *The Symbolic Dimensions of the American Presidency* (Prospect Heights, IL: Waveland Press, 1982); Robert E. Denton, Jr., and Gary

Woodward, *Political Communication in America* (New York: Praeger, 1985; 2d ed., 1990); Robert E. Denton, Jr., and Dan Hahn, *Presidential Communication* (New York: Praeger, 1986); and Robert E. Denton, Jr., *The Primetime Presidency of Ronald Reagan* (New York: Praeger, 1988).

2. Aristotle, *The Politics of Aristotle*, trans. Ernest Barker (New York: Oxford University Press, 1970), p. 5.

3. Aristotle, *Rhetoric*, trans. W. Rhys Roberts (New York: The Modern Library, 1954), p. 22.

4. Dan D. Nimmo and Keith R. Sanders, "Introduction: The Emergence of Political Communication as a Field," in *Handbook of Political Communication*, ed. Dan D. Nimmo and Keith R. Sanders (Beverly Hills, CA: Sage, 1981), pp. 11–36.

5. Ibid., p. 15.

6. Ibid., pp. 17–27.

7. Keith Sanders, Lynda Kaid, and Dan Nimmo, eds., *Political Communication Yearbook: 1984* (Carbondale: Southern Illinois University, 1985), pp. 283–308.

8. Dan Nimmo and David Swanson, "The Field of Political Communication: Beyond the Voter Persuasion Paradigm," in *New Directions in Political Communication*, ed. David Swanson and Dan Nimmo (Beverly Hills, CA: Sage, 1990), p. 8.

9. Sanders, Kaid, and Nimmo, *Political Communication Yearbook: 1984*, p. xiv.

10. Ibid.

11. Nimmo and Swanson, "The Field of Political Communication," p. 11.

Preface

Humans are, according to Aristotle's *Politics*, "political beings," and "he who is without a polis, by reason of his own nature and not of some accident, is either a poor sort of being [a beast] or a being higher than man [a god]" (Aristotle 1970, 5). And because nature makes nothing in vain, Aristotle continues, a human "alone of the animals is furnished with the faculty of language" (6). Thus, it was recognized over 2,000 years ago that politics and communication go hand in hand because they are essential parts of human nature. Both fields claim the subject matter of other fields as part of their own content. Nearly every topic that is fit for comment by someone contains the seeds for political and communication analysis. Neither field, of course, can claim an area of interest that is exclusively its own. Each necessarily crosses the boundaries and invades terrain with more neatly defined borders. Advances in medical technology, for example, can be praised or blamed by how they are described. And such descriptions usually have a significant impact on the discussions of the proper role of the state in the control of new technologies. The communication analyst is always a guest (if not an intruder) on someone else's turf. But communication is fundamental to all other fields of inquiry. What we know about events is always revealed first through the communicator's skill and art.

The focus of this edition has not substantively changed from that of previous ones. It concerns the roles and functions of communication in U.S. politics and not on the "politics of communication." In describing the processes common to "political communication," the priorities of the writers would be better reflected if the two terms were reversed. This volume is first about the possibilities and problems inherent to public discussion in an advanced industrial society. It is to a lesser extent about political institutions and controversial issues. Although the frameworks for our analysis utilize conventional categories of political activity—for example, campaigns, activity in Congress, the courts, the mass media, and the presidency—the essential points of our analysis hinge on what we consider to be pivotal communication processes.

We posit that the essence of politics is "talk" or human interaction. Such interaction is formal and informal, verbal and nonverbal, public and private—but always persuasive in nature, causing us to interpret, to evaluate, and to act. Communication provides the basis of social cohesion, issue discussion, and legislative enactment. While certainly not a new perspective today, fifteen years ago, upon publication of the first edition, the role of human interaction within the realm of politics was seldom the focus of study within the discipline of political science and was viewed as somewhat problematic within the growing social science perspectives within the discipline of communication studies.

As perhaps befits a work on politics, our work is still very much eclectic. The point of view developed in these pages consistently centers on the ideas common to the interactionist and dramatistic perspectives. Both now represent an important tradition in descriptive studies within the social sciences. But we are also indebted to the substantial body of survey research on political attitudes as well as traditional historical and biographical works that enrich our knowledge of the polity. Thus, we have built our case with a variety of materials and sources from the disciplines of political science, communication, history, journalism, and sociology as well as firsthand sources, including private memoranda, memoirs, speeches, and journalistic accounts.

Readers familiar with the previous editions will notice rather drastic changes in this new edition. Wherever possible, we have attempted to condense our arguments and make the book more accessible to both students and general readers. We have also updated sources from the wealth of recent publications in the area as well as ideas with newer examples. In addition, we retained references to classic historical works and examples that serve to not only illustrate a theory, practice, or concept, but also to remind us of critical turning points in the art and practice of American politics. In many ways, this is a "new" book with completely new chapters and organization. In comparison to the last edition, you will note new chapters on the topics of campaign management, congressional campaigns, politics and popular culture, and "unofficial Washington."

After political communication is defined in the introductory chapter, Part I focuses on the contexts of political communication. The chapters therein attempt to describe the social suspicion of governmental processes and public distrust of contemporary politics, to provide a theoretical perspective of the role of communication in society as well as identify unique functions and uses of political language, and to examine the role of media in politics. Part II examines campaign planning, management, and strategies as well as specific exploration of presidential and legislative campaigns. Part III focuses on governing—the functions, strategies, and tactics of political communication within the institutions of the presidency, Congress, and "unofficial Washington." Finally, we conclude with a discussion on the growing public interest in issues of crime, justice, and the courts as well as explore the communication of political themes in entertainment.

This edition, as others, reflects a reality that we did not wish to gloss over in deference to the heuristic device of a "single theme." Because the subject matter is necessarily broad, the work as a whole is more horizontal than vertical. While the first chapter provides useful groundwork for the later ones, the reader can successfully read the chapters separately as well as in the sequence in which they are published. We made no special effort to weave an artificial thread of continuity in what is a naturally complex and varied range of subjects.

We also resisted the temptation to give our observations and conclusions an air of finality. The reader may be surprised to see that points are argued as much as they are asserted. Many studies of political activity work from a framework of actual (or grammatically induced) certainty. Such certainty is often unjustified. We think the book speaks to a basic reality about polities that needs to be constantly acknowledged—namely, that political communication is about people making choices of indeterminate quality that will produce indeterminate effects. Of this much we are certain: No subject is more worthy of study than the communication processes that can nurture or starve a nation's civil life.

REFERENCE

Aristotle. 1970. *The Politics of Aristotle*, trans. Ernest Barker. New York: Oxford University Press.

Acknowledgments

We are both pleased and humbled by the response to the first and second editions of this book. To know that the book was useful to friends, colleagues, and students was reward enough for undertaking yet another revision. We have benefited from comments, suggestions, and reviews provided over the years. To those of you who were kind enough to share your reactions to the first and second editions, we sincerely hope you will do the same to this one.

In the nearly fifteen years since the first edition, the field of political communication as a distinct area of study has experienced tremendous growth. As was the case for the earlier editions, an incalculable number of communication and political writers have influenced our own thinking. We have borrowed and adapted material from all of them—we hope with some degree of success. But, of course, any shortcomings in our work are the fault of the "other" coauthor.

Although truly a joint effort, each author received help and support from individuals and institutions that deserve special recognition.

Robert Denton: I wish to thank my colleagues in the Department of Communication Studies at Virginia Polytechnic Institute and State University for their personal encouragement in completing the revision. I also want to thank Robert Bates, Dean of the College of Arts and Sciences, for his continued support of administrative, professional, and scholarly activities. Together they generate a rich environment that makes my job a privilege and pleasure. Finally, as is always the case, it is family and friends that sustain us, encourage us, and provide a sense of belonging and security that frees us to read, write, and pursue projects of interest. Thankfully, they provide a wonderful life beyond academe.

Thanks to Bobby, Chris, and Rachel for enriching, and in many ways, saving my life.

Gary Woodward: I am indebted to the generous support of the Faculty and Research and Sabbatical Committee at the College of New Jersey for several grants that provided time for writing. I also acknowledge the help of the National Endowment for the Humanities for a Summer Study Fellowship at the University of Wisconsin.

Chapter 1

Political Communication Defined

> Within the life of the generation now in control of affairs, persuasion has become a self-conscious art and a regular organ of popular government. None of us begins to understand the consequences, but it is no daring prophecy to say that the knowledge of how to create consent will alter every political calculation and modify every political premise.
>
> Walter Lippmann (1930)

As we approach the millennium, America is experiencing an unparalled period of peace and prosperity. We "won" the "cold war," interest rates are low, the rate of inflation is the lowest since World War II, and we are even reducing the national deficit with a united call from both political parties for a balanced budget in the future. Yet, voter turnout for the most recent presidential election was the lowest since 1924, where less than half of all registered voters participated in the defining act of democracy. So the question becomes, does this lack of interest reflect satisfaction with the candidates and the status quo or growing cynicism of our political system?

For over a decade, academics, journalists, and social critics have noted an increasing feeling of frustration and anger of Americans towards government and politicians. The watershed elections of 1992 and 1994 revealed increasing waves of anger among all voters. "Anger" became the political watchword of the 1990s and the unifying target of the social anger was *government* (Cappella and Jamieson 1997; Tolchin 1996; Craig

1996). Government became the scapegoat for all that was perceived wrong in our society.

According to Francis Fukuyama (1995), Americans are experiencing a "crisis of trust." In the aftermath of winning the "cold war," the political climate became one of public distrust, cynicism, and even fear. At least according to public opinion polls, many Americans have lost confidence in the government and trust in elected officials and politicians. Government and the political process are viewed as dominated by special interest rather than the common interests of all Americans. Citizens feel caught between the crossfire of self-interested politicians, special interest groups, and mega corporations. At the least, they are unhappy with the nature of politics itself.

But we recognize that one cannot escape "politics." Politics, broadly defined, is the "currency" of social life. From the sublime to the ridiculous, politics impact our lives on a daily basis. Just consider the wide range of activities determined by politics:

- Who serves in office and how long
- Where we send troops
- The laws that are passed
- When we can vote, drive, or enter contracts
- The rate of taxes and the level of services
- What is taught in school
- Is a road built or is a bridge safe
- When our garbage is collected

And consider the range of *feelings* that flow out of political discourse:

- Frustration that "our" group has been neglected by the state legislature
- Elation with a trial verdict that confirms our beliefs
- Annoyance with the president for backing away from a campaign pledge
- Pride in press reports that the president has decided to fight for a favored federal program
- Anger at the offhand remarks of a leader in the Senate
- Inspiration from a feature film in which the leading character demonstrates political courage

However one defines politics, it cannot be avoided.

Human communication is the vehicle for political thought, debate, and action. David Easton (Nimmo and Swanson 1990, 33), from a system perspective of politics and human behavior, demonstrates the role of communication in "politics." Our political system processes a multitude of inputs from our social environment that become outputs of political structures, values, and actions. Communication channels the inputs, structures the outputs, and provides feedback from political system to the environment. The vast multitude of interactions literally construct our political, economic, and social institutions. According to Nimmo and Swanson (1990),

> in its political dimensions, communication is a force for both conflict and consensus; political campaigns in liberal democracies are about both change and stability; strong empirical evidence can be adduced for, and valuable insights derived from, conceiving political communication as both empowerment and marginalization, produced and consumed by citizens who are more or less autonomous, cognitive, intentional, and creative actors as well as shaped by powerful historical, social, and other structures. (22)

GENERAL CHARACTERISTICS OF POLITICAL COMMUNICATION

While the forms and types of political messages are nearly limitless, there are commonalities among them. Although many features of messages that we discuss in this book are not exclusive to the political world, they are more than casual companions to it.

Short-Term Orientation

Among the most common realities governing political life is a general preoccupation with transitory issues and limited time frames. Messages are typically planned, prepared, and delivered with an eye to immediate outcomes. They must enter the continuous flow of public discussion within a period that is beneficial to the communicator and timely for the mass media and their audiences. The limited and specific time frames for political campaigns are rather obvious. But the public discussion and consideration of issues are comprised of many rather distinct "campaigns" and specific initiatives. Issues are discussed in a variety of ways, over periods of time. Yet, for each action taken, for each piece of legislation passed to deal with an aspect of a larger social issue, very specific and planned communication takes place within a specific time frame and with a specific outcome in mind.

The controversy over abortion, for example, did not end with the Supreme Court ruling of *Roe v. Wade*. Across the nation, political discussion, debate, and legislation has centered on various questions such as, When may abortions be performed? What constitutes "legal" versus "illegal" abortions? Who should perform abortions, technicians or physicians? Should there be some provisions for parental notification? Should procedures called "partial birth abortions" be allowed to continue? Each question leads to discussion, debate, and perhaps to referendums and legislation. Most political communication benefits from a "window of opportunity" that can pass as quickly as it appears. Every election generates calls for campaign finance reform, direct election of presidents, limitations of negative advertising, and banning of announcements of returns before the polls close across the nation. However, specific action in these areas is woefully lacking.

Political communicators seek practical and immediate results. Their effectiveness usually hinges on their adaptation to the transient nature of public opinion and the fleeting attention of the mass media. They are often criticized for "rudderless" and "hypocritical" beliefs. Yet, taken on its own terms, political communication can only be understood when there is a willingness to reconstruct the immediate political context—the relevant climate of opinion—that a public figure felt duty-bound to honor. While it may be the case that novels, inspirational speeches, movies, and other forms of communication may permit measurement against "timeless" standards, serious attempts to shape opinion rarely profit from comparisons against similar invariant critical yardsticks. The first major address by newly elected Jimmy Carter to confront the pending "energy crisis" was the unveiling of the National Engery Plan that included 113 separate initiatives that today appear naive and unrealistic. Even Abraham Lincoln's venerated speeches from the 1858 Senate campaign will appear to the modern reader as dated: intended for a different age with vastly different values and needs.

Communication Based on Objectives

Political behavior is almost always directed to some specific end, even when it takes on the appearance of predictable ritual. What is overlooked in the common complaint that political talk is a "meaningless" substitute for political action is the important fact that it is often intended to increase the prospects of the talker, the agent for the ideas. Every political campaign tries to fulfill this objective, giving credibility to a campaigner by making him or her the vehicle for reasonable proposals and familiar values. Perceptions of a candidate's intellectual honesty and authenticity typically rank high among these values.

According to Brian McNair (1995), political communication is "purposeful communication about politics" (4). This includes all forms of communication by political actors (politicians) for achieving specific objectives, communication addressed to political actors by nonpolitical actors, and communication about political actors and their activities. Political actors, according to Blair, are "those individuals who aspire, through organizational and institutional means, to influence the decision-making process" (5). Thus, "purposeful" communication is directive, "persuasive" communication designed to alter a belief, attitude, value, or lead to some action.

Importance of the Mass Media

The mass media are basic to the study of politics. Political communication is largely mediated communication. No claim about the conduct of modern political life seems more self-evident. Speeches, press conferences, pleas for support, and justifications of controversial decisions all imply the presence of constituencies—audiences for those acts. Most of those audiences are only reached by the extended coverage provided by public media.

Political reporting is dedicated—in philosophy if not always in practice—to a "watchdog" role over those public officials who are clearly within their own sphere of influence. In the familiar terms of this philosophy, the free press performs an "adversary" function that provides a check, a "fourth branch of government," to keep a wary eye on the other three. "The only security of all," Thomas Jefferson said, "is in a free press." This role is an obvious and largely undisputed objective of the political press in America. And yet for all of its familiarity, the norm of a constitutionally protected independent press is perhaps the greatest single contribution the United States has made to the lore of democracy.

The mass media function in an important second way, a way that reverses the familiar "reporter"/"subject" relationship. In forms that are detailed more fully in Chapter 4, the political press "controls" as well as "reports." Especially in this century, journalists have sometimes been able to lead rather than just follow the course of an unfolding political story. Critics claim that too many politicians lead by reacting to the whims of public opinion polls rather than leading by creating public opinion by argument, information, and public debate. Too often, the practice of U.S. politics requires the ability to respond to an agenda of issues and events largely fabricated or generated in America's newsrooms. The political newsmaker still initiates the raw materials for many stories, but the control and management of political information is now largely in the hands of privately controlled news and entertainment enterprises.

When Theodore Roosevelt denounced the "muckraking press" just after the turn of the century, he was not paying a compliment to the new investigative muscle of the William Randolph Hearsts or Ida Tarbells. He was making what has since become a familiar complaint based on the realization that the public media place their own commercial demands on those engaged in political discourse. Like nearly all politicians of his time and later, he savored the attentions of the press, but not their insatiable thirst for stories intended to capture the public imagination. The narrative thread of political news almost always carries within it popular images of good and evil, heroes and villians, and national fantasies of justice and injustice.

As we will discuss, the media compete with politicians to set public agendas, define issues, and frame public debate. For the public, the mass media become the primary source of political information, knowledge, and opinion on issues and campaigns of concern.

Politics as Audience-Centered

Political actors are motivated by the desire to gain the support of specific constituencies. "Political" messages are not neutral. Messages are created with a targeted audience in mind. Such an audience-centered approach properly forces the analyst to think in terms of the processes that govern the search for a consensus, or to its unmaking. The arts of compromise, emphasis, de-emphasis, and simplification are all very much a part of this process. Rather than lamenting the avenues for blatant manipulation that are implicit in such a point of view, we prefer to think of an audience-centered activity as wholly natural and nominally democratic. There can be no doubt that politics offers the potential for pandering to the lowest of human impulses. The price we pay for an "open" political system is the risk that there will be excesses. We think the greater danger lies not in the manipulation of audience allegiances to political ideas, but in the society that minimizes opportunities for the articulation of such ideas, or gives only lip service to the rhetorical rights of the politically active. At their best, democratic societies are strengthened by exchanges between those in a position of authority, and by citizens with countervailing rights to revoke it.

Generally, then, we conceive of political communication as a practical, process-centered, decision-oriented activity. Because it is dependent on the approval of specific audiences, its utility is strongly restricted by time, and by the willingness of the political media to make its messages accessible. We have necessarily cast our net quite broadly. It includes speeches and addresses, whether heard firsthand or reported in highly edited segments. It also includes many other forms of public discussion: reports, "public" letters, defenses of administrative action or inaction, hearings, "mediated" accounts of events from the press, and even ostensibly "nonpolitical" messages such as films and prime-time television. Ultimately, a crucial factor that makes communication "political" is not the source of a message, but its content and purpose.

POLITICAL COMMUNICATION DEFINED

Misguided Expectations about Political Life

There is something inescapably seductive about describing political communication so that it is nearly synonymous with "obfuscation." Analysts are frequently tempted to characterize it in terms of the abuse it gives to some set notion of "The Truth." This tendency is based in part on what we think is the mistaken assumption that political address is primarily about discovering the "right" solution to a problem, or concealing the "wrong" one. If an observer believes that one side in a debate has the "correct" answer, the only possible way to explain the other side is in terms of the obfuscation of ideas. George Orwell's (1949) widely admired description of political address is a case in point:

> In our time, political speech and writing are largely the defense of the indefensible. Things like the continuance of British rule in India, the Russian purges and deportations, the dropping of the atom bombs on Japan, can indeed be defended, but only by arguments which are too brutal for most people to face, and which do not square with the professed aims of political parties. Thus political language has to consist largely of euphemism, question-begging and sheer cloudy vagueness. (363)

In *Political Language and Rhetoric*, Paul Corcoran (1979) provides a similar expression of disillusionment that functions implicitly as a kind of operational definition:

> Contemporary political language . . . has assumed a peculiar and in some sense an inverted social function as a technique of linguistic expression. This is borne out in the uses to which political language is often put: not to convey information, but to conceal or distort it; not to draw public attention, but to divert or suppress it. In short, contemporary political language may play precisely the reverse role from that classically conceived for political rhetoric. Instead of a rhetorical "method" to inform, persuade and enlighten, contemporary political language aims at an etiolated monologue which has no content, which placates, and which bears no relationship to the organization, coherency and clarification of information and ideas. (xv)

These descriptions are superficially likable; criticizing the rhetoric of U.S. political leaders is something of a national sport. But they actually tell us very little because they render political communication deficient by definition. The only task that remains for the analyst of a generic rhetoric of camouflage is to point out its inherent irrationality. Not surprisingly, it is much easier to do that than to explain how it works: how audiences are affected by it, how converts are made, and how groups and institutions adjust to its more fluent advocates. The counterpart definition for another subject—architecture, to pick an example—might be to label it as the "design and building of what are largely inadequate and deficient structures by people intent on profiting at the expense of others." Without doubt, architects do build ungainly and inhospitable structures. But the essence of architecture, like the essence of political communication, involves more. The problem, of course, is that negative definitions masquerade judgments as descriptions, indicting general processes by inviting consideration of negative examples to stand in for the whole. If one dislikes a policy, the easiest way to attack it is to dismiss the general category of communication used to defend it.

This debate over the nature of practical persuasion is far from new. Aristotle's seminal discussion of public advocacy in *Rhetoric* over 2,000 years ago was partly a rejection of the low priority to which Plato had relegated it. Plato craved certainty and exactitude from human institutions. Yet, while science and other "hard" subjects might build on such closed systems, audience-centered politics cannot. Aristotle (1954) noted that the arts of rhetoric were like many other skills that can be used for evil or beneficial purposes: "A man can confer the greatest benefits by a right use of these, and inflict the greatest of injuries by using them wrongly" (23).

Even so insightful a political analyst as Walter Lippmann at times succumbed to the temptation to find a scientific basis for a "public philosophy." Lippmann (1955) was a shrewd observer of the American political scene, yet he sometimes believed that discourse devoid of self-interest could produce something close to universal agreement on many political questions. He wrote overoptimistically, we think, that "All issues could be settled by scientific investigation and by free debate if—but only if—all the investigators and the debaters adhered to the public philosophy; if, that is to say, they used the same criteria and rules of reason for arriving at the truth and for distinguishing good and evil" (134).

But even in the limited politics of one small group his conditions probably could not be satisfied. It is unrealistic to base an understanding of political debate on the hope that there can be a kind of universal standard from which to measure its validity. On most political questions (i.e., questions involving choices with competing advantages to different constituencies) "The Truth" is not easily located. This is because politics is not primarily about truth telling, but consensus seeking. Political conflict typically concerns itself with decisions implying values or preferences rather than determinations of fact, even though there may indeed be relevant facts that should inform political debate. The bulk of most practical discourse is centered on the mobilization of public opinion: a process that involves rationality and fact-finding, but frequently denies a "superior" point of view.

As long as policy lies at the heart of politics, values will have to be discussed rather than precisely reckoned. Values admit to no one standard for judgment. As Lloyd Bitzer (1981) has written,

> The fact that human valuation interacts with contingent subject matter helps explain why political rhetoric must ever remain unscientific—that is, why it will refuse to be held to statements of the true-false variety. Values and interests will exert such force that persons contending in the same context and about the same subject will disagree in what they perceive and say, a political speaker will be inconsistent from one situation to another, and the perceived truth of political discourse will vary markedly across contexts. (233)

We endorse what seems to be the enlightened distinction made by Chaim Perelman (Perelman and Olbrechts-Tyteca 1969, 509–14) between arguments of all forms that "demonstrate" and those that "argue." The former tend to be analytic, arbitrary, and *a priori*: as in the synthetic formulas of physics and mathematics where the same conclusions are generated by a wide diversity of individuals. A true demonstration provides no reasonable basis for dissent. On the other hand "arguments"—the ever-present products of what may be legitimate differences of opinion—exist in the realm of preferences. Political conflict is "legitimate" when it originates in pluralist thought about values and priorities. A position put forward in a dispute is necessarily a combination of the individual's own intellectual and social history, and the history of the group that he or she seeks to influence.

Consider, for example, the ongoing politics involved in the federal government's management of national forests. To what extent should the National Forest Service permit the harvesting of timber on federal lands by private companies? Furthermore, should such sales of public timber be at market price or lower? Policy for land use may be set by unelected officials in the Forest Service or its parent agency, the Department of Agriculture. But debate may also flare up on this question in Congress and within the president's own staff. Facts will help various interested parties determine a position on this continually renewed debate, but the answer finally depends on how we rank the service's obligations to conservationists, lumber industries and their employees, and to the aesthetics of "harvesting" woodlands. There are clearly moral, logical, and evidentiary bases for arbitrating questions like this. But to start from the premise that political address is a form of obfuscation because it fails to tally with some *a priori* standard is to force it into alien territory. Such a perspective carries a reassuring certainty, but it fails to provide the tools that are necessary to discover the processes and varied perspectives that mediate political decisions.

Toward a Definition of Political Communication

Democratic politics is concerned with the power to decide. Everyday political acts function to influence decisions or defend them. Certainly since the time of ancient Greece, rhetoric is the lifeblood of democracy. Public discourse and persuasion are modes of information, knowledge, and political power. The public communication that accompanies most forms of political activity serves to alter, justify, or clarify the range of choices that are in dispute in the public arena. The more "open" the society and the more active the political press, the better the chances that rhetorical disputes will be productive vehicles for governance.

Thus, any definition of political communication addresses issues of content, intentions, and structure of such interactions. Craig Allen Smith (1990) defines political communication as "the process of negotiating a community orientation through the interpretation and characterization of interests, of power relationships, and of the community's role in the world" (vii). By examining the major concerns of those who study "political communication," Nimmo and Swanson (1990) define it as "the strategic uses of communication to influence public knowledge, beliefs, and action on political matters" (9). G. R. Boynton (1996) offers a different perspective by defining political communication as "conversations flowing through institutionalized channels punctuated by the vote" (109). The notion of "institutionalized channels" recognizes "sanctioned" locations or places of political conversations such as the courts, legislatures, media, or campaign events, to name only a few. Boynton's notion of "punctuated by votes" also recognizes the "acts" of democracy to include elections and legislative actions as well as public opinion polls that influence outcomes of public "conversations."

Brian NcNair (1995, 5) suggests another way to investigate political communication is to focus on the relationships of various elements. He identifies three elements: political organizations, media, and citizens. Political organizations are broad social collectivities that include political parties, public interest groups, social movement groups, or government. Media is the generic term to include all modes, means, and levels of mediated communication. McNair also views citizens as individuals or social groups with common purpose. What is interesting about this perspective is that the forms of communication define the relationships among the elements. Citizens write letters, make speeches, or form groups to impact the political environment. Media also have a wide range of activities that include writing stories, editorials, or commentary as well as providing analysis, taking polls, or simply providing platforms for citizens and political actors, to name just a few. Finally, political organizations orchestrate events, make news, contact citizens, media, etc. For McNair, the patterns and channels of communication provide the most insight in considering the scope of political communication activities.

The Four Concerns of Political Communication

We think the above definitions of political communication are valuable. Political communication *is* a process, *is* strategic, and *is* unique in terms of content. We view political communication as public discussion about the allocation of public resources (revenues), official authority (who is given the power to make legal, legislative, and executive decisions), official sanctions (what the state rewards or punishes), and social meaning (what does it mean to be an American and the role of citizen, implications of social policy, etc.). Such discourse makes its way into the life of the nation, state, or community when there is conflict between competing interests about what the "official" positions of various agencies of the state shall be. At best, the language of political communication is a valuable mediating agent that replaces sheer violent conflict and makes orderly change possible. It serves to prepare the way for eventual compromise and acceptance by making arguments, facts, and opinions a part of the public record on an issue. But it is also the language of the faction, of the "friend" and the "foe." It may sharpen differences beyond the point of repair, or it may dull them. It can be a vehicle to mask what should be highlighted, or it may actually repair what has been deeply divisive. One can express optimism for its ability to transform the society for the better; but one can also despair over its widespread abuse. The rhetoric of politics can be many things: therapeutic, divisive, alienating, inspiring, or informational.

Revenue

The much-vaunted cliche that politics is about the exercise and control of power finds its best examples in discourse involving the power to spend. Protracted negotiations over the allocation of scarce resources are common to every society. Potential alterations in the way public money is spent inevitably produce organized advocacy and opposition. Whether to build local baseball fields or repair decaying roads, whether to permit federal funding of abortions for poor women or the leasing of federal lands to oil speculators, all only hint at the broad range of resource-based debates that reach Americans daily. Not all political issues involve conflict over the use of public funds, but the exceptions are rare. Especially in the legislative arena, real commitments to legislative action are revealed more in amendments specifying how a given piece of legislation will be funded than in general endorsements of the legislation. Every city mayor and agency executive that is guided by these actions knows that the intent of most legislation inevitably exceeds what scarce available revenues will actually permit.

Control

The question of who decides is the focus of the political campaign. In all levels of government elected public officials are given the power to act as trustees of "the public interest." They may be municipal judges, school board officials, legislators, governors, or presidents. The heart of American faith in republican democracy resides in the assignment of power based upon the "consent of the governed." Unlike any other political event, the political campaign galvanizes the public by giving ephemeral political ideals a universal reference point in the features of a specific personality. Appealing to the electorate's shared vision of its future, the candidate uses real and invented traits of character to enact one part in an ongoing drama of contested leadership. Arguably, the power of the ballot may be overestimated in this age when so many complex bureaucracies and civil service systems have replaced the citizen-politician. But even though decreasing numbers of employees in the public sector are accountable through the electoral process, the chain of responsibility ends most dramatically with the elected leader. He or she is at least nominally accountable for the massive "professional" government that can never be voted in or out of office.

Sanctions

A class of political discussion arises from official statements that accompany administrative decisions, court rulings, and the consideration of legislation. Political sanctions are typically initiated as governmental actions—either legislated or enforced—which require the compliance of certain segments within the population. Laws defining criminal conduct are the most obvious forms of sanctions, but they may include a presidential decision to deploy new weapons systems in a foreign locale, or an attempt by some members of the Congress to forbid it. They are represented by the decision of a big city mayor to give tax incentives to a commercial developer, or the federal judge's award of precious water rights to a state bordering on a river. Because sanctions are governmental and judicial responses to problems that have usually created social conflict, they often set in motion a cycle of public discussion that pit political officials against a range of opposing factions. With the exception of judges, disputes frequently surface between the sanctioning agents of government and a wide variety of traditional opponents, including journalists, corporate leaders, opposing political leaders, academics, and even television writers. Any of these advocates may play for the attention of the larger public by focusing interest on the wisdom or failures of a public policy. In doing so, they frequently initiate public discussion on the wisdom of a sanction's advocates and detractors as well. Some of this discussion creates high political drama, because deep public divisions about where the state should impose its official and moral weight involve the highest of stakes, including fine-tuned feelings of status and well-being.

Meaning

The process of political communication does more than enact legislation and elect officials. As we will discuss in Chapter 2, political discourse defines issues and candidates as well as our roles as citizens and government, our beliefs and values as Americans, and our sense of "place" and history. As Americans, we struggle with historical views of the purpose of the Civil War or our role in Vietnam. We debate whether the act of abortion is a "medical procedure" or "merely murder." We question whether federal subsidies are "corporate welfare" or "engines of economic growth." Does affirmative action perpetuate discrimination or ensure equal opportunity? The issues and questions are countless. Through political communication we come to understand our values, issues, and culture.

THE MANIFEST AND LATENT FUNCTIONS OF POLITICAL DISCOURSE

Modern studies of communication fall generally into two fundamentally different approaches. The older and broader tradition is to examine and judge messages largely in light of their publicly stated purposes. These purposes involve the formal and "official" functions of discourse. Our definition of political communication cited above fits into this general pattern. To use the pivotal terms provided by sociologist Robert Merton (1968, 73–138), the *manifest* functions of communication are objectives that are intended to achieve clearly understood ends. Individuals publicly express their intentions to exert influence, to promote understanding, to educate, and to reinforce. Studies of national figures written by biographers and political journalists largely operate at this level, though the best are not naive about the subtle latent purposes to which an artful political defense can be put.

The newer tradition owes its origins to the social sciences, and to the strong analytical motive to "discount" public actions in favor of concealed or unconscious motives. This pattern did not originate with Sigmund Freud, but it perhaps received its most forceful perspective in the Freudian notion that human expression is a product of the mediation between an instilled sense of public duty, and ego-defensive needs

(Freud 1938, 102–50). We speak out to serve ideas and honorable civic goals. But it is also now an unshakable article of faith that we seek to nurture a public regard for our fragile inner selves.

The social sciences are partly built upon this premise. Human behavior with apparently simple motivations signifies infinitely more complex latent objectives: based in the psyche and its inner logic—a psycho-logic—rather than on the idealized rhetorical logic of the public forum. For example, Harold Lasswell's (1962) *Power and Personality* starts with the hypothesis that an individual's psychology governs some of his political choices. The "power seeker," he notes, "pursues power as a means of compensation against deprivation. Power is expected to overcome low estimates of the self" (39).

The analyst primed for the discovery of latent functions and content profitably considers instances of political communication both for what they say and what they signify. Political language naturally invites consideration of the private "investments," the personal and group needs, that are served under the benign symbolism of "the public interest." Some of the most penetrating political analyses in recent years have explored relationships between personal motives and public rhetoric, or between groups separated and protected by hierarchical distinctions.

To be sure, an interest in exploring private objectives hidden behind the manifest content of language is no guarantee of insight. Freud's own excessively psychoanalytic study of Woodrow Wilson, written with William Bullitt (1967), has the effect of reducing the former president to a one-dimensional caricature whose every decision was apparently the product of earlier discontents. Even so, the study of public rhetoric has been revolutionized in the last two decades by the search for ideological motives underpinning justifications that present themselves as something quite different. Following the lead of Freud and Karl Marx, Kenneth Burke (1953) especially influenced a wide range of political communication scholars to search for doctrinal "investments" in all sorts of public discourse.

Our position, however, cannot be reduced to only one approach. Political communication demands analysis and criticism in terms of its own manifest content. But to go no further denies valuable insights about the complex social and psychological processes that contribute to political discourse. We therefore reject a focus that is exclusively centered on structural and social explanations of political acts. We equally reject a purely message-centered view that overlooks the important roles that social and psychological pressures have on political outcomes. It is both a challenge and a source of frustration that even so simple an act of communication as a campaign speech cannot be reduced to a single invariant system of analysis. We believe that the eclecticism that exists in a well-rounded study of political communication has an important role.

It should help fill the enormous gaps of knowledge left between the time journalists have finished their immediate assessments and history has had its final say.

Our perspective thus suggests a good deal more than apparent headlines, newscasts, or even academic writings of political events. How do presidents perceive their office and role? To what extent must a political leader "own" the feelings his rhetoric seeks to arouse in others? What does the presence of a permanent video record of a politician's statements do to enhance or undermine his leadership? These questions all seek to explore the dimensions of decisions taken by a political leader in a specific setting. Many others could be considered from the point of view of the intended audiences. For instance, does the American public believe that campaign speeches are "written" by the candidate? And how do they view the national press when it "unmasks" carefully constructed public personas?

All of these questions center on the subject matter of this book, and indicate that our goals in these pages are varied and pragmatic. Like most political observers, we are intrigued by the ever-shifting relationships that exist between political agents and their inherited roles, their strategists, and their publics. But our communication orientation leads us to consider politics as an expressive as well as instrumental activity. The subject matter of this book includes more than traditional areas such as policy and leadership. It also involves explorations of public communication as the expression of acceptance and rejection, rewards and punishments, threats and reassurances. In these pages we continue to measure political messages against long-honored traditions that foster vigorous public debate in a democratic society. But we are also interested in the ways political values weave themselves into subtle rituals of daily life that have very little to do with formal political structures.

REFERENCES

Aristotle. 1954. *Rhetoric*, trans. W. Rhys Roberts. New York: The Modern Library.

Bitzer, Lloyd. 1981. "Political Rhetoric." In *Handbook of Political Communication*, ed. Dan D. Nimmo and Keith R. Sanders. Beverly Hills, CA: Sage, pp. 225–48.

Boynton, G. R. 1996. "Our Conversations about Governing." In *Political Communication Research*, ed. David Palez. Norwood, NJ: Ablex Publishing, pp. 91–109.

Burke, Kenneth. 1953. *A Rhetoric of Motives*. New York: Prentice-Hall.

Cappella, Joseph N., and Kathleen Hall Jamieson. 1997. *Spiral of Cynicism: The Press and the Public Good*. New York: Oxford University Press.

Corcoran, Paul E. 1979. *Political Language and Rhetoric*. Austin: University of Texas Press.

Craig, Stephen C. 1996. *Broken Contract? Changing Relationships between Americans and Their Governments*. Boulder, CO: Westview Press.

Freud, Sigmund. 1938. *A General Introduction to Psychoanalysis*, trans. Joan Riviere. Garden City, NY: Garden City Publishing.

Freud, Sigmund, and William C. Bullitt. 1967. *Thomas Woodrow Wilson*. Boston: Houghton Miffin.

Fukuyama, Francis. 1995. *Trust: The Social Virtues and the Creation of Prosperity*. New York: Free Press.

Lasswell, Harold. 1962. *Power and Personality*. New York: Viking.

Lippmann, Walter. 1930. *Public Opinion*. New York: Macmillan.

———. 1955. *The Public Philosophy*. Boston: Little, Brown.

McNair, Brian. 1995. *An Introduction to Political Communication*. London: Routledge.

Merton, Robert. 1968. *Social Theory and Social Structure*. New York: Free Press.

Nimmo, Dan, and David Swanson. 1990. "The Field of Political Communication: Beyond the Voter Persuasion Paradigm." In *New Directions in Political Communication: A Resource Book*, ed. David Swanson and Dan Nimmo. Newbury Park, CA: Sage, pp. 7–47.

Orwell, George. 1949. "Politics and the English Language." In *The Orwell Reader*. New York: Harcourt, Brace.

Perelman, Chaim, and L. Olbrechts-Tyteca. 1969. *The New Rhetoric*, trans. John Wilkinson and Purcell Weaver. Notre Dame, IN: University of Notre Dame Press, pp. 509–14.

Smith, Craig Allen. 1990. *Political Communication*. San Diego, CA: Harcourt Brace Jovanovich.

Tolchin, Susan. 1996. *The Angry American*. Boulder, CO: Westview Press.

Part I

Contexts

Chapter 2

The Disenfranchised Polity

> There is no politics in a totalitarian society because conflict is looked upon as a form of illness.
>
> John Bunzel (1970)

It was a small moment, no more than a minute or two. But sometimes simple events capture larger truths. In the midst of interviewing a collection of voters from a Maryland suburb, pollster Peter Hart had hit a wall of silence. The goal of this focus group session was to determine what voters thought about Bill Clinton's pledge to establish a program of national service. During the 1992 campaign Clinton had pushed repeatedly for a federal program that would encourage students to devote a year or two to community service projects. In return, they would get a modest grant to be used toward college or technical school. Modeled on the Peace Corps and other national service programs, Clinton's plan would put thousands of young adults from very different backgrounds to work on projects benefiting children, the elderly, and others in dire social straits.

Putting together a program that could win congressional support would be no easy matter. Clinton badly wanted to implement community service nationwide, and that fact made its defeat a high priority for his opponents.

On this day Hart set out to gauge what ordinary voters of various backgrounds thought about the idea. But the session was not going well. This focus group knew little about what the candidate had proposed in the campaign and was skeptical of Hart's description of the high ideals of national service. Moreover, several members volunteered the conclusion that similar programs had failed in the past. Did they think it was a good idea? "No," some volunteered, arguing that any government program was likely to be more of a failure than a success. Grasping for some common ground from which to proceed, Hart backed up to a more general question. He asked if they could name any federal program that worked well. He waited in silence, as the presidential staffer responsible for developing the Clinton plan looked on in frustration. It was perhaps 30 seconds before someone offered the space program, and—after another prolonged pause—the Peace Corps. More silence followed, but they were done. None of the eleven participants on this day was eager to offer examples of federal programs that worked well and contributed to the common good or wealth of the nation.[1]

Clinton himself would have filled in the void of silence without a pause, perhaps citing in one breath Head Start, The Family Leave Act, Social Security, landmark civil rights legislation, and the rules of the federal agencies that made American food, air, water, and transportation among the safest in the world. But after being coaxed into a halfhearted murmur of two examples, this group could think of nothing else to praise. Their silence spoke for them and for the polity's collective disenfranchisement with the ideal of an activist, problem-solving government.

Signs of this national fatigue are easy to locate. Voter turnout is often under half of even those who bother to register. And approval ratings for the institutions of government have precipitously declined over the years. The percent of the public with confidence in Congress now hovers in the high teens or low twenties, well down from a rare "high" of 40 percent after the Senate Watergate hearings (see Table 2.1). Presidents, who traditionally score higher, now feel fortunate to win the approval of just half of the American public (Saad 1995). According to the Gallup Organization, among major American institutions only the military, the presidency, and the Supreme Court inspire significant levels of confidence. Congress, the news media, big business, and the criminal justice system lag far behind.

As E. J. Dionne has noted in a widely quoted book, Americans have come to distrust politics.

> Over the last three decades, the faith of the American people in their democratic institutions has declined, and Americans have begun to doubt their ability to improve the world through politics. At a time when the people of Poland, Hungary, and Czechoslovakia are experiencing the excitement of self-government, Americans view politics with increasing boredom and detachment. For most of us, politics is increasingly abstract, a spectator sport barely worth watching. (1991, 10)

Table 2.1
Confidence in Institutions: A Legacy of Political Distrust

(Percent of Americans surveyed by the Gallup Organization saying "a great deal" or "quite a lot" when asked about "how much confidence" they had in major American institutions)

	1995	1983	1975
Military	64%	53%	58%
Organized Religion	57	62	68
Presidency	45	NA	NA
Supreme Court	44	42	49
Banks	43	51	NA
Public Schools	40	39	58*
Newspapers	30	38	39*
Television News	33	NA	NA
Organized Labor	26	26	38
Congress	21	38	40
Big Business	21	28	34
Criminal Justice System	20	NA	NA

*data from 1973

Source: Adapted from Leslie McAneny and David W. Moore, "American Confidence in Public Institutions on the Rise," 6 May 1995, *Gallup Organization Newsletter* (May) [online].

The low esteem attached to politics can be attributed to three broad causes, each considered in the following sections of this chapter. The first is the historical American antipathy to governmental power and authority. The second is the rise of "identity politics," which has undermined faith that the great polity of the United States shares the same values and goals. The third is the intensification of partisan and nonconciliatory discourse, particularly in Congress. All of these causes are a reminder that political communication in the 1990s must be understood in the context of suspicion about governmental processes and the fundamental health of the nation's civil affairs.

THE POLITICAL CONNECTION: A HISTORY OF AMBIVALENCE

In some ways, Americans have not come lately to their concerns about the machinery of democratic institutions. Misgivings of all things political has always been part of the genetic code of the American body politic. The battle for independence was not so much a revolution in ideas as a rebellion against the financial and legal interventions of the British government. The colonists wanted less rather than more of King George's participation in their lives. As John Dewey noted, the American experience was "deeply tinged by a fear of government" and a desire to "reduce it to a minimum so as to limit the evil it could do" (Dewey 1954, 86).

In the founding documents of the Declaration of Independence and the Constitution's early amendments, government is defined by its limits, by the absence of controls and restrictions on the individual. The First Amendment, for example, grants freedom of the press, speech, and religion by declaring that "Congress shall make no law" that would abridge them. And Article Two is notably stingy in assigning powers to the president. He (or she) was to be no monarch.[2] In the strict terms of the Article, this elected official was to have little to do beyond functioning as commander in chief over the military.

The period of the revolution was energized by the idea that the rule of the crown was intrusive and unjustified. Nowhere was this more apparent than in the issue of taxation. The Boston Tea Party was only the most visible revolt against taxes. In 1766 members of Britain's Parliament questioned Ben Franklin at great length about rising American hostility to the Stamp Act, which had imposed taxes on a variety of goods ranging from playing cards to newspapers. The venerable printer-turned-statesman made it clear that the resentment of the colonies was such that they would only pay if "compelled by force of arms." The governments of the colonies had set up their own steep taxes for liquor, real estate, and business profits. Under the circumstances, he noted, citizens of the heavily taxed Pennsylvania and other colonies were hardly in the mood to pay even more to the Crown.[3]

It remained for others back home—among them the eloquent Thomas Paine—to argue to preserve our "native country" while it was still "uncontaminated by European corruption" (Hacker 1947, 204).

In this rebellion Americans thus began what has been a prolonged love-hate relationship with the political process. Having successfully made the defeat of the British government its object, the nation's early leaders had no choice but to invent a republic that glorified personal independence while still establishing governmental units—courts, legislatures, and executives—that were often similar to Britain's. Arguably, early pivotal figures like George Washington and Thomas Jefferson have retained their appeal to Americans because their own lives and words have managed to combine elements of an attractive and pervasive deception: that somehow the American experience is above the imperfections of the political process. Washington is often portrayed as the successful general who would not be king. He clearly relished his image as a war hero but largely shunned opportunities to turn his presidency into an American monarchy (McDonald 1975, 25–26). Jefferson had similarly left a personal legacy that captured the public imagination—notably the Declaration of Independence—that glorified a Rousseauian love of natural rights over the confining limits of human institutions (Becker 1958, 64–72). The Declaration held that the pursuit of life, liberty, and happiness are "unalienable rights," and that "it is the right of the people" to abolish governments which are "destructive of these ends."

By contrast, other brilliant engineers of early American political life—notably Alexander Hamilton and James Madison—have generally not become the same kind of icons. Their contributions were not popular acts of rebellion, but construction. They helped guide the fluent debate that produced and implemented the constitution.[4] It would fall to Jefferson, Franklin, Washington, and others to feed the more attractive myth of a nation that had thrown off the tyranny of a foreign government.

A DISAPPEARING CENTER

As we have seen, the foundations of American life are built on suspicions about political power. Revolutions naturally engender a certain level of distrust in the political. But even the simplified images of revolutionary America cannot account for the deep ambivalence toward politics that Americans feel today. In one study of public knowledge of issues only 10 percent of American adults could identify the name of the British prime minister (John Major), but 78 percent could identify the vegetable least liked by President George Bush (broccoli). At the same time, less than one-third of those surveyed said they followed important stories closely (the collapse of the former Soviet Union, the Bosnian Civil war), while nearly 75 percent said they had "Heard a lot recently" about the Teenage Mutant Ninja Turtles (Pew 1995). These numbers reflect a general decline in attention to news, especially in comparison to other media content. Only one-half of all adult Americans indicate that they regularly read a newspaper, and fewer than half (42%) indicate that they regularly watch a nightly network news show (Pew 1996).

Clearly, there is an increasing disconnection between the nation and its civic life. More Americans see the political process as something that is, at best, on the margins of their own lives. Paradoxically, while we have never had more access to the processes and moments of the political process—whether it is congressional debate televised on C-SPAN or interviews with the President and legislative leaders on CNN or the major news programs—we have never felt less a part of the process. For many politics is seen as a kind of running con game, an exploitative exercise intended to benefit those in power at the expense of an increasingly turned-off public. The rhetoric of politics is, by this logic, a rhetoric of deception: a collection of self-serving half-truths communicated to the nation by a powerful but compliant press (Entman 1989, 3–13).

As we have seen, the origins of this rising tide of disenfranchisement have historical roots, but additional causes have also surfaced in the last 40 years. The first is an expanding political dialogue on issues involving "identity politics," where identification with the broad political middle has been partly replaced by interest in the issues of specific groups. The second is a growing impatience with conflict as a necessary dimension of politics.

IDENTITY POLITICS, CULTURAL WARS, AND FRAGMENTATION

In the realm of civil affairs, America seems to be increasingly a nation at war with itself. Since Washington took office in 1789 there has always been a lively dialogue over broad questions of taxation, America's role in the world, and the extent to which government should be an active force for social change. But overlaying these older venues of political dispute is now another layer of more active fault lines that involve decisions about how governmental resources will be used to support or legitimize the status claims of specific segments of society. In this realm of "identity politics" groups within the polity (women, ethnic groups, older citizens, veterans, victims of crime or discrimination, labor, businesses, homosexuals, etc.) define their interests *in opposition* to the larger society rather than as a part of it (Gitlin 1995). In this context, the needs and rights of "my" group need to be considered in relation to the actions and injustices perpetuated by others. The rhetoric of affirmative action or gay rights is thus often a rhetoric of oppression. And the politics of these areas is about power in the society and its fairer redistribution.

The surfacing of identity politics as the flashpoint of contemporary public debate signals what may be a significant shift away from the discourse of consensus in favor of the discourse of difference. In this climate, politics becomes a means to separate oneself or group from a distrusted and increasingly fragmented culture.

Consider the question of what history textbooks the nation's public schools will use. Textbook selection is frequently now a matter of considerable public debate between various parties that compete for representation on the printed page. Battles over the political correctness of books in Texas and California have been particularly heated (Gitlin 1995, 7–30). Public hearings with page-by-page analysis of the narrative of American history have at times resembled riots rather than reviews. Should Columbus be credited with "finding" the new world? Were the first Europeans in North America seekers of religious and political freedom, or exploiters in their early settlements along the East coast? How should slavery be represented in the old South? And what is the preferred narrative about women in the western expansion of America? Were they victims of a strict patriarchal structure, or resourceful equals in the settlement of the west?

As analyzed by sociologist Todd Giltin, these debates over the portrayal of America's past no longer allow for a collective view of history. As a former left-wing political activist, Gitlin's sympathies are certainly with the multiculturalist traditions of American life. But after observing a continuous tide of fierce debate between Native Americans, African Americans, whites, Asian Americans and others testifying in Oakland, California, Gitlin wonders if America still allows shared regions of experience.

> Why are so many people attached to their marginality and why is so much of their intellectual labor spent developing theories to justify it? Why insist on difference with such rigidity, rancor, and blindness, to the exclusion of the possibility of common knowledge and common dreams? (32)

Like most Americans, Gitlin yearns for a nation that could find common themes and values that would transcend its ever-deepening differences, a culture that "federates" rather than separates "people of different races, genders, sexualities . . . religions and classes" (32).

This pattern of focusing on differences and nurturing a political cause by identifying (and often demonizing) the forces of opposition is especially evident on social or lifestyle issues, including questions over the rights of homosexuals, availability of birth control (including abortion), censorship of media content, and federal support of welfare and affirmative action programs. Activists interested in these issues tend to overlook the broad middle regions of compromise to the left or right of their own views. Their energy comes from a rhetoric of polarization.

The issues that now deeply divide Americans sometimes create a sense that winning or losing on a particular issue defines who we are as a society and who represents the moral authority within it. "Winning" on such issues confers legitimacy and power to some groups, and feelings of bitter defeat to others. As James David Hunter argues, two broad divisions have formed in America between those who want American life to reflect its traditional religious and social beliefs and those who favor more progressive change. These are two very different—if inexact—value systems that now feed the fires of America's so-called "culture wars." The traditionalist side favors older values and unquestioned definitions of good and evil that have been comfortably a part of the nation's religious orthodoxies. Those on the opposing side favor more progressive ideas, "the spirit of rationalism," and the willingness to admit that values and choices are open to a great deal of subjectivity.

Many on the progressive side of this widening divide, for example, accept homosexuality as a reasonable extension of the notion that people ought to be able to live as they wish, with the same protections at home and in the workplace that are offered to other Americans. For traditionalists, by contrast, the weight of scriptural admonitions against homosexuality cannot be simply set aside; the moral authority of church teachings is greater than the wishes or implied rights of any segment in society (Hunter 1991, 42–45).

This example oversimplifies views that are far more complex, but it is a reminder that issues that have become skirmishes in the culture wars are not easily bridged. Finding the middle ground is difficult, even in a society with a long traditional of political pluralism.

The effects these battles have had on the polity are far-ranging. Those activists engaged in conflict over an issue that they believe defines the essence of America are psychologically rewarded by carrying their banners into battle. No political fight is more satisfying than one that allows activists to express their moral indignation. But for the larger society one of the effects of identity politics seem to be alienation. This frustration sometimes plays out in the form of a generalized resentment against specific groups that have lobbied noisily for change. Questions about identity groups surface in the broader population as put-downs to "them" and what is seen as their excessive persistence. "What do *they* want?" "Will *they* ever be happy?"

For the larger polity a generalized fatigue seems to have set in. The vocal and polarized "extreme" on an issue turns off potential supporters and large segments of the rest of the population, a condition feminist writer Naomi Wolf describes as the fate of the women's movement in the late 1960s (1993, 66–72). In either case the broader outcome is a disenfranchised and frayed public, unwilling to subject itself to more exposure to public rancor and bruising partisanship.

INCREASING DISTASTE FOR THE PUBLIC FIGHT

In our time the inherently discordant nature of public life is often mistaken as a sign of the corruption or failure of politics. Politics is and always has been about conflict because it is about problems for which there are no self-evident solutions. "The essence of the political situation," notes John Bunzel, "is that someone is trying to do something about which there is no agreement." (1970, 7). Conflict is therefore not the problem of politics, but an inevitable part of its process. The competition of interests that creates political tension flows from the very pluralism that we pay tribute to in society.[5]

The irony, of course, is that we want pluralism without conflict, multiculturalism under the common laws of the states and federal government without the frictions that such diversity is likely to produce. As Robert Bellah has observed, we say we are an "individualistic" culture, but "it is consensus that is appreciated and the conflicts of interests that is suspect." (Bellah et al. 1985, 203). As the quote that opens this chapter suggests, if the conflict of political debate is allowed to become an "illness" in a society, then we have succumbed to the logic of totalitarian states which banish it.

There can be little doubt about the widespread dislike of contentious discourse—ranging from campaign advertising to the daily posturing of congressional leaders against their counterparts in the other party. What is less clear is whether we have changed as a society, or whether the discourse has become, in the words of Robert Hughes, "debased" and "corroded by fake pity and euphemism" (1993, 4).

It is easy to suggest that we have changed, that ours is no longer an age that sees much virtue in political argument at all. In the contemporary climate, "debate" is understood less as a form of knowing and learning than as the product of expressive excess. This view implies that conflict is a sign of a breakdown in the system, an unpleasant interruption in the inclusiveness and glossy good-naturedness that we admire in advertising and prime-time entertainment.[6]

By contrast, public debate in the last century had a vigorous but different role in American life. Newspapers of the mid to late 1800s were far more willing to take on partisan causes, with argument spilling from the editorial pages into the newswriting of the time. And from before the Civil War through to the 1930s lectures and speeches of social reformers, politicians, and activists were a recurring presence in towns and cities everywhere. Local Lyceums, Chautauquas, and forums regularly booked key figures like Susan B. Anthony, Anna Howard Shaw, Frederick Douglass, and William Lloyd Garrison. Between 1874 and 1886, for example, the preacher and former anti-slave activist Henry Ward Beecher traveled an estimated 300,000 miles, giving nearly 1300 lectures in virtually every state (Hance 1960, 120–26). Speakers like Garrison were a prime form of public entertainment, even when they challenged the beliefs of many of their listeners.

In addition there was less of a tendency then to link what we say with who we are. A century ago personality was not so intimately associated with a person's public rhetoric as it is now. This is a subtle point, but an interesting one. The 1800s was a time in public manners and discourse when the aim of civility was—in Richard Sennett's revealing phrase—to shield others "from being burdened with oneself" (1978, 264). Communication was not considered an act of intimate disclosure, as it now frequently is. An educated person's public statements where meant to articulate their reasons, less so their feelings. A person could more easily enjoy an advocate they disagreed with because an advocate's statements were more easily assessed out of the context of who they were.

It would take the work of Sigmund Freud and the popularity of psychotherapy to reposition speech and public discourse as a window into the soul (Duncan 1968, 13–16). Speech is now a signal of our deeper nature, the unique signature of our personality. As a consequence, as Sennett notes, meaning in political life comes from the personality of the leader. We judge them less by their works than in our estimates of their intentions as revealed by their rhetoric. "Political conflicts are interpreted in terms of the play of political personalities; leadership is interpreted in terms of "credibility" rather than accomplishment" (Sennett 1978, 219).

Our point is that conflict in public discourse carried less psychological significance a century ago than it does today. We are perhaps less inclined to tolerate verbal conflict today because we interpret it as a problem of character. Conflict carries more risk for us and our leaders now than it used to. In our time the idea of "divisive rhetoric" implies its own solution. The "scars" and "wounds" it creates must be healed by conciliation or the search for misunderstandings:[7] notions that would have been peculiar to those living in an earlier but equally tumultuous America. Few Presidents would follow Jefferson today in observing that "a little rebellion" is a "good thing and as necessary to the political world as storms in the physical" (Barone 1995, 44).

THE TRIUMPH OF EXPRESSIVE PARTISANSHIP

One of the problems that plagues contemporary politics is that the demeanor of its participants and their language now seems coarser than it used to be. Politics at the state and national levels seems increasingly to be a gladiatorial activity, a chance to punish the opposition with fighting words that tend to obliterate the more subtle distinctions of policy rhetoric.

THE PROMINENCE OF RHETORIC AT THE MARGINS

As noted above, our public discourse seems to include more rhetoric at the far margins, while real solutions seem far too subtle and complex to compete for our limited attention. A 1990 memo from Representative Newt Gingrich's political action committee, for example, laid out a formal set of terms suggested for others in the GOP as an aid to "define opponents." They included "traitors," "sick," "antifamily," "corrupt" "destructive," and so forth. Terms reserved for themselves had a distinctly different tonality: "caring," "moral," "humane," and "pro-family," among others (Woodward 1997, 101). "Polarization is addictive," notes Robert Hughes. "It is the crack of politics—a short intense rush that the system craves again and again, until it begins to collapse" (1993, 28).

The fierce venom and polarization of talk radio, television debate shows, and daily congressional struggles have all taken their toll on the public's patience. But it would not be entirely accurate to call this mean-spirited rhetoric new. In his own day, Lincoln was vilified and demonized in the press and by popular political figures on both sides of the slavery question, abolitionists as well as slave owners. For the enormously popular antislavery speaker Wendell Phillips, the south was a "great brothel," the Constitution a "curse," and Lincoln an example of "the white trash of the south spawned in Illinois" (Woodward 1990, 17–20). Through the years the rants of figures as diverse as the anti-Semitic Father Charles Coughlin, the red-baiting Senator Joseph McCarthy, and anti-war activist Jerry Rubin have always had their imitators and followers.

What has changed is that figures on the political margins have been given access to wider audiences because of their news value as sources of controversy. As Gloria Borger has noted,

> What is new is the size of the echo chamber, and every political performer knows it. Technology takes the message, amplifies it, personalizes it. Warped minds seeking self-justification can easily find it: When G. Gordon Liddy instructs listeners how best to kill a federal agent, or when Colorado talk show host Chuck Baker makes a gunshot sound effect when talking about government officials, paranoids hear allies. (1995, 46)

Civil affairs have become the center of uncivil rhetoric in part because political figures are now part of the celebrity mix that attracts media attention. Even mainstream outlets have found profit and large audiences in what Lance Morrow has described as "entertainer-provocateurs," (1996, 30) radio and television figures that promise to entertain by trashing their subjects. Radio's Rush Limbaugh and CNN's Patrick Buchanan have thrived on their abilities to condense issues to stereotypes, and their dismissive contempt of their enemies. Buchanan's 1992 GOP National Convention speech promising "a religious war for the soul of America" was among the most quoted of the entire campaign (Rosenstiel 1993, 227).

Presidents have always decried the polarized nature of political debate in the United States, even though their electoral campaigns have often featured it.[8] Journalist Steven Waldman has described Bill Clinton as "an integrationist in a separatist era" (1995, 88). In 1994 Clinton lamented the fact that talk radio has become a "constant unremitting drumbeat of negativism and cynicism" (Clinton 1994). John Kennedy was about to make similar remarks on the day he was assassinated in Dallas. The undelivered 1963 speech noted that "There will always be dissident voices . . . perceiving gloom on every side and seeking influence without responsibility . . . voices preaching doctrines wholly unrelated to reality" and fearing "supposed hordes of civil servants" (Borger 1995, 46).

Modern leaders who would like others to follow the more inclusive and nonpartisan language of the presidency are up against stiff odds. Shouting matches are not easily transformed into dialogues. And in the immediate future it will be difficult to refranchise those who have grown disillusioned.

PROCESS REPORTING IN THE SYNOPTIC MEDIA

Styles of reporting have also contributed to public disillusionment. Readers of newspapers or political reporting a century ago would have found long accounts of what presidents, corporate leaders and members of congress *said*. Political intelligence in the United States was altogether simpler and more direct. To be sure, newspapers were partisan and reporters were notoriously inaccurate. But reporting focused on actions and words: what people in power were saying and doing.

Today such basic informational reporting continues in some places and has never been better. Some major newspapers, along with C-SPAN, CNN, NPR, and other outlets provide detailed and extended accounts of political events and rhetoric. But the explosion of all kinds of information has been partly eclipsed by the continued attention the larger public gives to synoptic political reporting. C-SPAN may cover Congress all day, but its audience is still tiny compared to the millions of viewers who find time only to catch the headlines and sound bites of CNN and the three network newscasts. Their synoptic reporting of politics frequently emphasizes process over content. Process reporting accounts for why a political figure has said or done something. The lead-in of a print or broadcast story defines an event or remark in terms of the likely political catalyst that produced it. Such stories prime the viewer to look for the manipulative intentions behind a statement. "Hoping to paint the White House into a corner, the Democratic leadership in the Senate has scheduled a vote next week on health care legislation they know President Bush will veto." "In an effort to shore up flagging support in the West, President Clinton today released federal money to help ranchers." The subtext of these stories is that politics as a game of "gotcha!" or "winner-take-all." It dismisses substance as the mere vehicle to a more self-motivated goal.

To be sure, reporters have not made up their lead-ins. Politics has always involved calculations about how to best dominate opponents who are blocking your own objectives. Our point is that process reporting consumes more time and attention in the popular media, notably the television networks. From a journalistic perspective it represents a level of sophistication and professionalization that did not exist in earlier forms of journalism. Reporters covering Presidents Woodrow Wilson or Franklin Roosevelt were more deferential and less inclined to look for a message's subtext or the public opinion benefits of an action (Grossman and Kumar, 1981, 7–13). The norm that emerged after World War II—and intensified after the Watergate affair of 1972—was for a more skeptical and less deferential press; in the words of David Riesman, a press that would "never be taken in by any person, cause, or event." (1961, 182).

SUMMARY

The conduct of civil affairs in the United States has always occurred under a cloud of considerable public distrust. This distrust is an important but largely negative backdrop that conveys meaning to every other part of the nation's civil life.

By its nature, politics encourages a wary skepticism. And the traditions borne out of the nation's emergence honor the idea of freedom as a protection against governmental power that can easily be abused. Even so, as we have argued in this chapter, there has been an intensification of public distrust in many basic American institutions, especially Congress.

The reasons for the heightened concern about governmental affairs are many. At a simple level, the most widely seen forms of news reporting today are more "insider" oriented, sometimes substituting analysis of the political process in place of the discussion of political ideas. And the process itself has never been a source of admiration. In addition, more high-visibility issues today involve questions of group legitimacy and power. This realm of "identity politics" naturally unfolds against a backdrop of vituperation and opposition rather than conciliation. Groups gain prominence and supporters by representing themselves as the victims of other segments within the polity. As a result, the nation appears to be fragmented and divided, fighting various skirmishes in what increasingly looks like a prolonged culture war. The public discourse of this war seems to be more polarized, succeeding only when it can praise supporters and demonize opponents. The cohesion that activists gain in the process, however, comes at an effect that is precisely the reverse for the society as a whole. Polarizing political rhetoric turns off the polity and lessens the likelihood that they will find much merit in vigorous public debate.

NOTES

1. This session is reported in Steven Waldman, *The Bill, Revised and Updated Edition* (New York: Penguin, 1995), p. 102.

2. See Alexander Hamilton's description of the new office in *The Federalist Papers*, No. 67 (New York: Signet, 1967), p. 407.

3. "Examination of Dr. Franklin," in *The Shaping of the American Tradition*. ed. Louis Hacker (New York: Columbia University Press, 1947), pp. 196–97.

4. The brilliance of Hamilton and Madison is captured in their exchanges on the nature of the Constitution in *The Federalist Papers*.

5. Every January 22, for example, pro-choice and pro-life groups gather in various locations in Washington and elsewhere to rally in support of their beliefs. This date is the anniversary of the Supreme Court's 1973 decision that the constitutional right of privacy gives women the option to choose an abortion. In 1997, for example, Hilary Rodham Clinton and Vice President Al Gore addressed a luncheon meeting of the National Abortion and Reproductive Rights Action League while marchers opposing abortion gathered at the same time for what is now an annual parade to the Capitol. "Abortion Battle Heats Up on Roe's Anniversary," Reuters, January 22, 1997 [online].

6. That durable staple of prime time, the situation comedy, thrives on the avoidence of conflict or dispute. Characters are rarely an odds with each other over any question of substance.

7. I. A. Richards, the influential critic, noted that rhetoric "should be a study of misunderstanding and its remedies." See his *Philosophy of Rhetoric* (New York: Oxford University Press, 1965), p. 3.

8. Far more than Congress, the presidency encourages rhetorical inclusion rather than the segregation or polarization of audiences. Executives (presidents, mayors, and governors) generally gain more by building bridges to opponents than staking their political success on attacking them.

REFERENCES

"Abortion Battle Heats Up." 1997. Reuters, 22 January [online].

Barone, Michael. 1995. "A Brief History of Zealotry in America." *US News and World Report*, 8 May: 44.

Becker, Carl. 1958. *The Declaration of Independence*. New York: Vintage.

Bellah, Robert N., Richard Madsen, William Sullivan, Ann Swidler, and Steven Tipton. 1985. *Habits of the Heart: Individualism and Commitment in American Life*. Berkeley: University of California Press.

Borger, Gloria. 1995. "Debasing the Political Currency." *US News and World Report*, 8 May: 46.

Bunzel, John H. 1970. *Anti-Politics in America*. New York: Vintage.

Clinton, Bill. 1994. Remarks of the President in Phone Call to KMOX Radio, St. Louis, 25 June, Texas A & M Presidential Archives [online].

Dewey, John. 1954. *The Public and Its Problems*. Chicago: Swallow Press.

Dionne, E. J. 1991. *Why Americans Hate Politics*. New York: Simon & Schuster.

Duncan, Hugh D. 1968. *Communication and Social Order*. New York: Oxford University Press.

Entman, Robert M. 1989. *Democracy without Citizens*. New York: Oxford University Press.
Gitlin, Todd. 1995. *The Twilight of Common Dreams*. New York: Metropolitan Books.
Grossman, Michael, and Martha Kumar. 1981. *Portraying the President: The White House and the News Media*. Baltimore: Johns Hopkins University Press.
Hacker, Louis. 1947. *The Shaping of the American Tradition*. New York: Columbia University Press.
Hamilton, Alexander. 1967. *The Federalist Papers*. New York: Signet.
Hance, Kenneth. 1960. "The Later National Period, 1860–1930." In *A History and Criticism of American Public Address Vol. 1*, ed. William Norwood Brigance. New York: Russell and Russell, pp. 120–26.
Hughes, Robert. 1993. *Culture of Complaint: The Fraying of America*. New York: Oxford University Press.
Hunter, James D. 1991. *Culture Wars: The Struggle to Define America*. New York: Basic Books.
McAneny, Leslie, and David Moore. 1995. "American Confidence in Public Institutions on the Rise." 6 May, *Gallup Organization Newsletter* (May) [online].
McDonald, Forrest. 1975. *The Presidency of George Washington*. New York: Norton.
Morrow. Lance. 1996. "Stinking to High Heaven." *Time*, 4 March: 30.
Pew Research Center for the People and the Press. 1995. "Times-Mirror News Interest Index: 1989–1995." 28 December [online]
———. 1996. "TV News Viewership Declines." 13 May [online].
Richards, I. A. 1965. *Philosophy of Rhetoric*. New York: Oxford University Press.
Riesman, David, with Nathan Glazer and Reuel Denney. 1961. *The Lonely Crowd*, abridged ed. New Haven: CT: Yale University Press.
Rosenstiel, Tom. 1993. *Strange Bedfellows*. New York: Hyperion.
Saad, Lydia. 1995. "Congress and Clinton Encounter Smoother Waters." *Gallup Organization Newsletter* (February) [online].
Sennett, Richard. 1978. *The Fall of Public Man*. New York: Vintage.
Waldman, Steven. 1995. *The Bill*, rev. and updated ed. New York: Penguin.
Wolf, Naomi. 1993. *Fire with Fire*. New York: Random House.
Woodward, Gary. 1990. *Persuasive Encounters: Case Studies in Constructive Confrontation*. New York: Praeger.
———. 1997. *Perspectives on American Political Media*. Boston: Allyn and Bacon.

Chapter 3

Language and Politics

> And however important to us is the tiny sliver of reality each of us has experienced firsthand, the whole overall "picture" is but a construct of our symbol systems.
>
> Kenneth Burke (1966)

In Chapter 1, we offered a very broad definition of politics and argued for the centrality of human communication as the vehicle for political thought, debate, and action. In this chapter we provide a theoretical perspective of the role of communication in society as well as identify unique functions and uses of political language. We conclude with a discussion of contemporary "mediated political discourse" and the implications for campaigns, political debates, and issue discussions.

COMMUNICATION, SOCIETY, AND SOCIAL ORDER

At the heart of our perspective of government and politics is the notion of interaction. Interaction is not so much a concept as an orientation for viewing human behavior and, ultimately, society. Through interaction, people are continually undergoing change and, consequently, so is society. Interaction is a process involving acting, perceiving, interpreting, and acting again. This interaction among people gives rise to reality which is largely symbolic. Thus, it is through symbolic interaction with others that meaning is given to the world and the reality toward which persons act is created.

Interaction, as a concept, is not limited to spoken and written language. Objects exist in physical form that are given meaning through social interaction. Depending upon our social groups and frames of reference, specific objects may "communicate" success, status, and acceptance. The cars we drive, the watches we wear, and even the pens we use are more than means of transportation, instruments for telling time, and tools of communication. Compare a Mercedes to a Chevy, a Rolex to a Timex, or a MontBlanc to a Bic. Artifacts and objects should be viewed as social objects. For the peasant, a rake is a gardening tool as well as a weapon for revolution. Such a transformation results from social interaction. Objects take on meaning for individuals as they interact with others.

Interaction, as a concept, is also not limited to the notion of self-development. It is the very fabric of society. Societies, therefore, should be viewed as consisting of people in interaction. When people interact, they influence the behavior of each other. Behavior, then, is created by interaction rather than simply a result of interaction.

Individuals, of course, interact within larger networks of other individuals and groups. Although many of society's networks are far removed from individuals, the impact of such networks may be considerable. Social networks, formal or informal, social or political, provide a framework within which social action takes place. The networks, therefore, are not determinants of action. Even structural aspects of society, such as social roles or class, should be viewed as setting conditions for behavior and interaction rather than as causing specific behavior or interaction. Human interaction, then, is at the core of human existence. It gives meaning to the self, to symbols and languages, to social networks and societies, to worldviews, and to social objects.

Symbols

It is impossible to talk of human interaction without addressing the symbolic nature of humans. Distinctively human behavior and interaction are carried on through the medium of symbols and their attached meanings. What distinguishes humans from lower animals is their ability to function in a symbolic environment. Humans alone can create, manipulate, and use symbols to control their own behavior as well as the behavior of others. All animals communicate. However, humans are uniquely symbolic.

George Herbert Mead (1972) defined symbols in terms of meaning. A system of symbols "is the means whereby individuals can indicate to one another what their responses to objects will be and hence what the meaning of objects are" (122). The human, as a cognitive creature, functions in a context of shared meanings that are communicated through language (which is itself a group of shared meanings or symbols). Symbols, therefore, are more than a part of a language system. Joel Charon (1979) defines a symbol as "any object, mode of conduct, or word toward which we act as if it were something else. Whatever the symbol stands for constitutes its meanings" (40). This definition has important implications for individual action as well as for the nature of society.

We posit that nearly all human action is symbolic. Human action in all its forms represents something more than what is immediately perceived. Symbols form the very basis of our overt behavior. Human action is the by-product of the stimulus of symbols. Before a response to any situation can be formulated, the situation must be defined and interpreted to ensure an appropriate response to the situation. Meanings for symbols derive from interaction in rather specific social contexts. New interaction experiences may result in new symbols or new meanings for old symbols which may, consequently, change one's understanding or perception of the world. Our view of the world alters and changes as our symbol system is modified through interaction. This process suggests that our reality is made up of symbolic systems.

Social Reality

Simply stated, reality is a social product arising from interaction or communication. Reality for everyone, therefore, is limited, specific, and circumscribed. Of course, communication can be used to extend or limit "realities." To discover our own reality or that of someone else, we must first understand the symbol system and then the meanings the symbols have for all concerned. Mutual understanding and subsequent action is accomplished through communication or interaction.

The construction of reality is an active process. It involves recognition, definition, interpretation, action, and validation through interaction. Communication becomes the vehicle for the creation of society, culture, rules, regulations, behavior, and so on. From such a chain of actions grows a complex and constantly changing matrix of individual and societal expectations.

The capacity to learn culture (or the process of socialization) enables people to understand one another and at the same time creates behavioral expectations. Consequently, we are in a continual state of orienting our behavior to that of others.

Society

This perspective recognizes the dynamic, changing nature of society. Individuals are constantly interacting, developing, and shaping society. People exist in action and consequently must be viewed in terms of action. Society may be viewed as individuals in interaction, individuals acting in relation to each other, individuals engaging in cooperative action, and people communicating with self and others.

This interactivist orientation rejects the notion that human society is simply an expression of preestablished rules of joint action. New situations are constantly arising requiring modification or reinforcement of existing rules of society. Even "old" joint action arises out of a background of previous actions of the participants. Participants of any action bring unique "worlds of objects," "sets of meanings," and "schemes of interpretation." In this way all joint action is "new" resulting from interaction although, indeed, from a familiar pattern of action.

Self-control is inseparable from social control. The notion of free will is restricted and limited by the culture of an individual. The interrelationship between social control and self-control is the result of commitment to various groups that produce a self-fulfillment, self-expression, and self-identity. Social control is not, therefore, a matter of formal government agencies, laws, rules, and regulations. Rather, it is a direct result of citizens identifying and internalizing the values of a group so that the values become essential to their own self-esteem and thus act so as to support the social order. Adherence to the rules of society becomes a fair price to pay for membership in the society.

Don Faules and Dennis Alexander (1979) define regulation as "symbolic processes that induce change or maintain stability in self and others." (130). Of course language provides the major framework dictating ways of thinking and seeing society. Language and symbols may regulate behavior by creating expectations, producing negative bias, or by subordinating other considerations by allowing a norm or value to supersede other symbols. In addition to creating expectations of behavior, symbols create social sanctions (i.e., war as God's will) or function as master symbols (i.e., to die for freedom).

LANGUAGE AND POLITICS

When considering politics, it becomes necessary to link the functions and characteristics of government to the general nature of society. Richard Rose (1970, 196–97) identifies three criteria that gauge the impact of governmental actions upon the fabric of society. The first criterion is the scope of a government activity. How many individuals of the population are affected by the action? The second criterion is the intensity of the impact of the government's action. How much importance is attached to the action by the general public? Third, the frequency of impact of governmental decisions is important. Here, the key question becomes how often or how long are people affected by governmental policy or action? These criteria gauge the magnitude of influence of government over society.

Mass support for any individual, institution, or system of government is not automatic. Societal support is a long, continual, and active process. The greatest task confronting any government is to generate enough support for governmental authority and action to meet the needs of all segments of society. David Easton (1965) defines political legitimacy as "the conviction on the part of the [citizen] that is right and proper for him to accept and obey the authorities and to abide by the requirements of the regime" (279). Legitimacy, according to Easton, is a two-way proposition. It is desirable for citizens because it sustains political order, stability, and consequently minimizes stressful changes and surprises. A sense of legitimacy is advantageous for authorities because it becomes the most significant device for regulating the flow of diffuse support.

Political Settings

A political setting, as defined by Murray Edelman (1964), is "whatever is background and remains over a period of time, limiting perception and responses" (102–3). For him, "it is more than land, buildings, and physical props. It includes any assumptions about basic causation or motivation that are generally accepted" (103). The setting, then, creates the perspective from which mass audiences will analyze a situation, define their response, and establish the emotional context of the act that enfolds. Political actors must carefully assess the situation, calculate the appropriate action, and identify the proper roles to assume. Settings, therefore, condition political acts.

Implicit in the discussion is the need for governments to create appropriate political settings that legitimize a set of values. The assumption is that control over the behavior of others is primarily achieved by influencing the definition of the situation. In a democracy, the secret is to act in such a way that creates an image of the actor or scene that stimulates others to act voluntarily as desired. Getting others to share one's reality is the first step toward getting others to act in a prescribed manner. This is best achieved by creating or defining reality for others. In turn, the use of potent symbols, rituals, and myths is useful in creating commonalities in the midst of national diversity. The interrelationship of these is succinctly described by Dan Nimmo (1978):

> By inducing people to respond in certain ways, to play specific roles toward government, and to change their thoughts, feelings, and expectations, significant political symbols facilitate the formation of public opinion. As significant symbols of political talk, the words, pictures, and acts of political communicators are tipoffs to people that they can expect fellow citizens to respond to symbols in certain anticipated way. (69)

The entire process, however, yields more than desired behavior. Soon, the process becomes a commitment and total belief in the institutions and system of government.

Political Symbols

We have already argued that humans live in a symbolic environment. Our "significant symbols" arise through the process of social interaction. A significant symbol, defined by Mead (1972, 122), is one that leads to the same response in another person that it calls forth in the thinker. Thus, significant symbols are those with a shared, common meaning by group. Consequently, a political vocabulary of significant symbols may evolve which provides common understandings among individuals. They are socially constructed and provide common references for people to engage in more interaction to help solve the problems of the group life.

As a group, there are three ways an individual may respond or relate to a significant symbol. First, there is a content or informational dimension. The content dimension is rather easy to pinpoint and define. Facts can, of course, be manipulated but are rather readily recognizable. There is, second, an affective or emotional dimension to a symbol. Such responses are less predictable and result from years of cultural socialization. Politically, the trick is to use symbols where the affective responses are rather predictable. Finally, there is an evaluative dimension reflecting the importance of the symbol. Each of these dimensions is defined through interaction and hence becomes a rather potent motivator for action.

There are a large number of significant political symbols in society. They have evolved, according to Nimmo (1978, 67–68), in five ways. From "authority talk" arise laws, constitution treaties, and so on, which often sanction specific political orientations. "Power talk" usually creates symbols dealing with international politics. Detente, cold war, or perestroika are such significant symbols. In contrast, "influence talk" provides the domestic creation of significant symbols arising from such sources as party platforms, slogans, speeches, or newspaper editorials. Often, "complex issues," when condensed into a single term or phrase, become powerful political symbols. Such symbols include: busing, gun control, abortion, capital punishment, law and order, or civil rights. Finally, significant symbols arise from the "types of objects symbolized" such as democracy or Old Glory. This characterization emphasizes the dynamic, evolving, and emerging nature of political symbols.

Roger Cobb and Charles Elder (1972, 82–86) provide a hierarchical typology of political symbols which is also most useful. They identify four types of stimulus objects as the universe of political symbols. At the top of the hierarchy are symbols of the political community comprising its core values. Old Glory, democracy, equality, liberty, and justice fall within this category. The next type of political symbols is regime symbols or those relating to political norms of the society. These include such concepts as due process, equal opportunity, or free enterprise. Third in the typology are symbols associated with formal political roles and institutions such as the president, Congress, or FBI. The last type, situational symbols, is comprised of three components. These components include: governmental authorities (president, vice president, mayors, etc.), nongovernmental authorities (Ralph Reed, Jesse Jackson, Common Cause, etc.), and the political issues (deficit, gun control, health care, etc.). Those symbols high in the typology are the most abstract and general, whereas those in the lower divisions are more specific in nature. Abstract political symbols are more encompassing, applicable, salient, and less temporally specific. All politicians use abstract symbols, especially during campaigns. Although the typology is clear, the response to the symbols may not be as clear-cut. On the informational level, the same information may be gleaned from the more specific symbols but certainly debatable for those higher in the typology. The affective nature of all the symbol types depends upon the rather unique experiences, culture, and socialization of an individual or group. The same is true for the evaluative dimension. The point is, the classification of a symbol without the appreciation of the social construction and interaction aspects of symbol making is limited in utility.

How do political symbols work? It is their abstract semantic hollowness that makes symbols so powerful. Although political symbols function as objects of common identification, they simultaneously allow for idiosyncratic meanings to be attacked. Two individuals may disfavor abortion but do so based upon differing—religious or constitutional—arguments. The same individuals may disagree about abortion for rape victims but clearly support congressional or presidential action disavowing the practice of abortion. Political symbols are powerful not because of the broad commonalities of shared meaning but because of the intense sentiments created and attached to them resulting in the perception that the symbols are vital to the system. As elements of the political culture, political symbols serve as stimuli for political action. They serve as a link between mass political behavior and individual behavior.

There are aspects unique to symbols that endow them with power whether political or not. Myth, ritual, and ideology are three such symbolic forms. They are especially valuable in arousing public action.

Myth

Myth bridges the old and the new. Myths are composed of images from the past that help us cope and understand the present. Myth functions to reduce the complexity of the world identifying causes that are simple and remedies that are apparent. "In place of a complicated empirical world," Edelman (1964) observes, "men hold to relatively few, simple, archetypal myths, of which the conspiratorial enemy and omnicompetent hero-savior are the central ones" (16). Virtually all of our political behavior lies in the realm of myth. For James Barber (1980), myth is the essence of human politics. Barber writes:

> The pulse of politics is a mythic pulse. Political life shares in the national mythology, grows in the wider culture, draws its strength from the human passion for discovering, in our short span of life on this peripheral planet, the drama of human significance. Ours is a story-making civilization; we are a race of incorrigible narrators. The hunger to transform experience into meaning through story spurs the political imagination. (20)

Politics, then, relies upon a multitude of images constructed over time comprised of various values, prejudices, facts, and fiction.

Nimmo and Combs (1980, 9–13) provide four views or orientations to social myths. Each view shares insight into the social construction of myths. The "common sense" view of myths perceives them as simple distorted beliefs based more upon emotion than fact. They are dangerous, therefore, because of their falsification of truth. The "timeless truth" view of myths, in contrast, argues that what is important is the fact that people believe the myths. Thus, the issue of accuracy is not important. Myths must be dealt with as true because they are believed to be true by the general public. The "hidden meanings" view of myths is a compromise of the other two. Here, all myths are believed to contain some element of truth of moral principle. Consequently, all myths are grounded in truth. Finally, the "symbolic" view of myths defines myths as "collective representations" of society's beliefs, values, ideologies, cultures, and doctrines. Myths symbolize codes of approved beliefs, values, and behavior and thus function to legitimize authority. Each of these approaches to myths emphasizes the dynamic and utility aspects of myths. They are constructed through social interpretations of the past and become predictions of the future.

In light of this discussion, we prefer Nimmo and Combs's (1980) definition of myth as a credible, dramatic, socially constructed representation of perceived realities that people accept as permanent, fixed knowledge of reality while forgetting (if they were even aware of it) its tentative, imaginative, created, and perhaps fictional qualities (16). This definition acknowledges the dramatic nature of myths.

There are several different types of political myths (Nimmo and Combs 1980, 26–27). Master myths are national in scope and encompass the collective consciousness of a society. These are usually utopian in nature. One such prevailing myth in America is the myth of the American dream. We believe that if we work hard, there is no limit to our capacity for success. Such a myth serves to motivate individuals and reinforce societal values. Another prevalent form of political myth in America is myths of "us and them." These myths focus on social structures or collectivities. Specific groups, movements, and governmental institutions encourage myth development in order to generate credibility, to enlist support, and to sustain existence. The myth of American democracy and free enterprise reduces the complexity of our systems of government and economy to rather abstract notions. We all know that our government is a form of democracy and our economy is a variation of free enterprise. Nevertheless, the myths serve to legitimize the governmental institutions. Definitional myths are useful in another way as well. In addition to defining what is preferred, good, and proper, myths can also define what is bad, unjust, and evil. The notions of communism and socialism are fraught with criticism while most of Europe has been more socialist than democratic for many years. In defining, myths sanction and reinforce societal values. In contrast to "us and them" myths, "heroic" myths focus on individuals. Humans need heroes for motivation and emulation. To state that George Washington, our founding father, never told a lie not only adds esteem for the individual but also espouses the virtue of honesty for the citizenry. Finally, an increasing category of political myths are pseudomyths. They are myths in the making. Most politicians, especially during elections, are attempting to be perceived as "heroic underdogs," the "common man," or the "new maverick." Messages are created and disseminated by the candidate to reinforce desired images. The mass media, which will be investigated in Chapter 4, plays an important role in the development of pseudomyths.

Within the realm of politics, there are four basic uses of myths. The first and perhaps most obvious function of myths is to increase public comprehension and understanding of rather complex notions, theories, or structures. Second, myths function to unite a society and to create common bonds among the populace. Myths can reinforce and articulate common elements within a diversity of social mores. The careful construction of political myths can prescribe proper and legitimate public beliefs, attitudes, values, and behavior. Third, political myths offer unique identities for the citizens. They provide the link between the individual and the polity. Although broad in nature, myths become personalized and the views or morals expressed are internalized. Finally, myths are persuasive. Myths can legitimize, stimulate, and motivate behavior. They can sustain commitments to a specific polity.

Political myths, in summary, are socially conceived, created, permeated, and structured entities and are real. Because they are real, political myths are credible and pragmatic. And because they are socially constructed, political myths are dramatic, involving a story, actors, and morals.

Ritual

Ritual, in many ways, functions in the same way as does myth. Edelman (1964) defines ritual as "a motor activity that involves its participants symbolically in a common enterprise, calling their attention to their relatedness and joint interests in a compelling way" (16). Ritual is the bridge between the individual and society. It functions as a leveler providing instant commonality. By allowing one to become a part of a larger entity, ritual promotes conformity in a rather satisfying way. Myths unite people. Rituals also have special significance, for meaning can evoke and reinforce a certain value, belief, attitude, or desired behavior.

For example, Bruce Gronbeck (1986, 226–45) views presidential inaugurals as rituals and "moments of cultural transmission." Inaugurals link past and present in the symbolic acts of remembrance, legitimization, and celebration. Ronald Reagan's first inaugural especially followed this pattern. Although 1981 was not a time for great celebration, Reagan held out hope for future prosperity. He recognized Carter's help in transition of power, a direct appeal to legitimization. He talked of being confirmed by the people and asked for God's help. In terms of remembrance, Reagan went from the difficulties of the recent past to the heroes of the more distant past invoking the names of Washington, Jefferson, Lincoln, and Kennedy.

Ideology

Ideology is a symbolic belief system that functions to turn listeners into believers and believers into actors. Craig Smith (1990) defines ideology as "a set of socially shared preferences about the nature of life, built on shared values priorities, shared authorities, and/or shared derivations. Whatever a community collectively believes or imagines is its ideology" (29). From this perspective ideology is more than a set of political norms. Rather, it is linked to an individual's perception of political reality. Ideologies are socially constructed and are in a continual process of definition and interpretation. For the individual, internalizing an ideology requires a continual assessment of political acts based upon norms or values that become a permanent motivation for political action. America, however, is generally characterized as being less ideological than most nations. Our political system focuses on specific issues and personalities rather than political parties and abstract ideologies. Ideology, whether from the right or left, is seldom complicated. Nevertheless, to accept an ideology implies a commitment toward a specific social reality. On a larger scale, the commitment toward an ideology links one to a community of believers who largely share the same interpretation of the world. Thus, such a commonality of viewing reality provides a strong rationale for specific societal behavior or action.

By briefly discussing myth, ritual, and ideology, aspects of the unique nature of political symbols are well illustrated. First, political reality is socially constructed and created through the use of political symbols. There is a participant dimension to political discourse. Second, political symbols are pragmatic in nature. No matter how abstract the idea or concept, the evoking of political symbols affects behavior. Political discourse is persuasive, pervasive, and influences beliefs, attitudes, and values. Finally, political discourse is dramatic. This means that nearly all political discourse seeks to construct a certain reality. Of course, there is usually a great deal of competition in constructing realities.

Political Language

Socialization depends upon language and is key to the process of creating legitimacy. Language, as the means of passing cultural and political values, provides a group or individual a means of identification with a specific culture, set of values, or political entity. As people assess their environment, language is created which structures, transforms, or destroys the environment. Words are the molds for concepts and thoughts and become symbols reflecting beliefs and values. Thus, the creation of language, or symbol systems, is required before societies and political cultures can develop. Language serves as the agent of social integration; as the means of cultural socialization; as the vehicle for social interaction; as the channel for the transmission of values; and as the glue that bonds people, ideas, and society together.

Language, therefore, is a very active and creative process which does not reflect an objective reality but creates a reality by organizing meaningful perceptions abstracted from a complex world. Language becomes a mediating force that actively shapes one's interpretation of the environment. "Metaphorically, language and the words embedded in it," according to Claus Mueller (1973), "are posed between the individual and his environment and serve as an invisible filter. The individual attains a certain degree of understanding through the classification made possible by concepts that screen and structure perception" (16).

Political consciousness is dependent upon language, for language can determine the way in which people relate to their environment. At the very least, language should be viewed as the medium for the generation and perpetuation of politically significant symbols. Political consciousness results from a largely symbolic interpretation of sociopolitical experience. To control, manipulate, or structure the interpretation is a primary goal of politics in general. A successful politician will use rather specific linguistic devices that reinforce popular beliefs, attitudes, and values. Politically manipulated language can promote and reinforce the existing political regime or order.

From this brief discussion, it is clear that what makes language political is not its particular vocabulary or linguistic form, but the substance of the information the language conveys, the setting in which the interaction occurs, and the explicit or implicit functions the language performs. As Doris Graber (1981) observes, "When political actors, in and out of government, communicate about political matters, for political purposes, they are using political language" (196).

Political language, then, is about power, social relationships, morals and ethics, identity, to name only a few items. But, as Paul Corcoran (1990) warns, "while language shapes and empowers its users, the unhappy consequence is that language reproduces and reinforces exploitation, inequality, and other traditions of power" (53). Leaders win and lose, the public is empowered or enslaved, informed or misled by the *strategic* use of language. In fact, Corcoran argues that

> *All* language is political because every speech setting, however private and intimate, involves power relations, social roles, privileges, and contested meanings. It is not simply *difficult* to separate out the intermingling of politics and language. Rather, one *cannot* distinguish between politics and language because they do not occupy separate spheres of existence that merely "overlap." In a much stronger sense, language articulates and confirms all the things that we call political: the weak and strong, the valued and the rejected, the desired and the undesirable, "us" and "them." (53)

Just consider the policy implications of whether you consider abortion a "medical procedure" or "murder," or whether affirmative action is a program ensuring "equal opportunity" or "governmental discrimination." As Edelman (1988) reminds us, "the potency of political language does not stem from its descriptions or a 'real' world but rather from its reconstructions of the past and its evocation of unobservables in the present and of potentialities in the future, language usage is strategic" (108).

It is also important to understand that politics as talk does not imply politics is all talk and no action. Politics as talk *is* action, in very important, although sometimes very subtle ways. To win the public debate in defining abortion as murder is the first step toward legislative action.

As argued in Chapter 1, political language is about meaning, power, and resources. From a cultural perspective, political language has certain "symbolic capital," inherent shared truths (Lorenzo 1996, 13). These tend to be the more abstract and value oriented such as "freedom," "justice," "equal opportunity," etc. In some ways, the Declaration of Independence and the Constitution, as political discourse, defined the "rights" of humans and the relationships with government, elected officials, and the larger community.

Functions of Political Language

Doris Graber (1981) identifies five pragmatic functions of political language: information dissemination, agenda setting, interpretation and linkage, projection for the future and the past, and action stimulation (195–224). It is useful here briefly to discuss each of these functions, although they will be discussed in greater detail in other chapters.

There are many ways information is shared with the public in political messages. The most obvious, of course, is the sharing of explicit information about the state of the polity. Such dissemination of information is vital to the public's understanding and support of the political system. This is especially true in democratic nations where the public expects open access to the instruments and decision making of government officials. But the public, being sensitized to uses of language, can obtain information by what is not stated, how something is stated, or when something is stated. Oftentimes, especially in messages between nations, the public must read between the lines of official statements to ascertain proper meanings and significances of statements. Such inferences are useful in gauging security, flexibility, and sincerity. Sometimes the connotations of the words used communicate more truth than the actual statements. There are times, especially in tragedy, that the very act of speaking by an official can communicate support, sympathy, or strength. Thus, the act of speaking rather than the words spoken conveys the meaning of the rhetorical event.

The very topics chosen by politicians channel the public's attention and focus issues to be discussed. The agenda-setting function of political language primarily occurs in two ways. First, before "something" can become an issue, some prominent politician must articulate a problem and hence bring the issue to public attention. The issue can be rather obvious (poverty), in need of highlighting (status of American education), or created (The Great Society). A major way political language establishes the national agenda is by controlling the information disseminated to the general public. Within this realm there is always a great deal of competition. There are a limited number of issues that can effectively maintain public interest and attention. While certain self-serving topics are favored by a person, party, faction, or group, the same topics may be perceived as meaningless or even harmful to others. While President Nixon wanted to limit discussion and public attention to the Watergate break-ins and tapes, rival groups wanted public debates and revelations to continue. During the Carter administration, rival politicians maintained pressure on the president to resolve the Iranian hostage situation. Carter was unable effectively to address domestic issues during this period. His failure to end the ordeal led to his sound defeat in 1980. In Ronald Reagan's final years in office, the Democratic Congress attempted to discredit his administration by probing into the "Iran-Contra scandal." Investigations and public hearings of the charges of exchanging arms for hostages dominated public attention and restricted Reagan's domestic and foreign policy initiatives for over a year. Bush was successful in justifying the Gulf War, not on the basis of economic interests, but as a need to teach the "Hitler-like" dictator, Saddam Hussein, a lesson and to help our friends in Saudi Arabia. However, he lost the pending election because of his failure to convince Americans of his domestic policy concerns. And early in his first administration, Clinton wanted to reform our health care system, but failed in his attempt to persuade Americans that the system was in a state of "crisis."

The very act of calling the public's attention to a certain issue defines, interprets, and manipulates the public's perception of an issue. Causal explanations are often freely given. Such explanations may be suspect. Control over the definitions of a situation is essential in creating and preserving political realities. For Ronald Reagan, the rebels in Nicaragua were "freedom fighters" comparable to America's revolutionary war heroes. Some members of Congress, however, called the rebels "common criminals." Participants in election primaries, for example, all proclaim victory regardless of the number of votes received. The top vote-getter becomes the "front runner." The second-place winner becomes "the underdog" candidate in an "uphill battle." The third-place candidate becomes a "credible" candidate and alternative for those "frustrated" or "dissatisfied" with the "same old party favorites." Political language defines and interprets reality as well as provides a rationale for future collective action.

A great deal of political rhetoric and language deals with predicting the future and reflecting upon the past. Candidates present idealized futures under their leadership and predictions of success if their policies are followed. Some predictions and projections are formalized as party platforms or major addresses at inaugurals or state of the unions. Nearly all such statements involve promises—promises of a brighter future if followed or Armageddon if rejected. Past memories and associations are evoked to stimulate a sense of security, better times, and romantic longings.

No president since Dwight Eisenhower was more successful in projecting a positive future and glorious past than Ronald Reagan. The positive themes of the Reagan presidency, as noted, were heroism, faith, and patriotism. He welcomed heroes, espoused faith in God and country, and surrounded himself with icons of American myth and culture. In the reelection of 1984, his spots proclaimed that "It's morning again in America," showing a wedding, a family moving into a new home, fertile fields, and employed construction workers. His rhetoric provided a sense of momentum, tradition, and historical significance. The characters of his stories were historic and symbolic, reflecting the values of family, freedom, nationalism, and faith, to name only a few. Even with real, genuine stories, Reagan made complex operations the story of one person. An important function of political language, therefore, is to link us to past glories and reveal the future in order to reduce uncertainty in a world of ever-increasing complexity and doubt.

Interestingly, in the 1996 presidential campaign, Clinton spoke of the future with the notion of "a bridge to the twenty-first century" in contrast to Dole's portrayal of an America from the past. In his nomination acceptance speech, Dole wanted to be the "bridge to a time of tranquility, faith, and confidence in action." Clinton, in contrast, said he did not want to be a bridge to the past, but "a bridge to the twenty-first century" (Just 1996, 87). This single contrast highlighted the difference between the two candidates, in terms of vision, youth, and outlook. When Dole talked about why he was running, he used words like "duty," "honor," "integrity," "trust," "God and country." These are the words of previous generations, certainly not today's adults who never faced the challenges of a world war, the great depression, or securing the basics of life. Today, voters want to hear about opportunities, material goods, economic security, health care, and day care.

Finally, and perhaps most importantly, political language must function to mobilize society and stimulate social action. Language serves as the stimulus, means, or rationale for social action. Words can evoke, persuade, implore, command, label, praise, and condemn. Political language is similar to other uses of language. But it also articulates, shapes, and stimulates public discussion and behavior about the allocation of public resources, authority, and sanctions. Michael Osborn (1986) argues that political rhetoric today is dominated by strategic verbal and nonverbal visualizations that linger in the memory of audiences (80). It functions as presentation, intensification, identification, implementation, and reaffirmation. For him, political rhetoric presents the world, provides emotion, recreates a sense of oneness, sustains action, and reminds us of our history. Osborn's study challenges the notion that political rhetoric is primarily rational. Rather, it "emphasizes instead the symbolic moorings of human consciousness" (97).

Functions of Governmental Language

Craig Smith (1990) identifies five functions of governmental language: to unify, to legitimize, to orient, to resolve conflicts, and to implement policies (61–62). These are very pragmatic and programmatic uses of political language. From a governmental perspective, language serves to generate a sense of inclusion and participation among citizens. Language also serves to legitimize and confirm in the minds of the public the authority, role, and justification of governmental actions. Related to the agenda-setting function identified above, governmental language frames our national goals, policies, hopes, and desires as well as articulates our needs, problems, and shortcomings. Social conflicts are resolved by issue discussion, explanation, debate, and negotiation. Finally, government implements policy through the creation of legislation and regulatory interpretation. From this perspective, the language of government encompasses elected officials, government agencies, and government employees.

Styles of Governmental Language

Murray Edelman (1964) identifies four distinctive governmental language styles used to maintain the political order (133–48). They include: hortatory, legal, administrative, and bargaining styles. Hortatory language is the style most directed toward the mass public. It is employed by individuals and contains the most overt appeals for candidate and policy support. Consequently, the most sacred of national symbols and values are evoked. Legal language encompasses laws, constitutions, treaties, statutes, contracts, and so on. It is the specialized language of lawyers, courts, and legislatures. It attempts to be precise but is often ambiguous to the general public. Legal language compels argument and interpretation. Administrative language is certainly related to legal language. It is the language of bureacrats, the rules and implementation of laws and interpretation of regulations. The style usually encourages suspicion and ridicule by the public. Interestingly, administrative language, in its attempts to be clear and concise, is often as confusing to the public as legal language. Bargaining language style "offers a deal, not an appeal" and is acknowledged as the real catalyst of policy formation. Yet, public reaction or response politically is avoided. Once a bargain is created, the rationalization of the bargain often assumes the hortatory language style.

It is important to note that these language styles are content-free and are not limited to certain individuals or government agencies. For example, a president must utilize the linguistic devices in the bargaining style to win congressional approval of favorite legislation, the legal style to draft special legislation, administrative style for enforcing or providing the mechanics for operationalizing the legislation and the hortatory style for attempting to gain public support for a measure. Each style creates a different reality and subsequent behavior. The realities of crisis, confidence, patriotism, and action may all be created to achieve the final goal. For the basic assumption, as Edelman (1964) notes, that the public "responds to currently conspicuous political symbols; not to 'facts,' and not to moral codes embedded in the character of soul, but to the gestures and speeches that make up the drama of the states" (172). The task remains to investigate the types of political symbols and their impact upon societal behavior.

Strategic Uses of Political Language

We have drawn a rather large circle. We began the chapter by discussing the inherent symbolic nature of humans followed by a discussion of the role and importance of communication in society. Political symbols are the direct link between individuals and the social order. As elements of a political culture, they function as a stimulus for behavior. The use of appropriate symbols results in getting people to accept certain policies, arouse support for various causes, and obey governmental authority. Political symbols are the means to social ends and not ends in themselves.

There is, however, a long process for the creation, definition, acceptance, and subsequent behavior. Implicit in our argument is the notion that successful leadership and control is dependent upon the successful creation and manipulation of political language and symbols. Political symbols are perpetuated in order to preserve the prevailing culture, political beliefs, and values. Political language creates, alters, and maintains the "social state."

It is important to remember that the context and content of the interaction is what makes the use of language political. The contexts range from a local candidate talking at a reception, to speeches in the halls of Congress, to the rally of citizens outside a courthouse, to name just a few. In Chapter 1, we identified the broad content areas of political communication as dealing with resources, control (authority and power), sanctions (rules and regulations), and social meaning. Below are among the most common strategic uses of political language:

- *Argumentation and persuasion*—Political language is used to discuss, debate, and negotiate issues and legislation. As already mentioned, political rhetoric is not neutral, it's about the altering of attitudes, beliefs, and values. Political language is about advocacy, creating a "symbolic reality" from a particular perspective, for a specific purpose.
- *Identification*—Political language creates commonality, understanding, and unity. Language is a way to relate to others, to formulate bridges of understanding. Politicians, both verbally and nonverbally, attempt to demonstrate they understand their constitutents and are similar in beliefs, attitudes, and values. According to Kenneth Burke (1969), "you persuade a person only in-

sofar as you can talk the person's language by speech, gesture, tonality, order, image, attitude, identifying your ways with this person's" (p. 55). The importance of language as it relates to nationalism can be viewed in light of the debate over English as our "standard" language. A "homogeneous linguistic community" is argued in terms of shared values. Social identity is another important use of political language. Language links us as a social class or ethnicity or cultural heritage. Socialization, common experiences, and such appeals are very strong. Language can provides a rallying point for issues and commonality of efforts.

- *Reinforcement*—The process of persuasion, the altering of beliefs, attitudes, and values, is a very difficult process. In fact, despite conventional wisdom, most political communication is not about altering attitudes, but reinforcing existing beliefs and attitudes. Most political discourse and even advertising is about reinforcing public preferences. Much of presidential discourse is about reinforcing our national goals and values. Thus, to approach all political discourse as blatant attempts to change public attitudes will miss the dominant strategic use of political language.

- *Innoculation*—Innoculation is a message strategy that seeks to promote resistance to attitude change. By strengthening existing attitudes, individuals become less susceptible to subsequent persuasive attempts. What is intriguing about this strategy is that when persuaders acknowledge counter-arguments or introduce negative information related to their own position, audiences are not only more likely to believe them, but will be less likely to process or believe counter-arguments or information in the future. This is most useful in political campaigns, especially in generating resistance to the influence of political attacks by opponents. The result, you will note, is not about the altering of attitudes, but reinforcement of existing attitudes.

- *Polarization*—Political language can create likenesses and commonalities but also may distinguish or separate people, issues, and ideas. Interestingly, sometimes the best way to define an issue or position is by detailing what it is not, by contrasting the concept with its opposite. Reagan, for example, was good at articulating American values of freedom and free enterprise by comparing us with Russia. Of course, a more direct mode of polarlization is simply labeling the opposition, issue, or ideology as "bad." While polarizing issues and rhetoric may divide, it does unite in the sense that it helps clarify positions, actions, and even aspects of ideology. For example, while some people were fearful of the campaign rhetoric of Republican Pat Buchanan, he did unite and speak for a segment of conservative Republicans as well as provide clear policy alternatives to issues such as affirmative action, illegal immigration, and the practice of abortion.

- *Labeling*—As suggested above, labeling and defining issues, politicians, and policies forces us to make judgments and evaluations. In many ways, campaigns are really contests of prevailing (i.e., winning) definitions of social reality. Is the economy strong or weak? Is the crime rate high or low? Are our values strong or slipping? Is the opponent liberal or conservative? In essense, whose view of reality are voters going to believe? This perspective reflects the view, once again, that much political language is not about changing opinions, but reinforcing prevailing views or attempting to prevail in providing the dominant view of social reality.

- *Expression*—This represents more than the instrumental functions of political language. Much of the political symbols, rituals, and language is expressive in nature. Political language allows for the expression of frustration as well as specific policy ideas, for hopes as well as fears, for successes as well as failures. A review of the functions of political language identified above illustrates how much of political language is expressive rather than more programmatic. It is also important to recognize the growing importance of political language as an expressive function as entertainment in American popular culture. Novels, films, television, and popular journalism all contain messages about issues, politics, and society.
- *Power*—Much of political communication is about power, domination, or control. Kenneth Hacker (1996, 29) identifies three dimensions of power. The first dimension of power is conflict over concrete political interests revealed in policy preferences. In this case, language is objective and descriptive. The second dimension of power is control over how issues are defined, debated, and acted upon. Language is critical in framing issues, defining concepts, etc. The final dimension of power is control over agendas and decision making. Language here is more utilitarian once again. Power in language is exhibted in many ways: arguments grounded in language that legitimizes rule of those who govern, appeals to moral authority, or narratives of preferred behavior, to name a few. It is also important to recognize that *how* something is said gives language power as much as *what* is said.
- *Drama*—Most political events are dramatic. For some scholars, politics is living drama and worthy of study. For Hugh Duncan (1968), "failure to understand the power of dramatic form in communication means failure in seizing and controlling power over men" (25). It is important to remember that social dramas are not just symbolic screens or metaphors but they are social reality because they are forms of social interaction and integration. For example, to focus on dramas of authority one should ask: Under what conditions is the act being presented? What kind of act is it? What roles are the actors assuming? What forms of authority are being communicated? What means of communication are used? What symbols of authority are evoked? How are social functions staged? How are social functions communicated? How are the messages received? What are the responses to authority messages? The drama can involve one person or many, a symbolic (rhetorical) event or physical act, one moment or a specific period of time. Politics, in Burkean terms, is a study of drama composed of many acts. They are acts of hierarchy, transformation, transcendence, guilt, victimage, redemption, and salvation. With an act as the pivotal concept, Kenneth Burke (1967, 332) suggests that we investigate scenes that encompass and surround the act, for the scene provides the context for an act. Next, he suggests that we consider the agents involved in an act; the actors who mold, shape, create, and sustain movements. Likewise, consideration of the agency or the channels of communication in an act help reveal the impact of rhetorical activities. And consideration of purpose of an act aids in discov-

ering the ultimate motives or meaning of the act. Drama is part of the communication process where public issues and views are created, shared, and given life. Ernest and Nancy Bormann (1977, 306–17) call this process "group fantasy." A relatively small number of people may attach significance to some term or concept such as the notions of justice, freedom, or the American dream. These fantasies are shared and passed on to others. Fantasies are contained in messages that channel through the mass media to the general public. When a fantasy theme has "chained through the general public," there emerges a "rhetorical vision." "A rhetorical vision is a symbolic reality created by a number of fantasy types and it provides a coherent view of some public problem or issue" (Bormann and Bormann 1977, 311). Slogans or labels that address a cluster of meanings, motives, or emotional responses usually indicate the emergence of a rhetorical vision. There are several useful implications to the notion of fantasy themes. As a result of creating and sharing fantasies, there is a greater sense of community, cohesiveness, and shared culture. There are, then, common beliefs, attitudes, and values upon which to live and act. And communication is the foundation of it all.

All of these elements demonstrate the strategic power of language in politics. Our position is that public views on issues are mobilized rather than fixed. Issues are largely created, identified, and permeated throughout society. Neither issues nor specific positions on issues exist in a vacuum. Even governmental outputs are results of the creation of political followings and mass support.

THE CHANGING NATURE OF POLITICAL DISCOURSE

As society and technology change, so do the ways presidents campaign and govern. As a result, presidential rhetoric has undergone a fundamental change in both form and content.[1] Barnet Baskerville (1979) argues, in a book entitled *The People's Voice*, that "societal values and attitudes are reflected not only in what the speaker says but also in how he says it—not only in the ideas and arguments to be found in speeches of the past but in the methods and practices of representative speakers and in the role and status accorded speakers by the listening public. As public tastes and public needs change, so do speaking practices—types of appeal, verbal style, modes of delivery" (4).

The United States has a rich history of political oratory. For much of our history, public oratory provided the main avenue to success and popular esteem. Politicians were expected to frequently make long public orations. Such occasions were public spectacles with banners, bands, slogans, and fireworks. The famous "soap box" or "stump" campaigns were deliberative in nature. Politicians articulated elements of political philosophy. Political oratory was an instrument for conducting national business and a means of public education, and served as an end in itself—a mode of creative expression.

By 1900 political oratory had undergone its first fundamental change. This change was signaled by Lincoln in his Gettysburg Address. He established a trend toward brevity and simplicity in public oratory. But more important was the shift of the American hero from the politician to the businessman. Captains of industry espoused virtues of directness, conciseness, and pragmatism. Political speeches became shorter, more colloquial, and less "airy." In fact, political oratory became public speaking with an emphasis on utility of message and the sharing of information. The number of magazine articles and newspaper stories increased while their length decreased. Radio introduced lively discussion shows, news "reports" (unlike news stories), and time constraints upon both the speaker and audience.

Thus, there was a shift in the attitudes of Americans toward politicians, work and industry, and the outside world. The shift of attitudes also impacted how we talked to each other. Radio crossed ethnic and regional boundaries. Politicians had to speak "at" audiences, not "with" audiences. The press became "filters" rather than "vehicles" of political communication.

It was television, as you may have guessed, that initiated the third major change in political campaign rhetoric. In the 1970s, campaign politics was viewed as a mature science. The professionals believed the key to success was "poli-techs" or the use of computers to track voters and assist in precinct canvassing and direct mail activities. The better financed Republicans utilized such technology primarily because of scattered and rural party members. Democrats relied on organized labor and other groups to mobilize voters and garner support. Today, the key is "video politics" (Schram 1987, 27–28). This does not refer to policy discussion or political commercials but to the control and manipulation of local and national nightly news presentations. Campaigning and governing are done through the medium of television. As early as 1974, Kevin Phillips proclaimed that "in the age of the mass media, the old Republican and Democratic parties have lost their logic. Effective communications are replacing party organizations as the key to political success. . . . As the first communications society, the United States is on its way to becoming the first 'mediacracy' " (1974, v). We are witnessing the evolution of the "new presidential" rhetoric that differs in both form and content from that of only 20 years ago.

Today, it is only through the media that we come to know our leaders. And with the frequency of appearance we feel that we have come to know our presidents intimately. It is virtually impossible to distinguish between our political system and the media as separate entities. Television, as a medium, has changed the form and content of American politics. This change is not so much the result of how the medium is used as much as the requirements or essential nature of the medium.

As noted, the days of impassioned, fiery oratory presented to packed auditoriums of live human beings are over. Today, presidents invite us, through the medium of television, into the privacy of their living rooms, offices, or studios for informal, "presidential conversations." Kathleen Jamieson (1988) argues that the interpersonal, intimate context created through television requires a "new eloquence;" one in which candidates and presidents adopt a personal and revealing style that engages the audience in conversation.

Presidential Conversation as Mediated Discourse[2]

Scholarly attention is increasingly becoming focused on the nature of the "plebiscitary presidency" (Lowi, 1985) and the various strategies involved in "going public" (Kernell, 1985). Presidents who increasingly rely on the medium of television are forced into playing the communication game by television's rules. This not only means shorter speeches, it also means speeches that are crafted specifically for television. Presidential speech is increasingly familiar, personalized, and self-revealing. Reagan's use of contractions, simple and often incomplete sentences, informal transitions, colloquial language, and frequent stories transformed his "formal" Oval Office addresses to conversations with the American people (Jamieson, 1988, 166). His skillful adaptation to the camera simulated direct eye contact with individuals in his audience. It has all the appearance of conversation. This conversational style "invite[s] us to conclude that we know and like" presidents who use it (Jamieson, 1988). Ronald Reagan first excelled at this style, which stands in marked contrast even to the conversational style of Franklin D. Roosevelt, for example. For where the strength of Reagan's rhetoric is that we feel we know and understand him, the strength of FDR's was that he knew and understood us. Bill Clinton through his mediated conversational style accomplishes both, especially in the town hall meeting format.

Certainly with Clinton, presidential conversation was to be the primary means of conveying policy orientations and image projection. These "one-on-one" sessions, sometimes with viewer call-in or a live audience moved the president one step closer to the public. Participation and interaction are encouraged. Settings are becoming more informal, giving the appearance of a casual interaction where the audience simply "eavesdrops" on the conversation.

It is important to note, however, that mediated conversation does not parallel the process of human communication. We know, for example, in the media interview format, questions to be asked are often known ahead of time and presidents rehearse desired responses prior to a mediated event. In some cases, topics and areas of discussion are issues of negotiation. In addition to lacking spontaneity of interaction, there can obviously be no "turn taking" with the televised audience. Naturally, the interviewer gives a great deal of deference to the president. Thus the partners in the interaction, whether it is the audience or the interviewer and president, are not equal in terms of control, power, or reciprocity in any phase of the conversation. There is not a mutual exchange of asking questions, voicing opinions, or stating facts.

Presidents may make themselves "physically" available but not accessible in terms of openness and a willingness to share and disclose feelings, beliefs, and attitudes. Likewise, there is little commitment to the interaction or relationship and, from a presidential perspective, the "conversation" is more often a means to a political end. In short, there is no intrinsic value to the conversation. In mediated presidential conversation, competition over control and message rather than cooperation is the norm. Although interaction takes place, it is, quite simply, a different kind of interaction.

Not only is the structure of mediated presidential conversation different from nonmediated conversation, but the content of the interactions differ as well. Interviews on television differ greatly from those in print. On television, how one responds is as important as the content of the response. Was there a hesitation, a shift of the brow, an expression of emotion? Remember the shot of Bush, in the 1992 Richmond presidential candidate debate with Clinton and Perot, taking a quick glance at his watch? This simple action communicated a rather callous, cavalier attitude toward the audience and the event.

Perceptions of personal characteristics conveyed primarily in nonverbal communication influence viewer perception of specific presidential performances. Measures of cooperative attitude, equality, absence of superiority, warmth, interest, similarity and friendliness, sincerity, and honesty account for substantial variance in likelihood of viewers voting for a candidate, perceptions of credibility, and judgments about competence, sociability, and character (Pfau and Kang, 1991, 124). The secret, therefore, is a controlled response best suited for the medium of television. "More than print," Meyrowitz (1985) says, "electronic media tend to unite sender and receiver in an intimate web of personal experience and feeling" (96). The public's reactions are personal and "real," shaped by feelings and intuitions as much as by rational analysis and interpretation. In the end, the public believes they "know" the president.

Presidents should adapt to the medium of television through higher levels of intimacy and expressiveness. The "presumption of intimacy" attempts to make the audience feel as if they know the president as a dear friend and to force the audience to render positive, personal judgments. Frequent "conversations" lead to friendship, trust, and intimacy with the nation. Issue disagreements are less important and tolerated because of the appearance of friendship (Cathcart and Gumpert, 1986).

But these conversations are no more real than any televised performance. The "conversation" is at least loosely scripted and practiced for timing, camera angle, and content. Some subjects and areas are off-limits. The media tourist cannot spontaneously change the spaces to be included in the tour nor surprise the First Couple with a tough policy question. Finally, the product is edited to meet the constraints of the medium and the expectations of the audience. The audience receives its "televised invitation," a promotional advertisement, to the open house. It is both performance and production.

Because they are so revealing, politicians must at all costs protect their "true" back regions. Many Americans were surprised at the language of Richard Nixon revealed in the Watergate tapes. Americans were shocked at Carter's revelation that he too had "lusted in his heart" for women. Reagan's playful comments of blowing up Russia when testing a microphone before one of his weekly radio broadcasts frightened many Americans, perhaps revealing his true intentions towards the Soviets. Presidents must be on guard without appearing guarded.

While Reagan proved that television's intimacy could heighten audience identification, the 1992 presidential campaign moved a step further with an interpersonal mediated context—the televised town meeting. It is Clinton's mastery of the town hall meeting format that epitomizes "presidential mediated interpersonal conversation" (Denton and Holloway 1996).

Implications of Mediated Presidential Conversations

Political scholars, journalists and pundits raise concerns about the new presidential "public address." Mediated presidential conversation fails to properly inform and educate the public on political matters. Mediated presidential conversation encourages citizen's continued emphasis on character rather than substance of policy (Schram, 1991). As the public becomes even more reliant upon television as a source of political information, the medium increasingly simplifies the information and, consequently, the ability to recognize, perform, and appreciate complex social issues also decline. Ferrarotti (1988) observes that "as we are informed, we know everything about everything, but we no longer understand anything. It is purely cerebral information that does not manage to touch the deeper levels of human beings" (13). For Roderick Hart (1994), "television miseducates the citizenry but, worse, it makes that miseducation attractive" (12). In reality, the public does not know what they think they know and the public does not care about what they do not know. Politicians no longer try to change minds through argumentation; rather, they attempt to say something we in the audience can identify with, to project an image by what they say, to communicate something about their personalities by the audiences they choose to address.

The staged mediated presidential conversations offer a mode of discourse that Neil Postman (1985) characterizes as "accessible, simplistic, concrete, and above all, entertaining" (18). He argues that

> the problem is not that TV presents the masses with entertaining subject matter, but that television presents all subject matter as entertaining. What is dangerous about television is not its junk. Every culture can absorb a fair amount of junk, and, in any case we do not judge a culture by its junk but by how it conducts its serious public business. What is happening in America is that television is transforming all serious public business into junk. (15)

Not only does mediated presidential conversation trivialize public issues and thought but its overall effect is one of confusion.

Through mediated presidential conversations, our presidents become media celebrities or personalities. A celebrity is a "human pseudo-event" where people are "known for their well-knowness" (Nimmo and Combs, 1983). The mediated conversations provide a false intimacy because they do not reveal the true back regions of presidents' thoughts or ideas. They are backstage interactions performed on frontstage. The illusion is one of spontaneity and accessibility. In Clinton's case, Joe Klein (1992) noted that "there is a facile opacity to this style of leadership: even though we get to hear about his twelve-step program, his stepfather's alcoholism, his mother's cancer, his brother's drug addiction, the host himself remains elusive, a kaleidoscope of comforting images" (35). We participate vicariously in their life through "artificial interactions." At best, according to Roderick Hart (1984), "television gives us a one-dimensional presidency. It presents our presidents to us in their Sunday best but without their souls or feelings" (54).

Perhaps the most damaging aspect of all mediated conversations is the public's open acknowledgment that all political talk is performance. Martin Schram (1987) argues that the public's recognition that all presidents are ultimately "acting" merely leads to acceptance of the ability to perform as the essential qualification for office: "the quest for personal leadership becomes a self-destructive quest in which all pretenders are found to be just that. In the end, the grammar of electronic electioneering teaches people to be content with their inability to find a "real leader" and to be comfortable with elected officials who are comfortable faking it" (215).

The mediated conversations also create a short-term political environment. The focus is on the person, not the issue; the momentary emotion, not the long-term commitment; the immediate image, not the long-term solution. Through the conversations, presidents engender trust and identification rather than the process of rational decision making. There is, as Jamieson (1988) notes, a continual divorce between speech and thought, character and ideas (215).

The Future of Political Discourse

Ronald Collins and David Skover (1996) fear the "death of discourse" in America. They view an irony of "discourse dying in America, yet everywhere free speech thrives" (xix). For them, "discourse" is interaction characterized by reason, by method, and with purpose. It is not "trivial talk." Discourse is not mere expression for expression sake but, as in the Aristotelian sense, in the service of the public good. It is about values, policies, and national character.

A way of thinking about their question is to ask, do we engage in healthy political discourse? A candy bar is food, but is it nutritional? How much "junk food" do we consume? How much "junk food" can we ingest before the body becomes sick? We have plenty of food, but we are starving. Thus, Collins and Skover (1996) distinguish between the principles of political discourse characterized by rational decision making, civic participation, meaningful dissent, and self-realization and contemporary political "speech" characterized by entertainment, passivity, pleasure, and self-gratification. For them, we are on the border of equating "amusement with enlightenment, fantasy with fact, and the base with the elevated" (203).

One should note that the concern is not about *persuasive* oratory, genuine engagement of ideas. As Keith Felton (1995) argues, "there is power in purposive oratory. When poetic in its reach, when deservedly acclaimed, oratory outlives the moment of utterance, and enters a universal lexicon of expression to become a permanently recorded part of the march of ideas. The influence of language upon history is ineluctable . . . [it] buoys civilization over its perennial perils" (xv).

NOTES

1. Much of this discussion is based on Chapter 1 in Robert E. Denton, Jr., *The Primetime Presidency of Ronald Reagan* (Westport, CT: Praeger, 1988).

2. The definition and argument of "presidential conversation as mediated discourse" is based on Robert E. Denton, Jr., and Rachel L. Holloway, "Presidential Communication as Mediated Conversation," *Research in Political Sociology* 7 (1995): 91–115.

REFERENCES

Barber, James David. 1980. *The Pulse of Politics*. New York: Norton.

Baskerville, Barnet. 1979. *The People's Voice*. Lexington: University of Kentucky Press.

Bormann, Ernest, and Nancy Bormann. 1977. *Speech Communication: A Comprehensive Approach*. New York: Harper & Row.
Burke, Kenneth. 1966. *Language as Symbolic Action*. Berkeley: University of California Press.
———. 1967. "Dramatism." In *Communication Concepts and Perspectives*, ed. Lee Thayer. Rochelle Park, NJ: Hayden, pp. 322–55.
———. 1969. *A Rhetoric of Motives*. Los Angeles: University of California Press.
Cathcart, Robert, and Gary Gumpert. 1986. "Mediated Interpersonal Communication: Toward a New Typology." *Quarterly Journal of Speech* 69: 267–77.
Charon, Joel. 1979. *Symbolic Interactionism: An Introduction, an Interpretation, an Integration*. Englewood Cliffs, NJ: Prentice-Hall.
Cobb, Roger, and Charles Elder. 1972. "Individual Orientations in the Study of Political Symbolism." *Social Science Quarterly* 53: 82–86.
Collins, Ronald, and David Skover. 1996. *The Death of Discourse*. Boulder, CO: Westview Press.
Corcoran, Paul E. 1990. "Language and Politics." In *New Directions in Political Communication: A Resource Book*, ed. David Swanson and Dan Nimmo. Newbury Park, CA: Sage, pp. 51–85.
Denton, Robert E., Jr. 1988. *The Primetime Presidency of Ronald Reagan*. New York: Praeger.
Denton, Robert E., Jr., and Rachel L. Holloway. 1995. "Presidential Communication as Mediated Conversation." *Research in Political Sociology* 7: 91–115.
———. 1996. "Clinton and the Town Hall Meetings: Mediated Conversation and the Risk of Being 'In Touch.'" In *The Clinton Presidency: Images, Issues, and Communication Strategies*, ed. Robert E. Denton, Jr., and Rachel L. Holloway. Wesport, CT: Praeger, pp. 17–41.
Duncan, Hugh. 1968. *Symbols in Society*. New York: Oxford University Press.
Easton, David. 1965. *A Systems Analysis of Political Life*. New York: John Wiley and Sons.
Edelman, Murray. 1964. *The Symbolic Uses of Politics*. Urbana: University of Illinois Press.
———. 1971. *Politics as Symbolic Action*. Chicago: Markham Publishing.
———. 1988. *Constructing the Political Spectacle*. Chicago: University of Chicago Press.
Faules, Don, and Dennis Alexander. 1979. *Communication and Social Behavior*. Boston: Addison-Wesley.
Felton, Keith S. 1995. *Warrior's Words: A Consideration of Language and Leadership*. Westport, CT: Praeger.
Ferrarotti, Franco. 1988. *The End of Conversation*. Westport, CT: Greenwood Press.
Graber, Doris. 1981. "Political Languages." In *Handbook of Political Communication*, ed. Dan D. Nimmo and Keith R. Sanders. Beverly Hills, CA: Sage, pp. 195–224.
Gronbeck, Bruce. 1986. "Ronald Reagan's Enactment of the Presidency in His 1981 Inaugural Address." In *Form, Genre and the Study of Political Discourse*, ed. Herbert Simons and Aron Aghazarion. Columbia: University of South Carolina Press, pp. 226–45.
Hacker, Kenneth. 1996. "Political Linguistic Discourse Analysis." In *The Theory and Practice of Political Communication Research*, ed. Mary Stuckey. Albany: State University of New York Press, pp. 28–55.

Hall, Peter. 1972. "A Symbolic Interactionist Analysis of Politics." *Sociological Inquiry* 42: 35–73.

Hart, Roderick. 1984. *Verbal Style and the Presidency*. Orlando, FL: Academic Press.

———. 1994. *Seducing America*. New York: Oxford University Press.

Jamieson, Kathleen H. 1988. *Eloquence in an Electronic Age*. New York: Oxford University Press.

Just, Marion. 1996. "Candidate Strategies and the Media Campaign." In *The Election of 1996*, ed. Gerald Pomper. Chatham, NJ: Chatham House, pp. 77–106.

Kernell, Samuel. 1985. *Going Public: New Strategies of Presidential Leadership*. Washington, DC: Congressional Quarterly Press.

Klein, Joe. 1992. "The Bill Clinton Show." *Newsweek*, 26 October: 35.

Lorenzo, David. 1996. "Political Communication and the Study of Rhetoric." In *The Theory and Practice of Political Communication Research*, ed. Mary Stuckey. Albany: State University of New York Press, pp. 1–27.

Lowi, Theodore. J. 1985. *The Personal President: Power Invested, Promise Unfulfilled*. Ithaca, NY: Cornell University Press.

Mead, George H. 1972. *Mind, Self, and Society*. Chicago: University of Chicago Press.

Meyrowitz, Joshua. 1985. *No Sense of Place*. New York: Oxford University Press.

Mueller, Claus. 1973. *The Politics of Communication*. New York: Oxford University Press.

Nimmo, Dan. 1978. *Political Communication and Public Opinion in America*. Palo Alto, CA: Goodyear.

Nimmo, Dan, and James Combs. 1980. *Subliminal Politics: Myths and Mythmakers in America*. Englewood Cliffs, NJ: Spectrum Books.

———. 1983. *Mediated Political Realities*. New York: Longman.

Osborn, Michael. 1986. "Rhetorical Depiction." In *Form Genre and the Study of Political Discourse*, ed. Herbert Simons and Aron Aghazarion. Columbia: University of South Carolina Press, pp. 79–107.

Pfau, Michael, and Jong Kang. 1991. "The Impact of Relational Messages on Candidate Influence in Televised Political Debates." *Communication Studies* 42(2): 114–28.

Phillips, Kevin. 1974. *Mediacracy*. New York: Doubleday.

Postman, Neil. 1985. *Amusing Ourselves to Death: Public Discourse in the Age of Show Business*. New York: Penguin.

Rose, Richard. 1970. *People in Politics: Observations Across the Atlantic*. New York: Basic Books.

Schram, Martin. 1987. *The Great American Video Game*. New York: William Morrow & Co.

Schram, Sanford. 1991. "The Post-Modern Presidency and the Grammar of Electronic Engineering." *Critical Studies in Mass Communication* 8: 210–16.

Smith, Craig Allen. 1990. *Political Communication*. San Diego: Harcourt Brace Jovanovich.

Chapter 4

The Media of Politics: News and the Political Agenda

> In a political democracy, the media are a vital force in keeping the concerns of the many in the field of vision of the governing few.
>
> Michael Schudson (1995)

In 1952, what was to be just a small footnote to campaign history became a milestone in the use of political media. Democrat Adlai Stevenson and the venerable Dwight Eisenhower had begun their presidential campaigns. But it was Eisenhower's running mate, an aggressive young senator from California named Richard Nixon, who created much of the news. Many vice-presidential contenders pass in and out of public attention with a minimum of national interest. But Nixon was different. Early in the campaign it became evident that he was a lightning rod for attention and in deep trouble. The eventual outcome was one of those moments in history when a public figure's redemption hangs by the thread of a single event. In this case Nixon was able to preserve his political career in a single 30-minute nationwide television speech.

The address was a master political move and an early glimpse of the role the media would increasingly play in defining our national political life.

The episode began with the charge that Nixon had used campaign funds to establish a private "slush" fund of $16,000. The suggestion that he was skimming money from his fundraising efforts was severely aggravated by the fact that Eisenhower was slow to come to Nixon's defense, giving weight to press speculation that the scrappy senator was in deep political trouble. Hours and days passed until it became evident to Nixon that he would have to engineer his own political salvation. Speaking to the nation from a living room set in an empty Hollywood theater, he justified the necessity to seek outside financial support to run for the Senate. In the process, he saved his place on the ticket and probably rescued his future.

The address was both a masterful and tawdry apologia, dramatically recounting his own modest finances to an audience of perhaps 60 million (Nixon 1968, 126). In a perfect adaptation to the strengths of television, the speech translated the personal into the political. With his wife at his side, he reviewed his own modest finances to vindicate the implication that he was making a fortune in politics: the paid-off loan on his Oldsmobile, his mortgage on a modest home, a $4,000 life insurance policy. "It isn't very much," he noted. "But Pat and I have the satisfaction that every dime that we have got is honestly ours." And then the man known for his ability to play congressional hardball shamelessly extended himself into the unfamiliar vernacular of television to find the perfect Ozzie and Harriet touch. He regretted that Pat did not have a mink coat. "But she does have a respectable Republican cloth coat, and I always tell her that she would look good in anything." And there was the gift of a dog named Checkers that the kids had grown to love. "I just want to say this, right now, that regardless of what they say about it, we are going to keep it" (Nixon 1968, 122).

On television, the virtues of domesticity could have their own political benefits. Indignation over "smears" and "innuendo" was wrapped in a rhetoric of middle-class honor. The alleged use of a political fund had been transformed into something altogether more personal and visceral.

Nixon asked viewers to decide his fate by writing to the Republican National Committee. But he need not have worried. The appeal yielded thousands of telegrams of support, and forced Eisenhower out of his indifference. Arguably, 30 minutes of political rhetoric has never had a greater effect on the course of American history.

The speech was an omen of a new age in American political life where personal attributes would take on more vividness than policy decisions, where peripheral matters of conduct would begin to compete for attention with the substance of political ideas. The speech signaled a new reality brought on by the entry of television into the political world. The medium—which is more about attitude than information, style more than substance—has changed the nature of political discourse and challenged journalists and politicians to use it as effectively as the older discursive medium of the printed page. If the press could generate doubts and television could amplify them, the same popular medium could be used to create effective defenses.

To be sure, the news environment comprises more than television, but all of the news media have changed to deal with the staggering growth of the electronic media in America's recent history. Radio emerged in the 1920s and television in the 1950s. The expansion of cable and web access in the last few decades continues to bring together political agents and the news industry in an uneasy relationship. Those in public life seek power by having their messages heard and accepted. Their counterparts in the media have a commercial need to find interesting stories and pictures, and a professional need to demonstrate their independence.

This chapter explores the tensions built into this relationship. Although virtually every topic in this book touches on the news media, our goal in this chapter is to review some essential features and problems common to the political press. After beginning with four clarifications about what it means to talk about "political media," we explore basic frameworks for assessing how news and our nation's civil life interact. These include the essential concepts of agenda-setting and gatekeeping. Both are discussed in length, because public attitudes about politics are heavily shaped by the story-telling preferences of news organizations. We also examine the distinguishing features of "free" and "paid" media, as well as the "attack" and "news management" models of the press. The chapter closes with an estimation of the effectiveness of mediated political messages.

MEDIA AND POLITICS: TRAPS AND CLARIFICATIONS

Politics in the Larger Media Universe

By the term "media" we mean the news and entertainment industries—large and small—who sell their wares to the general public on a routine basis. We include newspapers, broadcast news programs, political advertising, Internet sites, and purchased media such as Nixon's television address. Our focus here is specifically on the news and public relations aspects of political media. The role of politics in other forms of entertainment is considered in Chapter 12.

The mix of media available to Americans is enormous, including nearly 12,000 radio stations, 1,700 television stations, 11,000 periodicals, and about 1,600 daily newspapers. Sixty-five million households subscribe to one of the nation's 11,600 cable systems. And about one household in two subscribes to a newspaper. No nation comes close to producing the sheer volume of mass media content. And our consumption of it is equally voracious. The average American family has a television on over 6 hours a day. In the course of a year an adult American will consume 1,500 hours of television, 1,100 hours of radio, and 175 hours reading newspapers (Woodward 1997, 204).

But establishing the enormous size of the American media environment is the easy part. It becomes more difficult to define the portion that deals—broadly speaking—with the political.

It is obvious that most media content is not news, at least in the traditional journalistic sense. And most news is not about politics. The dominant components of the most heavily consumed media include mixtures of information and entertainment, much of it centered on film and sports celebrities. Even the traditional center of "serious" television news—the three broadcast networks' prestigious half hour early evening news programs—represents only a brief interruption of a schedule dominated by entertainment. And their share of viewers has fallen to below half of all of those watching television at the time (Tucher 1997, 26, 29). At the same time "hard news" is also in competition with other features and information in America's newspapers. Even the most prestigious examples of the daily press such as the *New York Times* have come in for criticism about the softening of their journalistic rigor in favor of entertaining features (Diamond 1995, 381–86).

If the bulk of American media is about entertainment rather than information, there is still no shortage of political news for those who wish to seek it. Policy and political discussion abounds in newspapers such as the *Wall Street Journal, Washington Post,* and *Los Angeles Times*. It exists in abundance in periodicals like *The Nation, The Weekly Standard, The New Republic, Slate* (online), and *Washington Monthly*. It is also found on television's PBS stations, C-SPAN, CNN, MSNBC, and scores of related Internet sites. And pockets of thoughtful discussion can even be found on the airwaves, notably in public radio. If the output and audience for all of these sources is small relative to the entire universe of American media, it is still easily available to those who are interested.

Media and the Limits of What We Know about Politics

By their very nature, the events and participants of political culture are rarely witnessed first hand. Instead, they are reconstructed for us by intermediaries. Like any arena where the discussion of human motivations weighs significantly, politics invites narration, interpretation and summation. Debates in a state assembly, hearings on Capitol Hill, or thick reports issued by an executive agency research staff will often be incomprehensible. It often takes a press report appearing in a morning paper to make sense of them. As the great journalist Walter Lippmann noted, "The world that we have to deal with politically is out of reach, out of sight, out of mind. It has to be explored, reported, and imagined." Through the mass media an individual learns "to smell, hear, or remember. Gradually he makes for himself a trustworthy picture inside his head of the world beyond his reach." (1930, 29). In short, news offers a mediated reality.

In an important sense, news is also less a comprehensive mirror of events than an interpretation of what events mean; less about hard information than about the stories of key actors in our national dramas. News provides a window onto the "defining moments" of the present: an imperfect but frequently vivid narrative of pivotal events in our public life. In 1996, for example, the three major television networks devoted the greatest amount of time to five stories of national and international significance: the explosion of TWA Flight 800 over Long Island, the Bob Dole presidential campaign, the war in Yugoslavia, the trial of O. J. Simpson, and conflict between Israelis and Palestinians (Tucher 1997, 30). The extensive coverage given to each story not only defined important features of the news culture of that year, but also to a large extent determined our national consciousness: the private and public discourse of American life in a particular period.

The Shared Rhetorical Nature of Politics and Press

Members of the press and those in political life are—in many ways—working at the same enterprise. Both must attribute motives. Both must explain the nontangible principles that form the honorable rationales for political action. And both must please audiences with reconstructions of attitudes and events which are inexact and diffuse. If a politician chooses to talk about the plight of "the poor in America," the reporter assigned to cover her must exercise similar rhetorical options to relay the tone and nature of the event to the reader or listener. As Michael Novak notes, the political impulse to please a constituency is usually every bit as strong in the journalist as it is in the politician, and maybe more, as well as corrupting.

> The tradition of American journalism demands "news." An "angle." Something "different." Something "fresh." . . . The world isn't made that way—"There's nothing new under the sun," men believed for thousands of years—and good politics is seldom a matter of novelty. But journalism has a voracious appetite for novelty. . . .
>
> Commentators, I think, fail to see how corrupting the practices of journalism truly are: the cult of celebrity, the cult of "news," the manipulative skills of "riding the wire," supplying two new daily "leads," grabbing headlines," manufacturing "events" and "statements." Journalists speak as if money were the great corrupter of our times; but the corruption of intelligence and imagination by the demand for "news" is deadly. (1973, 174)

In a word, journalism—like politics—is a rhetorical endeavor. It uses communication to give order to a disordered world.

Media and Pluralism

It is important to remember that the term, media, is a plural concept and, as such, carries limitations. As a name representing what we know to be a major force in our lives, the idea of the media is irresistible. But the "singularizing" of media that is common in everyday discussion (i.e., "the media ruined his chances for reelection.") implies more than is sometimes justified. Media outlets can have starkly different owners, objectives, audiences, and ways of constructing and delivering their messages. A local television newscast in New York City, for example, shares little more than a few headlines with the *New York Times*, the *Newark Star Ledger*, the *Amsterdam News*, and other media from the same region.[1]

This inherent diversity often produces a conceptual muddle when we overreach for phrases that are sometimes too broad to be meaningful. The complaint that some elections are won by "media campaigns," or that the Reagan and Clinton presidencies were "media driven," means less when we assume that a unique species of political life has been defined. Virtually every political level in the United States is known through what is written or reported about it, from reports about school board actions in local papers and citizen's newsletters to the latest dispatch from the White House carried by CNN. All of politics is in a sense mediated, and always has been. Even in the life of George Washington one finds public relations problems thought to have been invented in the age of radio and television: press fascination with his personality, a chain of publicity-based "pseudo events" leading up to his appointment as president, "news management" in the publication of his Farewell Address, and the kind of elevation to celebrity status that would have made *People* magazine proud (McDonald 1975, 24–26). In describing the function of media sources that influence Americans, therefore, it is important to specify contexts, messages and audiences. Each moment in public life is unique, fostering different realities created by different media.

Media and the Tendency to Over-Attribute Causation

Since World War II researchers in the social sciences have been exploring the complex relationships that exist between news sources and public attitudes. The impulse for this research is enormous, because we tend to assume that the collective impression of the culture is a product of what the media delivers to us. This belief that our attitudes are direct products of media consumption could be called media determinism. We intuitively believe that media messages directly determine attitudes and behaviors. To say—as many did—that Bob Dole lost the 1996 presidential election to Bill Clinton because he looked sullen and angry on television, or that Clinton was the better television debater, is to posit a relationship between media exposure and what we think and do as citizens (Bennet 1996, B6).

Even so, attributions of causation assigned to various forms of the media are notoriously difficult to establish. Extensive research over the last 50 years has yet to resolve a number of questions. Are correlations between public attitudes and intense media coverage causally related, or simply two arbitrary points in a process that involves other hidden forces? How accurate are media usage studies? And are the media so collectively powerful that they function like "magic bullets," piercing the thought processes of everyone in their path?[2]

Generally speaking, survey research reflecting public attitudes, and monitoring studies summarizing media content are conceptually more solid than studies that seek to link exposure to media content with changes in attitudes.[3] To put it simply, it is easier to ask people what they think, or to summarize messages they are exposed to, (i.e, which news stories they follow closely, and how pervasive those stories are), than to determine how specific news content affects their judgments about a reported event. For example, we have a clear understanding of how people use their time processing the news (Graber 1984) and what that news contains.[4] But it is far more difficult to determine how specific subjects react to certain media and its content. This latter approach involves the use of elaborate attempts to manipulate message- and source-related variables and to assess how they have affected people who have volunteered to be experimental subjects.

One notable study undertaken by Shanto Iyengar and Donald Kinder subtly altered the order of news stories in pretaped television news broadcasts to test the idea that prior stories could alter people's reactions to latter ones. Most interestingly, by changing the sequence of stories, they could induce subjects to change their judgments of the effectiveness of the president. They found that early stories on topics like the rate of economic inflation "primed" viewers to assess the chief executive in terms of how he dealt with such issues (1987, 112–33).

But experimental design is prone to a host of problems. Experiments occur in artificial environments. Their duration is usually short term, even though the most important media effects are those that last. It is also hard to isolate subjects from other outside influences. And few experimental groups represent the diversity of the population.[5] As Kathleen McGraw and Milton Lodge note, it is tempting to make judgments about the effects of "a neatly packaged information environment" such as a speech. But "Even in controlled laboratory studies, we do not yet have a firm grasp of how much of what kinds of information gets attention and is used" (1996, 133). For all of these reasons, measuring the effects of media exposure is a relatively rare form of political research. The more common approach is to infer possible or likely effects based on evidence of wide and pervasive exposure to certain media and frequently repeated messages.

Even within the limits of current research and analysis, a number of important conclusions are clear about how news shapes our political attitudes. Among the most important are the following:

- No single mass media source commands total loyalty and certain credibility. There is little reflexive acceptance of persuasive or informative messages, including those of the most prestigious mass media.
- People are generally selective about what they hear, making the actual effects of any political communication difficult to predict. Conclusions other than those intended by the sender are sometimes reached. Messages may be considered, momentarily accepted, and then later rejected.
- There is a great deal of elasticity in the attitudes of individuals. Attitudes may be stretched and momentarily altered by the appeals contained in a news story, editorial, or political broadcast. But individuals with preexisting beliefs are likely to retain those beliefs.
- Because opinions and attitudes are the products of many experiences, the messages of the mass media must be treated as only a few among many causes. To imply that the media alone are prime causes in attitude formation is to overlook other sources of attitudes, especially those gained from interpersonal contact. Attitudes are produced interactively rather than unilaterally.

BASIC FRAMEWORKS FOR ASSESSING POLITICAL MEDIA

Among the many key ideas that can be used to productively assess how politics is reconstructed for public consumption, four seem especially useful. They include the pivotal concepts of media gatekeeping and agenda-setting, along with the crucial relationships that develop between participants and press in the use of free media and news management techniques. Each of these is considered in turn.

Agenda-Setting and the Political Landscape

It is both obvious and important to note that the media collectively exert a considerable influence in determining the agenda of topics that will surface in the public consciousness. "The press," Walter Lippmann noted, "is like a beam of a searchlight that moves restlessly about, bringing one episode then another out of darkness into vision" (1930, 364). As the pioneering studies by Maxwell McCombs and E. F. Shaw have suggested, our knowledge and interest about various news topics is largely governed by what the mass media decides to call news (1972, 176–87). The agenda-setting power of the media is their ability to focus their light on what would otherwise be a dark corner of our national life. Events previously unseen become known, moving to familiarity and perhaps gaining status as a defining cultural event.

Arguably the most significant political news story in America's recent past was the product of dogged reporting that eventually forced other media to follow suit. The 1972 break-in of burglars at the Watergate complex in Washington was initially a local crime story, of little interest to anyone beyond a few reporters and editors at the *Washington Post*. It obviously became much more, as links were established between the burglars discovered in the offices of the Democratic Party and members of President Nixon's reelection committee. Other media were slow to see the significance of the break-in, and the resulting cover-up that would lead to the resignation of the president on the eve of an impeachment trial (Woodward and Bernstein 1974).

More recently, a front-page story in the *New York Times* about a young female pilot facing a court-martial helped create widespread public discussion. Along with a few other major news outlets, the *Times* is read by other news organizations, and often triggers coverage in them. The woman was charged with disobeying orders to end a relationship with a married man.[6] Apparently none of the previous 67 prosecutions for adultery—which the Air Force believes violates its need for "good order and discipline"—had created any national attention. This case was different, however. Not only had the *Times* decided to make it a page one story, but previous stories about sexual conduct and intimidation in all the branches of the military helped prime public interest. Whatever the influential newspaper's reasons for giving the case a high profile, their decision put the case of Kelly Flinn and the Air Force's policies on "fraternization" under intense public scrutiny.

The news agendas of America's best newspapers seem to have changed little over the past ten years. But there has been a shift in the kinds of stories favored by the network news organizations. Between 1988 and 1996, according to information gathered by the Media Studies Center (1997, 6), the focus of television news shifted from foreign to domestic issues, with less attention to American elections and U.S. foreign policy, and more interest in regional affairs (see Table 4.1). To put it most simply, there has been a shift away from politics, institutions, and international affairs. At the same time, there was decidedly more internal criticism by reporters and other observers that news of all types had grown more irrelevant and hostile to the values of ordinary Americans (Fallows 1996, 3–73; Tucher 1997, 26–31).

The reasons for these changes are difficult to track, but many would concur that television news is more responsive to the commercial need to follow audience tastes, generally with greater attention to news they "want" to know rather than "need" to know (Woodward 1997, 74–87).

Table 4.1
Network Nightly News Agenda Changes, 1988–1996

The network nightly news agenda has changed between 1988 and 1996. This table shows the percentage of all stories (in rounded numbers) filed by reporters according to their bureau, focus, and topic.

	1996	1988	
Stories Filed From:			
Foreign Bureaus	13	24	% of total
DC Bureaus	28	25	
Other Domestic Datelines	59	52	
Story Focus:			
Federal Elections	13	19	% of total
Federal Government (Domestic)	13	12	
U.S. Foreign Policy	7	12	
International	14	24	
National (Non-government)	20	16	
Regional/Local (Domestic)	32	17	
Story Topic:			
Terrorism	7	4	% of total
Health and Medicine	7	3	
Transportation	7	6	
Crime	7	2	
Economy	6	6	
War	6	5	
Sex and Family	5	4	
Drugs/Alcohol/Tobacco	4	4	
Natural Disasters	3	4	
Sports	3	3	
Arts/Media/Show Business	3	3	
Race and Immigration	3	2	
Education	3	1	
Space/Science/Technology	3	2	
Defense	2	6	
Religion	2	1	
Animals	2	2	
Environment	1	2	

Note: These percentages are based on all stories filed by correspondents. These account for roughly 80 percent of the total editorial time on the network nightly newscasts. The remainder is devoted to the anchors or their substitutes. The anchor's role includes copy-only stories, voicing-over videotape, and interviewing.

Source: Media Studies Center, "Women, Men and Media: The Changing News Agenda," 3 June 1997: 6 [online].

Gatekeeping and the Political Landscape

Like agenda-setting theory, gatekeeping theory is also about story selection. But where the agenda-setting function assigns the role of focusing attention on certain topics and away from others, gatekeeping theory explores the bases used for determining how much space or time events will receive in a given media outlet. The rules of gatekeeping vary by media type. Local television news is heavy on crime reporting, for example, and limited in foreign or political news. Many observers consider the news output of most stations as little better than what supermarket tabloids offer their readers (Frankel 1997, 20). The so-called "prestige press" of major newspapers generally reverses these priorities, though even the best metropolitan papers are seeking ways to hold onto declining numbers of readers (Gleick 1996, 66–69).

The bases of story selection—and for the emergence of a leader or issue into public awareness—are diverse and represent some of the most interesting areas of exploration into the business of news. The issue of what gets reported is especially important in the political realm, because politics is generally less visual and entertaining than other kinds of news stories, such as those dealing with natural disasters.

Some analysts, such as Herbert Gans, have emphasized the traditional journalistic rules for story suitability. Something has news value if it involves public officials, affects the nation, has an impact on large numbers of people, or says something about where we are going (1980, 146–52). An event may be deemed worthy of coverage if it contains a degree of novelty, and element of action, actual or potential conflict, and so on (1980, 167–71). These are familiar journalistic standards—based in part on pleasing the largest possible audience, and in part on traditional journalistic criteria for assessing what is important for news consumers to know.

Others have approached the study of news and information content by exploring topic and story selection from a consensual perspective. In this view "news" is what our priorities, fantasies, and national history tell us it is. It is a group product: a matter of agreement based on shared attitudes and routines (Schudson 1995, 12–14).

One pioneering account of this consensus model of news focuses on the 1972 presidential campaign. In his study Timothy Crouse firmly planted the concept of "pack journalism" into the lexicon of political analysis. Crouse provided evidence that reporters traveling with a presidential candidate frequently let the work of their colleagues govern their own perspectives toward specific campaign events. Living and traveling together for days at a time, some members of the press became collaborators in developing their stories, reaching agreement on particular "angles" or "leads" (1972, 22–23).

Twenty years later, Republican consultant Mary Matalin noted that little had changed since Crouse's study. Waging the 1992 Bush campaign against Bill Clinton, she was particularly annoyed at what she saw as the tendency of major news organizations to "all bounce off each other and write stories to fit into a common contextual analysis." She particularly noted that the power of whatever the major wire services were reporting:

> First the wires file their stories. They service most newspapers and file continuously, and they keep updating their pieces as the day or event unfolds. Then the other political writers from the dailies file. If these writers vary significantly from what the wires ran as their lead, their editors will go back to them and say, "This is not what's running on the wires. Reconstruct your story." (Matalin and Carville 1994, 126–27)

Most of the journalistic values that govern the gatekeeping process have to do with what makes an interesting story. Presidents and congressional leaders, for example, are more interesting to editors than institutions. Personal details are usually better copy than policy ideas. Scores of observers have assessed the gatekeeping tendencies built into the story format (Gans 1980; Epstein 1974; Robinson 1981; MacNeil 1968; Bennett 1988; Nimmo and Combs 1990). While their conclusions vary, certain themes tend to reappear, including the following:

1. *Political action is framed within the conventions of melodrama.* No point of reference has proved more durable in popular reports of political behavior than the terms and concepts associated with drama. Political reporting rarely ignores the elements of theater. Roles, scenes, acts, and audiences are endemic to descriptions of political events (Combs 1980, 1–17). Television news in particular, notes Paul Weaver "is not governed by a political bias, but by a melodramatic one." (1976, 6) It is characterized by intensified peril, simplified values, and exaggerated intensity. Characterizations of melodramatic images of foolishness, villainy, and heroes are common. They are used in themes that are equally familiar: the triumph of the individual over adversity, justice winning over evil, redemption of the individual through reform, and the rewarding of valor or heroism. Stories may not always have happy endings. But the reader or viewer is usually left with the impression of what the ending should be. As Dan Nimmo and James Combs note, news reporting is "a literary act, a continuous search for story lines." (1990, 28) Reflecting the logic that has long dominated the writing style of the new weeklies such as *Time* and *Newsweek*, former NBC News Chief Reuven Frank vividly made the same dramatistic point in what has since become a widely reprinted memo to his staff:

Every news story should, without any sacrifice or probity or responsibility, display the attributes of fiction, or drama. It should have structure and conflict, problem and denouement, rising action and falling action, a middle and an end. These are not only the essentials of drama; they are the essentials of narrative. (Epstein 1974, 4–5)

2. *Personalization over policy*. News frequently encourages us to look at cases and examples rather than pure ideas. Melodramatic structure depends upon vivid characterization, including the sketches of a person's public persona and their private self. In contemporary news, we often understand issues by seeing how they play out in the lives of the famous and the ordinary. These subjects may be agents for change, the victims of inaction or social neglect, and the villains responsible for creating social unrest. To be sure, it has always been the case that the character of the public figure has been a subject of public interest. The politics of ancient Greece enshrined the role of *ethos* and its central idea that personal qualities are important to strong leadership.[7] Theatre and storytelling in general encourage explorations of linkages that connect specific personal qualities to public behaviors.

In our recent past the widespread acceptance of psychoanalysis, film, the novel, and gossip columns have all contributed to interest in the details of the individual life. And television has intensified this pattern. In Richard Sennett's phrase, television especially is "compulsively personalistic." (1978, 284). It easily serves as an instrument that invites the careful measurement of intention and motive. We frequently cannot conceive of the principles governing foreign policy until we see graphic portrayals of the residents who would be affected. We cannot tolerate extensive discussion of tax law revisions without seeing depictions of affluence or poverty. Television frequently reduces policy debates to their material and personal dimensions.

In a relatively typical week in 1997, for example, most of the time of the three major television network news shows was consumed with stories about the actions of particular people. Between June 2 and 6, top stories included the trial of Timothy McVeigh for bombing the Oklahoma City federal building, charges of sexual harassment brought against President Bill Clinton, charges of adultery raised against his nominee for Chairman of the Joint Chiefs of Staff, and the murder of the son of Time-Warner's chief executive (Tyndall 1997, 1). For this and many other weeks, policy discussion without an anchor in someone's personal story was less frequent.

The case of Clinton is especially interesting. His public life has been dogged with questions about his character and behavior, with far more indifference towards the policy proposals and ideas of his administration. Yet Clinton has clearly been in a unique league of presidents—

including Thomas Jefferson, Theodore Roosevelt, and Woodrow Wilson—in his love of ideas. One can make a compelling case that his greatest passion is for ideas, for the connections between public policy and reform (Maraniss 1995). Yet any president's fate, as Sennett implies in *The Fall of Public Man*, is tied to a shift in the landscape of American politics:

> A political leader running for office is spoken of as "credible" or "legitimate" in terms of what kind of man he is, rather than in terms of the actions or programs he espouses. The obsession with persons at the expense of more impersonal social relations is like a filter which discolors our rational understanding of society; it obscures the continuing importance of class in advanced industrial society; it leads us to believe community is an act of mutual self-disclosure and to undervalue the community relations of strangers. (1978, 4)

Americans sometimes wonder why our press has become so fascinated with the private lives of our national leaders. Sennett's answer is that we have forgotten the arts of formal public communication, where roles are clearly defined, and the decision to enter into public discourse carries the responsibility to put the needs of institutions before private considerations.

3. *"Official" voices are the prime interpreters of events.*

Routine versions of news usually give an enormous amount of credibility to presidents, leaders of Congress, heads of corporations or federal agencies, and other leaders. A "top-down" model for reporting events gives leaders a special place in the story because of their formal/structural role, and because stories are easier to tell when focusing on one rather than many.

Consider two pivotal events in recent American history, both of which were largely told through official sources. Todd Gitlin's assessment of debates during the Vietnam war convincingly points out how marginalized dissenters—groups such as Students for a Democratic Society—were in press accounts. Their arguments against escalations of the conflict after 1965 were largely ignored, or reported as arguments of a rebellious fringe. (Gitlin 1980, 21–77) The pattern was repeated in press reporting of the Watergate break-in and cover-up. David Paletz and Robert Entman conclude that most of the coverage was at least initially always careful not to undermine the legitimacy of official White House explanations (1981, 158). For a very long time President Nixon's participation in the cover-up was neglected in favor of reports about the possible involvement of other officials. Even while they are lauded as watchdogs, Paletz and Entman note that the press effectively protects "the powerful," giving them legitimacy as the primary interpreters of events (1981, 157).

4. *Political reporting has drifted toward an emphasis on "strategy" rather than ideology.* Perhaps reflecting the pace of television, or the natural interest it places on human motives, political reporting is somewhat different from what it was several generations ago. The reader of a newspaper earlier this century was more likely to find news reports of political activity dominated by long excerpts of speeches and remarks. For a number of years in the 1920s and 1930s even radio was content to carry political addresses with a minimum of commentary. This "journalism" was not necessarily better. But it was different. By contrast, the gatekeeping objective of much contemporary political reporting focuses on strategies and tactics. Faced with the choice of recounting to reader or viewers what a particular figure said, or analyzing the motives behind remarks addressed to a specific audience, more and more journalism seems to emphasize the latter.

This pattern is represented by the now familiar sight of a network correspondent delivering a "stand up" summary against the backdrop of a voiceless politician talking in the background. The option to let the politician's words speak for themselves is less often exercised. The reporter feels the need to act as narrator; not simply telling the viewer what has just been said, but assessing the "real" motivations behind the event. Consider Leslie Stahl's opening narration for a CBS report on the 1980 presidential campaign:

> President Carter chose the heart of George Wallace country for today's traditional campaign kickoff; he chose Alabama because he was concerned that the Wallace vote among Southerners and blue collar workers may be slipping to Ronald Reagan. (Robinson and Sheehan 1983, 214–15)

Joseph Cappella and Kathleen Hall Jamieson call this the "strategy structure" pattern of journalism, which presumes that politics is about winning, not about solving problems.

> In the strategy structure, policy positions are interpreted as a means of gaining a voter block to advance the candidacy or retain a position in the polls. Candidates' words and actions are seen as outward signs of strategic intent and cast as maneuvers rather than forms of self-expression. (1997, 34)

They argue that this structure comes at a big price for national discourse, because it inherently casts politics as a cynical and manipulative enterprise.

Gatekeeping is thus the process of editing content to fit into the limited space available for news. Giving officials preference, using the strategy structure, focusing on people rather than ideas, and emphasizing the melodramatic are only the most familiar of many processes for shaping the political realities we come to know.

Paid and Free Media

There is no greater threshold in the world of politics than that which separates messages which have been paid for and those which reach the public via "free" channels. The former include advertisements and tracts purchased by their proponents (like Richard Nixon's redemptive Checker's speech), campaign ads, or direct mail appeals sent out to mobilize supporters of an interest group. The latter includes information that reaches the reader, viewer, or listener in the context of news. Such journalistic coverage of a politician or group is obviously "free," though not necessarily positive.

Paid Media

It is easiest to see the distinction between free and paid media in the political campaign. Campaigners running for major elective offices purchase stunningly expensive blocks of television time to present messages wholly controlled by them. In the process, they have triggered an extensive public cynicism over the rapacious fundraising that has been required to keep the political marketing machine running (Bennet 1996, 136–53).

In the congressional elections of 1996, for example, members of the House of Representatives raised $660 million, those in the Senate, a total of $440 million. Representative Newt Gingrich lead the House, spending $5.4 million. And several in the Senate, including Massachusetts's John Kerry and New Jersey's Robert Torricelli, spent around $10 million in their campaigns (Wayne 1997, 1–2). To raise these huge sums candidates must set aside large blocks of time wooing contributors, inviting the widespread impression that campaign cash will buy useful access. To a large extent fundraising to pay for media efforts to reach voters has become the second occupation of incumbents.

For their part, candidates note that the modern campaign requires enormous cash to buy media access. With the exception of the smallest local media outlets, the price for a one-time message carried by a newspaper or local television station can run to several thousand dollars. Presidential candidates contend with national media such as television, which may require an outlay of $300,000 for one network 30-second commercial. And these figures are only the beginning. The only chance to have a sustained impact on voters is if media time and space purchases are duplicated many times over.

The place of advertising in the political process has divided many observers. It's effect on our civic life, notes broadcast historian Erik Barnouw, "has been devastating." (1978, 96) The literature of political communication is filled with case histories of national and regional campaigns that relied on misleading or fraudulent ads, especially those that "go negative" (Pfau and Kenski 1990). Joe McGinniss claimed that staffers packaged Richard Nixon in 1968 like a product (1969, 33–37). Theodore White declared that broadcast ads are subject to more innuendo and manipulation than comparable print messages (1973, 250). Others, such as Gary Mauser, have defended the idea that campaigns should more closely resemble the marketing processes used by commercial interests. Marketing theory, he argues, has a legitimate place in the electoral process (1983, 19). And in their own content analyses of campaign communication Thomas Patterson and Robert McClure reached the surprising conclusion that television ads for candidates were often richer in significant content than network campaign news.

> Although commercials are surely full of their own nonsense, blatant exaggerations, and superficial symbolism, presidential candidates do make heavy use of hard issue information in their advertising appeals. In fact, during the short period of the general election campaign, presidential ads contained substantially more issue content than network newscasts. This information is particularly valuable to people who pay little attention to the newspaper. Advertising serves to make these poorly informed people substantially more knowledgeable. (1976, 22–23)

The journalistic urgency for creating drama in campaign stories, for allowing reporters to have equal billing with their subjects, and for focusing on the "strategy structure," all point to the inadequacies that make campaign advertising something of a necessity. Seasoned political journalists may criticize advertising's "sterile" and "contrived" nature. But there is little evidence that those who cover the political beat are doing much to increase the public competence to master the substance of important political issues.

In her detailed study of the 1974 California gubernatorial campaign, Mary Ellen Leary amplifies this problem. The race produced significant press attention, and yet none of the six televisions stations Leary monitored allowed the candidates to speak in any sustained way to the public. The eventual winner, Jerry Brown, accumulated only 57 minutes of speaking time on all the newscasts over the course of the entire campaign. "With such abbreviated news exposure," she concluded, "advertising time became the critical avenue for getting a message across to television viewers" (1977, 90–91). Michael Robinson and Margaret Sheehan found a similar pattern in CBS's coverage of the 1980 presidential election. The network covered a good deal of personal information about Jimmy Carter and Ronald Reagan, along with their motivations and campaign plans. Less time was given to what they actually said (1983, 59). According to Thomas Patterson, even the *New York Times* has decreased coverage of election issues in favor of election strategies (1994, 72–76).

Radio and direct mail also play important roles as forms of paid media. Radio spots are easy to prepare. They are also relatively inexpensive and easy to target to particular regions and audiences. Voters in states like Delaware, New Hampshire, and New Jersey are more efficiently reached via local radio than television, which crosses more political boundaries.

Direct mail also has the virtue of being easy to target to particular audiences. As an advertising medium, it ranks with newspapers and television in total revenues. Adopting the techniques used by bulk mail marketing strategists, politicians and public interest groups now frequently use direct mail appeals distributed to thousands of preselected addresses. A number of firms specialize in the collection and sale of mailing lists tailored to meet particular target audiences. The goal is usually to find receptive supporters who will contribute money or time to a candidate or cause, often with great success. For example, in his effective 1996 win of a seat in the Senate, New Jersey's Robert Torricelli invested heavily in direct mail fundraising, spending a total of $122,677 in fees to a firm specializing in solicitations. The effort yielded handsome returns, producing 17 dollars in donations for every dollar spent "prospecting" for them (Morris 1996, 3).

What seems increasingly evident in assessing the use of paid media in campaigns and other settings is that the technology and cost continue to advance at a much faster rate than our knowledge of its effectiveness. Presidential campaigns now make extensive use of satellites to reach supporters and quickly capture opposition ads as they are broadcast. Phone banks are activated to mobilize preselected constituents who may contribute to a campaign or write a letter to a member of Congress. And sites on the web reach communities of like-minded voters and activists delivering reports on pending congressional votes, and recent political activity.

Free Media

Much has already been said about "free" media in our earlier discussions of agenda-setting and gatekeeping. From the perspective of the political agent, media are "free" if they give publicity to your cause in the context of a news story. Finding ways to court journalists is a necessity at all levels of American political life, because there is never enough money to purchase paid media. The process of winning favorable coverage involves a kind of courtship based on the principle of reciprocity. In return for the coverage newsgatherers give to a press conference or speech, publicity seekers make attempts to have these events conform to standard definitions of news. Their goal is to produce the "good press" that results when a story leaves a generally favorable impression with the reading and viewing public. The relationship is inherently loaded with tension, much like a troubled marriage. Politicians generally want favorable interpretations of their actions. They need to be heard and understood. But the press does not want to be "taken in" and "used." Elsewhere in this study we have more specifically detailed the nature of press relations in Congress (Chapter 9), the White House (Chapter 8), and political campaigns (Chapters 5–7).

This constant courtship and tension is evident on nearly every page of Katharine Graham's exhaustive 1997 *Personal History*. In her memoir she documents in fascinating detail the many channels and backchannels of communication between the *Washington Post* and the power structure of official Washington. Graham assumed leadership of the newspaper after her husband's suicide, and inherited an institution that had alternately befriended and alienated every modern presidential administration. The brilliant but erratic Phil Graham led the paper before his death in 1963. At the same time he had become an intimate friend of John Kennedy and many key officials in his administration. As she describes it, the paper seemed close to functioning as an administration mouthpiece in the early 1960s. The following terms of Lyndon Johnson and Richard Nixon were far more varied, with the paper alternately supporting and challenging their most visible and controversial actions. Katharine Graham was a frequent guest of Lyndon Johnson in the White House and at his home in Texas. Though press coverage of the Vietnam war strained their "intimate" and "friendly" relations, it was not until Richard Nixon's presidency that the proprietors of the *Post* broke dramatically with an administration. Watergate vividly enacted the "adversarial" model of journalism, attracting many more into its ranks as a result, but also making administrations much more wary of the impact of the national media. In its aftermath, neither the Grahams of the *Washington Post* nor the American public would be as unconditionally supportive of an American president.

Politicians and Reporters: Two Models of Their Uneasy Relationship

One useful way to assess the nature of free media is to consider two popular but contrasting models of the relationships that can exist between newsmakers and news reporters. One model that gives power to the former could be called the "news management model." The second which gives more power to the press might be called the "attack press model." The news management model emphasizes the power of key leaders and officials to control information that is released through the pipeline of the press. The power to dictate story lines, "the message of the day," and attractive pictures that leave a positive impression rests with those who can manage and manipulate information for their own advantage. Reporters covering the presidency often assume this model is dominant (Stoler 1986, 165–80). Many feel like they are hostages to an advance script prepared by the campaign to win favorable press coverage. And there is no shortage of "rules" for securing "good press," usually similar to those identified by Mark Hertsgaard (1989, 34–35) as part of the Reagan White House.

- Plan ahead
- Stay on the offensive
- Control the flow of information
- Limit reporters' access to the president
- Talk about the issues you want to talk about
- Speak in one voice
- Repeat the same message many times

A specific case that can be documented from the White House files of Lyndon Johnson is especially revealing of news management practices. Johnson was long aware of his inadequacies as a television spokesman for his own administration. Television captured all too well his turgid defenses of administration policies. At best, he was a slow and stiff public speaker, a style that concealed what others who knew the private Johnson recognized as a more animated and likable man. He sought help from Robert Kintner by making the former president of NBC television his special assistant. Although Kintner's duties varied, and his tenure was comparatively short, he worked to improve the sagging Johnson image.

A sampling of some of the confidential memos Kintner sent to the president just before and after the 1967 state of the union address points to the broadcaster's ability to tap the support of former colleagues for political gain. They demonstrate the tendency common in all forms of politics to build bridges between what are supposedly separate power blocks. In one case, Kintner sought to put Johnson's speech in a favorable context by using key White House figures to brief ("background") reporters from the *New York Times, Washington Post, Time* magazine, and the networks:

> I had a meeting with [Johnson advisors] Harry McPherson, Doug Cater, Joe Califano and Walt Rostow, particularly in relation to the meaning of the Civil Rights portion of your State of the Union address, but also in relation to the principal points of the talk. We divided up various key [journalism] people in town to

background including . . . [Max] Frankel . . . [James] Kilpatrick, [Joseph] Kraft, [Tom] Wicker . . . [Hedley] Donavan . . . [Charles] Bartlett, Joe Alsop, etc. . . . In addition, I will try to do some work with the news chiefs of ABC, NBC and CBS. (Kintner 1967)

In the news management model, then, key leaders have the power to shape coverage that is in their own interests.

The "attack press" model takes a different view, making the institution of journalism more powerful. In this form "the fourth branch of government" is a powerful check on the other three, a force to be reckoned with because its power to narrate events is also the power to judge. As James Fallows notes,

Everyone knows that big-time journalists have become powerful and prominent. We see them shouting at presidents during White House press conferences. We hear them offering instant Thumbs Up/Thumbs Down verdicts a few seconds after a politician completes a speech. We know that they swarm from one hot news event to the next—from a press conference by Gennifer Flowers, to a riot site in Los Angeles, to congressional hearings on a Supreme Court nominee. . . . (1996, 6)

Larry Sabato has similarly described what he sees as excessive press interest in stories that play on public suspicions that politicians are corrupt. We now expect the news media to seek out "wounded" politicians "like sharks in a feeding frenzy." Watergate, the Iran-Contra affair, and assorted lapses in judgment have primed the press appetite for stories that suggest investigative rigor.

The wounds may have been self-inflicted, and the politician may richly deserve his or her fate, but journalists now take center stage in the process, creating the news as much as reporting it, changing both the shape of election-year politics and the contours of government. (Sabato 1993, 1)

The reporting that came out of the Watergate Affair probably contributed to a feeling of romance and vindication for a probing and even hostile form of journalism. But in recent years there have been signs of public fatigue in what many see as an excessive press interest in sensationalistic reporting which offers little more than the appearance of investigative work. As one reporter noted after leaving a newsweekly in 1996, "I felt at *Newsweek* we were less interested in covering the essence of the Republican revolution than in the divorce rates of the freshman class" (Kurtz 1997, B1).

Aside from the goal of investigating wrongdoing, attack journalism has also taken another form that could be called the "journalism of attitude." It seems increasingly easy to find reporters and columnists who communicate more attitude than information: writers who use the sparest of facts or information as springboards into extended put-downs of political figures and their actions. Fed by television's fascination for punchy debate about political topics (i.e. CNN's Crossfire, The Captial Gang, the McLaughlin Group, and others), some journalists now make their reputations on their abilities to offer caustic one-liners at the expense of public officials. The popular *New York Times* political columnist Maureen Dowd, for example, sometimes writes with cutting wit about the imperfect physical appearance of a leader. At other times she invents a soliloquy, offering what she *thinks* may be going on in a politician's "nervous brain." In one such piece she portrays Vice President Al Gore as worrying about his appearance as well as his chances for someday winning the presidency after the Clintons and the Whitewater investigation move into history.

> Is the Spot getting bigger? Tipper says it isn't but I know it is. At this rate, by the year 2000 I'll look like Joe Biden. . . . Bill's the best. But c'mon—he and Hillary are time bombs. How long can they pretend not to remember anything about anything? (Dowd 1997, A21)

To be sure, politics has always had its satirists and cartoonists, ranging from Will Rogers to Jules Fieffer. And anyone going into public life needs a sturdy sense of humor. But many journalists have grown increasingly uneasy with the journalism of attitude which has edged into more traditional reporting. It's effect over time seems to be to pull reporting away from ideas and toward feelings that merely pander to the latent hostilities of the public. As one journalist who left daily reporting noted, "it's a business that grinds people up" (Kurtz 1997, B1).

MESSAGE SALIENCY: BASIC CONSIDERATIONS

Jimmy Carter once appeared on a game show just four years before he became president, and no one then knew who he was. The object of the show was to guess a person's line of work. But in 1973, the Georgia governor was a complete unknown (Glad 1980, 218). That he could go from obscurity to prominence in so short a period of time demonstrates the potency of mass media exposure.

By far the most vexing problem facing political advocates is attempting to predict the impact that individual messages or entire campaigns will have on mass media audiences. Our predicament at the end of the twentieth century is still much like that of tobacco magnate George Washington Hill at the beginning. He believed that half of the money that his company spent on advertising was wasted. The unsolved problem, Hill said, was to find out which half (Hacker 1984, 31). We tend to remember the spectacular successes—the effective speech or series of commercials that dramatically transformed a troubled situation into a victorious one. Richard Nixon's Checkers address cited at the outset of this chapter, Bill Clinton's masterful run for the presidency in 1992, the tide of negative publicity about the tobacco industry are but a few of the hundreds of catalytic events where attitudes changed in response to an effective marriage of media and message. Like television advertisers who can sometimes dramatically increase the market share for a given product, every public figure with access to the mass media audience is conscious of the benefits it can bring.[8]

But our knowledge of what makes successful appeals remains incomplete. "Some kinds of communication on some kinds of issues, brought to the attention of some kinds of people under some kinds of conditions, have some kinds of effects." That was Bernard Berelson's 1948 summation of the state of mass media research (Zukin 1981, 385). And it still seems valid. It is extremely difficult to accurately link media exposure to attitude change. And the matter is further complicated by increasing suspicions in the general public that the news media are often "unfair, inaccurate and pushy" (Pew, 1997b).

Probably the most compelling evidence of rapid impact comes in campaigns, where private tracking polls register the impact of heavy media advertising. These small sample polls are taken frequently—often everyday—as the campaign moves into high gear. Shifts in public interest in an issue, in approval for one political approach over another, and in candidate responses to attacks are all closely monitored and frequently lead to adjustments in daily tactics. Pollsters point out that they discover a great deal in tracking polls about what is working and what is not (Sabato 1981, 76–77). And reporters are quick to identify the "geniuses" running campaigns. But even in "textbook" cases of alleged advertising effectiveness—such as Richard Nixon's victory in 1968—it is possible to overestimate media power. As one member of that campaign has since conceded, the effect of the whole paid media blitz was "not large compared with the real determinants of the election's outcome," including an increasing dislike of Lyndon Johnson (Garment 1997, 136).

Consider as well some of the broad obstacles that must be addressed in assessing media impact in less volatile periods. One of the certainties regarding human attitude formation, for example, is that attitudes are highly resistant to short-term appeals. Opinions, beliefs, and attitudes tend to be elastic when pressed against the hard surface of an opposing point of view. They may momentarily give some ground to a persuasive appeal. But they are likely to assume their old shape when the stimulus for change is withdrawn (Graber 1993, 217–36). Individual speeches, occasional exposure to advertisements, and similar short-term encounters are unlikely to have much effect on what we think, and are even less likely to produce durable changes in attitudes and behaviors. When we concede as we must, that attitudes are shaped by long-term factors, we are also forced to recognize that simple experimental or survey research on attitude formation becomes extremely difficult to devise, given the pluralism of influences that exist in ordinary life. A corporation introducing a new product on the market may indeed be able to trace the effectiveness of advertising and other marketing strategies, because public knowledge of the new items will have started from a "zero" base. No similar information vacuum exists for most presidential candidates, national issues, or pending legislative questions. All usually have some public history and level of interest that has already been established.

It is also important to note that political attitudes or related behaviors, such as voting, signing a petition, or speaking in behalf of a position are more likely to be intensified rather than changed. This is because the process of changing attitudes is much harder for the persuadee than the process of forming them. The first involves the discarding of an inconsistent or conflicting attitude in favor of a new one, a process that is very slow and usually incremental. The latter is psychologically easier; something is simply added or intensified rather than replaced. This explains why most changes that occur in individuals subject to political appeals are defined in terms of the *activation* or *crystallization* of attitudes. If individuals have an interest in an event, they are more easily drawn to new information that confirms their interest, a factor that plays a big part in determining whether a news story is important or not. And—for better or worse—Americans have generally low levels of interest in political campaigns and policy debates (see Table 4.2).

If media effects are inexact, then what conclusions can still be drawn? We offer several. First, consumers of all forms of political discourse are selective rather than reflexive. Most are primarily attentive to messages that corroborate rather than challenge existing beliefs; they seek to confirm what they already know or believe. Change of any kind represents risk, work, and the readjustment of related attitudes. It is to be expected, therefore, that in the context of a campaign the most attentive listeners to a candidate's advertising tend to be solid supporters. Statements recalled after exposure to a candidate's positions tend to be those that fit preexisting beliefs (Lang and Lang 1981, 327–29).

Second, for most consumers there is an enormous gap between time spent with any mass medium and what one would normally expect in the way of effects. For all the rhetorical skills utilized by a side in a political conflict, recall and attitude change levels can be surprisingly low (Entman 1989, 32–26) As a form of protection against the constant buffetings created by new information, the typical consumer apparently shuts much of it out.

Third, political communication needs to be envisioned as occurring in

Table 4.2
Public Attentiveness to News Stories: a Selected Sample

Over the past ten years, the Pew Center for the People and the Press has tracked the extent to which random samples of Americans have followed over 550 news stories. In descending order, the list below is a sample of stories ranging from those often followed "very closely" to those rarely followed. Out of the total of over 550 stories, none of the top 20 (≥ 58% followed them "very closely") dealt with political processes, although several focused on war actions (i.e., in the Persian Gulf). Of the 20 stories with the lowest percentage of Americans who followed them "very closely" (≤ 6%), eleven were political (i.e., passage of the National Service Act, stories of political unrest in Ukraine).

Percent who followed these stories "very closely":

- 80% Explosion of the space shuttle *Challenger* (July 1986)
- 70% Verdict in the Rodney King case and the following riots and disturbances (May 1992)
- 69% The crash of Paris-bound TWA plane off the coast of New York (July 1996)
- 60% Destruction caused by Hurricane Hugo (October 1989)
- 58% The Oklahoma City bombing (June 1995)
- 55% The outcome of the 1996 presidential election (December 1996)
- 49% Clinton administration's health care reform proposal (September 1993)
- 47% Breakup of the Soviet Union (October 1991)
- 39% Passage of NAFTA (December 1993)
- 35% The burning of black churches in the south (July 1996)
- 32% The presidential election campaign (October 1996)
- 30% Freeing of jailed black South African leader Nelson Mandela (March 1990)
- 26% Debate in Congress over welfare reform (August 1995)
- 23% Charges that Newt Gingrich violated House ethics rules (January 1997)
- 22% Civil war in Bosnia (June 1995)
- 20% The trial of Timothy McVeigh, accused of bombing the Federal Building in Oklahoma City (April 1997)
- 19% The Democratic primary in New Hampshire (February 1992)
- 17% Nomination of Robert Bork to serve on the U.S. Supreme Court (September 1987)
- 14% President Bush's educational reform plan (May 1991)
- 13% Vice President Gore's program to reform the federal government (September 1993)
- 12% Negotiations to end the baseball strike (February 1995)
- 9% The purchase of the ABC Television Network by Disney (August 1995)
- 7% Russian presidential elections (July 1996)
- 6% The discussion about expanding NATO into Eastern Europe (April 1997)
- 4% Civil war in Cambodia (May 1990)
- 3% Woody Allen and Mia Farrow's family breakup (September 1992)

Source: Pew Center for the People and the Press, "Public Attentiveness to Major News Stories (1986–1997)," 22 May 1997: 1–25 [online].

tiers of influence, where the mass media functions as both the carrier as well as shaper of messages. Our constant focus on the media as a means of mass persuasion mistakenly gives it sole possession of the power to persuade. But such a simplification distorts what is a far more complex reality. In addition to being initiators of their own forms of influence, the mass media are acted on by many external forces. They are both the targets and agents of control. As noted above, their content can be subject to news management by some elites such as the President, a powerful institution like NASA, or their own corporate hierarchy. At other times the influence of the powerful may be more subtle. Paletz and Entman have pointed out the tendency of press reports to sanitize and justify the sometimes marginal performance of elites in government, making them appear more efficient and organized than they really are (1981, 151–54). Or the media may simply be uncritical and generous when it comes to certain groups. A study of Seattle's daily newspapers found that they generally suspended traditional journalistic skepticism in their coverage of the city's largest employer, The Boeing Company (Underwood 1988, 50–56). Boeing and its workers are perhaps too important to the Pacific Northwest to alienate. In general, the media are not exempt from the rule cited by Benjamin Ginsberg that "a successful regime caters more to the interests of the elites and more to the emotions of its masses" (1986, 47).

What we have described is a diffuse system of communication. None of the many contributors to the political process—the press, the advertising industry, campaign consultants, power blocks, and powerful individuals—have a complete franchise on the political process. At various times all are able to influence the news agenda, while at other times conceding its formation to others.

SUMMARY

The relationships between the news media and various types of political blocks are subtle and variable. As the opening sections of this chapter suggest, even the best crystal ball for exploring this process is bound to remain partly cloudy. The term "media" is itself a problematic concept, as are attributions of media power in shaping political attitudes. Even so, there are several basic frameworks for assessing how political agents interact with those in the media and information business. They include the core concepts of agenda-setting and gatekeeping, both of which explain the essential processes by which content is selected and shaped. As we noted here, the rules of media gatekeeping are especially important in understanding how political events reach the public. Among other things, those rules give preference to officials over dissidents, and to events that conform to the conventions of narration and melodrama.

Other basic frameworks for assessing the media's role in the political process hinge on distinctions between "free" and "paid," and on vary different models of the power relationship between members of the press and the groups they cover. The "attack press" model assumes that journalism is its own power center, able to shape and influence public perceptions about those who participate in America's civil life. The "news management" model reverses the arrows, and assigns greater control to newsmakers and their skillful public relations specialists. Both models can be useful in different settings. Although, as we have seen, there are limitations in our abilities to estimate the effectiveness of specific messages on specific channels.

A recurring theme throughout this section is that the media and the political world represent two blocks in an unsteady relationship. As we have described it, the press and the political world need each other, and frequently develop alliances of convenience. But each also remains capable of sustaining goals that are at odds with the other, frequently to the benefit of the American public. The "system" seems to work best when these elements are truly semiautonomous, when friction between them provides a larger window on the political landscape. We sometimes view this friction as a sign of our national disintegration. But in some ways events like the Watergate or Whitewater scandals—with their conflicting White House, congressional, and national press objectives—demonstrated the vibrancy of American pluralism. We should expect no less from a society so well-endowed with the technical means for creating a truly enlightened democracy.

NOTES

1. Local television is often criticized for promoting violent and sensational stories. See, for example, McClellan (1997), p. 34.

2. For a review of media effects studies and their limits, see DeFleur and Dennis (1996), pp. 533–606.

3. For examples of survey and monitoring data, see references in this chapter to data gathered by the Pew Center for the People and the Press, and the Media Studies Center of the Freedom Forum.

4. Along with others, *Tyndall Weekly* keeps track of how much time the networks are spending on major news stories.

5. Iyengar and Kinder (1987) address many of these issues in their own research, pp. 6–15.

6. See Sciolino (1997). Although the case was known to high members of Congress and the Pentagon, reporting of this story prior to this date seemed to be limited to the Minot, South Dakota press.

7. Aristotle discusses character extensively in Book II of *Rhetoric* (1954).

8. See, for example, our analysis of antitobacco campaigns in Woodward and Denton (1996), pp. 4–9.

REFERENCES

Aristotle. 1954. *Rhetoric,* trans. W. Rhys Roberts. New York: The Modern Library.

Barnouw, Erik. 1978. *The Sponsor: Notes on a Modern Potentate.* New York: Oxford University Press.

Bennet, James. 1996. "Despite Dole's Best Effort, Softer Side Loses Ground." *New York Times,* 3 July: B6.

Bennett, W. Lance. 1988. *News: The Politics of Illusion,* 2d ed. New York: Longman.

———. 1996. *The Governing Crisis,* 2d ed. New York: St. Martin's Press.

Cappella, Joseph N., and Kathleen Hall Jamieson. 1997. *Spiral of Cynicism: The Press and the Public Good.* New York: Oxford University Press.

Combs, James. 1980. *Dimensions of Political Drama.* Santa Monica, CA: Goodyear.

Crouse, Timothy. 1972. *The Boys on the Bus.* New York: Ballantine.

DeFleur, Melvin, and Everette Dennis. 1996. *Understanding Mass Communication,* 1996 ed. Boston: Houghton Mifflin.

Diamond, Edwin. 1995. *Behind the Times.* Chicago: University of Chicago Press.

Dowd, Maureen. 1997. "Al Agonistes." *New York Times,* 30 January: A21.

Entman, Robert M. 1989. *Democracy without Citizens.* New York: Oxford University Press.

Epstein, Edward. 1974. *News from Nowhere.* New York: Vintage.

Fallows, James. 1996. *Breaking the News.* New York: Pantheon.

Frankel, Max. 1997. "Live at 11: Death." *New York Times Magazine,* 15 June: 20.

Gans, Herbert. 1980. *Deciding What's News.* New York: Vintage.

Garment, Leonard. 1997. *Crazy Rhythm.* New York: Times Books.

Ginsberg, Benjamin. 1986. *The Captive Public.* New York: Basic Books.

Gitlin, Todd. 1980. *The Whole World Is Watching.* Berkeley: University of California Press.

Glad, Betty. 1980. *Jimmy Carter: In Search of the Great White House.* New York: W. W. Norton.

Gleick, Elizabeth. 1996. "Read All About It." *Time,* 21 October: 66–69.

Graber, Doris. 1984. *Processing the News.* New York: Longman.

———. 1993. *Mass Media and American Politics,* 4th ed. Washington, DC: Congressional Quarterly Press.

Graham, Katharine. 1997. *Personal History.* New York: Knopf.

Hacker, Andrew. 1984. "Poets and the Packaging of Desire." *New York Times Book Review,* 24 June: 31.

Hertsgaard, Mark. 1989. *On Bended Knee: The Press and the Reagan Presidency.* New York: Shocken.

Iyengar, Shanto, and Donald R. Kinder. 1987. *News That Matters.* Chicago: University of Chicago Press.

Kintner, Robert. 1967. Memo of January 11, White House Central File. Austin, TX: LBJ Library.

Kurtz, Howard. 1997. "The New Reform School." *Washington Post,* 12 May: B1.

Lang, Kurt, and Gladys Lang. 1981 "The Mass Media and Voting." In *Readings in Public Opinion and Mass Communication,* 3d ed, ed. Morris Janowitz and Paul Hirsch. New York: Free Press, pp. 327–29.

Leary, Mary Ellen. 1977. *Phantom Politics: Campaigning in California*. Washington, DC: Public Affairs.

Lippmann, Walter. 1930. *Public Opinion*. New York: Macmillan.

MacNeil, Robert. 1968. *The People Machine*. New York: Harper and Row.

Maraniss, David. 1995. *First in His Class*. New York: Touchstone Books.

Matalin, Mary, and James Carville. 1994. *All's Fair*. New York: Random House/Touchstone.

Mauser, Gary. 1983. *Political Marketing: An Approach to Campaign Strategy*. New York: Praeger.

McCartney, Laton. 1988. *Friends in High Places*. New York: Simon & Schuster.

McClellan, Steve. 1997. "Violence, Fluff Lead Local News, Says Survey." *Broadcasting and Cable*, 19 May: 34.

McCombs, Maxwell, and D. L. Shaw. 1972. "The Agenda Setting Function of the Mass Media." *Public Opinion Quarterly* (Summer): 176–87.

McDonald, Forrest. 1975. *The Presidency of George Washington*. New York: W. W. Norton.

McGinniss, Joe. 1969. *The Selling of the President: 1968*. New York: Trident Press.

McGraw, Kathleen, and Milton Lodge. 1996. "Political Information Processing: A Review Essay." *Political Communication* 13: 131–42.

Media Studies Center. 1997. "Women, Men and Media: The Changing News Agenda." 3 June: 1–11 [online].

Morris, Dwight. 1996. "Weeds in the Garden State." *PoliticsNow* 8 October: 1–5, [online].

Nimmo, Dan, and James Combs. 1990. *Mediated Political Realities*, 2d ed. New York: Longman.

Nixon, Richard. 1968. *Six Crises*. New York: Pyramid.

Novak, Michael. 1973. "Notes on the Drama of Politics and the Drama of Journalism." In *The Politics of Broadcasting*, ed. Marvin Barrett. New York: Thomas Crowell, pp. 169–177.

Paletz, David, and Robert Entman. 1981. *Media Power Politics*. New York: Free Press.

Patterson, Thomas. 1994. *Out of Order*. New York: Vintage.

Patterson, Thomas, and Robert McClure. 1976. *The Unseeing Eye: The Myth of Television Power in National Politics*. New York: G. P. Putnam's.

Pew Center for the People and the Press. 1997a. "Public Attentiveness to Major News Stories (1986–1997)." 22 May: 1–25 [online].

———. 1997b. "Press Unfair, Inaccurate and Pushy." 22 May: 1–3 [online].

Pfau, Michael, and Henry Kenski. 1990. *Attack Politics: Strategy and Defense*. Westport, CT: Praeger.

Robinson, John. 1981. "Mass Communication and Information Diffusion." In *Readings in Public Opinion and Mass Communication*, 3d ed., ed. Morris Janowitz and Paul Weusch. New York: Free Press, pp. 97–123.

Robinson, Michael, and Margaret Sheehan. 1983. *Over the Wire and on TV: CBS and UPI in Campaign '80*. New York: Russell Sage.

Sabato, Larry. 1981. *The Rise of Political Consultants*. New York: Basic Books.

———. 1993. *Feeding Frenzy*. New York: Free Press.

Sciolino, Elaine. 1997. "From a Love Affair to a Court-Martial." *New York Times*, 11 May: 1.

Schudson, Michael. 1995. *The Power of News*. Cambridge, MA: Harvard University Press.

Sennett, Richard. 1978. *The Fall of Public Man*. New York: Vintage.

Stoler, Peter. 1986. *The War Against the Press*. New York: Dodd and Mead.

Tucher, Andie. 1997. "You News." *Columbia Journalism Review* (May/June): 26–31.

Tyndall Weekly. 7 June 1997: 1.

Underwood, Doug. 1988. "The Boeing Story and the Hometown Press." *Columbia Journalism Review* (November/December): 50–56.

Wayne, Leslie. 1997. "Gingrich Tops Spending List in Campaigns for the House." *New York Times*, 3 January: 7 [online].

Weaver, Paul. 1976. "Captives of Melodrama." *New York Times Magazine*, 29 August: 6, 48–57.

White, Theodore. 1973. *The Making of the President, 1972*. New York: Atheneum.

Woodward, Bob, and Carl Bernstein. 1974. *All the President's Men*. New York: Simon & Schuster.

Woodward, Gary. 1997. *Perspectives on American Political Media*. Boston: Allyn and Bacon.

Woodward, Gary, and Robert E. Denton, Jr. 1996. *Persuasion and Influence in American Life*, 3d ed. Prospect Heights, IL: Waveland.

Zukin, Cliff. 1981. "Mass Communication and Public Opinion." In *Handbook of Political Communication*, ed. Dan Nimmo and Keith Sanders. Beverly Hills, CA: Sage, pp. 359–90.

Part II

Campaigns

Chapter 5

Campaign Planning, Management, and Strategies

Plans are useless. Planning is essential!

Dwight D. Eisenhower (1945)

The notion of "campaign" comes from the military vocabulary. In a general context, a campaign is a connected series of operations designed to bring about a particular result. It involves planning, strategy, competition, winners and losers. Republican Speaker of the House of Representatives Newt Gingrich, in motivating candidates for takeover of 1994, observed that "politics and war are remarkably similar systems. . . . War is politics with blood; politics is war without blood" (Faucheux 1998, 26).

Much has been written about political campaigns. The classic "limited effects model" of campaign communication research dominated scholars' views of the impact of campaigns upon voters for nearly 40 years. The model was based upon data from the 1940 elections presented by Lazarsfeld, Berelson, and Gaudet (1948) in *The People's Choice*. They found that most voter decisions were based upon attitude predispositions, group identification, and interpersonal communication. Thus, mediated messages would contribute little to the actual conversion of voters favoring one candidate over another.

But today, in terms of voters behavior and campaigns, political outcomes are less predictable than in previous decades. With the decline of political parties, the increase of single issue politics, the prominence of mass media, and the sophistication of social science research, the studies of the 1940s and 1950s are no longer apropos of today's electoral campaigns. Scholars are now recognizing the variety of factors that influence voter preferences.

Just 30 years ago, campaigns were conducted by volunteers and party activists. Face-to-face cavassing was essential to winning. Beginning in the 1960s, new communication technology and social science changed the way one conducted and ran campaigns. The changes in campaign technologies continue today.

Daniel Shea (1996) argues that campaigns have moved from an "old-style" to "new-style" of campaigning in four ways: new players, new incentives, new tactics, and new resources (7–10). In the old style, parties ran candidates for office. Today, individuals run for office. The party has less control over who runs, especially in cases of primaries. Individuals with money (like Steve Forbes in 1996 or Ross Perot in 1992), or people with recognition but little or no political experience, may now run self-identifying party–affiliated campaigns. Once nominated, the individual carries the campaign function with little but party endorsement. Access to television has become more important than party support. The decline of parties and increasing importance of political action committees have encouraged "lone-ranger" campaigns.

Campaign professionals have replaced volunteers. Campaign management and services have become an industry. For consultants, political ideology or public policy are less important than the number of clients. The notion of the citizen-legislator is replaced with the professional, career politician. Government service provides a path to corporate jobs and big money.

Old-style politics involved traditional strategies of group-based appeals with traditional party messages. The goal was voter education and broad mass appeal. Today, the strategies and tactics are more narrowly defined and targeted. Voter preferences are revealed through scientific research. Messages are targeted to voter segments. Technology plays an increasing role in voter targeting and fundraising.

Much of the change, of course, comes at the higher levels of electoral politics. There still are true "citizen-politicians" at the state and local level. However, there is an increasing professionalization of political campaigns, even at the local levels.

Historically, as already noted, party volunteers and activists played an essential role in generating grass-roots support and getting out the vote. Today, however, campaign people and money come from outside the geographic area of the race. Money rules the day in terms of staff, advertising, and the use of campaign technology.

Today, the "uses and gratifications model" of campaign effects is increasing in popularity. This model basically argues that campaign effects upon voters depend upon the needs and motivations of the individual voter. Voters may turn to campaign messages for information, issue discussion, or pure entertainment. There are a variety of motives, therefore, for exposure to campaign communication.

CAMPAIGNS AS EXERCISES IN COMMUNICATION

As we argued in the first chapter, politics is primarily a communication activity. William Swenney (1995) thinks that "a political campaign is fundamentally a communications exercise about choices between the aspirants for public office and the audience of voters" (14). A communication approach to campaign analysis challenges the basic assumption of behaviorists that political campaigns play a minor role or have little influence in election results. Communication scholars argue that too much emphasis of campaign research has been focused on voter conversion. Such research tends to ignore the long-term, subtle effects or cumulative effects of politics and political campaigns.

As argued in Chapter 3, political reality is created, manipulated, and permeated. Campaigns are exercises in the creation, recreation, and transmission of significant symbols through communication. Communication activities are the vehicles for action—both real and perceived. It is true, however, as Samuel Becker (1971) argues, that "any single communication encounter accounts for only a small portion of the variance in human behavior" (21). He characterizes our communication environment as a "mosaic" (21–43). The mosaic consists of an infinite number of information "bits" or fragments on an infinite number of topics scattered over time and space. In addition, the bits are disorganized, exposure is varied and repetitive. As these bits are relevant or address a need, they are attended. Thus, as we attempt to make sense of our environment, our current state of existence, political bits are elements of our voting choice, worldview, or legislative desires. As voters, we must arrange these bits into a cognitive pattern that comprises our mosaic of a candidate, issue, or situation. Campaigns, then, are great sources of potential information and contain, however difficult to identify or measure, elements that impact decision making. Information bits can replace other bits to change or modify our worldview, attitudes, or opinions.

Jonathan Robbin (1989), chairman of the Claritas Corporation, a marketing firm that specializes in geodemographics, recognizes the important role of communication in successful campaigns. "The essence of political campaigning is communications. A majority is built by repeatedly contacting voters and persuading them to register, turn out, and cast their ballot for the 'right' candidate or side of an issue" (106). For him, market data alone will not guarantee electoral success. How the market data is applied is critical to the campaign process. "The efficiency of a campaign depends on accurate delivery of elective communications"

(107). More recently, Dick Morris (1997), consultant to President Clinton's 1996 presidential campaign, claims that everything he writes, "a speech, an ad, a memo, a tract—[are] all text with a mission to convert, a goal to persuade" (xiii).

COMMUNICATIVE FUNCTIONS OF CAMPAIGNS

From a communication perspective, Bruce Gronbeck (1984) has constructed a "functional model of campaign research." The model, consistent with the uses and gratifications model, assumes that "receivers are active human beings who are subjecting themselves to communicative messages because certain needs can be satisfied and hence certain gratifications can be gained from exposure to those messages" (490).

In campaigns, there are both instrumental functions and consummatory functions. One of three instrumental functions is behavioral activation. Campaigns serve not only to reinforce voter attitudes or convert voters preference but also to motivate voters actually to vote or help in a campaign. Another instrumental function of campaigns is cognitive adjustments. Campaigns, by discussing issues, may stimulate awareness of issues, reflect upon candidate views, or result in voter position modification. Finally, campaigns function to legitimize both the new leadership and the subsequent rules, laws, and regulations.

Consummatory functions are those embodied in the communication processes that go beyond candidate selection and legislative enactments. They help create the metapolitical images and social-psychological associations that provide the glue that holds our political system together. Campaigns provide personal involvement in many forms: direct participation, self-reflection and definition, social interaction and discussion, and aesthetic experiences of public drama and group life. And campaigns provide the legitimization of the electoral process, reaffirming commitment to our brand of democracy, debate, and political campaigning.

Campaigns, then, communicate and influence, reinforce and convert, increase enthusiasm and inform, and motivate as well as educate. As Gronbeck (1984) argues, campaigns "get leaders elected, yes, but ultimately, they also tell us who we as a people are, where we have been and where we are going; in their size and duration they separate our culture from all others, teach us about political life, set our individual and collective priorities, entertain us, and provide bases for social interaction" (496).

CAMPAIGN MANAGEMENT

Campaign management today is a profession, not a hobby. Campaign professionals are used in races of all levels. Political consultants are the new power in American politics. As David Chagall (1981) observes, consultants "are the Merlins of the electronic age, the Vince Lombardis of modern electioneering. And, like it or not, they are here to stay" (400). In the days before consultants, the old party bosses served as the link between electoral politics and campaigns. Their job was to generate support, control conflict, and reinforce party discipline. Today, political consultants have access to the candidate and develop local campaign strategies and tactics from offices miles away.

When the general public thinks of a politician they are usually referring to an elected official or a candidate running for an elected office. Others may also include visible party leaders who serve over a period of time in various administrations. Few, however, consider the new campaigners as professional politicians. The new campaigners include consultants, pollsters, television producers and directors, fundraisers, speechwriters, and direct marketers—all professionals who shape the true character of modern political campaigning in America.

Larry Sabato (1981), one of the first scholars to recognize the growing role and importance of using professionals in campaigns, defined a political consultant as "a campaign professional who is engaged primarily in the provision of advice and services (such as polling, media creation and production, and direct mail fundraising) to candidates, their campaigns, and other political committees" (8). Because of the sophistication and technological advancement of mass communication and persuasion techniques, the trend is toward segmenting campaign activities into areas of specialization. The professional politician today, then, is more likely to be a specialist focusing on one activity of a campaign endeavor.

The number of firms and individuals who earn a living working on campaigns is increasing. Most firms, however, are rather small, often employing five to seven people. During a campaign the more specialized tasks of polling, advertising, and fundraising are subcontracted to firms specializing in such activities. Most political consulting firms are owned and operated by a well-known successful professional. Being associated with winning campaigns is vital to the professional political consultant. Matt Reese, a well-known consultant, states that the "trinity of necessity" for a political consultant consists of winning (or the reputation of winning), working for people whose names are well known, and winning when you're not supposed to (Sabato 1981, 18).

Beyond "big name" consultants are literally thousands of "political junkies" who work on numerous campaigns and staffs of elected officials. Within a political season, such people may change jobs and titles many times. Some will work on an elected official's staff—until the next election, when they will move to the campaign staff only to return to the official's staff after the election.

Today's professional politicians are politicians only insofar as they earn their living working for political candidates and campaigns. They are professionals in the sense that they possess unique skills and knowledge relevant to human motivation and mass communication technology. They are experts and specialists first, and politicians in the traditional use of the word second.

Political Consultants

Who was the first political consultant? Well, it's impossible to say. But Robert Friedenberg (1997) speculates that perhaps it was the individual who in 1758 suggested to a candidate of the Virginia Colonial Assembly that he should provide refreshments for the voters. The candidate, based upon this advice, bought 160 gallons of beverages for the voters and won the race. The candidate was George Washington (1).

Dan Nimmo (1970, 36) effectively asserts that today's political consulting industry is a direct descendant of the public relations profession that matured during the 1920s. Their task was to "propagandize" the activities of U.S. business. It is not surprising that the skills and techniques of advocacy became the mainstay of U.S. politics.

Edward Bernays, cited in *Time* magazine as "U.S. Publicist Number One," is considered the father of public relations. In the 1920s, Bernays introduced the "engineering of consent," scientific approach to public opinion formation and dynamics. President Calvin Coolidge was the first president to benefit from his skills. The press of the day portrayed Coolidge as "cold and aloof." To counter this image, Bernays invited Al Jolson and 40 other vaudevillians to a White House breakfast. The next day the *New York Times* headline read "Actors Eat Cakes with the Coolidges . . . President Nearly Laughs." This was, according to Sidney Blumenthal (1982), the "first overt act initiated by a media advisor for a President" (40). A decade later, Bernays called for the creation of a cabinet position titled Secretary of Public Relations.

The first political consulting firm was created by Clem Whitaker (a newsman and press agent) and Leone Baxter (a public relations specialist) in 1933 (Sabato 1981, 11–13). In that year the California legislature passed a bill authorizing a flood control and irrigation project. Pacific Gas and Electric Company viewed the project as a direct threat and thus initiated a campaign to reverse the decision. In turn, proponents of the project hired Whitaker and Baxter to develop a campaign that would defeat the electric company's effort. With a budget of $39,000 the team was victorious in stopping the opposition. Soon after the effort, Whitaker and Baxter formed Campaigns, Inc. Between 1933 and 1955 they won 70 out of 75 campaigns they managed. Their last campaign was the congressional race of Shirley Temple Black in 1967. They developed many of the techniques and strategies that are used in political campaigns today.

Whitaker believed that most Americans do not seek information during a campaign and have no desire to work at being good citizens. Thus, he argued that "there are two ways you can interest [citizens] in a campaign, and only two that we have ever found successful. Most every American loves a contest. He likes a good, hot battle, with no punches pulled. So you can interest him if you put on a fight! Then, too, most every American likes to be entertained. He likes fireworks and parades. So if you can't fight, put on a show (Blumenthal 1982, 164).

By 1950, advertising agencies handled national election campaigns. But by 1970, advertising agencies realized that handling campaigns was not as profitable as other products. A political campaign ends in a few months whereas selling soap, cars, or clothes goes on for years. And selling soap is less stressful. The last advertising agency campaign was Nixon's 1968 presidential race, well documented in Joe McGinniss's 1969 book *The Selling of the Presidency*. He writes of the role advertising played in creating and recreating a "new Nixon."

Public relations specialists were a permanent part of every campaign effort by 1960. Between 1952 and 1957, about 60 percent of all public relations firms had some kind of political account (Sabato 1981, 12). Part of John Kennedy's campaign staff included a research group, speechwriting group, and publicity group—all comprised of public relations personnel. At first, however, Republicans used public relations specialists in campaigns more than Democrats because of their natural ties to business firms, publicity firms, and available money.

Today, campaigns are run by professional consultants who coordinate the activities of media, advertising, public relations, and publicity. They understand both the new technologies and the unique requirements of campaigning. It is that blend of expertise and experience that makes them a sought-after commodity, even after the campaign is over.

There are several reasons why political officeholders and candidates need the services of campaign specialists. The modern campaign requires the performance of many specialized tasks to include advertising, issue research, strategy development, polling, and fundraising. Each of these tasks is complex, requiring training, experience, and knowledge of the industry. It is unrealistic to expect a candidate for public office to have the technical expertise in each of these areas or even to have the time to manage these activities in addition to campaigning or governing.

Another reason for campaign specialists is the impact of behavioral and social science concepts and theories of human motivation. The scientific approach to opinion formation and dynamics has become an essential element of every campaign. Predicting public attitudes and behavior is key to the development of campaign strategy. The measurement, tracking, and analysis of demographic and psychographic data forms the bases for issue positions and public appeals. Social science has provided the necessary tools and methodologies monitoring public beliefs, attitudes, and values.

The electoral process itself places unique requirements upon candidates and campaigns. Historically, Americans value the notion of candidates meeting the public and discussing issues. But as our society has become larger, more diverse, and complex, the requirements of campaigning have become more complex. For most campaigns, extensive direct voter contact is impossible. At the national level, each primary becomes an individualized contest requiring professional help and analysis.

But, of course, the greatest reason for the need of consultants is the role of mass media in our society. Every requirement and characteristic of the mass media impacts upon the nature of political campaigning. To reach the public through the media requires money, news exposure, and 30-second discussions of issues. Actions and statements are carried beyond the immediate audience. Television especially likes drama, a contest, and often favors an underdog. A mistake is recorded forever and subject to instant replay without contextual explanation. The media serve as a source of information, persuasion, and presentation of reality. To use a medium requires knowledge of the medium—its strengths, weaknesses, and nature. The growth and necessity of political consultants and professional politicians are directly related to the growth of the mass media and communication technologies.

Political consultants are also needed today because of what Blumenthal (1982) calls "the permanent campaign." The permanent campaign, a direct result of the new technology in the age of information, has become "the steady-state reality of American politics. In the new politics, issues, roles, and media are not neatly separate categories. They are unified by the strategic imperative . . . the elements of the permanent campaign are tangential to politics: they are the political process itself" (Blumenthal 1982, 10).

Political consultants are permanent, the politicians ephemeral. With the decline of party structure, discipline, and workers, television commercials and media appearances not only serve to mobilize voters but also play a role in governing the nation. Governing the nation, then, becomes a perpetual campaign where the public is constantly addressed and its support continually solicited. Ronald Reagan brought into the White House some of the most sophisticated marketers, pollsters, and media advisors to ever work for a president. Much of his success in opinion formation, information control, and law enactment is a result of Reagan's use of the new technologies. Bill Clinton also uses polls not only to direct public policy but to provide insight into how to generate public support. In the end, according to Dick Morris (1997), "we created

Table 5.1
The Campaign Plan

I. Contextual Information
  a. District profile
  b. Demographic profile
  c. Prior electoral targeting
  d. Candidate qualifications and background
  e. Opposition profile

II. Audience Considerations
  a. Issue paper abstracts
  b. Polling plan and schedule
  c. Voter concerns

III. Strategy and Tactics
  a. Campaign theme
  b. Overall time frame
  c. Paid media voter contact schedule
  d. Earned media activities
  e. Candidate activities

IV. Resources and Staffing
  a. Necessary resources (budget)
  b. Fundraising plan and schedule
  c. Staffing
  d. Organizational requirements

Source: Daniel Shea, *Campaign Craft: The Strategies, Tactics, and Art of Campaign Management* (Westport, CT: Praeger, 1996), pp. 17–23.

the first fully advertised presidency in U.S. history, which led to an extensive record of legislative accomplishment" (145).

A Campaign Plan

An important function of political consultants is the management of an entire campaign. They first establish the campaign organization consisting of professionals, committed party regulars, and citizen volunteers. Complete campaign management requires the implementation of campaign strategies and the allocation of candidate time, money, and talent. Today, even in congressional races, campaigns employ a team of consultants.

A campaign plan (see Table 5.1) is essential to any campaign. Money alone or tireless energy are not enough. Campaign plans are a reference tool, a timetable, that delegates responsibilities and keeps staffs focused on campaign tasks. The plan is a concrete document, although its sections and parts may differ depending upon level of race or consultant. The plan serves as a strategic blueprint for the campaign. A good plan reflects research, analysis, and reflection.

Daniel Shea (1996) identifies several major areas of a campaign plan. Contextual information details profiles of the district and demographic characteristics of the voting population to include prior electoral targeting. The section would also include profiles of the candidate as well as the opposition.

A section on audience considerations would include a polling plan and schedule as well as polling data that provides an overview of voter concerns. The section would also include all issue paper abstracts, which are one-page summaries of candidate's stand on issues.

A section on strategy and tactics identifies the campaign theme, paid media schedule, free media or press activities as well general candidate activities. Of course the candidate's specific daily schedule will change, but it is a good idea to identify special party or campaign events as well as general expectations of candidate and family members.

Resources and staffing focuses on budget and organizational items. Budget considerations include a fundraising plan, schedule of key fundraising activities and visits, and a proposed allocations by area. It is important for the staffing requirements detail both organizational needs as well as detailed duties and expectations of staff members.

Campaign Research

Campaign research is a highly specialized function and provides the basis for strategy development and execution. Campaign research provides a great deal of the data in the overall plan including voting patterns, voter turnout, demographic correlates of voting, voter attitudes, opinions, issues, registration, and election projections, to name a few. Most campaigns prepare a "bible" that summarizes the relevant issues of the campaign, profiles "friendly" voters, analyzes opposition strengths, weaknesses, and strategy, and provides local data for campaign stops. Like campaign planning and strategy development, research is a continual process, especially as election day approaches.

It was Stuart Spencer who introduced "tracking research" to political campaigns (Chagall 1981, 63). This marketing technique of taking frequent voter attitude measurements allows a consultant to isolate specific cause-effect relationships. Thus, the impact of various campaign events, such as radio or television commercials, is identified and adjustments are made.

An important element of campaign research today focuses on the opposition. Opposition research is more than simply finding "dirt" on one's opponent. It is detailed information that covers every aspect of an individual's private and public life. The key is how to interpret, to apply, and to communicate a piece of information. For example, during the 1992 presidential campaign, Pat Buchanan was challenging George Bush for the Republican nomination. Part of his campaign was based on the need for tougher trade policies that support American jobs and goods. The Bush campaign discovered that Buchanan owned a Mercedes Benz and developed an ad that portrayed Buchanan as being hypocritical owning a foreign automobile rather than an American product.

Opposition data is used in two primary ways. It may reveal past actions and behavior that disqualifies a candidate for selection or it may provide a basis to predict future behavior or attitudes about specific policies that may be contrary to prevailing public desires (Shea 1996, 97).

There are numerous sources for finding opposition data, especially in the age of electronic records and computer data banks. Daniel Shea (1996) identifies five types of opposition data: public service information, media-derived information, prior campaign details, business and career information, and personal information (98). Of course, the longer one is in office, the more media and public service information that is easily accessible.

For some, the use of opposition research has harmed the electoral process by making campaigns too personal and mean spirited. It also leads to distortion of views, redirects public attention from important issues, and contributes to the spiral of public cynicism about contemporary campaigns. However, many consultants claim the use of opposition research is good for the democratic process. They claim that such data makes candidates more accountable and makes campaigns more open and honest. At a minimum, it is important that any opposition information be true and obtained in a legal manner (Shea 1996, 95).

CAMPAIGN STRATEGY

Every campaign needs a strategy or a blueprint for winning an election. A strategy is how to position the candidate and allocate resources to maximize the candidate's strengths and to minimize the candidate's weaknesses. According to Ron Faucheux (1998), "message is the reason you give voters to select you over the opposition. How and when you communicate that message (sequence, timing, intensity, persuasion) and how and when you mobilize your resources are the strategic components of every campaign, large and small" (25).

Message strategies may be based on the personal "virtues" or "flaws" of the candidate (i.e., experience, competence, integrity, compassion, etc.); ideological or partisan differences (i.e., liberal, conservative, libertarian, etc.); or some combination of the two. The main point is that the campaign message must draw a line of distinction between the opposition and frame a clear choice for voters (Faucheux 1998, 25).

Faucheux (1998) argues that every campaign needs four strategies (26–32). A message sequence strategy identifies the order of presenting arguments to voters. A timing and intensity strategy specifies when the candidate acts and at what pace. A mobilization and persuasion strategy targets voter preferences and allocates resources to specific favorable voting groups. An opportunity strategy is finding ways to exploit situational events or obstacles. Table 5.2 provides several specific examples of each strategy.

According to Shea (1996), an overall campaign strategy will answer the following five questions: Who is the target audience? What is the message? What resources are needed to reach the target audience? When will the target audience be reached? How will the audience be reached? (172). Although rather simple and straightforward, the answer to each question is complex and multidimensional. It is important to remember that strategies must be compatible for the candidate. In implementation of strategy, you should remember that campaign messages should be consistent, coherent, and coordinated.

CAMPAIGN TACTICS

A tactic is a method or tool of implementing strategy. For example, the basic strategy for Bill Clinton in the 1996 presidential campaign was to demonstrate differences between himself and Dole on issues favorable to the Democratic core constituency (i.e., Medicare, Social Security, education, environment, etc.) and to blur or reduce the appearance of differences on issues favorable to traditional Republicans (i.e., crime, taxes, balanced budget, welfare reform, family values, etc.). The tactics Clinton used to implement the basic strategy included early television ads in targeted markets attacking the Republican positions on health care and Social Security, a series of speeches such as the State of the Union that declared such themes as "the era of big government is over," a series of legislative proposals such as school uniforms or the regulation of tobacco to combat teen smoking, and a series of very public bill signings such as the Welfare Reform Bill (Faucheux 1998, 25).

In executing the tactics described above, political consultants provide many services for candidates and elected officials. These countless services, ranging from day-to-day campaign operations, to fundraising, to image definition, depend upon three main services: advertising, public opinion polling, and direct mail. Each of these services is communication-based and has become an essential element of every campaign.

Table 5.2
Campaign Strategies

Message Sequence Strategies

1. "Ignore the Opposition"—Open positive and remain positive to the close, seldom if ever mentioning opponent.
2. "Classic"—Start positive, do not initiate attacks, respond to attacks, use comparative appeals, end positive.
3. "Aggressive"—Open positive, go negative before opponent, respond to attacks, close with dual track of positive and negative/comparative appeals.
4. "Frontal Attack"—Open negative/comparative, then go positive and respond to specific attacks, close on dual track of positive and negative/comparative appeals.
5. "Relentless Attack"—Open and maintain negative/comparative, introduce dual track of positive and negative/comparative, close with dual track of positive and negative/comparative appeals.

Timing and Intensity Strategies

1. "The Tortoise"—Start slow and build steady all the way, peaking at the end.
2. "Bookend"—Open big and loud, then a slow steady build, close big and loud.
3. "Pearl Harbor"—Open very quietly, causing opponent to underestimate strength and intentions, close loud and big.
4. "Hold Your Fire"—Slow, steady build with big and loud close.

Persuasion and Mobilization Strategies

1. "Classic Formulation"—Create/reinforce base, identify undecideds/opposition leaners, persuade undecided/opposition to your side, turn out supporters.
2. "Base Strategy"—Reinforce base, then turn it out.
3. "The Marion Barry"—Reinforce base, enlarge base, then turn it out.

Opportunity Strategies

1. "Setting a Trap"—Attack opponent while setting up a larger attack by withholding further information, opponent responds, unload additional information in an attack.
2. "Poison Bait"—Entice opponent to do something (i.e., go on TV, discuss an issue, etc.) that will cause unintentional, inadvertent harm to the opposition.
3. "Inoculation"—Identify biggest potential weakness before registered with public, take actions designed to turn weakness into strength.
4. "Lightning Rod"—Controversial individual person or group endorses individual who can't win but will receive most attacks while protecting another candidate; controversial candidate pulls out of race.
5. "Technological Advantage"—Use a tactic that opposition is not using or expected to use.
6. "Machine Gun Attack"—Attack opponent on item #1. As opponent responds, attack on unrelated item #2. As opponent responds to item #2, attack on unrelated item #3, etc.
7. "Critical Mass"—Overwhelm opposition with endorsements, money, activity, and so on at critical stage of campaign.
8. "Pincer"—Get opposition into a position that they cannot escape or avoid.
9. "Firewall"—Build solid pockets of support that cannot be penetrated by opposition.
10. "Three's a Crowd"—Enhance strength of third/minor candidate to draw votes away from major competition.

Source: Ron Faucheux, "Strategies that Win!" *Campaigns & Elections* 18(10) (January 1998): 24–32.

Advertising

Political advertising is the most recognized and controversial service provided by consultants. It is also, perhaps, the most important. In the 1996 presidential election campaign, Clinton and Dole spent nearly $100 million *each* on television advertising, not including amounts contributed by the national parties (Devlin 1997, 1058).

The media adviser was once primarily a technical adviser not privy to the overall strategy and tactics of the campaign. Today, however, the media consultant is a key member of the staff, often responsible for a campaign's total advertising and communication strategy.

According to Richard Armstrong (1988), nothing has changed the "business" of political advertising more than the advent of video (18). Video allows for quicker spot production as well as lower cost. The result is more different ads, more ads running, and because of the fast turnaround time, there are more reactive or response ads to counter opponents or to reflect a change in voter attitudes.

Of course, modern political advertising is a far cry from the distribution of flyers and campaign buttons of the 1800s. As radio and television became the primary means of communicating to a large number of people, it was natural for politicians to seek access to the media. But utilizing the commercial, business format of advertising as a way to gain voter acceptance was an evolutionary process. For Joe McGinniss (1969), the process was also a natural one. He wrote in 1968 that "politics in a sense, has always been a con game. . . . Advertising, in many ways, is a con game too. . . . It is not surprising then, that politicians and advertising men should have discovered one another. And, once they recognized that the citizen did not so much vote for a candidate as make a psychological purchase of him, not surprising that they began to work together" (26–27).

Although in 1948 only 3 percent of the population owned a television, Harry Truman produced a spot encouraging citizens to vote. It wasn't until 1952 when about 45 percent of the nation owned a television set that political ads became commonplace events. In that presidential contest, the Republicans spent $1.5 million and the Democrats only $77,000. Eisenhower's advisers felt television spots could be more controlled and counter his "stumbling press conference performances" (Sabato 1981, 113). Accounting for inflation, Eisenhower's television budget was greater than that spent in the 1980 presidential campaign (Devlin 1986, 25).

As discussed in the last chapter, it was also in that year that Richard Nixon, Eisenhower's vice-presidential running mate, took to the airwaves to deny charges of maintaining a slush fund of $18,000 and to save his spot on the ticket. The advertising agency of Batten, Barton,

Durstine, and Osborn purchased 30 minutes of network time for $75,000 for Nixon to answer charges. The presentation was carefully constructed, rehearsed, and successful. The medium was not only a way to communicate to an audience but was also a means to persuade them.

The dominant format of early political ads featured the candidate speaking directly to the camera. For media specialists, this format was lacking. It did not utilize the full capabilities of the medium and was certainly boring to the general public. Later, in a more creative use of the medium, campaign events were broadcast live. Live events are, however, difficult to control and staged interactions soon followed. In addition to 30- and 60-second spots, extended half-hour documentaries and telethons were a popular format from 1960 to 1972, but are much too expensive to broadcast today.

Contemporary political ads are creative, fully utilizing the medium of television with color, music, and a variety of technological manipulations. Lynda Kaid and Dorothy Davidson (1986, 199–208), in their study of political ads, found two very distinct video styles. The incumbent video style uses longer commercials, more testimonials, more candidate positive focus, more slides with print, and more formal dress. It stresses competence and is usually represented by an announcer. The challenger video style uses more opponent negative focus, talking head ads, cinema verite style, more eye contact with audience, and more casual dress. And most often, it speaks for him- or herself in the ads.

There are numerous functions of political ads: to create interest in a candidate, to build name recognition, to create, soften, or redefine an image, to stimulate citizen participation, to provide motivation for candidate support, to reinforce support, to influence the undecided, to identify key issues and frame questions for public debate, to demonstrate the talents of the candidate, and to provide entertainment. The content, approach, and thrust of an ad are based upon several considerations: the strengths and weaknesses of the candidate, the strengths and weaknesses of the opponent, available funds, the nature of news coverage of the candidate, public information and views of the candidate, and the general artistic and aesthetic inclinations of the consultant, to name only a few.

Although there are numerous specific advertising formats and strategies, there are four basic political advertising messages. Positive messages are those designed to promote the positive attributes of the candidate and to link the candidate to voters in a positive way. Such efforts range from rather basic biographical spots to more herotic "product of the American Dream" spots. Negative messages are specifically designed to attack the opponent. They may focus on the personal weaknesses of the candidate or aspects of one's voting record or prior public experience or behavior. Comparative messages are still designed to attack the opponent, but tend to focus on issue positions. The most effective comparison ads give the appearance of providing a "two-sided" argument, but the presentation is always slanted to favor the candidate sponsoring the ad. Some comparisons are implied, never specifically referring to the opposition. Audience interpretation favors the candidate sponsoring the ad. Finally, there are response messages designed to directly answer challenger charges, allegations, and attacks.

Specific ads may serve a variety of functions or purposes. Interestingly, however, there is a chronology of their use during a campaign (Diamond and Bates 1984, 303–45). Early in a campaign, advertising seeks to create name recognition and candidate identification. Biographical spots are most common as already noted during this phase. The next strategic use of commercials is to generate argument detailing the candidate's themes of the campaign often targeted to a particular demographic voting group. During the argument phase of the campaign; issues are treated in emotional terms seeking the approval and interest of voters. Following argument ads are attack commercials or what some call negative commercials. The focus of these ads is on the opponent, and they are seldom delivered by the candidate. Campaigns attack opponents to gain momentum, to move undecided voters, and to motivate people to vote against their opposition. Depending upon voter response and polling data, campaigns may simultaneously run positive messages to mitigate backlash to negative ads. Finally, by the end of the campaign, ads of resolution appear. In these spots candidates attempt to sum up the issues, their positions, and provide reasons for voting for them. Usually these ads are in the last week of the campaign and have the candidates speaking directly to the audience.

Many journalists and scholars argue that there seems to be an increasing trend towards negative campaigns in recent history at all electoral levels. Although there have always been negative ads, Richard Armstrong (1988, 18) argues that the elections of 1986 marked a new stage in electoral politics, a stage he calls "reactivity." New technologies allowed candidates to respond to opponents, public attitudes, and situations much faster, thus becoming more reactive, resulting in what appears to be more negative campaign activities. Today's technology has developed a kind of "punch/counterpunch" campaign.

In sheer numbers of ads, it does appear that each successive campaign is more negative or attack oriented. For example, Lynda Kaid (1998) claims that the ads of the 1996 presidential campaign were most negative in American history. Seventy-one percent of Clinton's ads were negative compared to 61 percent of Dole's ads (148–49). Both, however, reflect a predominate negative focus in their campaigns. According to Stephen Ansolabehere and Shanto Iyengar (1995), such continual negative campaigns have resulted in "record lows in political participation, record highs in public cynicism and alienation, and record rates of disapproval of the House of Representatives" (2).

Karen Johnson-Cartee and Gary Copeland (1997) provide an excellent review of contemporary research literature on the effects of political advertising (149–83). In terms of *cognitive or awareness effects* of political advertising, they found (150–51):

- Political advertising leads to more general knowledge about issues and candidates.
- There seems to be a point where information gain from political spots does not increase with increased exposure to the ads.
- Individuals who watch moderate levels of political advertising demonstrate the same level of information gain as heavy viewers of political advertising.
- Political advertising influences issues determined most salient to voters during a campaign.

Among the more important *affective effects* of political advertising, Johnson-Cartee and Copeland (1997, 151–52) report:

- Political advertising influences individual evaluation of candidates in terms of attractiveness, credibility, and status.
- Political advertising generates positive and negative emotions or feelings about a candidate.
- Issue-oriented ads increase a candidate's perceived leadership skills and feelings of warmth.
- Exposure to ads leads to greater positive effect toward candidates.
- Candidates are less persuading when expressing their own opinions than newscasters and retired politicians.

Determining how political advertising influences voting behavior is complex and difficult to isolate. Sometimes, findings of various studies seem to contradict each other. In their review of numerous studies, Johnson-Cartee and Copeland (1997, 152–53) found:

- Most people report that political advertising does not influence their vote.
- There is a positive relationship between money spent on political advertising and voter turnout and electoral outcome.
- Increase in political advertising tends to encourage voter ticket splitting (i.e., voting for members of different parties during an election).
- Political ads have often been identified as an important criterion affecting an individual's vote in an election.

- Impact of political advertising tends to be the strongest in "low-level," or more "low-involvement" local races as well as primary nomination campaigns, nonpartisan races, and state races.
- Political ads have greater influence on undecided and late decider voters.

Political advertising is also very important in influencing candidate issues and image. Both notions are multidimensional and can be very subtle. Candidate image deals with attributes of a candidate's character. Issues are matters of public concern or potential policy positions of candidates. In terms of issues, broadly defined, in political advertising, Johnson-Cartee and Copeland (1997, 156–57) found:

- The majority of ads in races usually mention some issue or issues.
- While ads may discuss an issue, the candidate's position on those issues may not always be presented in the ad. More often, the "favorable" stance is assumed.
- When mentioned, issues are usually treated in a rather superficial and broad manner.
- When issues are clearly identified in ads, they tend to be targeted to specific demographic voting groups.

Candidate image, like that of political issues, is a broad theoretical construct rather than a specific concrete variable. Studies investigating image have ranged from considering how a candidate looks to the personal moral behavior of candidates. In reviewing empirical studies on candidate image and advertising, the authors note (157–58):

- Television has increased the importance of how a candidate looks over issue positions.
- Personal characteristics of candidates are more important to a large number of voters than candidate issue positions.
- The way issues are treated in political ads influences image perceptions of candidates.
- The most common image appeals in political ads include experience, competence, special qualities, honesty, leadership, and strength.
- Candidate image influences how favorably voters view the candidate.
- Image-oriented ads are best for content recall and candidate name recognition.

Campaign ads from any election, whether a mayoral race or a presidential race, provide in a capsule form the basic issues, strategies, and tactics of a campaign. Together they provide the psyche of the public—their likes and dislikes, their concerns and worries, their hopes and dreams. They indeed provide future historians snapshots of American politics.

Public Opinion Polling

The art and science of polling have become the major influence in strategic decision making in modern political campaigns. Polling is used in all stages of campaigns. Pollsters gather data, suggest strategy, monitor campaign status, and evaluate communication tactics.

The *Harrisburg Pennsylvanian* published in 1824 contained the first political opinion poll in America (Sabato 1981, 69). It consisted of a survey of presidential preferences of the constituents between Andrew Jackson and John Quincy Adams. Jackson won the straw vote two to one. But scientific polling did not begin until the 1930s. Mrs. Alex Miller was the first candidate to use polling by her son-in-law George Gallup. She became the first female secretary of state in Iowa by utilizing sampling techniques that Gallup developed in his doctoral thesis. He founded the polling industry in 1935. Franklin Roosevelt's use of public opinion polls was to gauge his popularity and not to form issue or policy. Although Eisenhower's advertising agencies consulted Gallup in the development of themes to use in the 1952 television ads, extensive use of polling did not begin until 1960. John Kennedy used Louis Harris to analyze public opinion in a key primary state. Upon Harris's urging, Kennedy entered the West Virginia primary—and West Virginia is a heavily Protestant state. Kennedy nearly lost the primary and lost faith in Harris's predictions.

Political polls most often focus on three major variables: the candidate, the public, and specific issues or topics. In terms of the candidate, polls assess electoral viability, strengths and weaknesses of personality characteristics, profile matches with voters or specific voter groups, and current status of the election. In terms of the public, polls seek to identify what kinds of people plan to vote for the candidate and against the candidate, what they are thinking, why they are thinking the way they are, and how their thinking will impact the election. Finally, polls attempt to reveal issue positions in terms of support, strategy development, and electoral impact. For example, polling and focus group research was used extensively by the Clinton campaign in 1996, not only to ascertain which issues generated the most support but also to develop ways to attack the opposition. Consultant Dick Morris (1997) reveals that "we formulated each ad according to our polling. Mark Penn and Doug Schoen and I prepared poll questionnaires. . . . The poll measured public reaction to each element of the president's legislative program to that of the Republicans. . . . We prepared several different rough versions of the ads, called animatics, which Mark Penn would arrange to test at fifteen shopping malls around the nation. . . . Based on the mall tests, we decided which ads to run. . . . I felt like a violinist suddenly surrounded by a great orchestra or a baseball player in an all-star lineup" (146–47).

In a campaign, polls are used to assess name recognition, issue preferences of voters, check distribution of knowledge or beliefs about particular topics, discover underlying attitudes about social and political values, test hypotheses, or issue positions among voter groups as well as reveal basic demographic characteristics of potential voters.

Shea (1996) identifies four major types of polls in political campaigns (124–25). Focus groups consist of small number of individuals talking about their beliefs, attitudes, and values. If done correctly, they can provide insight in how to link issues and positions to specific voter groups. Benchmark polls are conducted very early in the campaign process to provide baseline information about candidates and their standing among voters. The information gathered helps campaign staff to develop strategy, identify key issues and appeals. Tracking polls are conducted on a regular basis to identify trends and to follow the status of the campaign. While limited in scope, they usually attempt to track name recognition, candidate support (including favorable and unfavorable impressions), issue support, and effectiveness of campaign activities and ads. Finally, campaigns may conduct quick response polls intended to assess the effect of specific events, usually those that are unplanned such as a barrage of attack ads.

Of course news organizations conduct many polls and these are much less informative than campaign polls. They tend to have higher margins of error and are much more limited in scope.

Although polling has become very sophisticated and scientific, it still remains problematic despite its popularity. Critics claim that polls do not distinguish between awareness of an issue and intensity of opinion. There is often no link between an attitude and subsequent behavior. By far the greatest concern is that polls alone become the basis for decision making. Dick Morris (1997, 83), for example, claims that President Clinton uses polls to help determine *how* to change people's views, not on what they should favor. Political opinion polls, unlike public polls of Gallup and Harris, are more tools of persuasion, image control, and creation, than reports of information. They are, simply, an important element of a consultant's service arsenal.

Direct Mail

Of all the services provided by consulting firms, the public is probably less aware of the importance and role direct mail plays in a campaign. As a relatively new industry, direct marketing has rapidly become the cornerstone for mounting a political campaign. In fact, if one considers all levels of political campaigns from presidential to school board elections, more money is spent on direct mail than television (*Campaign & Elections*, 18(5) [May 1997], p. 22).

Richard Armstrong (1988) claims that the direct mail "has utterly revolutionized American politics . . . it has drastically changed the role of the national parties . . . created an enormous shadow government of special interest groups . . . completely revolutionized the nature of campaign finance . . . abetted the rise of political action committees . . . created a new form of political advertising . . . changed the way incumbents communicate with their constituents . . . and dramatically altered the nature of lobbying" (28). Direct mail specifically is a powerful and persuasive communication medium. Larry Sabato (1981, 220) refers to direct mail as "the poisoned pen of politics" and Armstrong (1988) writes, "like a water moccasin, persuasion mail is silent, it is poisonous, and it has a forked tongue" (60). As the fastest growing advertising industry, direct mail utilizes the latest technology and theories of social science research.

In terms of politics, it was the 1972 presidential campaign that demonstrated the power and effectiveness of direct mail (Blumenthal 1982, 242–44). George McGovern was generally unknown and had great difficulty obtaining endorsements from party regulars, wealthy supporters, or organized groups. He was forced to use direct mail to generate funds from individual citizen supporters. Even in a difficult campaign, by 1972 direct mail was bringing in over $200,000 a month.

But Republicans have benefited most from direct marketing. In 1974, following Nixon's resignation, Congress enacted legislation that set a $1000 limit on individual political contributions. The Republicans immediately began developing a sophisticated direct mail program utilizing the latest technology, consistently raising four or five times more money using direct mail than Democrats (Armstrong 1988, 116). Democrats relied on direct mail primarily for fundraising, not for general advertising purposes. According to Richard Viguerie, Republicans and conservatives were forced to use direct mail because of the need to bypass the "liberal mass media." It became, for them, "a way of mobilizing our people, it's a way of communicating with our people; it identifies our people, and it marshals our people. It's self-liquidating and it pays for itself. It's a form of advertising, part of the marketing strategy. It's advertising" (Blumenthal 1982, 245).

Viguerie discovered that direct mail responders are more interested in principles than in winning elections. During the 1980s, he churned out direct mail solicitations concerning one hot issue after another. The "new right" began to generate more and more money. Conservative causes used direct mail to finance campaigns and sympathetic PACs through direct mail solicitation.

Thus, fundraising is the primary function of direct mail in political campaigns. Candidates use direct mail to supplement federal financing of elections. Fundraising objectives include reaching new contributors as well as maintaining contact with previous ones. Other uses of direct mail include targeting voters, developing issues, recruiting volunteers, molding opinions, getting out the vote, and laying the groundwork for future campaigns by establishing a list of donors and supporters.

Direct mail tends to work best for both fundraising and general advertising purposes in campaigns expecting a low voter turnout, if district or geographic area is not part of a major media market, or if race is "down-ballot" in expensive media market.

Direct mail is powerful because the package is carefully constructed. Starting with the envelope, there is some teaser or attention-getting statement that leads the reader to open the correspondence. The letter usually begins with a startling or dramatic statement by the politician or a celebrity. The letter is conversational and personal using a lot of I's and you's. There is an early identification of an enemy which is either the opponent, a group, or an issue position. The situation is described as being critical, desperate, and urgent. Of course, most letters conclude with an appeal for support and financial assistance. In short, the copy must get attention, arouse interest, stimulate desire, and ask for action.

At the heart of political direct mail is "emotional isolation." The target is an angry person who is politically frustrated. Direct mail acknowledges the anger and shows that someone or some group cares.

Techniques of emotion and motivation are well known by the professionals. They know that a letter is more likely to generate a response for funds if the letter is very specific as to what the money will be used for—television advertising, for example. Experts know that participation devices stimulate interest and focus concentration upon the issues or action discussed. Many mailings include opinion surveys, boxes required to be checked, or sample ballots to be marked. In terms of fundraising, the size of a contribution will be greater if not only the amount is specified but also if the suggested amounts start with the largest (i.e., $500, $250, $100, $50, rather than $50, $100, $250, $500). Ironically, a two-page letter is more likely to be read than a one-page letter, and the signature should be in blue ink and appear to be personally signed.

The timing of a mailing is critical to its impact and success. Generally, it is best to mail just before or after an announcement of candidacy, before a primary or general election, and to coincide with a major media blitz. For example, in the 1997 Virginia gubernatorial race, the primary issue for Republican candidate Jim Gilmore was the elimination of the personal property tax. On the day of the tax notices, the Gilmore campaign conducted a major mailing of nearly 2 million pieces of mail that looked just like a tax notice with "Important Personal Property Tax Information. Immediate Attention Requested." Of course, inside voters found a brochure detailing Gilmore's tax cut proposals.

And finally, experts know that direct mail donors are more committed to the candidate and issues than single-event donors. Single-event donors are usually one-shot contributors who like being near the candidate or at a party whereas the direct mail donor will be responsive even in tough times. Thus, the list of contributors is a valuable commodity.

There are several advantages to the direct mail medium. There is more complete control not only over the construction of the message but also over who receives the message and where the message will be sent. The message appeals can be tailored and targeted and tell the full story and present a detailed issue position. The message is not limited to 30 seconds. In direct mail there is wider coverage, personalized and guaranteed contact, and the ability to capitalize on current events. It is also less costly and very effective. The importance and impact of direct marketing techniques will continue to be a factor in every campaign endeavor.

New Technologies and Tactics

There are several new technologies that are playing an increasing role in campaigns. The state of the art in telemarketing was reflected in the Jesse Jackson presidential nomination campaign of 1984 (Armstrong 1988, 139–48). He used a computerized interactive system that would automatically dial random numbers and in his voice would inquire, "How are you doing?"; "Are you registered to vote?"; "Give us your name and telephone number,"; and "Remember, you are somebody and your vote counts." The impact was almost as if Jackson had called the person directly.

With this system, contacting thousands of people, everyone hears the same message. Thus, increased productivity and quality control are guaranteed. In addition, telemarketing is more aggressive than direct mail and generally produces a much greater response rate. The key is to personalize, dramatize, and create the illusion that the donor is talking to a high-ranking member of the campaign.

As cable television increases segmenting audiences, it becomes an important tool for reaching specific audiences at a reasonable cost. For the first time in history, Bush and Dukakis in 1988 spent more in spot and cable buys than on general network advertising. Cable television allows geographic, demographic, and psychographic targeting. It also provides much more time flexibility in terms of spot or programming format. Mark Weaver (1996) observes, "the narrow interest classification of cable channels provides a radio-like opportunity to reach certain kinds of voters" (208).

The proliferation of satellites has provided yet another tool for communication specialists. Frank Greer was the first political media consultant to use communication satellites (Armstrong 1988, 196–98). He argues that they can be used in four ways: for remote press conferences, to feed news stories to local media, for fundraising, and for local coordination and organization. During the 1996 presidential campaign, Clinton used satellites to conduct five-minute interviews with local, nonmajor media markets. Such interviews provided much free publicity in the smaller markets, invited more "friendly" questions, and bypassed the national media.

Audio and video press releases provide material for local stations. For example, The Senate Republican Conference has established a miniature news bureau. It covers statements and activities of party senators. Every afternoon, while the Senate is in session, footage of various senators is sent to hometowns on Westar IV or Galaxy I satellites. Both the Democratic and Republican conferences receive nearly $1 million each from the federal government for these video press releases.

Video mail is becoming very popular in congressional races. The short campaign videos are usually ten to fifteen minutes in length. Most often, they focus on the historical background and work of the candidate. They also include testimonials from community leaders and individuals matching a targeted group. While used early in a campaign, they are excellent for enhancing candidate image and name recognition. The total production cost today for a ten-minute video is only around $2.00. Many consultants find video mail more powerful and influential than direct mail. Most people will view a videotape but are more likely to discard "junk mail." The visual impact is much greater than mail.

The newest innovation in campaign technology is the use of the Internet. In 1996, over 25,000 of the more than 100,000 candidates who ran for public office posted home pages on the World Wide Web (Friedenberg 1997, 204). Exit polls from 1996 reveal that more than 25 percent of voters were online and nearly 10 percent made their candidate selection based upon some information obtained from their Internet sites (Connell 1997, 64). Internet users are more wealthy, better educated, and more likely to vote than nonusers. According to Mike Connell, "the web's value lies less in convincing undecided voters than it does in activating—and communicating with—your own supporters" (65). For example, the Dole campaign used their web site not only to provide information to voters but also to recruite volunteers and potential contributors. It offered opportunities to order campaign items, features personalized to the home state of the site visitor, and schedule of appearances. The campaign even offered weekly newsletters e-mailed to all visitors who registered with the site. By the next campaign cycle, virtually all candidates will have web sites.

SUMMARY

One cannot consider the role of the new politician without also considering the impact upon our political process of new technologies and media consultants. For some, consultants are now "king makers" and are at the heart of our electoral process. An industry has developed, according to Nimmo and Combs (1990), to communicate "political celebrities" much like the Hollywood star system and movie gossip magazines (96). Politicians have become fantasy figures and symbolic leaders because they represent more than politics. They also represent values, lifestyle, visions, and glamor.

There are two factors that have contributed to the development of today's political celebrity. First, historically Americans have believed in democratic politics, which implies that the best, most qualified individual will rise to lead the people, representing their desires and reflecting their values (Denton 1982). To succeed, politicians must honor this illusion. The public has a host of expectations relevant to behavior, beliefs, and values for those in public life. Second, what most Americans know about politics comes from the media. Few citizens experience the process of politics through direct experience. Political realities are mediated through group and mass communication. Thus, mediated politics give consultants a great deal of influence and power. This trend alarmed Herbert Schiller (1973), who over a quarter of a century ago observed that when media people "deliberately produce messages that do not correspond to the realities of social existence, the media managers become mind managers" (1). The ultimate danger is that by "using myths which explain, justify, and sometimes even glamorize the prevailing conditions of existence, manipulators secure popular support for a social order that is not in the majority's long-term real interest" (1).

But are the dangers that great? Consultants, of course, believe that they are actually making the electoral process more democratic. They claim that they cannot control votes as the old political bosses did through the patronage system. Also, consultants can't enforce voter discipline or the voting behavior of elected officials. There is even no empirical evidence of a direct causal relationship between watching a commercial or series of commercials and voting. Consultants further argue that they make elections more open and provide access for reporters to candidate strategy, views, and campaign information.

Of course there is nothing inherently wrong or evil in the new technologies or even the desire of politicians to present their best attributes to the public. But the pressure of winning for both the candidate and the consultant cannot be ignored. Therein lies the potential for abuse. For consultants to get business, they must continue to win elections. They are more likely, then, to accept only sure bets and, once in the battle, they may not recognize any limits to winning. The fact is, most candidates are willing participants. They seldom question the advice or strategy of consultants. Candidates are paying a great deal of money for consultant services. They seldom understand the new technologies, nor do they have the time to develop the necessary expertise to become a full partner in media decisions.

In the demise of political parties, consultants have taken their place in generating supporters, motivating voters, and raising money. For major elective offices, consultants rather than parties have become the intermediaries between politicians and the public and the press. The consequences, according to Sabato (1981, 313), are the continuing decline of party organizations; emphasis of images over issues; candidate independence from party ideology; more narrow elections with focus on single issues that can be packaged; dissemination of communication tools and techniques to political action committees or issue groups; resorting to factual inaccuracies, half-truths, and exaggerations; using deceptive and negative advertising resulting in voter distrust and apathy; emphasis on emotional themes over rational discussion of issues; and drastically increasing costs of elections.

The professional politicians of today are not the political officeholders, for the latter are paid for governing while the former are paid for managing and winning elections. For professional politicians, politics is a permanent, continual campaign and not the process of governing. Political consultants possess the tools, skills, and techniques of mass communication and human motivation. The functions and services of political consultants, while communication based, have a profound effect upon our electoral process.

REFERENCES

Ansolabehere, Stephen, and Shanto Iyengar. 1995. *Going Negative*. New York: Free Press.

Armstrong, Richard. 1988. *The Next Hurrah*. New York: William Morrow.

Becker, Samuel. 1971. "Rhetorical Studies for the Contemporary World." In *The Prospect of Rhetoric*, ed. Lloyd Bitzer and Edwin Black. Englewood Cliffs, NJ: Prentice-Hall, pp. 21–43.

Blumenthal, Sidney. 1982. *The Permanent Campaign*, 2d ed. New York: Touchstone Books.

Chagall, David. 1981. *The New King-Makers*. New York: Harcourt Brace Jovanovich.

Connell, Mike. 1997. "New Ways to Reach Voters and Influence Public Opinion on the Internet." *Campaigns & Elections* 18(8): 64–68.

Denton, Robert E., Jr. 1982. *The Symbolic Dimensions of the American Presidency*. Prospect Heights, IL: Waveland Press.

Devlin, Patrick. 1986. "An Analysis of Presidential Television Commercials: 1952–1984." In *New Perspectives on Political Advertising*, ed. Lynda Kaid, Dan Nimmo, and Keith Sanders. Carbondale: Southern Illinois University Press, pp. 21–54.

———. 1997. "Contrast in Presidential Campaign Commercials of 1996." *American Behavioral Scientist* 40(8): 1058–84.

Diamond, Edwin, and Stephen Bates. 1984. *The Spot*. Cambridge, MA: MIT Press.

Faucheux, Ron. 1998. "Strategies that Win!" *Campaigns and Elections* 18(10): 24–32.

Friedenberg, Robert. 1997. *Communication Consultants in Political Campaigns*. Westport, CT: Praeger.

Gronbeck, Bruce. 1984. "Functional and Dramaturgical Theories of Presidential Campaigning." *Presidential Studies Quarterly* 14(Fall): 487–98.

Johnson-Cartee, Karen, and Gary Copeland. 1997. *Inside Political Campaigns*. Westport, CT: Praeger.

Kaid, Lynda. 1998. "Videostyle and the Effects of the 1996 Presidential Campaign Advertising." In *The 1996 Presidential Campaign: A Communication Perspective*, ed. Robert E. Denton, Jr. Westport, CT: Praeger, pp. 143–60.

Kaid, Lynda, and Dorothy Davidson. 1986. "Elements of Videostyle." *In New Perspectives on Political Advertising*, ed. Lynda Kaid, Dan Nimmo, and Keith Sanders. Carbondale: Southern Illinois University Press, pp. 184–209.

Lazarsfeld, Paul et al. 1948. *The People's Choice*. New York: Columbia University Press.

McGinniss, Joe. 1969. *The Selling of the President: 1968*. New York: Trident Press.

Morris, Dick. 1997. *Behind the Oval Office*. New York: Random House.

Nimmo, Dan. 1970. *The Political Persuaders*. Englewood Cliffs, NJ: Spectrum Books.

Nimmo, Dan, and James Combs. 1990. *Mediated Political Realities*, 2d ed. New York: Longman

Robbin, Jonathan. 1989. "Geodemographics: The New Magic." In *Campaigns and Elections*, ed. Larry Sabato. Glenview, IL: Scott, Foresman, and Co., pp. 106–25.

Sabato, Larry. 1981. *The Rise of Political Consultants*. New York: Basic Books.

Schiller, Herbert. 1973, *The Mind Managers*. Boston: Beacon Press.

Shea, Daniel. 1996. *Campaign Craft: The Strategies, Tactics, and Art of Campaign Management*. Westport, CT: Praeger.

Swenney, William. 1995. "The Principles of Planning." In *Campaigns and Elections*, ed. James Thurber and Candice Nelson. Boulder, CO: Westview Press, pp. 14–29.

Weaver, Mark. 1996. "Paid Media." In *Campaign Craft*, ed. Daniel Shea. Westport, CT: Praeger, pp. 201–18.

Chapter 6

Presidential Campaigns

> Every four years a gong goes off and a new presidential campaign surges into the national consciousness: new candidates, new issues, a new season of surprises. But underlying the syncopations of change there is a steady, recurrent rhythm from election to election, a pulse of politics; that brings up the same basic themes in order, over and over again.
>
> James Barber, *The Pulse of Politics* (1980)

In the last chapter we noted that campaigns are complex communication acitivities with the growing influence of communication specialists in every level of political campaigns. There are numerous channels of campaign communication to include: public appearances (speeches, rallies); interpersonal (luncheons, meetings with opinion leaders); organizational (party machines, workers); display media (buttons, posters, billboards); print media (campaign literature, ads, newspapers), auditory media (radio, telephone); and television (advertising, news coverage, programs). Interestingly, some local campaigns are as complex, long, and expensive as national campaigns. Local and state campaigns differ only in scope and money spent—not in basic task requirements. But the U.S. presidential contest is unique in the world. Because of the magnitude of the office, every presidential election is historical and impacts upon the rest of the world.

The formal criteria for becoming president as set forth in Article 11, Section I of the Constitution are threefold: natural born citizen, at least 35 years old, and a resident of the United States for 14 years. But the informal criteria are numerous and include political experience, personal charisma, fundraising, and audience adaptation. Today, the presidential contest extends beyond the traditional three-month campaign between Labor Day and November every four years. In fact, the contest has become continual and, for some participants, a matter of lifelong training and maneuvering. The "right" person for the job is not just found but is created, demonstrated, and articulated to the American public. The distinction between being a president and being a presidential candidate has virtually disappeared. Godfrey Hodgson (1980) even argues that the presidential election campaign is no longer simply the way a president is chosen; it actually influences the kind of person chosen and the priorities they will have as president (211). Thus, the strategies and tactics presidential candidates use to present themselves and to communicate with the American public are of vital importance and are the focus of this chapter.

THE PROCESS

Since World War II, our political system has undergone a fundamental change in how candidates for the presidency have been selected. In fact, one of the most striking features of our presidential nomination process is its constant change of rules, financing regulations, and primaries. Changes to the electoral process have resulted in longer campaigns and increased influence of media coverage. Some "reforms" impact the process in ways unkown at the time. The focus of the changes has been on the role of the public in the process. The citizenry rather than party activists increasingly determine which candidates will meet in the general election. Since 1968, presidential primaries have become the critical factor in capturing nominations and the public have become the true power brokers. We have, in effect, blurred the distinction between nominating and electing candidates.

By 1976, with the Carter campaign, Larry Bartels (1989) claims the public witnessed the strategic success inherent in the contemporary presidential nominating process. The key to success is not "to enter the campaign with a broad coalition of political support, but to rely on the dynamics of the campaign itself . . . to generate that support" (3). The new system is dominated by the candidates who seek public support. A critical issue becomes, of course, whether or not the increased roles of the public and media have resulted in better candidates.

Historically, we have experienced three presidential nominating systems. The congressional caucus system existed between 1800 and 1824. Successful candidates had to appeal to congressmen and the national political elite. Party congressmen controlled the nomination and the role of party grass-roots voters, and the press was minimal.

The brokered convention system, 1832 to 1968, emerged as a result of the deaths of the founding fathers, general population growth and movement to the west, and the initiation of more democratic political customs. During this system, nominations occurred at national conventions involving a great deal of bargaining. Popularity with state and local officials as well as with major officeholders was critical for the successful candidate. Although presidential primaries began in 1908, regular party leaders and national officeholders controlled the nomination. As late as 1968, Hubert Humphrey won the Democratic party nomination without contesting in a single presidential primary. Once again, party grass-roots voters and the press had little influence upon candidate selection.

The system of popular appeal began with the 1972 presidential election. The old systems functioned under the philosophy of "consent of the governed" and the new under the auspices of "government by the people." Conventions normally ratify state primaries, conventions, and caucuses. Candidates have to maintain popularity with party voters, activists, and media representatives. The new system, initiated by the Democratic Party, was heralded as open, democratic, deliberative, and responsive to popular preferences.

Many political scientists are alarmed at how we nominate and elect our presidents. They challenge Al Smith's maxim that "the cure for the ills of democracy is more democracy." Scott Keeter and Cliff Zukin (1983) argue that the new system of presidential nomination makes for uninformed choice both by the individual and for society as a collectivity. For them, quality of citizen input is not a function of the capacity of the public to participate, but the nature of citizen input is a function of the structure and environment in which it is made. Keeter and Zukin (1983) conclude "that the contemporary system of presidential nomination presents a most inhospitable climate for rational and informed participation" (vii–viii).

The presidential nomination system of popular appeal raises several concerns and issues:

1. Officeholders are at a disadvantage seeking nominations because of the need for full-time personal campaigning for years prior to a general election.
2. The role of political parties decreases, diminishing peer review of candidates and weakening the ties between campaigning and governing.
3. Some states' primaries are more important than others based upon such factors as size, time of primary, and so on.
4. Rules for delegate selection vary from state to state.
5. Voter eligibility rules differ among states.
6. Sequencing of primaries changes the number of candidate choices in later primaries.

7. Most citizens learn very little about the candidates during the primary process.
8. General public opinion seldom corresponds to those of specific or important state primaries.
9. Convention delegates are not representative of the general public.
10. Journalists play a major role in the campaigns.
11. The current system favors people who have a burning desire for power and who can campaign full time.

ELEMENTS OF A COMMUNICATION MODEL OF PRESIDENTIAL CAMPAIGNS

Campaigns, from a communication perspective, are exercises in the creation, recreation, and transmission of "significant symbols." Political campaigns are an essential part of our national conversations—conversations about our national goals, social objectives, national identity, and future courses of action. Communication activities are the vehicles for social action. This model attempts to locate, isolate, analyze, and describe the communication variables of the presidential campaign process.[1]

There are two basic assumptions underlying the model. First, there are several essential elements of the campaign that are common to all candidates and that cut across all phases of a campaign. Second, these common elements differ dramatically in terms of rhetorical functions and impact across the phases of campaigns. Thus, while the elements remain the same, the roles they play and their impact upon strategy and outcomes differ over time.

The model explores the interaction of six key elements over the four stages of a presidential campaign. Both campaigns and communication more broadly understood are social processes rather than discrete events. The model attempts to capture the dynamic nature of communication within the evolving structure of a presidential campaign.

The Keys to a Presidential Campaign

There are six elements that are crucial to developing an understanding of the presidential campaign process. These elements are: the strategic environment, organization, finance, public opinion polls, candidate image, and media. Each of these functions independently as well as interactively. That is, they have both an independent effect upon the rhetorical strategies and tactics of the candidates as well as affecting one another. The interaction of the elements establish clear expectations of the campaign process. A brief overview of these elements follows.

The Strategic Environment

The term "strategic environment" was coined by Nelson W. Polsby and Aaron Wildavsky (1980) in their seminal work, *Presidential Elections*. For Polsby and Wildavsky, the strategic environment includes voters, interest groups, political parties, finances, control over information, television, and the issue of incumbency. The strategic environment may be defined as the broad context within which the electoral process is played out. According to Daniel Shea (1996), "the most significant element in a modern campaign is the context" (27). For him, the elements of the context are "those pieces of the campaign that cannot be altered by your candidate, the opponent, or by anyone else" (27). Such elements include the candidates' status, candidates' qualifications, opponents' qualifications, the media market, and national trends, to name only a few. Ultimately, all strategies, tactics, and campaign messages originate from the social context.

This context varies depending on the electoral phase. There are two general areas of concern: political and social (Wayne 1992, 56–84). Political concerns include party identification, party nomination rules, number of likely opponents, incumbency, voter behavior and attitudes. For example, elements of voting behavior such as turnout, group ties, and partisanship will have very different strategic implications during the primary versus the general election phase of a campaign. Social concerns include dominant social issues, issues "created" by candidates, and unforeseen or unexpected events. Some social issues may dominate a campaign such as the economy, crime, or abortion. Candidates, of course, hope to "own" issues, or at least unique positions on issues. While the broad issue of family values was salient in the presidential campaign of 1988, it was markedly less important in 1992, when the economy became the dominant issue.

Electoral laws are also important as broad determinants of candidate behavior. In the pre-primary period, they are a factor as candidates decide which races to enter and which to avoid; getting on the ballot may require a strong enough organization to obtain requisite signatures and may require an early decision. In the primary period, these laws govern the allocation of delegates to state and national conventions. The allocation procedure is not neutral, and will inevitably favor some candidates, or some types of candidacies, above others. Finally, in the general election, the electoral college is a crucial determinant of candidate strategy. All candidates naturally want the largest vote total they can amass, but because of the peculiar arithmetic required by the electoral college, candidates are inclined to spend less time in "safe" states and in those they have given up for lost, and will concentrate their efforts on close state races, or those where they are likely to succeed.

A candidate's rhetorical strategies will also be affected by the partisan structure of the race. This structure determines the strategy to the degree that it requires the candidate to appear centrist, right or left wing. The structure during the pre-primary and primary is clearly different from that of the general election, for the relevant electorate is also different. Similarly, the volatility and expected turnout will affect candidate strategy, for candidates design appeals to those most likely to vote. In a very real sense, support only matters to the extent that it can be measured in the voting booth.

Elections do not occur in a vacuum. Citizens bring their histories, beliefs, attitudes and values to the voting booth. The social and political contexts of elections greatly influence strategic considerations. Political consultants and activists are quick to note that no two campaigns are alike. What "worked" in one cycle will not likely be successful in the next electoral contest.

Organization

In any campaign effort, candidate organization is vital. At the presidential level, campaign organizations are large, specialized, and complex. At a minimum, most campaigns have a director who coordinates all activities and acts as liaison among the candidate, the organization, and the party; a campaign manager who oversees the day-to-day activities; division chiefs for specialized tasks such as polling, media, issues, fundraising, etc.; and geographic coordinators that encompass regional territories down to congressional district levels with states (Wayne 1992, 173–80). From a macro perspective, the organization plans, develops, and implements campaign strategies and tactics.

This organization is both internal and external. Internally, the organization consist of all the advisors and strategists; those people who plan the strategy, coordinate the effort, and manage the overall campaign. According to political scientist John H. Kessel (1988), this internal organization can be broken up into two specific groups: the core group and the strategy group. "The core group consists of the candidate's own confidants, persons he has known well or worked closely with for some years. . . . The strategy group is made up of those persons who are making the basic decisions about the campaign. Its membership is quite restricted, and should not be confused with a publicly announced 'strategy committee.' " (88).

The majority, and some would argue the most critical members of a campaign staff, are the paid political consultants (Chagall, 1981). Political consultants have come to dominate the presidential election scene, becoming in the process political actors of some note themselves. Consultants are important in their own right as well as because of their input into other strategic considerations. Larry Sabato (1981) notes that

> The consultants successfully recruited by a candidate have become status symbols. . . . Through the consultant he is purchasing acceptance from other politicians, insurance that his campaign will be taken seriously, and a favorable mention by journalists. He is also buying association with a consultants' past clientele, particularly the winners. He is securing access to the web of relationships that a consultant and his firm have developed. Finally, he is accepting the public services of a surrogate. (20)

Campaign professionals and consultants include, as noted in Chapter 5, pollsters, media consultants, direct mail experts, lawyers, accountants, marketers, to name only a few. While consultants occupy the role that used to belong to the party bosses, they play that role very differently. They lack the party boss's loyalty to a larger institution, the boss's personal and individual connections to the electorate, and most seriously, "The party boss might tell a candidate what to do, but he does not instruct him who to be" (Blumenthal 1980, 4).

The external candidate organization is also very important, although it is becoming less essential as the mass media increasingly dominates the electoral scene. Such organization is more important in some locations than in others. The rule of thumb is that the larger, more urban, more heterogeneous the state, the more likely it is that candidates will rely more heavily on media appeals than the precinct workers of old. National campaigns rely upon state and local partisan "get-out-the-vote" efforts.

Finance

Along with organization, campaign finance is a critical element in any campaign. A long-standing maxim is that money is the lifeblood of politics. According to Daniel Shea (1996), "the foremost resource in any campaign is money" (178). The organization and other campaign accoutrements have to be paid for: "primary success, poll standing, and the ability to raise money are all interrelated" (Asher 1980, 254). Financial concerns are more than just raising funds. There are also considerations of where to obtain funds, how to obtain funds, how to allocate funds, and how to insure compliance with complex legal requirements of political fundraising. Such concerns have strategic and tactical implications. While one cannot simply assume that the candidate with the most money wins, "money contributes to success, but potential success also attracts money" (Wayne 1992, 51). Money is most critical early in a campaign and for those less known to the general public. Edward Walsh (1992) argues that "the more seed money, the better the harvest" (50). Early money is needed for candidates to hire consultants, conduct polls, and for travel expenses. In 1992, successful open-seat congressional candidates enjoyed a two-to-one fundraising advantage over unsuccessful ones. In short, better financed candidates generally win (Shea 1996, 182).

New regulations governing campaign finance insure that raising money is increasingly problematic and time-consuming (DiClerico and Uslaner 1984, 87–98; Edwards and Wayne 1990, 30–32). Instead of relying on "fat cats" or political parties for money, candidates are turning, ever more frequently, to professional fundraisers (Kessel 1988, 147) and the technology of direct mail (Sabato 1981, 224). These have largely replaced large individual contributions with small, grass-roots contributors and political action committees.

No one can discuss modern campaign finance without including a discussion of political action committees (PACs). Their impact upon local, state, and national elections are phenomenal. In fact, PACs provide about 40 percent of incumbent congressional and senatorial campaign funds (Shea 1996, 181). Because PACs can raise and disburse large amounts of money, candidates simply can not ignore them. Yet, relying heavily on PAC money can reduce a candidate's strategic and rhetorical options, and the candidate risks being identified as the "candidate of special interests."

Public Opinion Polls

Political public opinion polls have become an essential element of both campaign management and news coverage. Technology has increased the types, frequency, and sophistication of opinion polls. There are numerous data collection techniques: phone surveys, door-to-door surveys, mail surveys, dial 900 surveys, and focus groups, to just name a few (Selnow 1991, 177).

From a campaign perspective, polls provide much needed information about voters: who are they, what they think, how they feel, and how they will behave in the voting booth. In addition to providing information on voters, they also provide valuable feedback to the campaign allowing for message adjustments and refinements. During the course of a campaign, the types of polls include benchmark, follow-up, panel surveys, tracking, and basic data analyses, to name only a few (Selnow 1991, 177–78).

An increasing percentage of campaign funds go to the support of polls and pollsters. A candidate's standing in the polls is a crucial determinant of that candidate's ability to raise money (Asher 1980, 254). As noted in the last chapter, polls have several uses: they allow candidates to identify constituencies and issues, to tailor their image, to target their opponents' weaknesses, to allocate resources, and to influence media strategy.

One visible result of the importance of polls to campaigning, according Larry Sabato (1981), is that "the onset of polling in an election campaign, like the campaign itself, has been moved steadily forward on the calendar. In past years, the benchmark survey for a campaign was usually scheduled in the spring of an election year, but now it is done in the prior autumn or even summer or spring of the previous year." (77). The earlier a candidate begins, the more money must be invested, so the more important fundraising becomes. The polls themselves are important; an early solid standing in those polls can be vital to getting a campaign off the ground.

In addition to candidate-sponsored polls, there has been an incredible growth of media public opinion polls. In the 1972 presidential campaign, there were only 3 media polls conducted. By 1988 it had risen to 259. A 1990 Roper Center survey revealed that 82 percent of large circulation newspapers and 56 percent of television stations were involved in news polling (Ladd and Benson 1992, 22).

Polls dramatically impact election coverage. According to Diana Owen (1991), the reporting of poll results "represent news manufactured by journalists themselves through the production of statistical data that can be reported as fact. News stories that contain polls gain a heightened aura of authenticity by assigning a numerical figure to a political trend" (91). Polls influence how candidates are covered, how much airtime they will receive, which reporter will be assigned to cover them, and the portrayal of a candidate's campaign (Ratzan 1989). For some scholars, however, media polls lead to biased reporting and misrepresentation. In 1992, there were more media polls than ever before. Yet, during the general election, 80 percent of network news stories were negative in tone for the Democrats and 87 percent for the Republicans (Patterson, 1994, 18).

There are both direct and indirect impacts of polls in campaigns beyond organizational strategic considerations. They influence voters, politicians, political elites, opinion leaders, and members of the media (Traugott 1992, 126–46). For example, media polls influence candidate image, status, momentum, funding opportunities, candidate performance expectations, volunteer help, to name a few. From a voter perspective, polls may influence candidate interest and support as well as motivation to seek out additional candidate information. Polls may also influence voter turnout.

Image

Campaigns involve a multitude of persuasive messages from a diverse variety of sources. Citizens select, sort, prioritize and attend to messages that develop images of candidates. Some studies find that voters may be more persuaded by their cognitive responses to messages than to the messages themselves. Kenneth Hacker (1995) claims, in fact, that voters often respond more to their perceptions than to objective realities about campaigns and candidates. "Voting behavior," according to Hacker, "occurs in relation to the ways in which voters perceive the election, their own circumstances and concerns, the messages and behaviors of the candidates, and how commentators and other voters talk about the candidates" (xii).

Image is more than public perceptions of a candidate. As Stephen Wayne (1992) observes, "it is difficult to separate a candidate's image from the events of the real world." (207). Michael Lewis-Beck and Tom Rice (1992) argue that the three factors that influence voting most are issues, partisanship, and candidate attributes. Today, candidate image is more than a reflection of one's political philosophical orientation or issue positions. In our media age, it includes such elements as personality, job performance, dress, character, and lifestyle, to name a few. Today's mode of campaigning and new technologies provide more opportunities for candidates to create, to reinforce, and even to reinvent their public persona and image. Every American can cite a list of desirable traits that makes a "good" president. Candidates compete to demonstrate that they meet public expectations of presidential performance.

Some scholars argue that a candidate's image is that set of attributes given to a politician by the electorate. Others argue that candidate images are those created by a candidate. A key factor in determining a candidate's standing in the polls is image, and designing a viable one is the chief and most controversial task of the political consultant. However, "Image-making, no matter how manipulative, doesn't replace reality; it becomes part of it. Images are not unreal simply because they are manufactured" (Blumenthal 1980, 5).

There is at least some evidence that "perceptual defenses are lower during the primaries than in the general election, and hence images of the candidates formed during the primary season, especially early on, are more likely to be stimulus-determined" (Asher 1980, 250). This means that the earlier candidates begin to communicate an image, the more control they—and their organization—have over the image building process. Obviously, however, this process does not occur in a vacuum, no matter how early the candidate begins, especially on the presidential level. Most presidential contenders have been in public life and in the public eye for many years. They cannot create new images out of whole cloth, but must design images that are appropriate for both a presidential bid and their public past.

Increasingly, character is becoming an important part of candidate image, as candidates as diverse as Robert Dole, Gary Hart, and Joseph Biden discovered in 1988 (Lichter et al. 1988, 7), and Bill Clinton in 1992 and 1996. The candidates' private lives are no longer considered sacrosanct by the media, and posing with the spouse, kids, and family dog no longer constitutes sufficient evidence of moral integrity. It is not enough merely to design a presidential image and hope for the best; the candidate must also be careful not to undermine that image through inappropriate or inconsistent behavior.

Once an image has been designed, it must also be communicated. The mass media is one way of accomplishing this communication. As Larry Sabato (1981) says, this can be done in a variety of ways:

> Commercials can be used to establish name identification and draw attention to a candidate, increasing his visibility. The candidate's personal image can be developed, evoking certain feelings about him based on selected personality characteristics. . . . Advertisements can link the candidate directly with his party or other groups, winning support for his cause through association. . . . Finally, campaign commercials can be used to attack opponents. (121)

But the mass media, either paid or free in the form of news, is not the only means through which a candidate communicates image. In fact, other forms of communication are important elements in preparing voters for television advertising, familiarizing them with campaign themes, and providing an element of fun. Bumper stickers, placards, and other campaign toys are useful campaign aids and should not be overlooked (Sabato 1981, 192).

Candidate image is an important element, if not to create, at least to control through paid media, news coverage, campaign events, speeches, and debates. Most Americans do not cast their vote based on a single issue but rather for an individual.

Media

Presidential campaigns are essentially mass media campaigns. In fact, Matthew Kerbel (1994) finds television "brokering the relationship between candidate and voter to an unprecedented extent. . . . It is not by design, but television has come to function as a political institution. By this I mean that television is structured in such a way and newsgathering is conducted in such a fashion as to have an enduring role in American political decision making" (xiv, 208). The media, in all of its forms (broadcast and print, news and entertainment, free and paid) are the principle means of conducting presidential campaigns. As the influence of political parties decreases, and as the size of the potential electorate increases, campaign organizations increasingly rely on "the durable communication structures in order to communicate with the electorate" (Arterton 1978, 6). Without being too deterministic, at the very least the mass media provides substantial "political and candidate" information that works in conjunction with preexisting public political orientations to influence candidate images and issues (Owen 1991, 173).

The mass media have caused both quantitative and qualitative changes in presidential elections (Denton 1988, 35). Daily news coverage of the campaign, debates, political ads, and pseudo-events produce more campaign messages than ever before. From a qualitative standpoint, the media demands more sophisticated techniques of presentation, message creation, and targeting.

Media coverage can make or break a candidacy, as candidate organizations are painfully aware. While few if any candidacies are planned solely around media strategies, all candidate organizations plan with a view toward media interpretations of events. These interpretations are most important during the early stages of a campaign, when the standards of victory are less clear (as in multicandidate primary races) and the level of information is low (Asher 1980, 252). As the level of information increases, and as the structure of competition simplifies, making decisions easier, the role of the media as interpreter correspondingly diminishes.

The media do not lack for powerful roles as the race continues, however. These roles include agenda-setting and the defining of candidate images. Much of their ability to perform these roles depends on access to the candidate, and campaigns can, within limits, control coverage by controlling access (Edwards and Wayne 1990, 34–38). Candidate organizations also use staged events and similar techniques in their effort to control and dominate the news.

A recent concern for scholars is the role or impact of the news media upon the electoral process. Based upon his analysis of the 1992 presidential campaign, Kerbel (1994) argues that "television finds itself brokering the relationship between candidate and voter to an unprecedented extent. . . . During the 1992 campaign, reporters routinely inserted themselves and their experiences into election text, becoming co-stars in a drama of their own creation while sending a strong, cynical message to the audience about the evils of the political system" (xiv, 2).

In his study, Kerbel found that television coverage of elections encompass five distinct themes: horse race, issue, process, image, and nonissues. Horse race coverage alludes to stories of who's on top, who's ahead, and the electoral status of the race. Issue coverage are stories about policy concerns and positions of the candidates. Process stories actually focus on the media's role of covering the election—media coverage of the coverage. Image stories focus on the personae of the candidates. Their concerns are more than candidate resume items, but also include aspects of character, deeds, and past actions. Nonissue coverage are those unplanned, unexpected, and surprise elements and events of campaigns. They may be dramatic moments, campaign crises, or breaking stories that dominate news interests. In 1996 such items include speculation about Clinton's health care records or Dole's tumble off the podium. For Kerbel, each theme becomes part of the television story or portrayal of a campaign (4–6).

While candidates and elected officials are frequently criticized for "news management," it is equally true that candidates and elected officials who fail to manage the news are not likely to be candidates or elected officials very long. A presidential candidate, in particular, must communicate a strongly focused image to gain success in the polls and at the polls, maintain an organization, and raise needed funds. No candidate can afford to rely on the media to safeguard his or her image; attempts at controlling the news is the logical result.

Summary

There are six elements essential to all phases of every presidential campaign: the strategic environment or context; the organization, both internal and external; finance and fundraising; public opinion polls; candidate image; and finally, the mass media. While each of these is important in its own right, their role and functions are affected by and affect one another. This dynamic process is played out over time in a roughly predictable fashion. An analysis of the time periods that provide context for this process follows.

A Communication Model of Presidential Campaigns

Scholars have identified various stages or phases of presidential campaigns. For example, Trent and Friedenberg (1995) identify the stages as surfacing, primary, convention, and general election. They argue that various communication functions differ across the stages of a campaign (17–54). Likewise, the essential elements of a campaign differ in rhetorical functions and impact across campaign stages. Thus, while the elements remain the same, the roles they play and their impact upon strategy and outcome differ over time.

While all the various elements are interactive and interdependent during each stage of a campaign, some are more "important" or dominant. The dominant elements for each campaign phase are not only essential in defining the strategy but also in impacting the other elements. When considering the model, it is important to note that "issues" are considered to be part of candidate "image." In addition, the direction of the arrows indicates "pressure" or "initiative" of impact upon the other elements.

The Surfacing Phase

During the surfacing stage, candidates must achieve visibility, establish credibility or "fitness" and begin to build a viable organization (Trent and Friedenberg 1995). As Judith Trent (1978, 1995) says, this period is important because the public begins to establish expectations of the candidates, the important issues begin to emerge, and the frontrunners begin to be determined. All of these stress beginnings—images are being framed, altered, and reframed, much discussion centers on who

Figure 6.1
Pre-Primary Campaign Phase

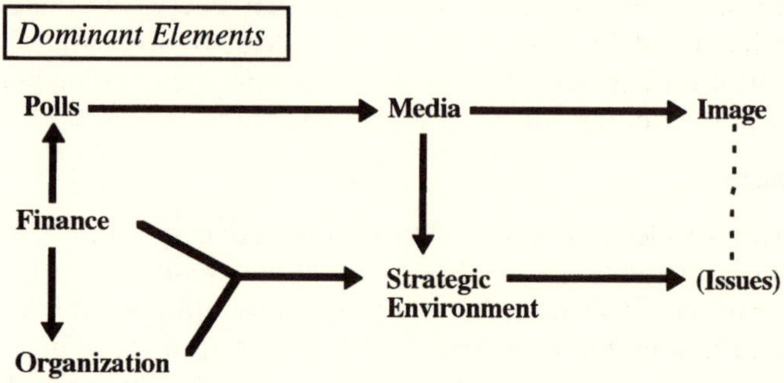

will and who won't be running, and the debate is characterized by uncertainty.

The dominant elements of this stage of the campaign are finance, polls, and organization (see Figure 6.1). Fundraising and organizational development are critical and time consuming at this point of the campaign. Key donors provide the necessary funding to identify early staff members and to pay for modest travel. Potential large-sum donors and contributors are personally contacted, consulted, and courted. The campaign identifies and begins "to work" likely sympathetic or supportive political action committees. Immediate money is needed as well as the structure for future fundraising efforts.

In the 1996 presidential contest, finance dominated all other considerations. Because of the front-loading, or the placing of so many primaries close together early in the season, interested candidates had little choice but to engage in fundraising and very visible campaign activities long before the general public was interested in the pending contest. The means and magnitude of fundraising efforts by both parties generated news coverage and public debate. The 1996 Presidential campaign broke all records in terms of money collected and spent by both political parties. The 17 major presidential candidates raised $244 million, twice the amount raised in the 1992 presidential contest (Corrado 1997, 135, 137).

From an organizational perspective, state coordinators and congressional district supporters are identified. A campaign organization is needed in every state. Nomination politics impacts the duties and behind-the-scenes activities of grass-roots supporters. Candidates must "wheel and deal" with party bosses. Again, as with fundraising, although the actual number of supporters may be low, the structure must be established at this phase of the campaign. Campaigns need a small but highly skilled and professional staff. By the primary season, it's too late to hire important, high-level staff members.

For the 1996 contest, the Clinton campaign began holding regular strategy meetings in early 1995 with more than 20 advisors and specialists. At the beginning of the primary season, 17 states would be contested in just 16 days. Thus, the front-loaded primary process required both early fundraising and organizational efforts.

While one can argue that political opinion polls are always critical to candidates, they serve a dual function in the pre-primary period. Straw polls provide legitimacy for the candidacy to the media as well as to potential key donors. For the media, early polls create candidate performance expectations, front-runner status, and initial candidate image and issue positions. For candidates, early campaign polls aid in surveying issues and developing positions.

The strategic environment is characterized by a lack of formal rules, emphasis on many candidates, and talk of various factions needing appeasement within the political parties. This lack of clear context means that the media have an important role: the media, or "Great Mentioner," provide predictions of candidate viability and/or potential weaknesses. The importance of labels cannot be underestimated. Few candidates have well-defined images, and are in the process of defining and shaping their image portrayal.

The task in the surfacing period focuses on emerging and announcing the candidacy. There is always the risk of entering the race too soon or too late. In the former case, public apathy may result, and in the latter case there may be too little time to raise funds and generate adequate support.

The collective media set the agenda for the surfacing period and may help or hurt a candidate's early image. The reputation of a candidate will dictate the frequency, slant, and tone of coverage. In addition to routine struggles of garnering favorable free media coverage, a candidate's use of paid media attempts to position them for the forthcoming primary season.

Both uses of the media were unprecedented in the 1996 presidential contest. Even with a dozen active potential Republican candidates, Colin Powell received the most positive attention from the media throughout 1995. Speculation about his candidacy virtually froze the attention and efforts of other candidates to gain media access and attention. Because of his relative poor standing the polls, the Clinton campaign started an early "air war" of ads targeted against Republicans in the summer of 1995, some 17 months before the election

In creating a rhetorical vision, the candidate must develop and articulate the campaign theme. This theme extends beyond specific issues and allows the candidate to share their vision of America and the American Dream. The rhetorical agenda, which is part of the rhetorical vision, consists of key issues that the candidate will emphasize during the campaign. These issues, of course, are based on poll results and in the early campaign are localized to maximize impact.

Of course, unexpected events outside the campaign may suddenly impact the strategic environment. National or international events may dominate the headlines and force candidates to respond.

Campaign rituals during this period include fundraising events, speaking engagements, and countless parties and dinners. These rituals function to create media attention, introduce the candidate to the voters, build group support, and help the candidate to sharpen skills for the primary period that follows.

Finally, perhaps the most difficult element of building candidate image in the pre-primary phase is the need to demonstrate that the candidate is "presidential timber." It is essential that the candidate be perceived as a "statesman" and a credible candidate. They attempt to convey this by exhibiting knowledge and expertise as well as by taking trips abroad or introducing legislation. Image in the surfacing period is a task of creation, definition, and demonstration rather than reinforcement or expansion. As already mentioned, the media play a major role in this early candidate image definition.

The best recent example of image definition, and in this case, redefinition was Clinton's early use of advertising in 1996. The three-spot campaign portrayed Republicans as cold, mean spirited, and champions of the rich. The anticrime, anti-assault weapon spots were attempts to enter the "policy game" on Clinton's terms and a way to inoculate himself against Republican criticisms of being soft on individual rights and being a typical "liberal" Democrat. The ads were aimed at "swing voters." By June of 1996, Clinton's popularity and favorable ratings were at an all time high.

The keys to the surfacing period are finance, organization, and both candidate and public opinion polls. Strength in these areas will propel the candidate into the next phase—the primary campaign.

The Primary Phase

This phase of the presidential election process has changed the most over time. Until the twentieth century, primaries were not a part of the presidential campaign. By 1916, twenty-six states were holding primaries as part of the presidential election process. It was not until the 1970s and 1980s, however, that primaries played an important role in the nomination process. Before 1968, party bosses controlled delegate selection. Candidates were forced to "lobby" party leaders to win the nomination. Winning primaries was not necessary, and entering them was often a sign of weakness rather than strength. Delegate selection was not necessarily connected to electoral strength, and was not representative of the overall population (Keeter and Zukin 1983, 6). Women and minorities in particular were largely excluded from the process.

Network televised news events such as Vietnam and the civil rights demonstrations in 1968 brought about a new "informed" or "activated" public. Everyone saw the same news and limited or very similar coverage. Candidates soon realized that they could reach all the public via the network news. The nomination system became nationalized (Keeter and Zukin 1983, 7). Party leaders were soon seen as out of touch with their constituency, and were less able to influence that constituency's behavior. The lack of representativeness in the nomination process and the new "informed" public led the Democratic Party to reform its delegate selection process.

In 1971 the McGovern/Fraser Commission of the Democratic Party implemented many changes in delegate selection. The two most important changes were first, a quota system for delegate selection that required a certain percentage of minorities, women and young people, and second, published uniform rules for all delegate selection (Keeter and Zukin 1983, 8). These changes made primaries more important by attempting to take away the power of party bosses and make the process more representative. Primaries were the easiest way for states to comply with the new rules.

In 1976, the Democrats implemented a percentage rule calling for the elimination of "winner-take-all" primaries. Candidates who received some percentage of the vote would earn a proportional number of delegates to the national convention. This rule further stressed the importance of running in the primaries and caucuses. Thus, by 1976 the nominating system was based almost entirely on elections, with most of the convention delegates selected in primaries and bound by those results.

As the Democrats made their reforms, the Republicans were swept into the new system. Most of the Democratic election reforms were passed into law, which required Republican compliance as well. All of these rule changes during the early 1970s helped to create and magnify the importance of primary and caucus elections as a means of determining delegate selection. Since 1968, the number of primaries has gone from 16 to 38 and the percentages of delegate selection has increased from 52 percent to 77 percent (Wayne, 1992, 11). Candidates could no longer win the nomination as John F. Kennedy or Hubert Humphrey had done. Primaries and caucuses were the only way to the nomination.

These changes have not occurred without controversy. Delegate selection rules are not neutral, and there is evidence that they are "biased against lesser-known minority candidates" (Edwards and Wayne 1990, 28). However, sometimes primaries encourage more partisan candidates at the expense of an inclusionary candidate. For example, in 1992, Pat

Figure 6.2
Primary Campaign Phase

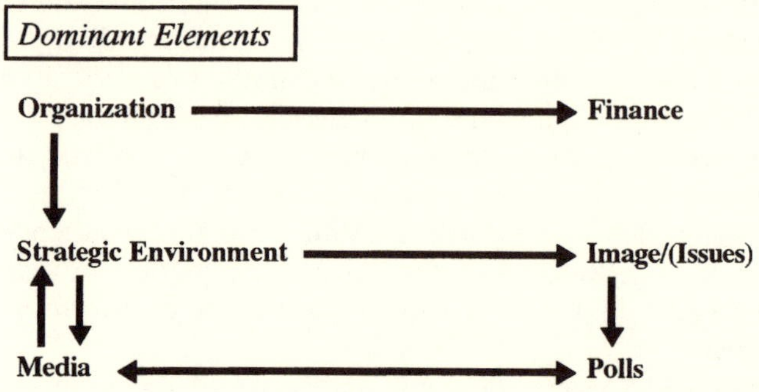

Buchanan was helped by party activists who voted in early primaries. In the old convention mold, he would have had less of a forum. The same may have been the case for McGovern back in 1972. The strategic environment is conditioned by these rules, and how they affect candidate image and fundraising efforts.

The dominant elements of this phase of the campaign are media, the strategic environment, and campaign organization (see Figure 6.2). The key tasks a candidate faces during the primary is the identification of their solid vote, the persuasion of the uncommitted vote, and maintenance of preferred image across parties, etc.

Media become the gatekeepers of access to the public as well as judge and jury of electoral performance. Campaigns are simplified, dichotomies are created, winners and losers are labeled. As a result, frontrunners emerge more quickly from media analyses and labels than from actual votes. Media expectations often determine magnitude of candidate success or failure. The news media become active participants in shaping the strategic environment by reporting polls, candidate issues, images, and strategies.

Media reports can greatly impact poll results which impact future primary elections and caucuses. Poll results justify media labels and become the mainstay of most primary period coverage. Michael Traugott (1992) argues that polls have the greatest influence during this phase of the campaign (131). The public use polls to assess candidate viability and electability. They can also help candidate name recognition and even provide momentum for candidacies. From the candidate perspective, targeted media, such as radio and direct mail are particularly valuable, since the relevant electorate is small, and it is relatively easy to tailor candidate appeals directly to them.

A strong organization is vital to primary success. The strategy team must decide which contests to enter, and develop an appropriate strategy for each. These strategies must be designed specifically for each state or region, and yet, because of the nationalization of the election process, must also be consistent across states and regions. A sound strategy will reinforce specific images in every contest, help avoid direct contradictions, and focus on relatively few themes. The result is often grand sounding mush, potentially effective on television, but is relatively free of policy content.

At this point, early funds are needed for specific state campaigns. Availability of funds will dictate primary strategies. In many ways, beyond advertising and day-to-day operations, finance has less impact on candidate image. The media have greater influence in determining winability, amount of news coverage, etc.

External organization is also central, for these are the people who wear the buttons, listen to the speeches, place the yard signs, and carry the placards. They are also the people who are instrumental in getting out the vote, and they are critical in a primary, when voter turnout is low.

The strategic environment is fully energized at this point. In a contested nomination battle, candidate organizations must be ready to respond to new issues, charges, or allegations. The contest feeds the media which impacts candidate polling numbers and issue positions, and candidate image. In many ways, candidates are more concerned with image, leadership, and personality qualities than issues; especially in terms of media coverage.

Thus, the strategic environment and the media influence the other elements while the organization's operational support should be one of routine implementation.

The Convention Phase

Today, political nominating conventions are simply media events. They no longer serve as decision makers, but as ratifiers of the party's nominees. Larry David Smith and Dan Nimmo (1991) characterize conventions as "a week-long hyped, publicized, televised spectacle that recognizes politics for what it is as currently practiced. . . . Teleconventions . . . showcase what is normally a concealed side of the contemporary conciliation of interests" (218).

However, conventions do provide some drama and follow a pattern (Smith and Nimmo, 1991). First, there is some conflict either over the nomination or various platform positions. Second, party leaders generate some compromises among the various factions. Then comes the big celebration with the focus on the candidate and the pending campaign. Finally, the media passes judgment and begins forecasting the race.

Conventions serve several functions (Trent and Friedenberg 1991, 41–45). They provide legitimization of the nomination process and the party's nominees. They also provide an opportunity for the party to

Figure 6.3
Convention Phase

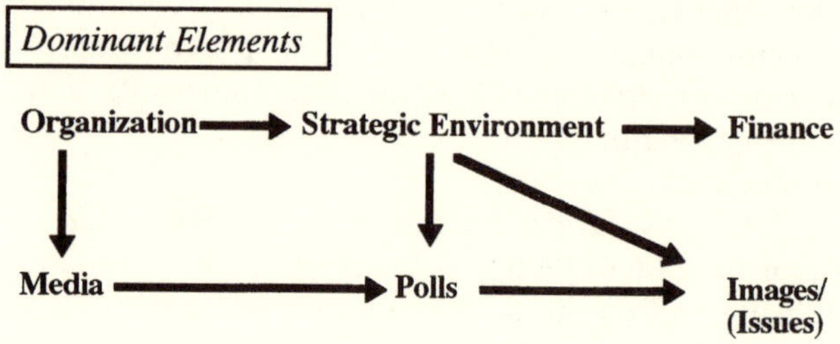

show unity and showcase party principles. Finally, conventions provide the opportunity for candidates to share their social agenda and issue positions. Thus, party conventions are highly "orchestrated" events resulting from the "process of give-and-take among party members, the news media, and various governmental institutions" (Smith and Nimmo 1991, xiv–xv).

The dominant elements of the convention phase of the campaign are organization and media (see Figure 6.3). The candidate's campaign organization plans the convention. Maximum control of all events and no surprises are the operative goals of convention management. The length and tone of media coverage become strategic concerns. Prime time becomes the place for noted speakers, rallies, and events to ensure a large audience and positive reception of party message. Media judgment and interpretation impact tracking polls long after the convention as well as projections of nominee viability. The nominee's organization attempts to maximize the traditional "convention lift" in polls and positive reporting hoping to frame the political agenda and environment for the fall campaign. A successful convention will lead to increased fundraising support. By this time, candidate image and issue positions are set in the public's mind. In fact, many voters have already made up their mind on who they will support. Entering the final phase of the campaign generates a drastic shift in the elements.

For the first time in 1996, the three major networks were less than happy about their "co-conspirator" role in bringing the carefully scripted events into American homes. In fact, Ted Koppel of ABC's *Nightline* left the Republican convention on the second day declaring that the proceedings were "more of an infomercial than a news event" concluding "nothing surprising has happened. Nothing surprising is anticipated." Although each party spent over $30 million for the four-day event, networks reduced their coverage to an all-time low. Overall, both parties were successful in presenting positive orchestrated events, but their im-

Figure 6.4
General Election Phase

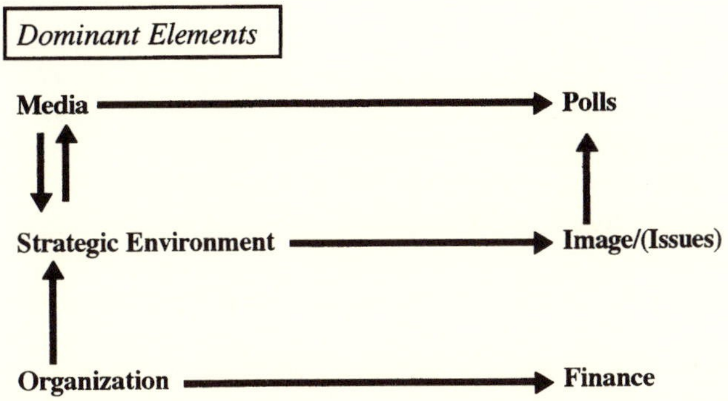

pact upon the strategic environment was limited by media coverage and portrayal.

The General Election Phase

This phase is the shortest and most intense of the entire election cycle. The political parties are mobilized, the electorate is finally interested or becoming so, and the context is national rather than state or regional.

The dominant elements in this final phase of presidential campaigns are strategic environment, media, and organization (see Figure 6.4). The strategic environment is critical to all decision making. It is dominated by the peculiar calculus demanded by the rules of the electoral college. Candidates write off some states as irretrievable, minimize the attention given to others, and focus on building the largest coalition possible given the requirements of securing 270 electoral votes. Issue positions and image maintenance are also concerns of the strategic environment. If behind in the race, corrective positions and strategies must be developed.

Of course, the media are the primary means of reaching the voters in two ways: paid advertising and news coverage. How campaigns are covered impacts public perceptions of the status of the candidates and the race. The coverage and general consensus among reports of "how the race is shaping up" impacts the strategic environment and candidate standing in the polls. Above all, there is a sense that time is running out; a sense that is heightened and "reinforced by polls that repeatedly announce the candidates' standings; these serve as reminders that only so many weeks remain until the election" (Kessel 1988, 81).

In 1996, network coverage was only half of that of 1992. In addition, Robert Lichter, director of the Center for Media and Public Affairs, reports that network coverage was more favorable to Clinton than Dole.

He found that 50 percent of the news stories on Clinton were positive compared to just 33 percent for Dole ("Washington Whispers," 1996, 20).

Much of the campaign money is earmarked to be spent on television. Media usage during the latter stages of the campaign is concentrated on reinforcing existing images and motivating the potential electorate. Negative or attack ads attempt to "push" undecided voters as well as detract support from opponents.

More and more campaigns are using a targeted state media strategy rather than making large national ad buys. Naturally, key electoral states are saturated with ads. For example, from April 1 through October 1996, nearly 170,000 spots aired in the nation's top 75 markets (Owen 1997, 209).

Candidate images are, by this phase, established. Voters pretty much know who the candidates are, and what they stand for. Candidates, in Fenno's (1978) terms, stress empathy above identification, for voters must be motivated at all costs. Advertisements become more emotional, less issue-based than before.

The organization is running at full speed. While day-to-day operational concerns are primarily event planning and coordination, finances are also important—when to spend, what to spend on, and where to spend are the big questions, made increasingly difficult as the laws governing spending limits and disclosure become more complex. Candidates increasingly rely on soft money to allow them to save funds for the final days of the campaign, when massive spending can make the difference between victory and defeat (Caddell and Wirthlin 1981, 8). Thus, the main focus is on where to spend money, not in raising it.

Summary

The foregoing discussion is useful in describing and analyzing the rhetorical functions of each of the six elements common to all campaigns within each phase of a presidential campaign. The role, function, and importance of the elements vary depending upon the phase of the campaign process. The model or paradigm attempts to capture the dynamism of the elements by exploring the interactions among the elements in various phases. Of course, presidential campaigns are not separated into tidy phases, each separately and individually packaged. They are a process, and must be understood as a process. While the model attempts to recognize the dynamic elements of a campaign, it also allows for the stable elements to be separately analyzed within the context of each phase that make up the entire campaign process. That way, one can achieve a more solid understanding of both the separate elements that form the process as well as of the process as a whole.

CAMPAIGNS

At the microscopic level, each presidential campaign is a unique historical event. Each possesses its own cast of characters, issues, conflicts, and contexts. A presidential campaign, according to James Barber (1980), "is a rousing call to arms. Candidates mobilize their forces for showdowns and shootouts, blasting each other with rhetorical volleys. It is a risky adventure; its driving force is surprise, as the fortunes of combat deliver setbacks and breakthroughs contrary to the going expectation, and the contenders struggle to recover and exploit the sudden changes" (3). Yet, from a macroscopic level, modern presidential campaigns are all very similar. There are a limited number of issues, images, tactics, and strategies available for any campaign. In fact, Barber (1980) even argues that "from the turn of the century to present day, three themes have dominated successive campaign years: politics as conflict, politics as conscience, and politics as conciliation. That sequence runs its course over a twelve-year period and then starts over again" (3). Thus, there are strong similarities in all presidential campaigns. The role and nature of communication is the structure that provides for the commonalities. In this section we will consider the role of communication in determining candidate campaign strategy and techniques.

The Role of Marketing

In Chapter 5 the importance and role of the political consultants were discussed in great detail. Suffice it to say that presidential politics are big business, complicated and high tech. Many aspects of politics are becoming more scientific with each election. Especially with the supreme importance of the mass media, politicians are utilizing marketing techniques and research tools. Gary Mauser (1983) argues that candidates and marketers have the same basic problems and goals. They both are competing for the support of a specified, target group under the constraints of time, money, and personnel. It is rather natural, then, for politicians to utilize the techniques of product marketing for election campaigns.

This development, according to Jack Honomichl (1984), reached a new high during Ronald Reagan's 1979 presidential campaign (67). It was, from a marketing standpoint, the most sophisticated and well-funded research program in the history of U.S. politics and provided the blueprint for the 1984 election and Bush's 1988 campaign. Reagan's 1979 presidential bid was based on a marketing plan developed by Richard Wirthlin, president of the firm Decision Making Information (DMI). He developed a 176-page strategy statement that became the "bible" of the campaign.

However, for Bruce Newman (1994), it was Clinton's 1992 presidential contest that fully implemented contemporary marketing concepts and strategies. He argues that

> the Clinton campaign organization resembled the best-run marketing organizations in this country, such as Procter & Gamble, McDonald's, Quaker, and others. And as in these finely tuned marketing-driven organizations, Clinton's campaign organizers kept their finger on the pulse of the consumer, the voter. Just as McDonald's uses marketing research to decide where to open up new restaurant locations, Bill Clinton's pollsters used the same technology to determine which states to target with commercials. Just as Quaker uses focus groups to decide which new products to bring to the marketplace, Bill Clinton's researchers used focus groups to decide on how best to communicate their message of change about the economy to the American people. (xv)

In effect, the marketing of a presidential campaign refers to the use of most standard marketing tools such as polling, advertising, direct marketing, focus groups, etc. and marketing concepts such as consumer segmentation, product positioning, push and pull marketing, etc.

The point is rather obvious. Often it is not concrete issues that win elections but the images, visions, and persona communicated to the electorate. And the use of marketing techniques goes beyond the simple identification of key issues or public concerns. Rather, they help to focus on the subtle likes and dislikes as well as motivations for human behavior in rather quantifiable terms.

Channels of Communication and Communication Strategy

There are four basic communication channels: the electronic media, the print media, display media (i.e., billboards, etc.), and personal contact. It is a most difficult task to determine the best combination of media to reach the potential audience and that which best communicates the desired theme. In addition, the factors of timing, money, and distribution are also important considerations. Candidates must decide when and where they will concentrate their communication efforts making sure that they do not peak too soon or spend too much in areas of little consequence.

The last chapter discussed in great detail campaign strategies and tactics. To determine the communication strategy, the target audience must be identified and segmented. This includes both committed loyalists and potential voters. Next, most campaigns attempt to "map" voter perceptions. The goal here is to identify the ways voters classify the candidates and issues viewed as important in the decision process.

As mentioned in Chapter 5, a great deal of time is also spent on identifying and characterizing the competition. By mapping voter preferences, candidates can better identify specific strengths, weaknesses, and likely patterns of competition. From all this information, various strategies can be identified, discussed, and evaluated. Ultimately, a budget is allocated, a strategy determined, time and content of appeals isolated, and a detailed media and marketing plan established.

But despite all this activity, there is a high degree of homogeneity in the political perceptions of the American people. It is difficult for well-known politicians to radically alter their image once it has become fixed in the minds of the public. There is little advertising can do to drastically change or convert voter perceptions, beliefs, and attitudes, especially in the middle of the general campaign period. Thus, most strategies seek to reinforce and link campaigns to existing perceptions, beliefs, and attitudes.

There is a standard, well-known marketing and advertising dictum. Products compete best against each other as long as they are perceived as being similar to each other. As Mauser (1983) observes, "the patterns of competition for any new product can be predicted from its pattern of perceived similarity with the other products in the markets" (267). Thus, challengers must appear presidential, and presidents must act presidential. With this in mind, Mauser (1983, 267) argues that the following communication strategies are probably most effective: Stress importance of features that are most attractive to target electorate; avoid, or state euphemistically, the features that are deemed to be undesirable; coordinate all information and advertising to reinforce the most important features of the candidate; and, if possible, attempt to move the candidate along those dimensions that can place him in an advantageous position.

Public Statements about Strategies

There is a rather clear distinction, as Henry Ewbank (1983) observes, between campaign strategies and public statements about campaign strategies. Public statements about campaign strategies come from three sources: the candidate, the candidate's spokesperson, or an opponent. Often strategy statements result from a direct challenge by an opponent, the media, or a specific voting bloc of citizens. Sometimes, in an effort to gain media attention or redefine the campaign issues, a candidate will provide a statement articulating a position or campaign strategy. Most public strategy statements deal with specific actions to be taken if elected, feelings or emotions relevant to the current state of affairs, and intentions relating to the execution of the campaign. The latter serves to establish appearances of fairness, openmindedness, and honesty. The themes of most public statements about strategy are twofold: consistency and uniqueness. Consistency is related in terms of how the candidate will meet the needs and expectations of the public, and uniqueness is related in terms of how the candidate will provide new leadership and new solutions to old problems.

For Ewbank, strategy statements can be classified in five ways according to apparent intent: offering an interpretation of a past great event, offering an explanation of current campaign events, offering a description of the future, soliciting reaction to some aspect of the campaign that may serve as a "trial balloon" for future reference, and construction of a desired perception of an event or issue position that is about to become a visible part of a campaign.

The most public view of strategy, from a communication standpoint, is the candidate's discussion of issues. Critics and scholars claim that with each contemporary campaign, true issues become less salient and less understood. This is simply not the case. Even in political ads, issue content is a major component (Kaid 1998, 144). In fact, in the 1996 presidential contest, 90 percent of Clinton's ads and 71 percent of Dole's ads stressed issues (Kaid 1998, 150).

Issues, from a communication perspective, should not be viewed as abstract or complicated constructions. They are simply what concerns the voters illustrated in concrete examples. Jean Elshtain (1989) is correct when she argues there is no real difference between "real" or "symbolic/rhetorical" issues." To claim, then, that candidates are trafficking in non-issues because they immerse themselves in weighty symbolism is to presume that which does not exist—a clear-cut division between the symbolic and the real, between issues and emotional appeals. . . . Thus, the speeches and symbols and rhetorical acts of our presidential candidates are co-authored by 'we the people,' depending upon how we receive their efforts" (117–18). And one cannot distinguish between "rational" issues and "emotional" issues, because even the issue of abortion may be based upon the tenets of a religion or interpretation of the Constitution. Audience response is the key. The real question may be whether or not citizens understand the scope, complexity, or relevance of some issues like cloning, health care, Bosnia, and so on. Perhaps, as Elshtain observes, the way issues are constructed becomes the issue.

For example, in 1996, Rachel Holloway (1998) argues that the challenge for both candidates was to define the issues in ways that resonated with the middle ground and favored their election. For Clinton, "the challenge was to preserve traditional democratic commitments while moving away from traditional democratic 'big government' methods" and for Dole "to convince voters that the country was not on the right track and their lives would be better with a Republican in the White House" (124).

In politics, the goal is to win the election. To do this, of course, requires getting individuals to become committed to one's candidacy, and then, of equal importance, to actually vote in the election. This is indeed a long, complicated process. No single variable, issue, event, or personal characteristic can motivate enough people to become committed and to vote in sufficient numbers to win an election. Likewise, no single strategy can win an election. But we argue that there are a limited number of communication approaches or strategies for motivating voters. Whether or not the candidate is an incumbent or challenger does impact strategy.

Incumbent Strategies

Judith Trent and Robert Friedenberg (1995) have identified several incumbent campaign strategies (65–80). An incumbent has many more strategy options than challengers. Some of the strategies involve maximizing the symbolic, subtle aspects of the office. Incumbents are certain to surround themselves with the purely symbolic trappings of the office. Such trappings include the use of the presidential podium and seal, "Hail to the Chief," and various official backdrops. Such devices communicate the strength and grandeur of the office. They serve to remind the audience that they are listening to the president of the United States and not just an average citizen.

The Reagan presidency was one of the best at maximizing the visual power of the presidency. In April of 1984, President Reagan changed the location of his televised press conferences. He stood before an open doorway in the East Room of the White House that reveals a long, elegant corridor. The cameras record a majestic setting and a stately exit that dramatizes the importance of the office. President Clinton followed the Reagan precedent.

In addition to the physical artifacts that enhance the prestige of the incumbent, the office itself evokes a sense of legitimacy, competency, and charisma. Any individual who holds the office is perceived as rational, intelligent, and is granted deference. The pageantry, history, and majesty of the office is transferred to its occupant. In a campaign, such perceptions are worth a great deal.

Presidents have immediate and almost total access to the media. It is very easy for them to create pseudo-events for the purpose of gaining favorable media exposure. Such pseudo-events include making special announcements, appointments, or proclamations that have more political impact than policy impact. Leading up to the 1996 reelection campaign, Clinton recognized the importance of "incremental achievements." Instead of attempting major social programs, he advocated and supported "minireforms" that directly affected middle-class Americans such as family leave, educational standards, handgun control, television violence, and control of tobacco advertising (Morris 1997, 13, 341).

During the campaign period, presidents make many appointments to jobs and special committees. This is a way to line up supporters early in the campaign, tap talent for the reelection bid, and identify people for key positions after the election. Also reports of special task forces are usually revealed during the campaign period. Task forces are effective ways to address special issues or concerns of the voters without committing resources or personal support. The very act of forming a task force communicates concern about an issue and the promise of future action. Actually, it allows the candidate to postpone taking a stand on controversial issues while at the same time making an appeal to a particular group of voters.

An incumbent president will appropriate billions of dollars to "cooperative" public officials for cities and projects in return for support. By the 1980 election, Carter had given over $80 billion in the form of federal grants. In 1992, Bush granted government contracts in states where jobless rates were higher than the national average.

Without doubt, incumbent presidents will visit world leaders during an election year. Such trips provide great drama and show the president as a world leader respected by other countries. The foreign visits also provide a repertoire of future references that can be worked into debates and discourse to reinforce notions of leadership and experience. How ironic indeed in 1980 when President Reagan, who spent most of his political career opposing the Chinese Communists, not only visited mainland China but offered U.S. economic and technological assistance. But most important, the trip was a television spectacular. Michael Deaver, a presidential aide, spent nine days in China scouting locations for the president to visit. The Republican National Committee sent a special film crew to record footage to be used in political commercials. Even Reagan's itinerary was influenced by the potential of media coverage. A trip down the Yangtze River was canceled because there was no way to get the tapes to the networks for showing. Some of the footage from the historic trip was included in the most effective "Morning Again in America" biographical video shown at the 1984 Republican Convention (and the nation) to introduce Reagan.

Incumbent presidents have the opportunity to manipulate domestic issues. This is done in two ways. First, presidents can divert or lessen the impact of news by creating competing pseudo-events. Of course, "good news" comes from the White House, "bad news" is released with little notice from related agencies. Another way to manipulate domestic issues is to take short-term actions that will provide at least a temporary impact. This is especially true in the economic realm. Usually, by election time, interest rates and inflation are down. In fact, the stock market has gone down only six times in the 25 years in which presidential elections were held since 1900. Administrations in the final two years of a term tend to focus on economic expansion to enhance the party's reelection endeavors.

A strategy that is especially useful for incumbent presidents is to obtain the public endorsements of local respected, successful, and well-liked politicians. Here the candidate is trying to link himself with already established leaders.

Presidents can also use surrogates to campaign for them. Popular members from the administration or locals who are part of the administration can have a very positive effect upon a campaign. Simply because of the daily job requirements, nearly all presidents are forced to rely upon the help of others during the campaign season. In 1972, Nixon used over 50 surrogates, and in the midterm elections of 1982, the Republican National Committee developed a program called "Surrogate 82" where all cabinet members were required to give 15 days to campaign activities. During the 1980 presidential campaign, Carter was forced to use surrogates because of his statement that he would not campaign while Americans were still held as hostages in Iran. As their length of captivity lengthened, Carter had to rescind his statement. Family members, both close and rather distant, all hit the campaign trail attempting to cover as much of the country as possible. However, there is a limit to the use of surrogates. The American public expects candidates to travel and press the flesh—up to a point. An incumbent president must not appear to be neglecting the job of running the country. Thus the use of surrogates best complements the campaigning of an incumbent president rather than replacing it.

Somewhat related, most incumbents try to create the image that they are above the political battle and removed from the day-to-day charges and countercharges of politics. Early presidents, as already noted, seldom actively participated in campaigns or even attended the party conventions. Such participation appeared undignified and unstatesmanlike. In contemporary times, the extreme of such a strategy is called the "Rose Garden" strategy. Very strong candidates can stay at the White House appearing presidential, committed, and serious. Only until close to election day will incumbents enter the campaign full time.

Nearly all presidents claim that reelection will communicate to the world a sense of stability. Most incumbents intensify their description of foreign policy problems to create an illusion of crisis to motivate voters to rally around and support the administration. Franklin Roosevelt was most successful using this strategy. History has shown that regardless of the crisis, Americans offer support to their leaders rather than condemnation.

Finally, the major strategy of every incumbent president is to emphasize administration accomplishments. They must demonstrate tangible results to promises made or problems solved. If not, they must deny problems are problems or clearly place blame on a single individual or group. Actions often speak louder than results. To propose a constitutional amendment to balance the budget, even though such a proposal would never be taken seriously, is at once to fulfill a campaign promise and to place blame if not accepted. For every action, there is an official interpretation that must be provided.

Despite the appearance of an almost limitless number of strategy options, Trent and Friedenberg (1995, 80–81) are correct in claiming that there are several major disadvantages of incumbency campaigning. First, as already mentioned, every president must run on his record. All actions or interactions must be explained and justified. Naturally, the challenger will blame the incumbent for all ills and problems of the nation. As the total presidential campaign period lengthens, challengers literally have years to question, second-guess, and negate the efforts of the current president. In the real world and especially in politics, there are seldom complete victories. Most victories are partial and it becomes demoralizing for every effort to be criticized or questioned. Finally, the media create a climate of expectations, conflict, and excitement during a campaign. There is a great deal of pressure associated with being the incumbent. America traditionally favors the underdog and a good fight. Thus, there are more restrictions on behavior and performance pressure associated with the incumbent than with the challengers.

Challenger Strategies

When campaigning against an incumbent president, challengers must take the offensive position in a campaign. Every action, issue, and stance of the president is questioned, challenged, and sometimes ridiculed. This often goes beyond simply attacking the record of the incumbent. The probing and questioning seldom results in the presenting of concrete solutions. John Kennedy never provided the details to the New Frontier, nor did Nixon say how he would end the war in Vietnam or Reagan explain on how he would end inflation. In fact, being too specific can lead to counter-questions and attacks. For example, in 1972 McGovern provided the details of a tax plan and guaranteed income that caused many problems. Mondale's call for higher taxes virtually ended any hopes for a close race in 1984. In fact, most contemporary candidates articulate broad policy hopes and desires and avoid offering specific policy details.

Most of the time, challengers call for a change—a change in direction and leadership. They emphasize optimism for the future and share a vision of future prosperity and peace. In 1996, Dole wanted America to return to the values of its past, while Clinton spoke of a bright future full of hope and promise. In the end, Dole was perceived as a "bridge to the past" in contrast to Clinton as a "bridge to the future."

Challengers focus their appeals on traditional values as Carter did in 1976 (honesty, self-rule, humility, morality); as Reagan did in 1980 and 1984 (free enterprise, capitalism, democracy, and moral courage); and as Clinton did in 1996 (stronger families, smaller and more efficient government, and strong economy).

Challengers must create constituency groups and will always claim to speak for the forgotten American, the silent majority, and middle America. This transforms into a strategy of articulating the values and feelings of an average American. The philosophical center is the road to follow.

The Campaign Promise

An important feature of American politics is the campaign promise. In theory, an elected official is obligated to fulfill promises made during a campaign as a result of the electoral mandate. Despite jokes about campaign promises, each election generates countless promises from candidates. To demonstrate the seriousness with which they are made, Carter's transition team compiled a 114-page listing of his 1976 campaign promises. But promises are difficult to keep or fulfill. In 1980 Reagan promised to reduce federal spending, cut federal taxes, reduce inflation, balance the federal budget, and increase defense spending. By 1984, Reagan's federal budget had the highest deficit in American history. In fact, all presidential candidates have promised to balance the federal budget since 1976. Only Bill Clinton, in the budget year 1999 was able to achieve this promise with the help of a Republican-dominated Congress.

Some might argue that the fulfillment of three out of five major campaign promises is not a bad record. Of course, for test purposes that represents a score of 60 percent—a failing mark by most standards. Others would argue that even to promise reduced federal spending and a balanced budget reflects supreme naiveté. But keeping campaign promises is a difficult task and their fulfillment depends upon the cooperation of others. Few promises can be met with a simple presidential declaration. The public today recognize that politicians as a group seldom deliver on their promises.

From a communication perspective, there are four observations about campaign promises. First, the degree of importance attached to a promise depends upon how much the fulfillment of the promise affects each of us. Thus, of the promises made during a campaign, only those relevant to us as a group or as individuals are to be remembered. Second, what constitutes fulfillment of a promise is likely to be an attempted action rather than a complete fulfillment of the promise. To lower inflation by one percent is to fulfill the promise of lowering inflation, but this may be of little value in real economic terms. The issue of what determines fulfillment of a campaign promise, then, is a matter of interpretation and campaign debate. Third, it is best not to make specific promises that may come back to haunt the candidate in future elections. That's why value statements are better than issue statements. Finally, there is indeed a rhetoric of campaigning that differs from a rhetoric of governing. One is the rhetoric of hope, promise, and certainty. The other is one of negotiation, persuasion, and compromise.

The Basic Campaign Speech

Local appearances by candidates demand a few appropriate remarks. With the frequency of travel and the nature of national campaigning, candidates develop a series of speech modules resulting in a basic campaign speech, often called the "stock speech" (Friedenberg 1997, 74). The stock speech is not just one speech. Rather, it contains units tailored to the specific audience, but the core themes remain the same for each speech.

Campaigns will generally develop a speech module on the major issues or likely policy questions confronting candidates. For example, in 1992, the Clinton campaign developed over 30 speech modules on topics ranging from AIDS to welfare reform (Friedenberg 1997, 76). Each module is an independent two- to seven-minute speech unit that can easily be incorporated into a larger speech. According to Friedenberg (1998), most modules are organized around three key points and follow a similar pattern (76–77). They open with a typical attention-getting device or identify a problem, followed by a brief discussion of the problem, and concluding with a presentation of the candidate's proposed solution to the problem. Often, as part of the solution phase of the module, candidates will include an effort to visualize the problem, a full exploration of detailed impact.

The basic campaign speech has four purposes (Reiss and Hahn 1981). First, the basic speech defines the crucial issues of the campaign. Most issues fall within the areas of policy issues, personal issues, or leadership issues. Issues in campaigns also display similar characteristics. They tend to be very broad, be small in number, lack definition, and are seldom defined in terms that will arouse controversy. Also, campaign issues are often linked to claims about the personal qualities of the opponent. Finally, some issues are indeed localized—for example, education for the South, unemployment for the Northeast, farming for the Midwest, and environmental protection for the West.

The second purpose of a basic campaign address is to identify and emphasize the failures of the opposition. Here past issue positions, actions, and voting records are used to demonstrate either a lack of ability to lead by the opponent or a lack of proper position on the issues by the opponent. The speech must at least attempt to show why the opponent should not obtain the office. Statements concerning actions, positions, or personal characteristics are offered as evidence of failure.

Another important purpose of the basic campaign speech is to appeal to the audience. This is achieved through style and substance of the address. Stylistically, the candidate hopes to use common words and phrases unique to the area. The goal is to give the appearance of being one of the locals, sharing their concerns and speaking their language. Dress is also a part of this process. When speaking to farmers, candidates often wear jeans and open shirts.

Finally, the basic campaign speech offers a vision of the future. The vision is usually a carefully constructed articulation of the American dream: a world of peace, prosperity, justice, and equality. The vision often involves evoking a sense of duty and obligation to make the future better than the present for the sake of our children and grandchildren. The vision portion of the speech need not be logical but rather uplifting and inspiring.

For the basic speech, the writer will depend upon poll data or identified intended audiences for guidance to determine the "hot" issues. Focus groups can be used to test key ideas and phrases as well as to discover the best ways to handle certain issues rhetorically. Often the speech-writing staff will include an audience analysis unit and a research unit.

The basic stump campaign speech is truly a localized affair. The major issues of the campaign have long been decided. But the candidate meeting the public face-to-face has become an important part of presidential politics. Such events, however, hold little interest for the national newspeople traveling with the candidate. They hear the basic speech hundreds of times. What interests them most are the question-and-answer exchanges that follow most addresses. Here the candidate may show unexpected emotion, share a new statement or position, or stimulate some newsworthy event. With an eye toward the evening news, the candidate may begin the address with a timely retort or challenge to the opponent. Thus, although the basic speech is given over and over again, the national audience is unlikely to have heard the speech. The campaign event is new and appears spontaneous to those hearing the candidate in person. However, journalists pay attention to the beginning of each speech for any "new" charge, allegation, or issue discussion and wait for their chance for the give-and-take of postspeech "Q & A" sessions.

Presidential Campaign Debates

Presidential debates are an expected element of presidential campaigns. Historically, the Lincoln-Douglas debate of 1858 provided the precedent for the debating of political issues. But the Kennedy-Nixon debates of 1960 firmly established the debates as a part of presidential politics. In fact, the 1960 presidential debates attracted the largest television audience at that point in history—over 100 million viewers. Historically, incumbent presidents viewed debating opponents as too risky. Gerald Ford became the first incumbent president to debate his opponent, Jimmy Carter. Four years later, Carter also debated his challenger, and the tradition has continued until today. However, it is interesting to note that incumbents Ford, Carter, and Bush lost their reelection bids with only Reagan and Clinton winning a second term. Both Reagan and Clinton performed well in their debate challenges.

Television has had the greatest impact upon the form and content of presidential debates. According to Susan Hellweg (1992) and her colleagues, "the demands of television have dictated the structure and formats of contemporary debates and that the visual content of presidential debates plays an important role in the way candidates exercise influence in televised debates. Television manifests a unique symbol system, which fundamentally shapes what is communicated to receivers, apart from content, and has changed the very nature of presidential debate discourse" (xxii). Thus, today's debates are an interesting combination of the old and the new (Jamieson and Birdsell 1988, 118). The common audience, opposing candidates, time limits, right to rebut, and agreed upon rules are vestiges of traditional debate. Multiple topics, question-and-answer formats, and use of "interrogating" reporters are contributions from press conferences. Television technology has contributed various production techniques and time constraints. Television does more than simply "carry the debate"; the medium is an element of the debate.

Debates have several benefits for the electorate. They provide an opportunity to compare the personalities and issue positions of the candidates in a somewhat spontaneous setting. They also invite serious consideration and attention to the campaign and the candidates, thus stimulating voter interest in the election. And finally, they certainly increase candidate accountability. What they say, support, and promise become a matter of record for future evaluation. But contemporary presidential debates are not as freewheeling or spontaneous as most voters think. They are as planned, rehearsed, and constructed as any other speech, commercial, or public presentation. The candidates place a great deal of importance on the debates. Image definition and confirmation is supreme to issue development and debate.

To get candidates even to debate requires a great deal of negotiation. In the debates of 1976, the issues of lighting, staging, position of cameras, use of reaction shots, camera movement, and the height of the podiums became major points of discussion and negotiation between the candidates prior to agreeing to debate (Tiemens 1978, 362–70). In the 1980 debates, an issue of discussion was whether or not the candidates would sit or stand. Carter favored sitting while Reagan favored standing. The compromise was to have stools for both candidates such that if seated the candidate would still appear to be standing. In 1992, the Commission on Presidential Debates suggested a new format—90-minute debates with a single moderator. President George Bush preferred the traditional panel of questioners. In the end, there were three debates with three different formats: a panel of reporters, a talk show format with audience questions, and the combination of single moderator and panel of reporters (Friedenberg 1994, 91–92). One of the big issues of negotiation for the 1996 presidential debates was whether or not to allow independent candidate Ross Perot to participate. Dole wanted to debate Clinton one-on-one, while Clinton was more concerned about utilizing the "town hall" format for the debates. In the end, both candidates got their wish. Perot was barred from the debates and the "town hall" format was used for one of the two confrontations (Friedenberg 1998, 101–3).

Are such issues, totally irrelevant to running the nation and current problems, really important? Most campaign organizations believe so and there is a growing body of research to support such conclusions. For example, one study of the 1960 presidential debates reports that those listening to the debates on the radio thought neither candidate won the debates but those watching the debates on television thought Kennedy clearly won the debates (Katz and Feldman 1962). Robert Tiemens (1978), in investigating factors of visual communication in the 1976 presidential debates, found that differences in camera framing and composition, camera angle, screen placement, and reaction shots seemingly favored Carter (370). More recently, Bush's lack of adaptation to the more informal "town hall" debate format and the lack of awareness of camera shots greatly hurt perceptions of his debate performance in 1992.

The 1980 debates, according to Myles Martel (1983), represent the ultimate in candidate planning and preparing for presidential debates. Reagan's preparation for the debates was much more elaborate than Carter's preparation. As early as August, Reagan developed a Debate Task Force that would perform the following tasks: negotiate the formats, prepare briefing materials, conduct research, develop debate strategies and tactics, and provide professional consultation on presentational aspects of the debates. Reagan spent three intense days prior to the debates practicing before knowledgeable panelists. In addition to strategy, they discussed such things as how he should arrive at the debates (they chose by airplane because it would appear more presidential), whether or not he should shake hands (they decided to shake hands first to give appearance of friendliness), and when to smile (Martel 1983, 12–76). The Reagan campaign even had a Debate Operations Center where 50 researchers carefully monitored the debates to see if Carter committed any errors in statements so they could contact the media immediately.

Edwin Diamond and Kathleen Friery (1987, 43–51) argue that perhaps the media coverage is more important than the actual debates. Debates attract a large quantity of news coverage and analysis. Diamond and Friery identify five media themes of debate coverage. First, the media begin weeks in advance "signaling the big event." Issues, strategies, preparation, and negotiation are discussed in print and broadcast. There is a great deal of speculation as to the role and importance of the debates. The week before the event all the networks engage in a lot of self-promotion in coverage and analysis. The countdown begins and dominates all newscasts and front pages of national and local newspapers.

Second, the media spend a great deal of time "picking the winners and losers." They speculate on who won and why, and what the impact will be. This analysis function has led to the development of the use of "spin doctors," campaign professionals who attempt to shape media interpretation of campaign events. After debates, each candidate has their "doctors" before the cameras proclaiming victory and points scored.

The third media theme is that of "assessing the candidate's appearance." This includes special stories on the candidates' performances on such items as oral competence, personality, and image. Even such aspects as candidate nervousness and ability to handle questions are noted. The focus of such stories is on the style of performance rather than the issues discussed.

Another theme tends to focus on the "debate as theatre." Journalists want excitement, drama, and confrontation. The language of reporting the event reflect and the need for "color" commentary. Comments such as "stinging attacks," "dullness," and "striking a death blow" are common. The athletic, fight image of the event pervades most commentary.

Finally, the authors would add the theme of "avoiding the facts." The press is too concerned with reporting impressions of the debate and not concerned enough with the facts of the debate. Television is an especially poor medium for the presentation of facts and "pure" information. Their general concerns about the coverage of debates include the inability of reportage to advance knowledge of what is said, the tendency to separate viewers from the central enlightening purpose of debates, and a general lack of balanced coverage.

From a strategic perspective, the most successful debaters are those most able to

- direct their remarks at highly targeted audiences
- develop an overall theme throughout the debate
- avoid specifics and make use of proven safe responses
- present themselves as vigorous active leaders
- identify themselves with national aspirations
- identify themselves with the dominant political party/philosophy
- personify themselves as exemplifying a desirable characteristic (Friedenberg 1998, 104)

For more than a decade, much research has been done on the impact or effects of presidential debates.[2] Some of the findings are contradictory. However, it is important to remember that debate effects are more than the outcome of any specific debate and cannot be viewed outside the context of the total campaign environment. Nevertheless, the primary effect suggests that they play more of a confirmatory than persuasive role in voter decision making. Pre-debate preferences tend to crystallize opinions and confirm voting decisions. Preference reinforcement tends to be the major effect when candidates amplify major themes, when viewers discuss the debate with others, and when candidate performance corrresponds to poll position and public expectations of candidates. Thus, few voters convert or favor different candidates after a debate.

However, they can be most important during the primary season when citizens are less committed to specific candidates. Some research indicates that debates may have influence upon undecided voters and provide some issue information, but most voter impressions revolve around candidate image and character rather than issue stances. In addition, post-debate analysis by the media generates the most influence on voter perceptions of winners and losers.

Finally, most scholars agree that debates do focus audience attention on the pending election and increase audience attention to the candidates. For some voters, debates can increase knowledge of issues and issue positions of candidates.

There are numerous strategies and tactics one can use during debates. Each one must be carefully analyzed to assess the potential gain or loss for the candidate. Trent and Friedenberg (1995) identify several debate strategies (221–28). Prior to the debate, campaigns attempt to lower expectations of candidate performance. It is better to exceed media predictions and public expectations of performance than to do well but be expected to do well. Related to this strategy, campaigns engage in "mind games" attempting to set up their opponent. Public statements about debate strategy or issues are often designed to mislead or misdirect opponents, influencing debate preparations and expectations. In the meantime, campaigns determine their primary audience and message points. Finally, candidates will spend several days preparing for the debate, practicing potential questions and responses to opposition attacks. During the debate, candidates want to make sure they continually mention their issues and campaign themes. They also want to reinforce images of leadership, create opportunities for audience identification, and reflect desired character personality traits. After the debate, surrogates for the candidates proclaim victory and attempt to put their special "spin" on the debate.

Post-Campaign

Ruth Weaver (1980) argues that there are rather strong rules that govern victory and concession statements made by candidates on election night. Acknowledgment of victory and defeat have almost become a ritual of American politics. There are three rules that govern post-campaign statements. The loser of the contest must concede before the winner can claim victory. The loser reads the congratulatory telegram sent to the winner, and the winner rereads the telegram before supporters. The loser appears before supporters surrounded by family. Thus, the sequence of messages, the reading of loser's telegram, and personal appearances of candidate surrounded by family members provide the contextual expectation associated with victory and defeat statements.

But the content of such statements is also familiar. Losers usually, first of all, offer thanks for family, friends, workers, and supporters during the campaign. They often then provide a statement of support for the newly elected president. Such support, depending upon the margin of defeat, may make reference to the notion of loyal opposition. Weaver (1980) observes that the greater the margin of defeat the more prevalent the theme of continual challenging of the opponent becomes in the concession statements. Support statements often contain explicit offers of help and direct assistance to the newly elected president.

Victors also thank their supporters, workers, and family. In addition, they are often laudatory in the comments about their opponents. They acknowledge a good campaign and express respect for their opponent. Next, the winner must make overt appeals for national unity. They are or will be president of all the people regardless of issues or views. Most of these statements are less policy-oriented and more general in nature. The victors, without doubt, express humility and offer a pledge to all the citizens that they are dedicated to the principles that make America great. Finally, most winners reassure the public that there will be a continuity in the transition of power or, if an incumbent, a continuation of the administration without an interruption of government.

Election night statements of victory and defeat are only the first elements of the process that ultimately unites the citizens behind the reign of a new president or the continuation of an old one. In the months prior to the inauguration, the media floods the nation with background information about the new president. The person is set within a historical perspective of the office. Anticipation of the members of the new administration mounts. The newly elected leader, when speaking before groups, makes appeals to national unification, support, and rearticulates a vision of the future that inspires hope, confidence, and excitement. By inauguration day a candidate has emerged as president. A tremendous transformation, at least in the eyes of the public, has occurred. The citizens are committed to the democratic process and the notion that one of them has been elevated to the position of leader, fully deserving a chance of success. In fact, a large majority of citizens will report voting for the new president regardless of the actual size of electoral victory (Mullen 1976, 2–3). The inauguration activities and speech culminate the process of acknowledgment and acceptance of the new administration.

CONCLUSION

Political campaigns are long and expensive. They offer numerous messages about our past, future, and current situations. As primarily communication phenomena, they influence and impact our behavior in both obvious and subtle ways. Their importance transcends the preference of one individual over another.

Although many countries have elections, U.S. presidential elections are unique. Political campaigns are truly communication events: communication of images, characters, and persona. Presidential campaigns are long, nearly continuous events. The burden is on the candidate to appear presidential, capable, and worthy of trust and confidence.

The pre-primary is when most of the candidate creation takes place. During this period the public is more susceptible to the ideas and arguments of future candidates. The groundwork for the campaign is carefully planned and constructed during this period.

For most Americans, the political season really begins during the primary period. The period tests the fabric of the candidates, the depth of their views, and the dimensions of their persona. Election interpretations and presentations are most important during this period.

Presidential campaigns follow rather predictable patterns. There are a limited number of issues, images, tactics, and strategies that are available for any campaign. Today, as never before, the tools of marketing and research are the instruments of electoral victory. American presidential politics is not based upon issue development as much as on specified images, visions, and persona targeted to identified and segmented audiences.

Most campaign strategies are designed to do more than get votes. They are designed to project a certain image, alter a perception, or counter the opposition. Communication is at the heart of every campaign strategy. Strategies can be grouped based upon whether the candidate is an incumbent or challenger. In terms of American presidential politics, the incumbent has many more strategy options than challengers. From the strategies, the promises, the basic speeches, and even the acceptances of victory and defeat, the rhetorical patterns are predictable in both form and content. In the end a president is elected who must confront new communication challenges.

The challenge for the future was clearly articulated in a press conference the day after the landslide defeat of Walter Mondale in 1984. In running against Reagan, Mondale acknowledged that he was at a distinct disadvantage in the television age. "Modern politics requires mastery of television. I think you know that I've never warmed up to television, and it's never warmed up to me. By instinct and tradition I don't like these things [twisting the television microphones in front of him]. I don't believe it's possible to run for president without the capacity to communicate every night." Mondale continued his observations about the impact of television upon the quality of a presidential campaign. "American politics is losing its substance. It is losing the debate on merit. It's losing the depth that tough problems require discussion. More and more it is those 20-second snippets. I hope we don't lose in America this demand that those of us who want this office must be serious people of substance and depth and must be prepared not to handle the 10-second gimmick that deals with things like war and peace."

Despite the problems and ills of our presidential election process, it's still important for citizens to participate and vote. Whether we like it or not, the results of every election impact the future. Presidents determine foreign and domestic policy, appoint justices to the Supreme Court that influence public policy for decades, and set our national agenda. Pragmatically, every election is important.

NOTES

1. A version of the model was first presented at the annual meeting of the Southern Political Science Association, Political Communication Division, Atlanta, Georgia, November 6, 1992, entitled "A Communication Model of Presidential Campaigns: A 1992 Perspective" by Robert E. Denton, Jr., and Mary E. Stuckey. A revised formulation of the model appeared as "A Communication Model of Presidential Campaigns: A 1992 Overview" by Robert E. Denton, Jr., and Mary E. Stuckey in *The 1992 Presidential Campaign: A Communication Perspective*, ed. Robert E. Denton, Jr. (Westport, CT: Praeger, 1994), pp. 1–42. The current presentation is based on the model presented in "Communication Vari-

ables and Dynamics of the 1996 Presidential Campaign" in *The 1996 Presidential Campaign: A Communication Perspective*, ed. Robert E. Denton, Jr. (Westport, CT: Praeger, 1998), pp. 7–50.

2. For summaries of research on presidential debates see: Diana Carlin and Mitchell McKinney, *The 1992 Presidential Debates in Focus* (Westport, CT: Praeger, 1994); Susan Hellweg, et al., *Televised Presidential Debates* (Westport, CT: Praeger, 1992); and Judith Trent and Robert Friedenberg, *Political Campaign Communication*, 3d ed. (Westport, CT: Praeger, 1995), pp. 209–43.

REFERENCES

Arterton, F. Christopher. 1978. "Campaign Organizations Confront the Media-Political Environment." In *Race for the Presidency*, ed. James D. Barber. New York: Prentice-Hall, pp. 3–24.

Asher, Herbert. 1980. *Presidential Elections and American Politics*, rev. ed. Homewood, IL: Dorsey Press.

Barber, James. 1980. *The Pulse of Politics*. New York: Norton.

Bartels, Larry. 1989. *Presidential Primaries and the Dynamics of Public Choice*. Princeton, NJ: Princeton University Press.

Blumenthal, Sidney. 1980. *The Permanent Campaign*. New York: Touchstone Books.

Caddell, Patrick, and Richard Wirthlin. 1981. "Face Off: A Conversation with the Presidents' Pollsters." *Public Opinion* (December/January): 2–12.

Chagall, David. 1981. *The New King-Makers*. New York: Harcourt Brace Jovanovich.

Corrado, Anthony. 1997. "Financing the 1996 Elections." In *The Election of 1996*, ed. Gerald Pomper et al. Chatham, NJ: Chatham House, pp. 135–71.

Denton, Robert E., Jr. 1988. *The Primetime Presidency of Ronald Reagan*. New York: Praeger.

Diamond, Edward, and Kathleen Friery. 1987. "Media Coverage of Presidential Debates." In *Presidential Debates*, ed. Joel Swerdlow. Washington, DC: Congressional Quarterly Press, pp. 43–51.

DiClerico, Robert E., and Eric Uslaner. 1984. *Few Are Chosen: Problems in Presidential Selection*. New York: McGraw-Hill.

Edwards, George C., and Stephen Wayne. 1990. *Presidential Leadership: Politics and Policy Making*, 2d ed. New York: St. Martin's Press.

Elshtain, Jean. 1989. "Issues and Themes in the 1988 Campaign." In *The Elections of 1988*, ed. Michael Nelson. Washington, DC: Congressional Quarterly Press, pp. 111–26.

Ewbank, Henry. 1983. "Public Statements Concerning Campaign Strategies." Paper presented at the Annual Central States Speech Association Convention, Lincoln, NE, April 8.

Fenno, Richard. 1978. *Home Style: House Members in Their Districts*. Boston: Little, Brown.

Friedenberg, Robert. 1994. "The 1992 Presidential Debates." In *The 1992 Presidential Campaign: From a Communication Perspective*, ed. Robert E. Denton, Jr. Westport, CT: Praeger, pp. 89–110.

———. 1997. *Communication Consultants in Political Campaigns*. Westport, CT: Praeger.

———. 1998. "The 1996 Presidential Debates." In *The 1996 Presidential Campaign: From a Communication Perspective*, ed. Robert E. Denton, Jr. Westport, CT: Praeger, pp. 101–22.

Hacker, Kenneth. 1995. *Candidate Images in Presidential Elections*. Westport, CT: Praeger.

Hellweg, Susan et al. 1992. *Televised Presidential Debates*. Westport, CT: Praeger.

Hodgson, Godfrey. 1980. *All Things to All Men*. New York: Touchstone Books.

Holloway, Rachel. 1998. "Clinton's Rhetoric of Conjoined Values." In *The 1996 Presidential Campaign: A Communication Perspective*, ed. Robert E. Denton, Jr. Westport, CT: Praeger, pp. 123–41.

Honomichl, Jack. 1984. *Marketing Research People: Their Behind-the-Scenes Stories*. Chicago: Crain Books.

Jamieson, Kathleen Hall, and David Birdsell. 1988. *Presidential Debates*. New York: Oxford University Press.

Kaid, Lynda. 1998. "Videostyle and the Effects of the 1996 Presidential Campaign Advertising." In *The 1996 Presidential Campaign: A Communication Perspective*, ed. Robert E. Denton, Jr. Westport, CT: Praeger, pp. 143–60.

Katz, Elihn, and Jacob Feldman. 1962. "The Debates in the Light of Research: A Survey of Surveys." In *The Great Debates*, ed. Sidney Kraus. Bloomington: Indiana University Press, pp. 173–223.

Keeter, Scott, and Cliff Zukin. 1983. *Uninformed Choice*. New York: Praeger.

Kerbel, Matthew. 1994. *Edited for Television*. Boulder, CO: Westview Press.

Kessel, John. 1988. *Presidential Campaign Politics: Coalition Strategies and Citizen Response*. Chicago: Dorsey.

Ladd, Everett, and John Benson. 1992. "The Growth of News Polls in American Politics." In *Media Polls in American Politics*, ed. Thomas Mann and Gary Orren. Washington, DC: Brookings Institution pp. 19–31.

Lewis-Beck, Michael, and Tom Rice. 1992. *Forecasting Elections*. Washington, DC: Congressional Quarterly Press.

Lichter, S. Robert et al. 1988. *The Video Campaign: Network Coverage of the 1988 Primaries*. Lanham, MD: American Enterprise Institute.

Martel, Myles. 1983. *Political Campaign Debates*. New York: Longman.

Mauser, Gary. 1983. *Political Marketing: An Approach to Campaign Strategy*. New York: Praeger.

Mullen, William. 1976. *Presidential Power and Politics*. New York: St. Martin's Press.

Newman, Bruce. 1994. *Marketing of the President*. Thousand Oaks, CA: Sage.

Owen, Diana. 1991. *Media Messages in American Presidential Campaigns*. Westport, CT: Greenwood Press.

———. 1997. "The Press' Performance." In *Toward the Millennium: The Elections of 1996*, ed. Larry Sabato. Boston: Allyn and Bacon, pp. 205–21.

Patterson, Thomas. 1994. *Out of Order*. New York: Vintage.

Polsby, Nelson W., and Aaron Wildavsky. 1980. *Presidential Elections: Contemporary Strategies of American Electoral Politics*, 7th ed. New York: Free Press.

Ratzan, Scott. 1989. "The Real Agenda Setters." *American Behavioral Scientist* 37 (2) (November/December): 451–63.

Reiss, Lenny, and Dan Hahn. 1981. "The Dichotomous Substance and Stylistic Appeals in Kennedy's 1980 Basic Speech." Paper presented at the Annual Convention of Eastern Communication Association, Pittsburgh, PA, April 24.

Sabato, Larry. 1981. *The Rise of Political Consultants*. New York: Basic Books.

Selnow, Gary. 1991. "Polls and Computer Technologies: Ethical Considerations." In *Ethical Dimensions of Political Communication*, ed. Robert E. Denton, Jr. New York: Praeger, pp. 171–98.

Shea, Daniel. 1996. *Campaign Craft: The Strategies, Tactics, and Art of Campaign Management*. Westport, CT: Praeger.

Smith, Larry David, and Dan Nimmo. 1991. *Cordial Concurrence: Orchestrating National Party Conventions in the Telepolitical Age*. New York: Praeger.

Tiemens, Robert. 1978. "Television's Portrayal of the 1976 Presidential Debates: An Analysis of Visual Content." *Communication Monograph* 45: 362–76.

Traugott, Michael. 1992. "The Impact of Media Polls on the Public." In *Media Polls in American Politics*, ed. Thomas Mann and Gary Orren. Washington, DC: Brookings Institution, pp. 125–49.

Trent, Judith. 1978. "Presidential Surfacing: The Ritualistic and Crucial First Act." *Communication Monographs* 45: 281–92.

Trent, Judith, and Robert Friedenberg. 1995. *Political Campaign Communication*, 3d ed. New York: Praeger.

Walsh, Edward. 1992. "The More Seed Money, the Better the Harvest." In *The Quest for National Office*, ed. Stephen Wayne and Clyde Wilcox. New York: St. Martin's Press, pp. 50–56.

"Washington Whispers." 1996. *U.S. News & World Report*, 18 November: 20–21.

Wayne, Stephen. 1992. *The Road to the White House 1992*. New York: St. Martin's Press.

Weaver, Ruth Ann. 1980. "Acknowledgment of Victory and Defeat: The Reciprocal Ritual." Paper presented at the Annual Convention of the Central States Speech Association, Chicago, IL, April.

Chapter 7

Legislative Campaigns

> Reelection is the fundamental task of every House Office, and legislators are becoming increasingly sophisticated in campaigning.
>
> Timothy Cook (1989)

In Chapter 5, we provided an overview of campaign planning, management, and strategies. In the last chapter, we identified six elements crucial to a presidential campaign. The elements are also important to congressional campaigns. The basics of campaigning are true whether you are running for president, mayor, or the local school board. They differ, of course, in size and scope which, in turn, impact specific campaign strategies and tactics.

Running for Congress is unique. Although a national office, congressional contests are very local races. Representatives are people you may see on local or national television but may also see at the local grocery store. Serving in Congress is a difficult job. While in Washington, representatives review and enact legislation. While home, they attend countless functions, explain their votes, and continually raise funds. They attempt to portray themselves as working on behalf of their constituencies. Sometimes, they attempt to separate themselves from the more common national views of politicians and the institution of Congress.

Campaigns are very important to the outcomes of congressional elections. As Paul Herrnson (1998) argues, that "national conditions are significant, but their impact on elections is secondary to the decisions and actions of candidates, campaign organizations, party committees, organized interests, and other individuals and groups" (p. 2). In addition, candidates themselves are the focus of congressional campaigns, not political parties, ideologies, or national issues. This is why party fortunes may not influence specific races. Some argue this forces congressional candidates to focus on issues and themes of their constituencies rather than those of party leaders or even the president. Thus, above all else, congressional races are candidate-based, local campaigns.

CANDIDATE-CENTERED CAMPAIGNS

Herrnson (1998) argues that because of candidate-centered congressional campaigns, a successful candidate is likely to be one with "strategic ambition, which is the combination of a desire to get elected, a realistic understanding of what it takes to win, and an ability to assess the opportunities presented by a given political context." Strategic ambition, he says, is a "characteristic that distinguishes most successful candidates for Congress from the general public" (30). Yet, despite the money spent on congressional campaigns, voters base their decisions on very little information. In most races, only 20 percent of voters can recall the names of the candidates (Herrnson 1998, 158). Of course, incumbents enjoy the major advantage of name recognition among voters. Most voters base their decision on three factors: incumbency, partisanship, and the relative state of the nation. In general, if the public is content, incumbents, regardless of party, are very safe.

Incumbents

For most congressional elections, the question for voters is simply whether the incumbent should be removed from office. In effect, all elections with incumbents are referendums on the incumbent. Incumbents have enormous advantages: name recognition, fundraising contacts, previous supporters, issue knowledge and experience, and press contacts. In addition, it is easy for incumbents to assemble professional staffs. They have more money, but they also already have the talent to work on campaigns. Many staff members take temporary leaves of absences to work on the member's campaign. Incumbents also have job resources available to them: free mailings, district offices, travel, staff to write speeches, etc. Between 1950 and 1990, house incumbents enjoyed a reelection rate of 90 percent. Even in the "revolt" elections of 1994, those who wished to remain did so with the same average.

There are four national environmental factors that most influence congressional incumbent campaigns. First, every 10 years each state must reapportion or redistrict House seats based upon population growth and shifts. The party in power in the state legislature can enhance their prospects for new seats or preserve current incumbents. Second, presidential or nonpresidential election years may well influence congressional races. Historically, the party in power tends to lose congressional seats in midterm elections. Also, during presidential elections, the national party candidate may have coattails to help, or hurt if the candidate is unpopular. For example, Ronald Reagan's 1980 campaign helped Republicans gain 33 seats in the House. However, in 1992, despite Clinton's Democratic victory, the party lost 10 seats in the House. By 1996, Clinton's victory helped Democrats gain 10 seats, but not enough to regain control of the House.

Third, the popularity of a president may well influence congressional elections. Midterm elections with an unpopular president spells disaster for an incumbent party. In the wake of Watergate, Republicans lost 49 seats in the House in 1974. Similarly, Democrats lost 52 seats in the House in 1994 largely due to the public's sense of Clinton being out of touch with the American people.

Finally, sometimes a single, national issue may influence voting behavior along party lines. During the later 1960s and the early 1970s, Vietnam dominated some elections. Over the decades, several races were influenced by such issues as civil rights, the economy, and gender issues.

In reality, incumbents are more concerned about maintaining and reinforcing their lead than attempting to gain new voters. Interestingly, most incumbents begin the race with a core vote of 65 percent. According to Herrnson (1998, 250), incumbents who are more likely to be in trouble are those who represent marginal districts, have been implicated in scandal, have failed to keep in touch with voters, or who have cast too many votes out of line with constituencies.

Challengers

Challengers or nonincumbents who decide to run for Congress tend to fall into several distinct groups. The obvious ones are prior local or state officeholders. They often have the advantages of name recognition, proven electoral viability, and a constituency base. The "unelected politicians" are those who have significant prior political and campaign experience, but who have never run for public office. These include campaign consultants, former staffers, and state and local party officials. Finally, "political amateurs" are those with very little political experience but who run out of a sense of civic duty or because of feelings about a specific issue (Herrnson 1998, 35).

Interestingly, in 1994, there was a decline in the number of candidates with elective experience who ran for Congress. There were more genuine amateurs running and winning for both parties than ever before. However, by 1996, both political parties reported difficulty in recruiting candidates for a variety of reasons. Among those most mentioned are the rough and tumble of contemporary campaigns, the enormous cost of elections, and the general lack of respect for national elected institutions.

Although incumbents begin elections with 65 percent of the vote, challengers begin with only 27 percent of potential vote. Thus, challengers must mount aggressive campaigns, build name recognition, give voters reasons for support, and overcome the early advantages of incumbent opponents.

Opponents in open-seat contests usually begin races more closely matched in terms of name recognition and potential support. Each candidate support usually begins with 43 percent of the vote. In open races, local media tend to pay more attention to the contests.

Because congressional campaigns are very candidate-centered, it is especially important for challengers and nonincumbents to understand themselves, their motives for running, and the campaign environment. For novices, it is helpful for them to do the following things:

1. *Develop a demographic profile of the district.* It is useful to get to know the constituency by such factors as age, sex, income, occupations, education, etc. A statistical picture of the district will help understand the needs and problems of the citizens as well as the likely routines of their daily lives.
2. *Develop an attitudinal profile of the district.* Polling data will reveal issues of concern, hopes, and attitudes that will provide insight in identifying issues to discuss and how to frame campaign messages and theme.
3. *Develop a coalition profile of potential voters.* It is important to identify groups or parts of groups that may well support a candidacy. Beyond partisanship, a percentage of support may come from social group affiliations or issue positions. This profile will identify groups to target during a campaign.
4. *Make a list of strengths.* This list should include personal, ideological, and strategic considerations.
5. *Make a list of weaknesses.* This list will help a candidate to develop strategies to overcome potential weaknesses.
6. *Make a list of strengths and weaknesses of the opposition.* This list will help to develop a variety of campaign strategies. It will also highlight areas requiring special attention. It is also useful to note strengths and weaknesses unique to your campaign.

There are two national party organizations that help local congressional campaigns with money, services, and advice. The Republican and Democratic National Committees are somewhat limited. They primarily offer candidate training seminars providing "talking points" and party platform information. The congressional campaign committees offer more direct support. At the national level they raise money, set priorities for the party, recruit candidates and provide some direct help to specific campaigns. In 1996, for example, the Democratic Congressional Campaign Committee spent $39 million on congressional races and the Republican Congressional Campaign Committee spent nearly $93 million. Both organizations employed 64 full-time employees (Herrnson 1998, 75).

The committees focus on competitive races. They provide help first to incumbent races facing serious challengers. Second in priority are races preceived as "winable" by party challengers. Generally, if the president is popular, the party committee of the president tends to invest more in challenger and open-seat races. The out-party committee tends to allocate more resources to incumbent races. In general, in-party committees tend to take a defensive posture favoring incumbent races, and out-party committees tend to be more aggressive, favoring challenger races.

Committees use several criteria for considering contributions to a race: competitiveness of district, incumbency, strength of candidate, and whether the seat is open, to name a few. Of course, committees closely monitor races and over the course of a campaign, some candidates may receive help while others that received early help may receive less support toward the end of the campaign.

Committees serve as a major source of information for local candidates. They keep lists of consultants and preferred vendors for all campaign activities. They also are involved in training seminars for potential candidates. In 1996, the Republican National Committee held seminars in forty-one states helping over 6,000 potential candidates, and the Democratic National Committee held three sessions in Washington and four in various states, training more than 3,000 candidates. (Herrnson 1998, 86). Historically, the most assistance campaigns receive from national committees is public opinion polling. National committees commission hundreds of polls during a campaign season. They often allocate a few questions for local candidates. As noted in Chapter 5, a good showing in a party poll will increase fundraising potential. Increasingly, national committees provide opposition research for party contestants.

POLITICAL ACTION COMMITTEES

Outside of campaign technology, the role of political action committees (PACs) have the greatest impact on congressional campaigns. Special interests groups form PACs to provide direct financial support to candidates in order to influence electoral outcomes and, hence, the formation of public policy. PACs tend to fall within four main categories: corporate, labor, trade (includes health care industry), and "nonconnected" (no sponsoring organization; the PAC is the organization itself).

The increase of PACs is a somewhat recent phenomenon. Since 1974, the number of PACs has gone from just over 600 to more than 4,500 organizations. Their financial influence has also increased dramatically from over $12 million in 1974 to more than $215 million in 1996 (Herrnson 1998, 105).

The goal of most PACs is access to legislators, especially powerful ones who are in leadership positions on various committees impacting legislation of interest to the sponsoring organization. Other PACs are ideological, hoping to increase the number of legislators who share their values and views on social issues. From these two broad motives, PACs follow several strategies of influence. Ideological PACs tend to give most of their money to candidates in close races where they have the best chance of influencing the outcome. Access-oriented PACs tend to contribute most of their funds to incumbents and open-seat races. For example, in 1996, PACs made 88 percent of their contributions to incumbents (Herrnson 1998, 116). During the 1970s, most PAC support followed rather strict partisan lines. Corporate and trade PACs largely supported Republican candidates, and Labor PACs the Democrats. Over time, business-oriented PACs have become more concerned about issues of access than ideological issues. It is interesting to note the shift in support when leadership changes in the House. With the Republican control resulting from the 1994 elections, PACs gave most of their funds to Republicans, reversing their previous contribution pattern of giving.

COMMUNICATING WITH VOTERS

When we argue that campaigns are primarily communication activities, campaign budgets support our assertion. Approximately 76 percent of the average House campaign budget is spent on communicating with voters, 18 percent on overhead, and 6 percent on polling and research. Among the communication activities, the typical House race will spend 18 percent of its budget on television, 18 percent on direct mail, 11 percent on radio, and just 4 percent on newspaper ads. The remaining 25 percent is spent on such activities as travel, voter registration, billboards, yard signs, campaign literature, and get-out-the-vote efforts. Interestingly, challengers usually allocate 10 percent more of their budgets for communication activities than incumbents (Herrnson 1998, 68–69).

As with most campaigns, congressional campaign communication seeks to accomplish several objectives: to improve name recognition, project a favorable image, set the campaign agenda, exploit issues, undermine opponent's credibility, and defend against or respond to attacks.

Most House campaigns were low-key affairs, relying upon friends and volunteers during the 1950s and 1960s. However, by the 1970s, congressional campaigns routinely used professionals for management and media activities. Today, professional staff members or paid consultants handle all press relations, issue and opposition research, polling, advertising, and fundraising activities. Leading up to the 1996 congressional campaigns, the average House incumbent spent over $200,000 on organizational activities (Herrnson 1998, 60).

As we have mentioned, House races are fought on local issues, whereas Senate races tend to focus more on statewide or national concerns. If there is a large national issue impacting congressional races, House candidates tend to focus on local implications. National party organizations routinely provide candidates with issue handbooks or "talking papers" for national issue discussions.

Perhaps the most successful national coordination of issues for local congressional campaigns was the Republican effort of 1994. Their national agenda had two main points. The first focus was on the ethical and policy failures of the Clinton administration and Democratic members. Of course, the most noted factor of the election year was the Republican "Contract with America." The "Contract" contained 10 program points calling for a balanced budget, welfare reform, and term limits, to name a few of the more prominent items. Nearly 400 Republican House members and candidates signed the "Contract" at a formal, highly publicized ceremony on the steps of the Capitol. Although only about a third of voters heard of the contract prior to the election, it did provide a unified, national message for Republicans.

According to Herrnson (1998, 172), the focus of most advertising in House campaigns is on the candidate's issue positions (45%) followed by the candidate's image (25%). Surprisingly, just over 10 percent of advertising focuses on the opponent's image (12%) or issue positions (11%). Of course, these allocations vary greatly depending on whether the candidate is an incumbent, a challenger, or running in an open-seat race. For example, challengers focus more on opponent image and issues (21%).

Chapters 5 and 6 detailed the strategic use of media during campaigns. There are more considerations and constraints of media usage in congressional campaigns. Television, of course, is the best medium for image presentation and agenda-setting. However, television is expensive and congressional districts may cross several media markets or none at all. Nearly 70 percent of House campaigns use television. In contrast, radio is a major medium for congressional campaigns. Radio allows candidates to target voters based upon listener profiles. Newspaper ads are used primarily for announcing campaign events and last day get-out-the-vote efforts. Congressional campaigns usually spend more on direct mail than any other form of advertising. Direct mail is used to raise funds, attack the opponent, and deliver a specific message to a highly targeted group of supporters or likely voters. Counter to popular belief, the most negative and vicious attacks occur in direct mail advertising rather than television advertising.

Congressional campaigns work hard to generate "free" media coverage of the candidate and the campaign by the news media. Coverage depends on many factors: competitiveness of race, market, news focus of outlet, etc. Among the most common activities campaigns use in attempt to gain coverage include a steady stream of press releases, press conferences, and editorial board meetings, to name a few. Newspapers and radio are more likely to devote extensive coverage to congressional races than television.

Daniel Shea (1996, 226) suggests several ways and techniques for candidates to earn free media.

1. Make events as "visual" as possible. Local news, especially television, are more likely to cover an event if it is visually interesting. Candidate walks or special clothing will gain notice. Most people in Virginia remember Oliver North's plaid-shirt senatorial campaign of 1994. The consultant worked on Lamar Alexander's Republican presidential nomination bid in 1996. Alexander wore the same plaid shirt on the campaign trail in attempts to appeal to the "average citizen."
2. Develop sound bites for the media for each issue of the campaign. Again, in order to get seen speaking on television or quoted in the newspaper, the candidate needs clever phrases to express ideas and issues.
3. Identify a target and attack it consistently. The media love drama, conflict, and a fight. Consistent and constant attacks will gain media attention and coverage.
4. Release new information or new perspectives on issues and topics of concern. Innovative or new approaches will likely garner media attention.
5. Campaigns must be timely. This means responding to events in the news with prepared statements. During a campaign, local candidates may be asked about national stories and news events. Such questions reflect local news values and interests and thus are more likely to be included in newscasts.

Direct voter contact is especially important for congressional races. Although it may be less efficient in reaching a large number of voters, it is very effective per voter. In fact, it appears that any direct request for support tends to be effective. After the candidate, candidate family members, friends, volunteers, party and interest group activists are all also effective in soliciting voter support. According to Shea (1996), there are several reasons why direct voter contact is valuable. First, contact with the candidate brings the voter to a different cognitive level than other communication contacts. The voter becomes more engaged and attentive when meeting with the actual candidate. Second, direct contact allows two-way communication. Voters value the opportunity not only to meet candidates, but to interact with them. Third, voter interaction humanizes the candidate. Media portrayals of campaigns are less real than face-to-face interaction. Finally, direct voter contact brings more commitment and enthusiasm to a campaign (241–42).

Voter contact is an organizational responsibility. There are two types of voter contact activities: low-intensity and high-intensity. High-intensity activities are personalized, direct contact with voters providing opportunities for interaction and feedback. In addition to candidate speeches and visits, phone banks, neighborhood canvasses, and door-to-door contact are high-intensity and high-impact activities. Low-intensity activities are nonpersonalized voter contact. These activities include direct mail, literature distribution, yard signs, bumper stickers, and billboards, to name a few. Low-intensity activities help shape the political environment and impart information to voters. Campaigns focus high-intensity efforts in areas where party performance is low and with competitive audiences.

At the heart of any high-intensity voter contact activity is the neighborhood walk. Candidates usually first canvass prime swing areas within a district and then areas of lower support in the last election. A serious district canvass or "walk plan" has several elements (Shea 1996, 243–45).

1. The first step is to develop "walk sheets" listing the names of voters at each address and party affiliation, if available. To maximize time and effort, one can avoid visiting homes of nonvoters or supporters of the opposing party.
2. A volunteer from the area should accompany the candidate. The volunteer can introduce the candidate and provide information about households that may enhance the visit.
3. A week or so before the walk, "pre-walk cards" should be mailed to each household. The card will announce the date and approximate time of visit by the candidate.
4. After a visit, candidates should leave a phamplet or brochure for the household. The phamplet should contain very general biographical and issue position information.
5. After each visit, the volunteer should take notes describing factual information about the visit, i.e., name of person, concerns expressed, intention to vote, etc.
6. If no one is at home, the candidate should leave a handwritten note on the literature. These can be written ahead of time with the name just dropped in at the time of the visit. Even this attention to detail will have an impact upon potential voters.
7. Within a couple of days of a visit, any information or questions requested during a visit should be mailed, telephoned, or delivered to the citizen.

Candidate image is important in any campaign. The public will already have some image of an incumbent, based upon their record, prior speeches, actions, and published statements. Challengers are usually less well known than incumbents. This provides an opportunity for them to construct a positive public persona. Style is a factor of candidate-oriented campaigns. How the candidate looks and acts is important in defining the candidate's image. How something is said, how a candidate responds to criticism—the total demeanor impacts candidate image. A third factor influencing candidate image is the political environment. Issues may indeed influence perceptions of candidates, especially from an ideological perspective. For example, close identification with specific issues may portray a candidate as liberal or conservative.

As is true with most campaigns, there are a tremendous number of activities a candidate must accomplish. Table 7.1 identifies the task priorities of a campaign. Notice how many are communication related.

SUMMARY

There are many similarities to all campaigns. The elements, strategies and tactics of campaign communication have been discussed in the last three chapters. Although congressional candidates seek a national office, congressional contests are very local. In addition, they are candidate-driven campaigns. Incumbency is the greatest predictor of electoral viability.

Interestingly, members of Congress are simply not representative of the general population. For example, although much less than one percent of the public are attorneys, 35 percent of House members are lawyers. Although 12 percent of the general public work in business or banking, 22 percent of members of Congress have that occupational background. Twenty-six percent of the general public are agricultural or blue-collar workers, while just 4 percent of Congress comes from this background. In short, members of Congress simply do not reflect the occupations of American society. They don't reflect the gender or racial composition either. While over 50 percent of the population are women, fewer than 10 percent of House members are women (Herrnson 1998, 47–55).

Both parties are finding it more difficult to recruit candidates for local, state, and national offices. Campaigns are time-consuming and difficult activities. Yet, the quality of our government is directly related to the quality of our elected officials.

REFERENCES

Cook, Timothy. 1989. *Making Laws & Making News*. Washington, DC: Brookings Institution.

Goldenberg, Edie, and Michael Traugott. 1984. *Campaigning for Congress*. Washington, DC: Congressional Quarterly Press.

Table 7.1
Campaign Tasks and Priorities

First Six Months

I. Fundraising
   a. Find a treasurer
   b. Meet personally with potential contributors
   c. Send out fundraising letters
   d. Follow up contributions with phone calls

II. Getting Endorsements
   a. Meet with prominent members of the community
   b. Meet with influential leaders of constituencies (i.e., labor, education, etc.)
   c. Meet with elected officials

III. Hire Outside Staff
   a. Hire a public relations and/or advertising consultant
      1. Create budget for media
      2. Create timetable for media

IV. Keep a Calendar of Events
   a. Create a list of community organizations and contacts
   b. Schedule speaking dates for each group

V. Research Issues to Create a Platform
   a. Keep a record of issues important to your community
   b. Meet with experts on the issues
   c. Develop a position on the issues

Last Six Months

I. Walk Door-to-Door
   a. Prepare a walking route or list
   b. Develop campaign literature, signs, and bumper stickers
   c. Buy a list of voters' phone numbers and keep a record of those contacted
   d. Contact volunteers for walking

II. Hire Volunteer Coordinator
   a. Organize lists of volunteers for various activities
   b. Organize walks
   c. Organize phone bank
   d. Organize poll workers
   e. Organize Election Day events
   f. Organize volunteer parties before and after election

III. Hire In-house Staff (i.e., Campaign Manager, etc.)
   a. Schedule appearances and events
   b. Manage calendar
   c. Research speeches and answers to questionnaires

Source: Susan Guber, *How to Win Your First Election*, 2d ed. (Boca Raton, FL: St. Lucie Press, 1997).

Guber, Susan. 1997. *How to Win Your First Election*, 2d ed. Boca Raton, FL: St. Lucie Press.

Herrnson, Paul S. 1998. *Congressional Elections*, 2d ed. Washington, DC: Congressional Quarterly Press.

Shea, Daniel. 1996. *Campaign Craft: The Strategies, Tactics and Art of Campaign Management*. Westport, CT: Praeger.

Part III

Governing

Chapter 8

The Presidency

> Style is the President's habitual way of performing his three political roles: rhetoric, personal relations, and homework. . . . A President's world view consists of his primary, politically relevant beliefs, particularly his conceptions of social causality, human nature, and the central moral conflicts of the time. . . . Character is the way the President orients himself toward life.
>
> James David Barber (1972)

When Ronald Reagan left office in 1989, he did so with the highest approval rating of any president since Franklin Roosevelt (Gallup 1989). His 63 percent approval rating is near Roosevelt's 66 percent and considerably ahead of Eisenhower's 59 percent and Kennedy's 58 percent. At the end of George Bush's first year, his approval rating exceeded Reagan's first year, but by the end of his term and failed reelection bid, less than half of the American public approved of his handling of the presidency. Despite the personal problems and allegations during both terms, by 1998 Clinton enjoyed the highest continual approval ratings of any president since Roosevelt. Yet, only about half of the American people personally trusted the president and thought he was routinely honest. There is no doubt that Clinton was well liked by the public and viewed as competent, but will he be viewed as a good leader by historians?

For years, scholars have noticed the increasing difference between campaigning and governing. Today, scholars are noting a new form of leadership, one based on style and public popularity rather than performance and accomplishment. In this chapter we review the current trend toward symbolic executive leadership and how the president governs by focusing on the role of communication in creating, defining, and sustaining our relationship with the institutional presidency.

EXECUTIVE LEADERSHIP

Leadership is a term that is often used in connection with politicians and specifically the presidency. "Good leadership," according to Barbara Kellerman (1984, 349), "is said to be the result of good fit between leaders and followers and between leaders and the tasks at hand." Theodore Sorensen (1984), an advisor to President Kennedy, renewed the argument for a strong and powerful presidency in the mid 1980s. He believes that "Congress can legislate, appropriate, investigate, deliberate, terminate and educate—all essential functions. But it is not organized to initiate, negotiate or act with the kind of swift and informal discretion that our changing world so often requires. Leadership can come only from the presidency" (10). It is, however, much easier to call for strong leadership than define the concept.

Dan Nimmo (1970) argues that political leadership "actually refers to a particular relationship that exists between a leader and his followers in specific settings" (8). The focus of much modern leadership theory is upon the willingness of followers to follow. There are no specific lists of traits that constitute leadership, although certain traits are helpful in any specific situation. It is more useful, according to Murray Edelman (1971), to look for leadership dynamics "in mass responses, not in static characteristics of individuals" (73).

Americans have generally denied hero status to contemporary politicians, unlike that granted to sports figures and stars of Hollywood. Our revolutionary heritage and democratic institutions have perpetuated a general mistrust toward governmental and centralized authority. The difficulty for leaders, argues Bert Rockman (1984), is the balancing of governability and legitimacy. Leaders must have powers to confront and solve problems, yet be accountable to various groups and constituencies. This is difficult because while we demand inspired leadership we also encourage a basic lack of trust and respect for autocratic decision making and formal institutions. Many politicians traditionally run against government. This has contributed to a shift of focus from issues and policies to candidates and officeholders.

Several scholars have noted this trend. Theodore Lowi (1985, xi) calls today's presidential government a "plebiscite," a government based on "popular adoration." Inability to meet expectations of performance is masked by shows of personal popularity. Lowi suggests that Reagan was so good at creating the appearance of success that he earned the title of

"Teflon presidency." His popularity literally protected him from political scandal or inefficiencies of his administration.

Dennis Simon and Charles Ostrom (1988) argue that "maintaining public support has become a key instrumental goal of the modern president" and the officeholder must actively engage in the "politics of prestige." They conclude that "the value of public support reveals that presidents have an incentive to manage, manipulate, or otherwise control how they are evaluated" (755).

George Edwards (1983, 1) recognizes that the "greatest source of influence for the president is public approval" and Raymond Moore (1988) predicts that "the leadership style most likely to win in the future will be 'political presidents' who exhibit a high degree of salesmanship but low managerial skills" (60). Barbara Kellerman (1984) describes today's "presidential politicking" as a process of "transactional leadership" based upon private bargaining and public interaction. The result is a personalized presidency that requires an engaging personality, an endless campaign, the maintenance of public relations activities, and public approval.

Rockman (1984) speculates that the reasons we lean toward the personalization of the presidency are the slack between the social system (the public dimension) and the political system (the operational, organizational dimensions), the American culture of individualism, the structure of institutions that stress individual autonomy, and the contemporary role of political polls and public opinion (177–78). There is a cost, however, in personalizing the presidency. Presidencies based solely on public approval and popularity will have a positive impact upon the legitimacy and prestige of the office but will have little influence on party cohesion or legislative programs. In contrast, a president who is elected based upon political reputation and bargaining skills has a better chance of impacting society through legislative enactments, very much like Lyndon Johnson.

For Ryan Barilleaux (1988), the trend toward the personalization of the presidency and Reagan's success in maintaining personal popularity established a new era of presidential leadership and government. He argues that "the office occupied by Ronald Reagan and his successors is not merely an extension of the modern presidency created by Franklin Roosevelt, but is sufficiently different to warrant a new label" (2). He calls it the "post-modern" presidency. Although Reagan did not create the post-modern presidency, he consolidated and maximized efforts and activities that have revised the institution and its occupant forever. There are several key characteristics of the post-modern presidency: revival of presidential prerogative power; governing through public politics; a large, specialized and centralized staff; policy-making through public support and staff appointments in the courts and various regulatory agencies; the president serving as chief whip in Congress and the vice president serving as a key adviser, envoy, and surrogate. Barilleaux (1988) poses a relevant question: "How do post-modern presidents govern in this environment?" The answer is that they do not. "The post-modern presidency does not govern, but is the premier part of a governing system" (77).

What these various scholars are acknowledging is that today presidential communication activities are a source of tremendous power: power to define, justify, legitimize, persuade, and inspire. Everything a president does or says has implications and communicates "something." A president surrounds himself with communication specialists. Every act, word, or phrase becomes calculated and measured for a response. Every occasion proclaims a need for utterance.

James Ceaser (1983), with several other colleagues, argues that three factors have attributed to the rise of the "rhetorical presidency." The first factor is the modern doctrine of presidential leadership. The public expects a president to set goals and provide solutions to national problems. To be a leader is a cherished concept and a political expectation and, hence, a necessity for our presidents. The second factor giving rise to the rhetorical presidency is the development of the mass media. The mass media have increased the size of the audience, provided immediate access to the public, and changed the mode of communicating with the public from primarily the written word to the spoken word delivered in dramatic form. The final factor contributing to the supremacy of the rhetorical presidency is the modern electoral campaign. Contemporary presidential campaigns require national travel, public performances, image creation, issue definition, and the articulation of problem solutions. A "common man" can become known and win an election. Competition for communication opportunities is great.

Craig Allen Smith and Kathy Smith (1994, 16) identify six features of presidential leadership that point to presidential persuasion as the essential element:

- The presidency of the late twentieth century is fundamentally different from the presidency envisioned by the founders.
- The presidency of the late twentieth century is actively engaged in policy-making and the legislative process.
- Presidential leadership in the late twentieth century entails the creation, mobilization, transformation, and maintenance of coalitions.
- The creation, mobilization, transformation, and maintenance of coalitions requires presidents of the late twentieth century to influence a variety of other citizens: the Congress and the courts, political parties and interest groups, reporters and pundits, the powerful and the powerless, foreign and domestic groups, public opinion and posterity.

- Presidents of the late twentieth century attempt to influence those other citizens by informing them, by bargaining with them, by persuading them; in short, by communicating with them.
- The effectiveness of a president's leadership in the late twentieth century depends heavily on his persuasive abilities.

Thus, the rhetorical presidency refers to more than a collection of speeches delivered by any one president. It refers to the communicative attributes of both the institution and its occupants. The presidency is an office, a role, a persona, constructing a position of power, myth, legend, and persuasion. Although the presidency is indeed a real office with an elected official, space, desks, and staff, it remains elusive and undefined. When consulting the ultimate authority—Article II of the Constitution which delineates the functions and duties of the president—one notices how short, sketchy, vague, and almost trivial the description of the office appears. In reality, as Grant McConnell (1976) argues, "the presidency is the work of the presidents" (9). Yet, virtually every American from seven to 70 has a list of criteria of what makes a good president. Expectations are created through presidents' rhetoric, use of symbols, rituals, and sense of history. At home and in schools we are taught that America is the home of freedom, equality, opportunity, and democracy. Within such an environment, as Rossiter (1962) notes, the president becomes "the one-man distillation of the American people" reflecting their perceived dignity and majesty" (16). Consequently, elaborate criteria are envisioned for the person who desires the sacred office.

In terms of the presidency, one should recognize the importance of what Orrin Klapp (1964) calls "symbolic leadership." The real appeal of public officials is what they symbolize rather than what they have done. Klapp argues that certain persons have enormous effect, not because of achievement or vocation but because they stand for certain things; they play dramatic roles highly satisfying to their audiences; they are used psychologically and stir up followings. Symbolic leadership is an emergent phenomenon resulting from the interaction of the public and the politician. As political drama begins, according to Klapp, roles are identified, interpreted, and projected upon the politician, and no distinction is made between what a thing "is" and what the audience sees that it is. The key, therefore, in becoming a symbolic leader is to take advantage of the dramatic elements in any setting. Settings become drama when "things happen to audiences because of parts played by actors; the function of the actor is to transport an audience vicariously out of everyday roles into a new kind of 'reality' that has laws and patterns different from the routines of the ordinary social structure" (Klapp 1964, 32).

The sources of images or preconceptions people have of the qualities of leadership are vast. There are, however, a couple of major influences upon such leadership construction. First, history rather carefully characterizes past national leaders. Washington was a man of integrity (the cherry tree episode), determination (Valley Forge), and was democratic (refusal to be king). Lincoln was a man of patience ("to preserve the union"), forgiveness ("with malice toward none"), and a lover of freedom (The Emancipation Proclamation). Second, television greatly contributes to the creation of leadership ideals. The open forums give the impression of being able to assess candidate qualities. In addition, the media allows the dramatic creation and presentation of heroic figures through media events, advertising, and international crisis events.

Thus, the greatest American mythic endeavor is to find a great person as leader. As a people, Americans find pleasure and comfort in searching as well as in finding heroes. "Two centuries ago," Daniel Boorstin (1962) argues, "when a great man appeared, people looked for God's purpose in him; today we look for his press agent" (72–75). Yet, ironically, hero worship counters democratic dogma. The heart of hero worship, however, is not reverence for divine qualities but appreciation for popular virtues. In addition, Walter Fisher (1982) argues, presidential heroes as romantic figures express certain American ideals, such as individualism, achievement, and success. A true American hero will be visionary, mythic, and a subject for folklore and legend (299–310).

In short, the presidency is a national political symbol. And political symbols are the direct link between individuals and the social order. As elements of a political culture, political symbols function as a stimulus for behavior. They can provide insight into macro- and micro-level behavior. The use of appropriate symbols results in getting people to accept certain policies that may or may not provide tangible rewards, arousing support for various causes, and fostering obedience to governmental authority. Political symbols are actually means to material and social ends rather than ends in themselves.

There is, however, a long process from symbol creation, definition, acceptance, and subsequent behavior. For implicit in the argument thus far is the notion that successful leadership and control is dependent upon the successful manipulation of political symbols. There is a constant competition and struggle for national symbols. At one level, a president attempts to manipulate symbols in order to mobilize support, deactivate opposition, and insulate from criticism. On a broader level, national symbols are perpetuated in order to preserve the prevailing culture, beliefs, and values. Thus, the ongoing manipulation of political symbols takes place in the context of an existing set of symbols grounded in the political culture.

THE "INSTITUTIONAL" PRESIDENCY

Of all the major clauses in the Constitution, the one governing the presidency is the shortest. The members of the Constitutional Convention simply did not delineate in great detail the powers and responsibilities of the presidency. According to Rossiter (1962, 72–75), eight key decisions were made at the convention which really created the form and structure of the American presidency:

1. A separate executive office should be established apart from the legislature.
2. The executive office should consist of one man to be called president of the United States.
3. The president should be elected apart from the legislature.
4. The executive office should have a fixed term subject to termination by conviction of impeachment for high crimes or misdemeanors.
5. The president should be eligible for reelection with no limit as to the number of terms.
6. The president should derive power from the Constitution and not simply from Congress.
7. The president should not be encumbered with a specified body to seek approval for nominations, vetos, or other acts.
8. As president, one may not be a member of either house of Congress.

These key decisions created the office, but they contain little information as to what the office entails. Nearly half of Article II simply deals with tenure, qualifications, and election of the president. Section 2 of Article II states that the president "shall be Commander in Chief," "shall have power to grant reprieves and pardons," "make treaties, provided two-thirds of the Senators present concur," "appoint Ambassadors, other public Ministers and Consuls, judges of the Supreme Court, and all other officers of the United States . . . by and with the advice and consent of the Senate" and "shall have power to fill all vacancies that may happen during the recess of the Senate." Section 3 adds that the president "shall from time to time give to the Congress information of the State of the Union," "convene both Houses . . . on extraordinary occasions," "shall receive Ambassadors and other public Ministers," and "shall take care that the laws be faithfully executed." These, then, are the duties as specified in the Constitution. On the surface, they appear rather simple and straightforward. It is the fulfilling of these functions that complicates the office.

Contemporary scholars, when addressing presidential functions, seldom delineate constitutional provisions. Rather, they group presidential tasks into broad, general categories. These categories, of course, differ in number. For Thomas Cronin (1975, 250–56), the job description of the president involves six major functions:

1. Symbolic leadership which must generate hope, confidence, national purpose;
2. Setting national priorities and designing programs which will receive public attention and a legislative hearing;
3. Crisis management, which has become increasingly important since 1940;
4. Constant legislative and political coalition building;
5. Program implementation and evaluation, which has also become increasingly difficult in modern times; and
6. General oversight of government routines, which forces the president to be responsible for governmental performance at all levels.

Somewhat related to Cronin, Bruce Buchanan (1978, 29) identifies four "generic" functions of the presidency: national symbol, policy advocate, mediator among national interests, and crisis manager. George Reedy (1970) believes, however, that what a president must do can be boiled down to two simple fundamentals: "He must resolve the policy questions that will not yield to quantitative, empirical analysis; and he must persuade enough of his countrymen of the rightness of his decisions so that he can carry them out without destroying the fabric of society" (29).

From this brief discussion of presidential functions, the Constitution as a job description is vague and general. A president clearly does more than what is outlined in the Constitution. Even as commander in chief, the president may undertake crisis management, legislative and political coalition building, and so on. It is how one meets or carries out the functions that provides insight into how the institution influences behavior.

Edward Corwin (1948, 20–23) was the first to mention presidential roles as sources of power. A president's power is based upon five constitutional roles: chief of state, chief executive, chief diplomat, commander in chief, and chief legislator. These roles are roughly analogous to the various areas of responsibilities outlined in the Constitution. A president who creates additional roles and hence additional power approaches a dangerous "personalization of the office."

As chief of state, the president functions as the ceremonial head of government, not unlike the monarch of England. Some would argue that the majority of presidential activity is ceremonial. Projected upon the president is the symbol of sovereignty, continuity, and grandeur. As chief executive, the president is manager of one of the largest "corporations" in the world. Whether the president likes it or not, he is held responsible for the quality of governmental performance ranging from a simple letter of complaint to military preparedness. In event of war, the president as commander in chief must ensure strategic execution and victory. Within modern history, the field of foreign relations has become extremely important. The formulation of foreign policy and the conduct of foreign affairs force the president to serve as the nation's chief diplomat. Finally, by providing domestic leadership, the president must guide Congress by identifying national priorities for legislation. These legitimate constitutional roles are obviously interrelated. Yet, the various hats require rather distinct approaches, strategies, and temperament. Even these, however, may be situationally bound.

Clinton Rossiter (1962, 28–37), building on Corwin's analyses, argues that five extraconstitutional roles must also be recognized: chief of party, protector of the peace, manager of prosperity, world leader, and voice of the people. Rossiter, as Corwin, believes that the source of presidential power lies in the combination of the various roles. Rossiter, at least, recognizes the expanding nature of the presidency. These extra roles resulted from the growing activities of a president plus the growing expectations of the public. When speaking of presidential roles, most scholars cite Rossiter's classic *The American Presidency*. Hence, the list of roles is fairly stationary. Yet, as the functions or duties of the presidency grow, so do the roles. As the various tasks become more complex, numerous roles may be required to carry out one function. One should also note that each role may require very different skills and techniques. Roles, then, are more numerous than functions. They are labels or characters that people see and each has a distinct mode usually congruent with public expectations, which will be discussed later. Finally, if a role set is good or successful, the set may become a model. The model may thus serve as an overall approach to the fulfillment of the functions. The role set, as a model, may be praised, condemned, imitated, or serve as a guide to performance.

THE SYMBOLIC PRESIDENCY

Most all political scientists recognize that the presidency is both an institution and a role. As such, the presidency has a great deal of influence upon those who occupy the office as well as upon the general public.

Certainly, the American presidency has established a rather clear traditional role set. The title of president implies more than simply a job description. To know that a person is president is to know in a very general way how the individual is likely to behave and how others will behave toward the individual. The title not only provides a means for anticipating a range of behaviors, but also confines the range of behaviors possible. Thus, behavioral expectations and restrictions are attached to all social positions. Richard Rose (1970) notes that "empirical investigation usually reveals that leaders are often constrained by the expectations of their followers and in some cases compelled to follow their followers or risk deposition as leader" (110).

Emmet Hughes (1972), in *The Living Presidency*, states that a president faces two constituencies: "the living citizens and the future historians" (26). This certainly is not an easy task. Nearly all scholars agree that any American president inherits a vast, complex set of role expectations. Roles create expectations but societal expectations can create political roles. Murray Edelmam (1971) perceptively notes that expectations also evoke a specific political role and self-conception for those individuals who accept the role in question. When Alfred deGrazia (1969, 50) speaks of "the myth of the President," he is referring to "a number of qualities [that] are given to every President that are either quite fictitious or large exaggerations of the real man." He further notes that "the myth is not alone the property of the untutored mind, but of academicians, scientists, newspapermen, and even Congressmen."

Thus, the office of the presidency has grown because of interaction; interaction of the office with the public and the public with the office. As public expectations increase, so does the job. Concurrently, the job is forced to expand to meet public expectations.

There appears to be a growth in public expectations of the presidency. However, twentieth-century presidents, because of the use of mass media, have encouraged the public to identify with the candidate and potential of the office. Theodore White asserts that especially since 1960, our idea of government consists of promises—promises to take care of people, the cities, the sick, the old, the young. According to White, "by 1980 we had promised ourselves almost to the point of national bankruptcy" (Sanoff 1982, 59). Consequently, the public has responded by holding the president accountable for meeting various demands. David Easton (1965, 273–74) has identified two types of expectations that citizens have of political leadership. One focuses on the office and the other focuses on the individual who holds the office. Thus, public expectations are vast and complex. Upon investigating the research on presidential and public expectations, Herzik and Dodson (1982) conclude that indeed "a consensus does exist concerning public expectations of the President—a consensus focused around general traits of personality, leadership, and individual virtue" (172–73).

Disappointment in presidential performance is not the only consequence of false expectations. False expectations also encourage presidents to attempt more than they can accomplish in any term of office. Thus, false expectations invite presidents to overpromise and overextend themselves. This, in turn, creates the need for image-making activities. Such activities, in some cases, become the major task or work function of an administration. "The public-relations apparatus," as Cronin (1974) argues, "not only has directly enlarged the Presidential work force but has expanded public-relations expectations about the Presidency at the same time. More disquieting is the fact that, by its very nature, this type of press agency feeds on itself, and the resulting distortions encourage an ever increasing subordination of substance to style" (168).

Many attitudes about the presidency stem from messages received in childhood about the virtues of various presidents. Studies continually find that the president is ordinarily the first public official to come to the attention of young children (Greenstein 1969). Long before children are informed about the specific functions of the presidency, they view individual presidents as exceptionally important and benign. David Easton and Robert Hess (1962) found that children stressed personal characteristics of the president which include: honest, wise, helpful, powerful, good, and benign (241–42). Such attitudes probably result from parents not mentioning negative aspects of the political world in front of children, plus the general tendency of children to selectively perceive more supportive characteristics of individuals in a wider environment. Generally, by the age of nine, virtually every American child has some detailed awareness of the presidency and can identify the incumbent president. Thus, esteem and respect for the office independent of the occupant is established at a rather early age. Every year since World War II, the majority of the ten most admired men and women are involved in national politics. And the president, regardless of performance, is usually among them.

Doris Graber (1972, 142), in a study designed to analyze images of presidential candidates in the press during campaigns, found that citizens tend to selectively extract information about a president's personal image that is beyond the media content which ignores issue elements. In addition, Michael Pfau (1993) and colleagues, found that voters form perceptions of candidates in two stages during primaries. First, the public forms "relational perceptions" about the candidate's sincerity, honesty, and caring qualities. Then the public assess job competencies based on mediated statements and appearances. Therefore, citizens apparently perceive and evaluate a president as a person in addition to his policies and skill in office. According to Greenstein (1969), when people are asked to indicate what they like or dislike about a president, they usually cite aspects of personal image.

Another result of childhood socialization is the heavy dependency for leadership on the presidency, especially in times of national crisis. Richard Pious (1979) argues that in times of national emergency, we discard skepticism and return to childhood images of the presidency. As adults, we still desire to see the president as a combination of Washington and Lincoln, making wise decisions and working harder than the average citizen to preserve the quality of life.

A presidential campaign emphasizes the childhood visions and qualities of the office. Hence, campaigns themselves perpetuate the mythic and heroic role demands of the office. To mobilize a nation is indeed a somewhat mysterious process. Although a campaign may be rather contentious and even disorderly, the process allows the opportunity to assess and project presidential qualities upon the candidates.

Media advisers must project appropriate images of the candidates that are always simplified depictions of reality. In a memo to Richard Nixon, Ray Price argued, "It's not what's there that counts, it's what is projected—and carrying it one step further, it's not what he projects but rather what the voter receives" (Pious 1979, 90). James Wooten (1978), in addressing the 1976 Carter campaign, wrote that Carter "believed that the candidate who took clear positions on every issue was not long for the political world. There would be only one issue on which a successful candidate would be judged that year, the amorphous, ethereal concept of integrity, honesty, trustworthiness, credibility" (35). Patrick Caddell is quoted as warning Carter during the transition that "too many good people have been beaten because they tried to substitute substance for style" (Pious 1979, 91). Is this ethically, logically, or even morally right? Carter's pollster Gerald Rafshoon believed that there was nothing wrong with a candidate adjusting himself to an ideology or "rhetorical stance" judged to be acceptable by the voters. Rafshoon argued to Wooten (1978), "He was always Jimmy Carter.... Hell, you wouldn't expect Sears Roebuck to step into a big multimillion dollar promotion without having the benefit of consumer research on what people are most interested in purchasing" (277). Consequently, the image projected by a candidate should meet the expectations and childhood visions of presidential behavior. The best image is one that is vague enough for voters to complete. In the simplest terms, this means that conservatives should be able to see the candidate as conservative and, likewise, liberals should be able to see the candidate as liberal. Above all, this should be done without seeming contradictory or insincere.

By inauguration day a candidate has emerged as president. A tremendous transformation, at least in the eyes of the public, has occurred. Americans want and even need to believe that the common man they elevated to the presidency is a Lincolnesque bearer of infinite wisdom and benevolence. The perceived qualities are confirmed as soon as the candidate takes the oath of office.

The public's relationship with the presidency is more than a search for the fulfillment of childhood notions of the office. For some time empirical and clinical evidence has shown that the office provides, for a large portion of the population, an outlet for expression of deep, often unconscious personality needs and conflicts. Harold Lasswell, as early as 1930 in his classic *Psychopathology and Politics*, argued that private needs become displaced onto public objects and rationalized in terms of general political principles. Greenstein (1969), a student of Lasswell, continually investigated these phenomena in relation to the presidency. He recognizes six major psychological uses of the presidency for the population.

1. The office serves a cognitive aid by providing a vehicle for the public to become aware of the functions, impact, and politics of government.
2. The presidency provides an outlet for affect, feelings, and emotions. The office serves as a focal point of pride, despair, hope, as well as frustration. It can easily be responsible, in the eyes of the public, for all that is bad or for all that is good.
3. The office serves as a means of vicarious participation. The president becomes an object of identification and consequently presidential efforts become citizen efforts resulting in a sharing of heightened feelings of potency.
4. Especially in times of crisis or uncertainty, the presidency functions as a symbol of national unity. When a president acts, it is the nation acting as one voice expressing one sentiment.
5. Likewise, the office serves as a symbol of stability and predictability. We assume that the president is knowledgeable and in control of events, thus minimizing danger or surprise.
6. Finally, the presidency serves as a lightning rod or an object of displacement. The office is the ultimate receptacle for personal feelings and attitudes, which become national. The president becomes either idealized or the ultimate scapegoat. Truman's cliche, "the buck stops here," is true—at least in the minds of the public.

Of all the political myths of the nation, Theodore White (1975) argues that the supreme myth is the ability of the citizens to choose the "best" person to lead the nation. From this belief followed the notion that the office would ennoble anyone who holds it. "The office would burn the dross from his character; his duties would, by their very weight, make him a superior man, fit to sustain the burden of the law, wise and enduring enough to resist the clash of all selfish interests" (White 1975, 324). Thus, the presidency is a combination of symbol and reality. However, the symbolic dimensions of the office are increasingly becoming more important as the role of mass media has become both "maker and breaker" of presidents. As Edelman (1974) notes, "the symbolic component is more crucial to the degree that people lack meaningful social commitments that provide a benchmark for evaluation" (160). In fact, the manipulation of salient symbols clouds issues and blurs situations resulting in emotionally charged but nebulously defined symbols.

Perhaps the forefathers were aware of the fact that the most practical method of unifying people was to give them a symbol that all could identify. When the symbol is manifested in a person, the efficacy and effectiveness are greatly enhanced. Clearly the president of the United States is the focal point of the political system. Every action by the president is symbolic because he is not merely an executive, he is also a carrier of meaning. What the individual symbolizes to each person or group depends upon the system of interpretation of the person or group. "Political symbols bring out in concentrated form those particular meanings and emotions which the members of a group created and reinforce in each other" (Edelman 1964, 11). Consequently, according to Michael Novak (1974), "from the beginning to the end of his term in office, his every action is a means by which citizens interpret life in the United States" (8).

The very potency of the presidency as a symbol gives the office purpose and pragmatic nature. Americans expect presidents to prod and unite as well as to provide direction and a sense of purpose. As such, the presidency fulfills the parental functions of supreme leader, guide, and teacher. It is important to note, however, that symbolic power is the precondition of pragmatic power. Much legislation and many programs have failed because they were not symbolically acceptable. The key to success, of course, is presidential leadership. Not surprisingly, the most frequent complaint of the presidency since the Vietnam War is the lack of leadership. But leadership, from an interactionist perspective, is more than effective management and the ability to isolate and derive solutions to problems.

Recognizing the symbolic importance and dimensions of leadership is not to support the old notion that one is born a leader or that leadership is simply a matter of charisma. Rather, true leadership is granted by people, comprised of their own unique perceptions, needs, and expectations.

Generally, most presidential scholars, although using somewhat different terminology, believe that the American people expect three major aspects of presidential behavior. First, the president is expected to be a competent manager of the vast machinery of government. Second, the American people expect the president to take care of their needs by initiating programs, legislation, and safeguarding the economy. Finally, the people want a sense of legitimacy from the president. The office, while providing symbolic affirmation of the nation's values, should faithfully represent the opinions of the public as well.

The importance of presidents meeting the expectations of the public cannot be overemphasized. Carter was very successful in rising from obscurity in 1976 to becoming president of the United States. As a presidential candidate, Carter was most successful in presenting himself as a common man and a man of the people. James Wooten (1978) noted that Carter "worked hard at establishing himself in the eyes of the public as a common man, just another American hired to do a particular job"

(361). Carter also effectively articulated the traditional values of an average American citizen. Carter's campaign rhetoric reflected how Americans wanted to conceive of themselves and the myth they wanted to live by as evident in Carter's slogan of "a government as good as its people." A vote for Carter became a vote for us reaffirming our national values and virtues in the wake of Nixon's disgrace.

But an interesting paradox of the American presidency is that once elected we demand uncommon leadership, great insight, and vast knowledge from our presidents. A president must appear presidential as defined by history, culture, and status of the position. Carter was often criticized for his lack of presidential behavior, dress, and demeanor. Carter wore a blue suit for his inaugural rather than a morning coat and top hat; took the oath of office as Jimmy Carter rather than as James Earl Carter; walked down Pennsylvania Avenue rather than rode in a limousine; prohibited the playing of "Hail to the Chief"; sold the presidential yacht Sequoia; sent Amy to a public school; carried his own luggage; and wore blue jeans at the White House.

In July 1977, Carter received a 64 percent positive rating on the question of restoring public confidence in government. Just one year later, however, Carter received a 63 percent negative response to the same question (Lasky 1979, 16). There is evidence to suggest that the public soon resented and rejected Carter's attempts to reduce the perceived stature and dignity of the presidency. Carter, much too late, realized the fact. In his memoirs he writes:

> However, in reducing the imperial Presidency, I overreacted at first. We began to receive many complaints that I had gone too far in cutting back the pomp and ceremony, so after a few months I authorized the band to play "Hail to the Chief" on special occasions. I found it to be impressive and enjoyed it. (Carter 1982, 27)

Simply stated, the presidency is both our administrative office and our ceremonial office. Our president must meet and entertain kings and rulers of other nations. The office, and hence the individual, embodies the hopes, desires, dignity, and wealth of our nation.

GOVERNING

It has become a truism in political science literature to recognize the distinction between campaigning and governing. For the rest of the chapter, we consider the more operational or pragmatic communication concerns of the institutional presidency.

Communication

Smoller (1990) argues that presidential communication follows a continuum ranging from full control to virtually no control over content, timing, or context. For example, a presidential address offers the most control while evening newscasts offer the least amount of control. Of course, every White House wants as much control over presidential communication as possible, especially in terms of news coverage and presentation. As a result, there are three presidential institutions that attempt to influence news coverage and public reception of presidential communication: the White House Office of Communication, the press secretary, and press conferences.

The White House Office of Communications

Richard Nixon created the Office of Communications to combat the White House press corps, whose coverage was a constant source of frustration and irritation. According to John Maltese (1992, 2), the goal of the office is to set the public agenda, to make sure all elements of the executive branch stay on the specified agenda, and to promote the agenda through mass marketing. More specifically, the office is charged with long-term public relations planning, disseminating the "line of the day," and circumventing the White House press corps by orchestrating direct appeals to the American people. On a daily basis, the office is usually responsible for media relations, public affairs activities, speechwriting, and research.

Each subsequent president has retained the office. However, it was the Reagan White House that strategically used the office in a proactive way to carefully manage public images and portrayals of Reagan.

According to Richard Perloff (1998), Reagan advisors decided to "sell the country on Reagan the man—the charming political leader" (61). They developed several rules of information management: plan ahead, stay on the offensive, control the flow of information, limit reporter's access to the president, talk about the issues *you* want to talk about, speak in one voice, and repeat the same message several times (62). The communication team also developed the strategy of the "line of the day." Each morning, staffers would decide on a major theme they would emphasize that day with every encounter with members of the press corps. This strategy also included considerations of how to get the president and the selected message point in the evening news and next day newspapers. All officials were instructed to speak only about the selected theme to insure coverage and consistency of message. The communication staff also paid very close attention to visuals, the backdrops and positioning of the president for television and photo opportunities. Nothing was left to chance. Virtually every moment of an event was planned, every word carefully scripted, and everywhere the president would stand or move clearly marked (Perloff 1998, 63). Finally, the Reagan administration perfected the notion of White House spin control—concerted efforts to provide their interpretation of events and actions. From press releases to public statements by cabinet officers, the Reagan White House would bombard the press with "official" accounts and reactions of the day's national and international news. Such ochestrated efforts reduced the likelihood of presidential gaffes and promoted consistency of message and a favorable portrayal of the president.

While successive presidents have attempted to utilize many of the Reagan strategies, Presidents Bush and Clinton have been less successful. President Bush simply did not see the full value of such concerted efforts of news management. He preferred more informal meetings with the press and was comfortable with his public persona. Although the Clinton administration wanted to emulate the Reagan successes in media management, the staff was simply less experienced and more disorganized. In addition, Clinton was more difficult to keep on script and would speak on many issues rather than just one or two. After the midterm elections of 1994, staffers determined that Clinton was actually "overexposed." He was too accessible to media and the public through the informal town hall meetings. His casual approach had eroded the dignity and stature of the presidency. As a result, the staff increased the ratio of press conferences to other appearances in order for Clinton to appear more "presidential" (Denton and Holloway 1996, 34).

Press Secretary

The press secretary is the primary spokesperson for the president. The secretary releases news and information as well as provides the official interpretation of events, words, and actions of the president. "How" something is said is as important as "what" is said. Without exaggeration, the words of the press secretary become the words and expressions of the president. The job is difficult and challenging. In addition to balancing policy and political demands, the secretary must also accurately reflect the thoughts and positions of the president. Press secretaries must also maintain the trust and confidence of the press corps.

Usually before noon, the press secretary conducts the daily news briefing. The briefing contains announcements about pending policy issues, presidential appointments for the day, and any other items of interest. During the typical "question-and-answer" portion of the briefing, secretaries provide the White House spin on topics of interest (Perloff 1998, 68).

Press Conferences

Presidential press conferences have become major national media events. They provide the president a national audience and an opportunity to express their views and to frame political debate on issues of importance to the public. According to Carolyn Smith (1990), "the presidential press conference has evolved into a semi-institutional, quasi-spontaneous, inherently adversarial public encounter between the president and the press" (65). For her, "the main obligation of the president in this dialogue is to persuade. The main obligation of the press is to hold the president accountable for his policies and his actions. These contrary obligations produce a delicate but natural tension—a balancing act, if you will—that should be played out in each and every good press conference exchange" (65).

While not a constitutional requirement, press conferences have become institutionalized. Presidents differ in the number and frequency of press conferences they hold. Usually, the longer a president is in office, the fewer formal press conferences they conduct. Press conferences are useful to make a special announcement, to sustain policy momentum, or to make a diplomatic response (Smith 1990, 132–39).

Press conferences are risky because there is limited control over the questions and agenda. After the openning statement, regardless of any prior agreements with the press, reporters are free to ask virtually any question. Many reporters want to be called upon to ask a question of the president that will generate interest and headlines. Some reporters, like Dan Rather and Sam Donaldson, build a reputation for asking tough questions, leading to better career opportunities.

Presidents must prepare for a variety of questions. Some questions solicit an attitude about a policy or situation while others seek specific information. Some questions attempt to put the president "on-the-record" forcing the president to take a public stand on an issue. The phrasing of some questions may advocate positions often counter to that of the administration. In each case, the president must remember his ultimate audience, the American public. Once again, from a political perspective, how a president responds to questions is as important as the content of his response. For Smith (1990), "the best press conference *questions* are those which compel a president to divulge a new piece of information about his public self, his administration, or his policies. The best presidential *answers* are those which enhance the president's leadership image to the American people. The best press *exchanges* are those which reveal that the president is exercising legitimate leadership and the press is exercising its legitimate watchdog role" (109).

It is important for the president to demonstrate a broad knowledge of issues, to use humor, and to connect with the viewing audience. From a strategic perspective, a president hopes to avoid controversy and to gain a lift in the polls and approval ratings.

Press conferences have declined in importance in recent years. Networks find them too scripted and less informative. Presidents experience less control over the agenda and more hostile questions.

News

We have already noted how the media have impacted the way candidates run for office. It is also important to recognize the impact of the media upon governing. Prior to television, presidents governed by accommodating broad coalitions and interests groups. But leadership in the age of television requires the mobilization of public opinion. Public opinion has become a critical element of political influence.

The institutional presidency relies upon the news media to communicate strategically to a variety of audiences: the general public, opinion leaders, members of the other branches of government, and the international community, to name only a few. Timothy Cook (1998, 124–40) identifies three reasons why presidents use the news media as a strategic tool for governing the nation. First, just making news can be making policy itself. For example, at the noon White House briefing, public statements about a whole range of issues become "official" policy, which influences subsequent actions and behaviors. President Clinton used press briefings to articulate our view of international sanctions against Iraq and to send a clear message to Saddam Hussein of our intention to enforce site inspections. Especially in the international arena, presidential statements become the basis for negotiation and for the terms of our relationships with other nations. Second, making news is a way the president can call attention to preferred issues and frame public debate. Each time President Jimmy Carter delivered a speech about energy, there was an average increase of 10 network news stories on the subject (Ansolabehere et al. 1993, 198). Publicity about issues influences the public's demand for action. Finally, making news is itself a form of public persuasion. News coverage of an event influences public opinion in several ways. Media provide very basic information and facts about issues necessary for opinion formation. The tone of coverage may influence public perceptions about issues. The duration or frequency of coverage of an item influences the sense of urgency or magnitude of an issue.

There is a rather clear cycle to media coverage and cooperation with the White House, regardless of whether it's a Democrat or Republican administration. Grossman and Kumar (1981, 273–98) identify three stages of a relationship between a newly elected president and the media. First, in the alliance stage, there is a high degree of mutual cooperation between the media and the president. Next follows the competition phase of the relationship where both sides are attempting to get their specific views heard. Manipulative strategies and more aggressive tone characterizes this stage of the relationship. Finally, late in a president's administration, the detachment stage develops and the relationship becomes rather formal and very structured. After much competition and contentiousness, both sides settle into a pattern or routine of interaction.

In a similar fashion, Smoller (1990, 66–74) writes about the "four seasons of presidential news." Each season is distinguished by the content and tone of news coverage. In general, coverage proceeds from positive to negative in tone. The first stage of coverage is a personal profile of the president, staff, and family. This tends to be the most favorable, highlighting past accomplishments and unique events in the lives of the first family. The second stage moves to coverage of the president's legislative agenda and policy initiatives. The tone becomes more negative as the press focuses on the president's persuasive attempts to push programs through Congress. In the third stage, the legislative program and initiatives are prematurely evaluated. The press judges competency and program effectiveness long before the impact of any specific piece of legislation or program can be implemented. During this stage, the media also focus on internal staff conflicts or scandals. Washington elites pass judgment and opposition members of Congress are granted greater access to the news media. In the final stage of coverage, the president is reevaluated. The skills and competency of the president are openly questioned. The portrayal is now one of crisis, failure, and decline. "In short, the president is profiled, and then his policies are examined; these policies are evaluated, and then the president is reevaluated" (67).

Richard Perloff (1998, 84–89) identifies five characteristics of presidential news. First, it tends to be very cynical. Journalists, especially since Watergate, have become less trusting and more adversarial in dealing with all issues of politics and with politicians in general. Second, presidential news tends to focus on very narrow political issues. As already noted in several other places, complex issues are reduced to winners and losers, right or wrong, and just two sides. The third characteristic of presidential news is that it focuses on conflict and controversy. Audience appeal and the need for drama encourages such an approach to covering politics. Television news especially needs to be very visual. And finally, as recognized by Smoller, presidential news tends to be personal.

Of course, presidents must develop strategies and tactics to combat such competitive and negative coverage. For example, some presidents take their message straight to the public rather than relying on the filtering or interpretation of policy by reporters. Others use surrogates to carry the word or use the "theme of day" approach to manage coverage. Still others simply retreat and reduce access of reporters to the president and White House officials. More and more time is spent by presidents managing news coverage and media portrayals.

Speechmaking

Presidents now talk to us more than ever before (Hart 1994). Even more significant, the way presidents talk and the medium through which they primarily talk also have changed. The days of impassioned, fiery oratory given to packed auditoriums of live human beings are over (Jamieson 1988). Today, presidents invite us, through the medium of television, into the privacy of their living rooms or offices, for informal, "presidential conversations" (Denton and Holloway 1995).

This change, of course, did not occur overnight. Radio signaled the change from flamboyant oratory to a more conversational style. Franklin D. Roosevelt initiated the fireside chats and brought live presidential communication into American living rooms. As the Roosevelt style became institutionalized, and as politicians became accustomed and adapted to the new medium, public addresses increasingly took on the style and tone of conversation. Speeches became talk. Television furthered this process, rendering presidential speech more intimate and conversational. The visual dimension of television also reinforced the apparently casual, intimate exchange between leaders and the citizenry. Cathcart and Gumpert (1983, 272–75) classify such exchanges as "media simulated interpersonal communication." Kathleen Jamieson (1988) argues that the interpersonal, intimate context created through television requires a "new eloquence," one in which candidates and presidents adopt a personal and revealing style that engages the audience in conversation.

Characteristics of "eloquence conversation" and research about nonverbal communication inform our understanding of the transformation of presidential communication strategies in the age of television. At the same time, television shapes the interaction in ways different from actual interpersonal communication contexts. The interaction of the television audience is "parasocial" (Cathcart and Gumpert, 1983; Pfau 1990).

Presidents who increasingly rely on the medium of television are forced into playing the communication game by television's rules. This not only means shorter speeches, it also means speeches that are crafted specifically for television. Presidential speech is increasingly familiar, personalized, and self-revealing. Reagan's use of contractions, simple, often incomplete sentences, informal transitions, colloquial language, and frequent stories transformed his "formal" Oval Office addresses into conversations with the American people (Jamieson 1988, 166). His skillful adaptation to the camera simulated direct eye contact with individuals in his audience. It had all the appearance of conversation. This conversational style "invite[s] us to conclude that we know and like" presidents who use it (Jamieson 1988). Ronald Reagan first excelled at this style, which stands in marked contrast even to the conversational style of Franklin D. Roosevelt, for example. For where the strength of Reagan's rhetoric is that we feel we know and understand him, the strength of FDR's was that he knew and understood us. Bill Clinton through his mediated conversational style accomplishes both, especially in the town hall meeting format. For Clinton, the town hall meetings best represent the power and potential of successful mediated conversation as a strategy of public discourse and persuasion in the age of telepolitics (Denton and Hollway 1996).

Presidential Discourse

Roderick Hart (1987) provides the most systematic and detailed study of presidential discourse. He and his colleagues coded every address from Truman through the Reagan administrations. He found that the presidents during this time period averaged twenty speeches per month ranging from Eisenhower's low of ten to Ford's high of 43. Interestingly, the first year each new president gave more speeches than the previous president, and more speeches were given in the second year of each presidency than in the first. The speech sample reveals that 37.5 percent were ceremonial in nature, 26.5 percent were briefings, 15 percent at political rallies, and 10.3 percent at organizational meetings, with the remainder at miscellaneous speaking activities (69).

Hart's (1984) analysis also finds that presidential language is more optimistic and contains more realism, less complexity, and more self-references than langage of other leaders (50). When comparing media versus nonmedia appearances, Hart found that presidential television language has more self-references, familiarity, human interest, and optimism than the language of personal appearances.

Richard Perloff (1998) argues that the rhetorical presidency is a broad theoretical construct. He summarizes (105) that

- presidents' addresses can be as important as their policies;
- presidents' words are deeds since they bring the force and majesty of the office with them;
- even presidential directives will not achieve their goals if presidents cannot persuade the public and the press to support their aims;
- presidents have a variety of ways to influence opinions, including speeches, press conferences, and the news;
- presidential messages are the outgrowth of modern marketing techniques.

From a strategic perspective, presidential discourse is required (Perloff 1998, 104) because

- presidential persuasion is no longer a private game, but a very public endeavor;
- presidents are increasingly appealing to the public for support;
- going public can take different forms, including public addresses, presidential appearances, political travel, and the use of new technologies.

The Process of Speechmaking

Throughout history ghostwriters have lived in the shadows of public awareness, at least since a Sicilian named Corax received payment to coach awkward orators over 2,000 years ago. Academics such as Plato might later quarrel about the presumptuous ethics of teachers and writers who would help "the weaker look the stronger." But the existence of republican government has always required coaching in the arts of rhetoric. Like other arts, political persuasion must be learned. The propriety of using a collaborator is arguably as acceptable as the relationship between mentor and apprentice, legal counsel and client, or expert and layman.

But there is a threshold that is crossed at some risk. Most Americans know that a high proportion of the president's rhetoric originates in the minds of subordinates. Few journalists even bother to inquire about the writers who assisted in preparing a particular message. While this sharing of a political burden is an accepted folkway, public figures must not seem to relinquish control over what is issued in their name. Collaboration cannot be capitulation. With the presumption of authorship comes the burden of responsibility.

When rumors were broadcast that John F. Kennedy's Pulitzer Prize–winning book, *Profiles in Courage*, was actually the handiwork of the senator's aide, that boundary had been crossed. Kennedy angrily denied the charge and started legal action against ABC Television for allowing columnist Drew Pearson to make the accusation. He admitted that Theodore Sorensen provided extensive help in gathering part of the book's materials. Sorensen's collaboration was acceptable; his alleged total responsibility was not (Sorensen 1965, 68–70). Arguably more harmful was the 1988 admission by Press Secretary Larry Speakes that he had drafted presidential statements for release to the press that were never actually made by Ronald Reagan. During a 1985 meeting in Geneva with Soviet General Secretary Gorbachev, Speakes prepared upbeat "remarks" allegedly spoken by the president on the positive nature of the talks. His motive, he noted, was to offset the favorable publicity the Soviet leader received for his own candid comments. The revelation and public furor over these fabrications embarrassed the president, who was already seen as too disengaged from his responsibilities (Johnston 1988, A29). In the first instance, what eventually appeared in the book went out with the approval and knowledge of Kennedy; in the second, however, Reagan apparently had no such opportunity to approve the comments.

A romantic but not entirely inaccurate view of the presidency is that it once nurtured a grandiloquent rhetorical tradition. Washington's inaugural, Jefferson's first inaugural, Jackson's popular challenges to Calhoun on the issue of nullification, and Lincoln's wartime and emancipation statements have all become part of America's political literature. The sonorities and spaciousness of eighteenth- and nineteenth-century rhetoric vividly recalls the heyday of the orator, but also what seems at first glance to be an old art in a state of advanced decay. The conciseness and ordinary prose of today's political rhetoric often renders it incapable of provoking the range of emotions that a Lincoln-Douglas debate could muster in the mid-1800s. Its metaphors and images are more mundane—taken from the broken rhythms and incomplete sentences of conversation rather than the fuller images of the printed word. Where Lincoln drew images from Shakespeare and the Bible, Presidents Reagan and Bush found models in Hollywood characterizations of Knute Rockne and Dirty Harry ("Make my day," "Read my lips"). "Few species of composition seem so antiquated, so little available for any practical purpose today," Richard Weaver (1953) noted, "as the oratory in which the generation of our grandparents delighted."

If the style of political discourse has changed, and if the less-than-monumental scope of contemporary address shows more pragmatism than vision, the immediate political consequences of many presidential statements remain important. Even the self-disclosing prose of Bill Clinton can surpass in immediate impact the profoundest efforts of presidents in power before the age of the microphone. Jefferson's inaugural, for example, was uttered in a barely audible voice before just several hundred members of Congress in the still uncompleted Capitol building. Clinton, in sharp contrast, easily reached over 100 million Americans in his own 1997 inaugural, with several other millions watching worldwide.

The potential for rhetorically altering the nation's climate of opinion has never been greater. With the evolution in the 1920s of mass radio audiences for a single speech, presidential utterance was rendered cautious and tactical rather than spacious and all encompassing. Franklin Roosevelt addressed the rough equivalent of all of Jefferson's presidential audiences in just one 15-minute "fireside chat." Changed most dramatically by radio, oratory that previously had to be suited to only the immediate audience on hand (and a secondary audience of newspaper readers) suddenly had to suit a nation of diverse constituents and accidental listeners held together by the invisible thread of the radio network. The temptation to use this medium and to widen the appeal of key speeches made the speechwriter an attractive addition to the White House staff. By allowing a writer to undertake what had been for Woodrow Wilson and Theodore Roosevelt an immensely time-consuming task of speech drafting or dictation, a president not only saved time, but gained the confidence of knowing that someone was available to flag an ill-conceived remark.

The broadcasting of presidential addresses and increased reporting of all public appearances naturally meant that political rhetoric had to be adapted to a wider audience than ever before. The risks of an unintended slur were increased and this meant that others would now intervene in what had been to most presidents the least delegable of all their tasks. As a public document having the widest possible distribution, it was thought a speech could no longer risk the candor expected by a gathering of a limited size. Presidents after Theodore Roosevelt were largely unwilling to jeopardize their political power by depending on their own memories, or their skills at speaking "off the cuff." The broad dissemination of virtually every message now meant that too much was at stake.

The growth in the number of special assistants and aides concerned with public relations and speech writing is what presidential scholar Thomas Cronin (1975) considers "one of the more disquieting aspects of the recent enlargement of the presidential establishment" (137). The first speechwriter hired to assist a president was Judson Welliver, who joined the Harding administration with that designated role in 1920 (Cornwell 1965, 70). By any standard Harding needed all the help he could get to defend what became an increasingly troubled and corrupt administration after the Teapot Dome and Justice Department scandals in the early 1920s. Even earlier, in the 1880s, Chester Arthur employed a friend named Daniel Rollins from New York to help draft a number of presidential messages clandestinely. Perhaps because ghostwriting would have been an unthinkable sharing of responsibilities at the end of the nineteenth century, Rollins went to great pains to keep his help to the ailing Arthur a total secret (Medved 1979, 73).

To a large extent speechwriters were to remain a rarity until the administration of Calvin Coolidge in 1923. Prior to Coolidge, the White House worked at whatever pace its officeholder set. Theodore Roosevelt not only answered the phone on occasion, but relished the chance to write speeches on as broad a range of topics as a president has ever claimed to conquer. War, physical fitness, politics, conservation, human rights, corporate monopolies, and natural history were frequent topics heard from his "bully pulpit." For Woodrow Wilson, who followed William Howard Taft in 1912, speeches remained a high priority. Trained by a Scots Presbyterian minister who placed the highest value on his son's oratory, Wilson spent hours perfecting what still remains as some of the most thoughtful and coherent of all presidential rhetoric.

Calvin Coolidge managed to vastly increase the number of presidential speeches through the continued aid of Judson Welliver and others, thereby establishing both an important precedent and a harmful liability for the publicity-conscious executive branch. The precedent was that the enlarged staff became known to the public, and perceptions of the office changed accordingly. With the Coolidge administration, Americans began to think of a president in the contemporary sense: as a leader whose fate was determined by the quality of his staff as well as by his own efforts. The liability was that rarely again would an executive's words reflect the undiluted visions and attitudes of just one person. The impact of these changes did not go unnoticed for long. "It is a misfortune," wrote an observer of the Coolidge administration, "that as President he had permitted so many of his formal addresses to be written for him by members of his staff. These have made him seem prolix, jejune, and ordinary to a degree" (Cornwell 1965, 95).

"Silent Cal" had managed to double the number of addresses over his eloquent predecessor, but at a heavy cost. No longer would presidents be content to write their own speeches, offer them for review and comment to close friends and advisers, and then deliver them. The emerging pattern was to be a reversal of that process for all except the most important statements. Others would write early drafts, with varying degrees of guidance, while only the editing would be done by the president.

This basic pattern remains today. Though presidents occasionally write sections of important addresses such as convention acceptance speeches, inaugurals, and portions of state of the union addresses, they now more usually function as final editors of drafts written elsewhere. The highest praise that one usually hears from aides working with a president is not that he is a good cowriter, but a good editor. His ability to quickly rework an aide's manuscript so that it represents an authentic copy of his own prose "signature"—what is characteristic of him in terms of idiom, ideas, and style—is a major test of his editorial skill. The result is the synthetic duplication of a rhetorical style that only approximates what a president might produce, had he spent the necessary time.

In the recent past, key writers of important speeches have usually had a comparatively long association with the president, often in many capacities other than as speechwriter. Hartmann was a one-time staff coordinator for Ford, but not a very successful one. As Ford (1979, 184–85) tells it, disorder tended to follow Hartmann around. Bill Moyers was a personal assistant, press secretary, and general sounding board for Lyndon Johnson. Theodore Sorensen was one of Senator John Kennedy's legislative assistants.

When pondering a major speech, a president will typically seek out whoever has been a reliable writer among his closest aides. For Franklin Roosevelt it was Judge Samuel Rosenman, an old friend and former member of the New York Supreme Court. For Kennedy the call was inevitably to Sorensen, Arthur Schlesinger, Jr., or Richard Goodwin. Dwight Eisenhower used Emmet Hughes and the politically astute Bryce

Harlow; but Sherman Adams more regularly assigned first drafts to one of any number of subordinates. More recently, Aram Bakshian, Jr., Anthony Dolan, and Patrick Buchanan served as principal writers for Ronald Reagan. All of these individuals initiated first drafts themselves, or served as final editors in what has become an elaborate process of bureaucratic review.

Reflecting the inevitable tie between policy and the way it is articulated, a neat organizational chart outlining staff responsibilities misses the fact that key policymakers regularly function to subvert or intercept major addresses. What better method is available to ensure that a good intention is translated into a firm commitment than to write the script of that commitment in behalf of the president? As a matter of routine, new policy initiatives in foreign and domestic affairs are in effect sponsored by a cabinet head or presidential staffer with a deep interest in their success.

Lesser speeches usually involve one or two subordinate speech writers serving nominally under a senior aide and writer. These second-line staffers may also work on press releases, important mail, and reports. An assignment will usually come with advice on who should be contacted for background information. If a minor message directly involves a shift or new development in policy, a first draft or an outline of "talking points" is usually requested from the agency responsible for the area. If the address is political, it may incorporate the suggestions of a supportive member of Congress.

Only on rare occasions will a president be involved before several drafts have been refined and edited by senior writers. Normally he is given a final draft from a few days to several weeks before the speech is delivered. The draft may be rejected, sending the staff into frantic high gear to produce something new in a short period of time. More commonly, it is edited by the president, sometimes with the order to clean up or alter one or two passages. Except for Gerald Ford, no contemporary presidents have followed Franklin Roosevelt's occasional practice of permitting two teams of speech writers to come up with competing drafts for approval. That can be understandably trying on the morale of those laboring in front of the word processor. What is somewhat more common is a pattern whereby a formal speech is generated from within the normal White House channels, while at the same time unsolicited manuscripts or offers of ideas come from close aides or friends. John Kennedy, for example, received several unsolicited inaugural speech drafts from friends, newsmen, and complete strangers (Sorensen 1965, 240) Most of the suggestions that the primary writers receive usually carry a different emphasis in one area which reflects the sender's attempts to neutralize certain suspected biases. In the Nixon White House each of the three top-level writers earned a more or less accurate caricature reflecting what key staff members perceived as their strengths and weaknesses. If a speech was to offer heavy doses of compassion, the liberal Ray Price was said to offer the most philosophical and least partisan prose. Patrick Buchanan, in contrast, could carve up liberals with a sabre of righteous right-wing indignation, as was clearly evident in the well-publicized attacks on the press that he wrote for Vice President Spiro Agnew. William Safire was known for his ability to make almost any idea memorable and at least superficially eloquent.

Surprisingly, however, there is little evidence to suggest that a writer chosen for a routine speech is selected because of his or her expertise on the topic. The mundane realities of office work, such as who has the time, may be more important in determining an assignment than who will produce the best draft. What emerges from various memoirs and accounts is that as many as five or six writers might produce a first draft. There is also little support for what would seem to be the natural conclusion that a president at least oversees the assigning and outline of a speech. The memoirs of most presidents contribute to this false impression. They frequently speak of "the need for a speech" to the National Association of Broadcasters, the VFW, the National Press Club, or thousands of other potential audiences. In fact the decision to appear before a group and the secondary step of assigning a writer—may well fall to one of several of the president's chief political advisers.

In many ways the life of an American chief executive has been made more difficult since the advent of the Xerox machine. Twenty years ago the number of people who could get an advance look at a draft copy of a speech was limited by the goodwill of the secretary facing the tedious task of making multiple copies. As few as two copies of any presidential speech draft were produced in the Lincoln, Taft, or Roosevelt years. But today the copier makes it possible virtually to publish a draft copy of a speech by making hundreds of offspring. Circulating them to any or all of the mandarins of the White House staff can be achieved with the least amount of effort. In the past, when a president wrote his own drafts he was perhaps less compelled to permit the speech to circulate. But with delegated speech writing a fact of life, widespread circulation is a partial guarantee to a busy president that a foolish mistake will be caught. Even so, the widespread editing of speeches is a mixed blessing. Mistakes are found, but an enormous amount of gatekeeping can dilute rather than enhance a message.

A further problem with speeches that have been widely circulated is that presidential commitments to new ideas often seem to become diluted. Presidents do not seem to be immune from the "group think" phenomenon described by Irving Janis and others (1972). Janis has noted that one common outcome of group attempts at problem solving is that solutions tend to evolve out of the middle ground of ideas accepted by the largest number. In the process of finding an acceptable solution to all, the creative fringes tend to get ignored. As George Reedy (1970, 91–98) documented with regard to the Johnson administration's Vietnam policy, the deviant edges of individual opinion on what to do were frequently abandoned as the risk of holding them became greater. There was strong pressure to go along with the administration's ill-fated support for a military victory. Speeches are captive to this same kind of logic. The rhetorical equivalent to "group think" can be prose that offers offense to no one, and is easily forgotten.

Ghostwriting and Accountability

The equating of who we are with what we say is a basic article of faith in human relations. Oral language is rightfully thought to be "a fingerprint of the man" (Weaver 1953, 9). In ordinary life we can justifiably assume that cues to the inner person's dreams, values, and beliefs linger just under the transparent surface of speech. Prejudiced persons, for example, will probably betray their views in their choice of language and patterns of thought that are not easy to conceal. But political language is not like everyday discourse. It is more carefully constructed. It carries the burden of speaking for many rather than one or a few. And it obviously shares many of the same mixed signals common to other messages that are also "ghosted" by professionals, including advertising, popular biography, corporate reports, and endless forms of similar public relations activities. Ironically, we remain suspicious of politicians who use professional writers to help craft their messages, but we show no similar concern for the fact that corporations and organizations hire advertising agencies and public relations firms to shape their own identities.

Even so, the essential dilemma of ghostwriting remains. Few Americans would quarrel with Ernest Bormann (1960) when he notes that if an audience is to truly "know" a speaker by what he says,

> then he must be honest with them and present himself as he really is. When he reads a speech that reveals to his audience a quiet humor, an urbane worldliness, subtle and incisive intellectual equipment, then he should be that kind of man. If his collaborators . . . are responsible for the "image" revealed in the speech, and if the speaker has different qualities and intellectual fiber, the speech is a deceit and it can be labeled as ghostwritten and condemned as unethical. (p. 267)

Bormann raises the nub of the ghostwriting issue; there is little doubt that a person can conceal his or her identity behind a facade of rhetoric carefully constructed by someone else (288). But Bormann's determination of what is deceitful rarely looks so simple. Among many complications that arise, for example, is the realization that individuals may construct their own deceitful rhetoric without ever resorting to the help of ghostwriters. Novelists and psychologists have long demonstrated that we are all truly authors of many personal identities. Life requires a series of managed "performances" that grow out of our desire to construct personas we want others to accept. Harry Truman (1955) noted that "almost every presidential message is a complicated business" (36). But everyday communication is not necessarily simpler, especially when we take into account the resourceful techniques of "impression management" that are part of the survival skills of ordinary life.

This view that ghostwriting is not so far removed from the routines of most forms of communication is not widely accepted. Resistance to it stems from two broad assumptions that we believe apply less and less to modern executives. One is that the president—like other public figures in politics, religion, and business—is engaged in a form of communication that aspires to a kind of visionary rhetoric, with the appropriate aesthetic components that are part of other forms of timeless utterance. In this view presidential rhetoric must not only communicate information and attitude; it is also expected to provide a visceral feeling of pleasure, stateliness, and grace. The problem, of course, is that a committee consisting of a group of writers cannot usually write monuments of English prose. The more pens on the paper, the less unified and elegant the style. The entire process of clearing or "staffing" a speech has the effect of breaking down its potential unity and style. Whatever their value as documents of state, today's remarks are usually pale imitations of better attempts written by great presidential orators such as Lincoln, Wilson, and Theodore Roosevelt. "Style may be the man," Bormann (1960) notes, "but when that style is five men, it ceases to be any style at all" (288).

This loss of visionary grace flows from the fact that, since the end of World War II, political rhetoric has been homogenized. John Kennedy and Ronald Reagan perhaps rediscovered what used to be called "the grand style" in their campaign and inaugural addresses, but arguably more in the fleeting drama of the moment than as sustained expressions of a personal rhetorical style. For example, the most lauded phrase in the Kennedy-Sorensen inaugural was the famous "Ask not what your country can do for you, ask what you can do for your country." But even this seemingly eloquent balanced phrase was a deceit; it was actually at odds with the new administration's brand of activist federalism. Kennedy wanted his government to do more for individuals, not less.

Today, style is an after-the-fact consideration for what is often a rhetoric concerned primarily with the amplification of administrative policy. What was once a common form of ceremonial oratory is now used more and more to support specific political policy objectives. Where Lincoln could construct what was essentially a poem to the dead at Gettysburg—noting the anguish and human sacrifice necessary to preserve the Union—a modern president more regularly lives by his wits as a tactician defending specific policy goals. To be sure, the elements of celebration, eulogy, and effusive hyperbole have not disappeared from the presidency. Indeed, they were revived by Ronald Reagan's fondness for homilies to America's virtue and "spiritual values." But in comparison to the Lincoln, Wilson, or Roosevelt eras, little of what is said today will become part of the nation's oral literature. The ideas of a single great statesman have gradually but consistently lost ground to the policy defenses of an administration. As such, this applied rhetoric invites the contributions and involvement of alliances and groups frequently represented by ghostwriters. A pluralism of viewpoints in, means a pluralism of viewpoints out. A president today speaks not only for himself and his party, but for an enormous bureaucracy with diverse constituencies and obligations. The result is a rhetoric that is more corporate than individualistic, and one that seeks to cast a wider net in which to capture temporary allegiances.

This is not to say that presidential speeches are devoid of style. Rather, the style that remains is less a matter of the accidents of a president's biography and more the product of the calculations of professionals. Much like characters appearing week after week in a television series, presidents must now bring to their roles specific sets of traits and predispositions that cannot be abandoned by those who help script their performances. The rise of radio after 1920 especially required collaboration with professional writers in scripting a consistent political persona. In place of oratory intended for one audience in a large hall, the radio address was intended to reach listeners with a new in-the-room intimacy that required issues of state to be discussed as if in a conversation. Radio dictated that Americans would pay less attention to the hall-filling thunder of a William Jennings Bryan and more attention to the calculated ease of Will Rogers. Along with television some 20 years later, radio became a new form of theater that politicians would have to learn to share. Like actors moving from the stage to the studio, they too would have to master the illusions of spontaneity and intimacy, but within the bounds of what were essentially performances scripted by writers with an ear for dialogue.

Franklin Roosevelt was especially attuned to radio's potential. To the surprise of many of his listeners, he read his "fireside chats." Such was the illusion provided by his skills that these radio addresses presented a seamless cloth of exposition made from the individual threads of many. With the help of Grace Tully, Raymond Moley, and Samuel Rosenman, he introduced and nearly perfected a dialogue within a monologue, the scripted conversation as a means of political persuasions.

A second assumption also leads to a suspicion about the influence and acceptability of ghostwriters. It is that if a president is not the author of his remarks, his commitment to them is indeterminant. In some ways it is easy to see why it might be believed that ghostwritten statements inherently carry less weight for a leader than those he utters under the power of his own creativity. Michael Medved (1979), once a speechwriter for a senate candidate, recalled his own feeling of awe in writing words someone else would ultimately have to be responsible for:

> I had been given the authority to issue statements in his name through our press office even if he had never seen the material before its release. It was an eerie feeling to read in the newspapers "the candidate said today . . ." and to know that all the press was really reporting were words that a totally obscure . . . aide had put into the candidate's mouth. (4)

How committed could any politician be under a similar situation, if asked to defend positions put forth by an inexperienced subordinate? Surely common sense tells us that ghostwritten remarks carry a broken and dangerously obscured line of responsibility.

But what would seem to be the case often is not. National politicians are in fact very loyal to both their staffs, and staff decisions taken in their name. None of the numerous memoirs cited in this chapter, for example, provide evidence that writers misdirected the intention of a president in any significant way. To the contrary, most presidents have been somewhat reluctant to give full credit to their writers, not only for the best of their efforts but also for their worst rhetorical moments. Whatever doubts exist prior to a decision, once it is consummated by a public remark, presidents as least outwardly assume Harry Truman's dictum that "the buck stops here."

The key to this readiness to accept responsibility lies in the fact that ghostwriters are really subordinate collaborators, rather than independent authors. It is easy to overlook this middle ground and assume that presidents are essentially the captives of someone else's script. But there is no reason to believe that they are other than a free agents, fully able to decide what they will and will not say. The decision to choose to utter remarks prepared largely by someone else carries with it the full obligations of authorship. In various ways every president has signaled his adherence to this commitment. Eisenhower (1963), for example, in a barely veiled attempt to say that every speech was at least partially his own, reminded the readers of his memoirs that "I have never been able to accept a draft of a suggested talk from anyone else and deliver it intact as my own" (60). Even if the imprint of the president was minor and largely cosmetic, the superficial changes essentially made the speech his. Truman (1955) was also sensitive to this burden, noting that, regardless of who wrote the drafts of a speech, "The final version . . . is the final word of the President himself, expressing his own convictions and his own policy. These he cannot delegate to any man if he would be President in his own right" (36).

Whether the result of a corporate psychology, or a desire to seem to be at the center of all White House activities, taking responsibility for speeches is a source of personal pride. A clearly weak speech will be rejected, an occurrence frequently known to writers for Kennedy, Johnson, and Nixon. Other presidents have protected themselves by becoming skillful at improvising from the podium. What is used, therefore, reflects what a president authentically endorses, even if the wording of the ideas strays from their own personal idiom. "When the President walks to the podium with that black ring-binder notebook," noted LBJ aide Ben Wattenberg, "it doesn't make a damn bit of difference who wrote what paragraph—it's his speech. The speechwriter is a creature of the President, not the other way around" (Devlin 1971, 9).

Ghostwriting is thus a peculiar activity. Functioning as editors rather than true writers of their own prose, presidents have been forced to treat speeches as documents: more reflective of the joint decisions of an administration and less revealing of the inner person. But is is equally apparent that presidential rhetoric has not been rendered meaningless by the fact of ghostwriting. Writers are an adjunct to the executive, not a replacement for him. Anyone who has traveled so far and so successfully through the minefield of public life should rightly carry the presumption of full accountability. As Emmet Hughes (1972) has noted, the only politically meaningful fact is not what the aide writes, but what the president says. The former may give important inflections to the latter. But the only decision of political moment belongs, wholly and unqualifiedly, to the president. Whatever he publicly declares is profoundly his.

Richard Perloff (1998) thinks presidential oratory is important. But what is the impact of presidential discourse? Does it work? In attempting to answer these pragmatic questions, he observes:

- Presidential speeches do not always increase public support for the president.
- Presidential rhetoric is unlikely to influence public opinion if the president fails to make a clear and convincing case for the policy recommendations, and if the rhetoric is inconsistent with the chief executive's public image.
- Presidential rhetoric will fail if it does not mobilize elite members of the president's political party.
- Presidential oratory can change political cognitions.
- Presidential speeches can influence people's feelings and attitudes.
- Rhetoric can help a president hold together a fragile political coalition.
- Rhetoric helps to preserve the institution of the presidency.
- Presidential rhetoric can change the nature of public discourse.

- Rhetoric can influence public policy by mobilizing powerful interest groups and by capitalizing on favorable press coverage. (129–33)

CONCLUSION

The American presidency is a center of ever-accumulating functions, roles, obligations, and expectations. It is a universe unto itself that is constantly growing and expanding. From a distance one only notices singular "planets." But closer observation reveals a strong interdependence of the planets. As an individual interacts with the constitutionality of the office, roles develop. These roles not only constrain individual behavior but also help create expectations of specified behavior. As expectations grow, so does the job. The public's perceptions of the office are institutionalized into models, myths, history, and textbooks. Unrealistic demands and expectations produce reliance upon style over substance; image over issues. A president must appear active, moral, fair, intelligent, common, and so on. But appearances are deceiving and paradoxical. For how can one be both active and passive, common and uncommon, impotent and powerful?

Such ambiguity attests to the symbolic nature of the presidency. As an institution the presidency is synthetic, believable, passive, vivid, simplified, and ambiguous. The office is our symbol of justice, freedom, equality, continuity, and national grandeur. The presidency is itself a significant symbol, comprised of many levels and elements. The institution reflects the beliefs, attitudes, and values of the public that have already been established through socialization. All occupants, therefore, must demonstrate that they possess the perceived qualities of the office. Presidential authority is largely a matter of impression management. Presidents run and lead through a variety of communication activities and behaviors.

REFERENCES

Ansolabehere, Stephen et al. 1993. *The Media Game*. New York: Macmillan.

Barilleaux, Ryan. 1988. *The Post-Modern Presidency*. New York: Praeger.

Boorstin, Daniel. 1962. *The Image*. New York: Atheneum.

Bormann, Ernest G. 1960. "Ghostwriting and Rhetorical Critic." *Quarterly Journal of Speech* (October): 288.

Buchanan, Bruce. 1978. *The Presidential Experience*. Englewood Cliffs, NJ: Prentice-Hall.

Carter, Jimmy. 1982. *Keeping Faith*. New York: Bantam Books.

Cathcart, Robert, and Gary Gumpert. 1983. "Mediated Interpersonal Communication: Toward a New Typology." *Quarterly Journal of Speech* 69: 267–77.

Ceaser, James et al. 1983. "The Rise of the Rhetorical Presidency." In *Essays in Presidential Rhetoric*, ed. Theodore Windt. Dubuque, IA: Kendall/Hunt.

Cook, Timothy. 1998. *Governing with the News*. Chicago: University of Chicago Press.

Cornwell, Elmer E., Jr. 1965. *Presidential Leadership of Public Opinion*. Bloomington: Indiana University.

Corwin, Edward S. 1948. *The President: Office and Powers*, 3d ed. New York: New York University Press.

Cronin, Thomas. 1974. "The Presidency Public Relations Script." In *The Presidency Reappraised*, ed. Rexford Tugwell and Thomas E. Cronin. New York: Praeger.

———. 1975. *The State of the Presidency*. Boston: Little, Brown.

deGrazia, Alfred. 1969. "The Myth of the President." In *The Presidency*, ed. Aaron Wildavsky. Boston: Little, Brown.

Denton, Robert E., Jr., and Rachel L. Holloway. 1995. "Presidential Communication as Mediated Conversation: Interpersonal Talk as Presidential Discourse." In *Research in Political Sociology*, vol. 7. New York: JAI Press, pp. 91–115.

———. 1996. "Clinton and the Town Hall Meetings: Mediated Conversation and the Risk of Being 'In Touch.' " In *The Clinton Presidency: Images, Issues, and Communication Strategies*, ed. Robert E. Denton, Jr., and Rachel Holloway. Westport, CT: Praeger, pp. 17–42.

Devlin, Patrick. 1971. *Contemporary Political Speaking*. Belmont, CA: Wadsworth, 1971.

Easton, David. 1965. *A Systems Analysis of Political Life*. New York: John Wiley and Sons.

Easton, David, and Robert Hess. 1962. "The Child's Political World." *Midwest Journal of Political Science* 3 (August): 229–46.

Edelman, Murray. 1964. *The Symbolic Uses of Politics*. Urbana: University of Illinois Press.

———. 1971. *Politics as Symbolic Action*. Chicago: Markham Publishing.

———. 1974. "The Politics of Persuasion." In *Choosing the President*, ed. James D. Barber. Englewood Cliffs, NJ: Prentice-Hall.

Edwards, George. 1983. *The Public Presidency*. New York: St. Martin's Press.

Eisenhower, Dwight. D. 1963. *Mandate for Change, 1953–1956*. New York: Doubleday.

Fisher, Walter. 1982. "Romantic Democracy, Ronald Reagan, and Presidential Heroes." *The Western Journal of Speech Communication* 46 (Summer 1982): 299–310.

Ford, Gerald R. 1979, *A Time to Heal*. New York: Harper & Row/Reader's Digest.

Gallup Report. 1989. 280 (January).

Graber, Doris. 1972. "Personal Qualities in Presidential Images: The Contribution of the Press." *Midwest Journal of Political Science* 16 (February): 142–55.

Greenstein, Fred. 1969. "What the President Means to Americans" and "Popular Images of the President." In *The Presidency*, ed. Aaron Wildavsky. Boston: Little, Brown, pp. 121–47, 287–95.

Grossman, Michael, and Martha Kumar. 1981. *Portraying the President: The White House and the News Media*. Baltimore: Johns Hopkins University Press.

Hart, Roderick. 1984. *Verbal Style and the Presidency*. New York: Academic Press.

———. 1987. *Sounds of Leadership*. Chicago: University of Chicago Press.

———. 1994. *Seducing America*. New York: Oxford University Press.

Herzik, Eric. 1985. "The President, Governors and Mayors: A Framework for Comparative Analysis." *Presidential Studies Quarterly* 15(2): 354.

Herzik, Eric, and Mary Dodson. 1982. "The President and Public Expectations: A Research Note." *Presidential Studies Quarterly* 12 (Spring): 168–73.

Hughes, Emmet J. 1972. *The Living Presidency*. New York: Penguin Books.

Jamieson, Kathleen H. 1988. *Eloquence in the Electronic Age*. New York: Oxford University Press.

Janis, Irving. 1972. *Victims of Groupthink*. Boston: Houghton Mifflin.

Johnston, David. 1988. "Speakes Says He Told Reagan of Bogus Quotes, but Later." *New York Times*, 19 April: A29.

Kellerman, Barbara. 1984. *The Political Presidency*. New York: Oxford University Press.

Klapp, Orrin. 1964. *Symbolic Leaders*. Chicago: Aldine Publishing.

Lasky, Victor. 1979. *Jimmy Carter: The Man and the Myth*. New York: Richard Marek.

Lasswell, Harold. 1930. *Psychopathology and Politics*. Chicago: University of Chicago Press.

Lowi, Theodore J. 1985. *The Personal President: Power Invested, Promise Unfulfilled*. Ithaca, NY: Cornell University Press.

Maltese, John. 1992. *Spin Control*. Chapel Hill: University of North Carolina Press.

McConnell, Grant. 1976. *The Modern Presidency*. New York: St. Martin's Press.

Medved, Michael. 1979. *The Shadow Presidents*. New York: Times Books.

Moore, Raymond. 1988. "The Constitution, the Presidency and 1988." *Presidential Studies Quarterly* 18(1): 55–61.

Nimmo, Dan. 1970. *The Political Persuaders*. Englewood Cliffs, NJ: Spectrum Books.

———. 1978. *Political Communication and Public Opinion in America*. Palo Alto, CA: Goodyear.

Novak, Michael. 1974. *Choosing Our King*. New York: Macmillan.

Perloff, Richard. 1998. *Political Communication*. Mahwah, NJ: Lawrence Earlbaum.

Pfau, Michael. 1990. "A Channel Approach to Television Influence." *Journal of Broadcasting and Electronic Media* 34: 195–214.

Pfau, Michael et al. 1993. "Relational and Competence Perceptions of Presidential Candidates during the Primary Election Campaigns." Paper presented at the International Communication Association Convention, Washington, DC, May.

Pious, Richard. 1979. *The American Presidency*. New York: Basic Books.

Reedy, George. 1970. *The Twilight of the Presidency*. New York: World.

Rockman, Bert. 1984. *The Leadership Question*. New York: Praeger.

Rose, Richard. 1970. *People in Politics: Observations Across the Atlantic*. New York: Basic Books.

Rossiter, Clinton. 1962. *The American Presidency*. New York: Mentor Books.

Sanoff, Alvin. 1982. "A Conversation with Theodore H. White." *U.S. News and World Report*, 5 July: 59.

Simon, Dennis, and Charles Ostrom. 1988. "The Politics of Prestige: Popular Support and the Modern Presidency." *Presidential Studies Quarterly* 18(4): 742–55.

Smith, Carolyn. 1990. *Presidential Press Conferences*. Westport, CT: Praeger.
Smith, Craig A., and Kathy Smith. 1994. *The White House Speaks*. Westport, CT: Praeger.
Smoller, Fredric. 1990. *The Six O'Clock Presidency*. New York: Praeger.
Sorensen, Theodore. 1965. *Kennedy*. New York: Harper & Row.
———. 1984. *A Different Kind of Presidency*. New York: Harper & Row.
Truman, Harry S. 1955. *Memoirs: Years of Decisions*. Garden City, NY: Doubleday.
Weaver, Richard. 1953. *The Ethics of Rhetoric*. Chicago: Henry Regnery.
White, Theodore H. 1975. *Breach of Faith*. New York: Atheneum.
Wooten, James. 1978. *Dasher: The Roots and Rising of Jimmy Carter*. New York: Warner Books.

Chapter 9

The Congress

> Congress is a verbal culture . . .
>
> Harrison Fox and Susan Hammond (1997)

If, as the phrase goes, "politics is theater," then the activities of Congress represent something approaching grand opera. Its 535 members in the Senate and the House are at the center of American political culture, functioning much like two companies competing for our favor in an endless ten-month season. The repertory they offer rarely strays from the familiar sagas of conflict and revenge, posturing and conciliation. But the cast often changes, with new superstars taking leading roles in the legislative process, all supported by talented assistants, aides and writers operating in the wings. And like the typical opera house, the outsized stories acted on the stage are matched by similar struggles behind the scenes. Supported by four "insider" newspapers that feed an insatiable thirst for news of who is in or out of favor, Capitol Hill can seem like a world unto itself.

Arguably, no political institution in American life so clearly represents the strengths and weaknesses of American democratic processes because representatives must master so many of the political arts. In a routine day a senator or representative may meet with ordinary constituents in the morning, lunch with a lobbyist at noontime, question an expert witness in an afternoon meeting of a House or Senate committee, and receive an evening phone call from a cabinet official soliciting support on a close upcoming vote. In between these events he or she may consult with a dozen colleagues, plan strategy on the introduction of a piece of legislation, tape a radio report to constituents back home, and review the schedule for a busy weekend of campaigning.

Congressional life is primarily about talk. The member is both the object and source of it. Legislating is an endless round of exchanges in which information or support is sought from colleagues, the press, constituents, and interest groups. The currency of legislative life is communication with staff members, constituents, and peers (see Figure 9.1).

This chapter examines some of the major relationships and communications processes that characterize the modern Congress. While our primary focus is on the national legislature, much of what we note also applies to legislators in the states. Members of state assemblies and senates, as well as those serving in city councils, share many of the same processes and institutional obligations. Like their federal colleagues, they must learn to work as one among many, conceding power in most settings, and sometimes winning it back by forming alliances, gaining important committee assignments, and getting the attention of the mass media on issues about which they feel deeply.

LEGISLATIVE AND COMMUNICATION FUNCTIONS

Legislatures have two primary functions: to provide oversight in the administration of the government, and to pass laws. These two objectives are naturally related. The oversight of governmental operations—which today takes in nearly every facet of American life—includes the study of how agencies and commissions enforce laws or carry out administrative or court-mandated decisions. In the textbook model of such oversight, hearings and information from various committees and support units such as the Congressional Budget Office produce modifications or repeal of existing laws. Such hearings also serve an "educational" function, providing the committee with the opportunity to orchestrate public opinion as a prerequisite to the introduction of legislation or as a counterweight to the president.

On some occasions committee oversight of particular agencies or businesses consumes the attention of the entire Congress. The resulting publicity may create public pressure for change, as in the 1994 hearings of a House subcommittee in which tobacco executives were asked to defend the safety of their products (see Figure 9.2). Their denials of charges that they manipulated levels of nicotine in cigarettes helped feed new calls for the regulation of tobacco (Hilts 1994, A1, A20). At other times oversight may entail the more sensitive issue of an alleged breach of ethics by a member, such as the 1995 Senate inquiry into charges of sexual harassment by Oregon's Robert Packwood (Salant 1995, 1982).

The legislative function is equally complex, although the basic procedures and traditions are well known. Bills are introduced by members,

Figure 9.1
A Member's Schedule for Two Days in the House of Representatives

This schedule is for David Price, who represents North Carolina's Fourth District. A Democrat in an increasingly Republican state, Price lost his seat to a challenger in 1994 and won it back again in 1996.

	Wednesday, April 10, 1991
8:00 A.M.	Budget Study Group—Chairman Leon Panetta, Budget Committee, room 340 Cannon Building
8:45 A.M.	Mainstream Forum Meeting, room 2344 Rayburn Building
9:15 A.M.	Meeting with Consulting Engineers Council of N.C. from Raleigh about various issues of concern
9:45 A.M.	Meet with N.C. Soybean Assn. representatives re: agriculture appropriations projects
10:15 A.M.	WCHL radio interview (by phone)
10:30 A.M.	Tape weekly radio show—budget
11:00 A.M.	Meet with former student, now an author, about intellectual property issue
1:00 P.M.	Agriculture Subcommittee Hearing—Budget Overview and General Agriculture Outlook, room 2362 Rayburn Building
2:30 P.M.	Meeting with Chairman Bill Ford and southern Democrats re: HR-5, Striker Replacement Bill, possible amendments
3:15 P.M.	Meeting with Close-Up students from district on steps of Capitol for photo and discussions
3:45 P.M.	Meeting with Duke professor re: energy research programs
4:30 P.M.	Meet with constituent of Kurdish background re: situation in Iraq
5:30–7:00 P.M.	Reception—sponsored by National Assn. of Home Builders, honoring new president Mark Tipton from Raleigh, H-328 Capitol
6:00–8:00 P.M.	Reception–honoring retiring Rep. Bill Gray, Washington Court Hotel
6:00–8:00 P.M.	Reception—sponsored by Firefighters Assn., room B-339 Rayburn Building
6:00–8:00 P.M.	Reception—American Financial Services Assn., Gold Room

	Thursday, April 11, 1991
8:00 A.M.	Prayer Breakfast—Rep. Charles Taylor to speak, room H-130 Capitol
9:00 A.M.	Whip meeting, room H-324 Capitol
10:00 A.M.	Democratic Caucus Meeting, Hall of the House, re: budget
10:25 A.M.	UNISYS reps. in office (staff, DP meets briefly)
10:30 A.M.	Firefighters from Raleigh re: Hatch Act Reform, Manufacturer's Presumptive Liability, etc.

Figure 9.1 (continued)

11:00 A.M.	American Business Council of the Gulf Countries re: rebuilding the Gulf, improving competitiveness in Gulf market
11:15 A.M.	Whip Task Force meeting re: Budget Resolution, room H-114 Capitol
12:00 P.M.	Speech—One minute on House floor re: budget
12:30 P.M.	Party Effectiveness Lunch—re: banking reform, room H-324 Capitol
1:00 P.M.	Agriculture Subcommittee Hearing—Inspector General Overview and the Office of the General Counsel, room 2362 Rayburn Building
3:00 P.M.	Testify at Oceanography Subcommittee hearing re: naval vessel waste disposal on N.C. Outer Banks, room 1334 Longworth Building
3:30 P.M.	Speak to Duke public policy students re: operations of Congress, room 188 Russell Building
5:00 P.M.	Interview with Mathew Cross, WUNC stringer re: offshore drilling
6:45 P.M.	Depart National Airport for Raleigh-Durham

Source: David E. Price, *The Congressional Experience* (Boulder, CO: Westview Press, 1992), p. 38.

usually because they have a special interest in the subject, or because the legislation meets the needs of an important constituency. In what is usually a proposal's first test, it is routed to an appropriate committee according to what are sometimes unclear jurisdictional lines. The committee holds hearings, "marks up" the bill, votes it out to the floor, votes it down, or simply lets it die (as most do). A bill reported out of the committee is considered by the whole body, usually reshaped by key amendments, and voted on. It, or one similar to it, is considered by the other house and likewise voted on. Then differences between the two passed versions are worked out in a conference committee composed of a limited number of members from both the lower and upper houses. It then receives another vote in each house before it is forwarded to the president for signature or a veto.

Few bills actually move through the Congress in such a straight sequence. Most are tabled, defeated, and amended in what is often a multiyear process. Final passage often comes only after repeated attempts over several sessions. When a bill is passed, it is usually far different from what its initial sponsors had in mind. Its adoption occurs only after a good deal of private bargaining and carefully negotiated compromises between party leaders and the president on key provisions. In all of this process a vigorous floor debate before well-attended sessions may never

Figure 9.2
Anatomy of a Hearing: Tobacco Executives Testify Before Congress

On April 13, 1994, the House Commerce Subcommittee on Health asked top executives representing the nation's seven tobacco companies to testify. Each appeared and was sworn in, beginning a process that one executive described as a hostile kind of political theatre. Over six hours of testimony was taken, much of it involving heated exchanges between the executives and the committee chair, Representative Harry Waxman. Waxman's opposition to the tobacco industry is well known. The hearings were intended to dramatize a mountain of accumulated evidence demonstrating that nicotine in tobacco is addictive, and that smoking represents a significant health risk. Each was asked in turn if he thought nicotine was addictive, and each denied it, producing a stunning image of industry-wide denial that has been replayed in countless reports on smoking and health. The event, summarized below, is a dramatic example of the power of committee chairs and members to promote issues well beyond specific lawmaking objectives.

Health Subcommittee of House Energy and Commerce Committee

Formal goal of the hearings: Fact finding on industry practices, with the option to propose legislation or direct the Food and Drug Administration to review its own regulatory practices.

Political Context: Committee hearings are arranged by the Democratic majority, and its Chair, known as a foe of the tobacco industry. Recent media reports had also indicated that some companies seemed to adjust nicotine levels in cigarettes to increase their addictive power. The industry was also beginning to lose allies in Congress, and the states and public health groups stepped up their efforts to demonstrate the health-related costs of cigarette use. By 1996, the industry would be in full retreat, seeking to make generous cash settlements with a number of states for health care costs.

Sample Testimony

Representative Harry Waxman questions James W. Johnson, CEO of the American Tobacco Co.

Q: How many smokers die each year from cancer?

A: I do not know how many . . .

Q: Does smoking cause heart disease?

A: It may.

Q: Emphysema?

A: It may.

Sample Statements from Committee Members

Representative John Bryant read a letter from a Florida woman describing the death of her father from emphysema. "His death was not the bad part. His life was the real horror."

Representative Mike Kreidler tells a story of his father, who died of emphysema in a nursing home. "You know, it would be hard for me to imagine that there's one of you gentlemen sitting here that has ever witnessed something like that. It's progressive. It just goes until you die. You can't breathe any breath."

Media Coverage (selected)

New York Times, p. 1

ABC Evening News, first story after lead (2 mins., 30 secs.)

CBS Evening News, 2nd story after lead (2 mins.)

NBC Evening News, lead story (2 mins., 50 secs.)

Covered live by CNN and C-SPAN

Sources: Vanderbilt News Archive, News Abstracts of the Networks, 13 April 1994; Michael Wines, "Makers of Laws and Tobacco Joust," *The New York Times*, 15 April 1994, p. A20.; Philip J. Hilts, "Tobacco Chiefs Say Cigarettes Aren't Addictive," *The New York Times*, 15 April 1994, pp. A1, A20.

have occurred. But that is not to say that the legislative cycle does not involve a good deal of debate and discussion. The most widely reported summaries of the merits of bills are constructed by the news media out of the variegated fabric of press statements made by interested parties during hearings in committees and from pre-session publicity generated by lobbyists and others with financial or ideological stakes in the legislation.

What emerges as central to the heart of congressional communication is the vital role played by the standing committees and subcommittees. Most of the 15,000 or so bills that are introduced in a session of Congress, for example, will never be passed, but some may still get an initial hearing in a committee concerned with hunger, airline safety, terrorism, industry practices, medical insurance, monetary policy, and thousands of other concerns. Both houses must approve all bills that become law, although measures that raise funds must originate in the House. The task of passing on high-level presidential appointees to agencies and federal courts goes to committees in the Senate.

Committees are a primary source of rhetorical and legislative work. The Senate has 20 regular standing committees, with scores of subcommittees. The number is similar for the House. As a member of the Senate's prestigious Foreign Relations Committee, or the House's Appropriations Committee, a member gets an opportunity to become one of a limited number of voices in the discussion of vital national interests.[1] In the case of the Appropriations Committee, as in most others, power flows downward to members who sit on key subcommittees (i.e. Transportation, National Security, Interior, District of Columbia, Transportation, and so on).

THE BUILT-IN DILEMMAS OF LEGISLATIVE COMMUNICATION

From a communications standpoint legislatures present their occupants with a series of troubling limitations. Except for a few select leaders in the House and Senate—notably the Speaker, the minority leader, majority leader, and a handful of committee chairs—the individual member is usually subordinate to the power of others. There are a number of reasons for this. One is simply a result of the large group involved. Any topic of general public interest creates heavy competition for the change to be heard by a wider public. In the search for "opinion in the Senate" or "the sense of the House" a key leader is likely to be sought out by the press more than a less powerful member. More likely, editors and television producers are inclined to seek the unitary voice of the president rather than the less definitive statements of a congressional partisan.

A second problem is that members must consistently change the focus of their attention, and often their votes as well. This makes them agents of negotiation as much as agents of ideas, something the press finds difficult to track. A corporate president speaks for the corporation; a union leader speaks for the membership. Even the president is accepted as a figure who strives to speak for the nation as a whole. Such reductions are psychologically satisfying because they give frequently incomprehensible institutions a personal voice and a human face. But who does the member of the Congress speak for? What formal and official structure is symbolized in his or her communication?

There is no simple answer because legislative roles are so varied, and because deliberative bodies were set up to make representation intentionally diffuse. Every new legislative and oversight demand subtly shifts the meaning of a member's actions. A party that is abandoned on one vote may be embraced on another. A bipartisan coalition urging a particular health care program in one session may be hopelessly split when the issue arises again in the next session. And so it goes. The organized defenses of governors or presidents seem more hierarchical and orderly. As several observers of congressional press coverage note, "Searching for a single voice beggars the media. Covering all the conflicting subcommittees' and committees' mark up sessions, overlapping hearings, the floor deliberations, is an expensive proposition" (Paletz and Entman 1981, 80). Most journalists simply do not do it, or merely graft a reference to congressional debate onto a report centered on the more personalized presidency.

A third limitation is that party discipline in modern Congresses is uneven and often unreliable. Part of what has changed from the "old" hierarchical Congress is that members see independence as both a necessity and an advantage. In the age of the well-bankrolled congressional candidate, the professional political consultant, and the heavy dependency on television campaigning, there is less and less dependency on party organization. Members are less inclined than their predecessors to wait to be selected as advocates for party-sanctioned causes. They are more apt to take advantage of communications opportunities as they come. "People get elected right off the street," lamented a Massachusetts congressman. "They don't have any political loyalties or i.o.u.'s" (Roberts 1979, A20).

This pattern has it exceptions as the well-disciplined GOP Congress of 1995 illustrated. After elections that gave control of Congress to the Republicans, the new Speaker of the House, Newt Gingrich, was effective for some time in producing a more hierarchical party structure, with members willing to buy into an ambitious legislative agenda set by the forceful new Speaker. But by 1996 Gingrich had clearly lost some of his ability to organize GOP members for party-based legislation initiatives, especially after several disastrous showdowns with President Clinton over issues of federal spending.

A fourth problem facing all legislatures is that their structure generally casts their members into reactive rather than proactive roles. In the popular aphorism, the president proposes, and the Congress disposes. Presidential leadership in the setting of major legislative objectives became commonplace during the New Deal, with the flood of economic recovery initiatives introduced by Franklin Roosevelt. It remains true today, though there are periods—notably in 1994 and 1995—when the congressional leadership can take some of the legislative initiative away from the president.[2]

The presidency provides an endless range of opportunities for its occupants to take bold initiatives, propose necessary actions, and generate what appear to be innovative forms of legislation. A member of Congress may be equally bold in proposing solutions, but the member's efforts will occur in what is, comparatively speaking, a publicity vacuum. Ultimately, he or she is left with the necessity to deal with initiatives of the White House. This fact itself does not represent a flaw in the organization of deliberative bodies. After all, parliamentary democracies are supposed to examine and weigh the consequences of proposed legislation. But the reactive nature of the Congress naturally mitigates whatever sympathies Americans may be inclined to have toward it. There are several reasons for this.

One is that Americans generally expect that legislatures will cooperate with executives, that members will not use partisan differences as bases from which to fight a popular leader. Presidents exploit this presumption repeatedly, as Harry Truman did in his famous diatribes against the "do nothing" Congress in 1948, or as Bill Clinton did against the GOP Congress which shut down government operations twice in 1996. Another reason legislators are handicapped is that they must be more cautious and more deferential to an executive than the executive must be to them. The potent symbolism behind a single head of state works against those who disregard its inherent appeals for unity. Woodrow Wilson's analysis of this aspect of the president's power still seems valid today:

> His is the only voice in affairs. Let him once win the admiration and confidence of the country, and no other single force can withstand him, no combination of forces will easily overpower him. . . . If he rightly interprets the national thought and boldly insists upon it, he is irresistible; and the country never feels the zest of actions so much as when its President is of such insight and caliber. Its instinct is for unified action, and it craves a single leader. It is for this reason that we often prefer to choose a man rather than a party. (Warren 1967, 29)

Perhaps the most interesting communication problem facing the legislator is that reactive and frequently critical communication often has the effect of casting its source as a pessimist, if not a villain. All things being equal, it is easier to take an affirmative position than to hold back and deny the affirmations of someone else. It is more socially useful to seem to be reaching for new solutions and new ideas than to be attacking the proposals of others. To be sure, presidents also play the role of dissenter. They key difference is that they tend to exercise this power more privately. Their surrogates inside and outside the Congress are often the carriers of those objections, leaving the president with a higher rhetorical style. And their vetoes and objections are easily counterbalanced by the celebratory and unifying roles which chief executives customarily play. In 1996, for example, President Clinton vetoed many pieces of legislation submitted to him by the Gingrich-led Congress. But many Americans blamed Congress for these highly publicized moments of impasse, believing that they were more negative and short-sighted than the president (Pew 1996) His vetoes were frequently eclipsed by traditional executive acts of national conciliation that members of Congress could only observe: consoling families of terrorist victims, issuing grants of federal disaster aid, and defending wounded American pride in Japan, Bosnia and elsewhere.

Finally, it should be noted that some facets of legislative life are simply out of fashion today. So much of what goes on in legislative deliberation seems either troublesome to the average citizen or at odds with the needs of modern technology. Except for private constituency service, such as helping a citizen find a lost Social Security check, there appears to be little public admiration for legislative craftsmanship or coalition building. Legislative skill is unlikely to be seen as a special gift. The ability to write and modify legislation or master the politics of interparty and intraparty coalition building are rarely prized in general political reporting, or by the public.

The reasons have to do with the process itself, a process dependent on the mastery of arcane details, skills of negotiation and flexibility, and a patience to move through a legislative timeline that is often too long for modern sensibilities. The mediation that represents the essential work of lawmaking will never fire the ordinary imagination in the same way that a visionary executive can. A president dramatizes the affirmation of universal values and national goals; the Congress carries on the essential but far less attractive task of representing the divisive pluralism of the two-party system.

EXTERNAL AND INTERNAL AUDIENCES

Members of Congress learn to function in two very different communication settings. They must maintain visibility in their own states or districts. At the same they must also work to master the sometimes Byz-

Figure 9.3
The Washington Constituencies of Congress

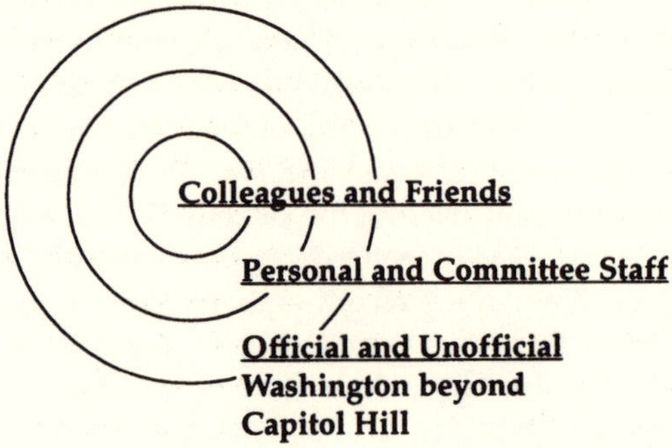

antine complexities of dealing with the internal support system on Capitol Hill. That structure includes an inner ring of colleagues and friends, an increasingly important middle ring of Capitol Hill staffers, and an outer ring of contacts represented by employees in federal agencies, members of the press, and interest group representatives (see Figure 9.3).

Most legislators naturally prefer to work primarily in one of these two arenas, either building support through external appeals or mastering the internal "inside game" of governing. But neither can be totally ignored. Senator Ted Kennedy, for example, has been considered a national resource and a tireless advocate on issues related to health care. In addition, since 1992 he has emerged as national voice for the liberal wing of the party, a segment that has sometimes felt abandoned by President Clinton. By contrast, Alaska's Frank Murkowski has maintained a much lower national profile (Hess 1986, 140–42), preferring instead to gain power through the internal channels of the Senate. If Murkowski is rarely featured in the national media, his position as chairperson of the Senate's Energy and Natural Resources Committee carries obvious importance to the citizens of his home state.

As with all elective politics, the home constituency provides the member's ticket to the capital. A member of the House, for example, can never really afford to think of the District of Columbia as "home" in the way it is for other high-level governmental employees. The congressional district generates a large chunk of the member's workload, particularly in the first few terms of service when the skillful exploitation of incumbency can pave the way for easier reelection. For many members of Congress and most state legislatures, the local constituency is the prime reason for being in politics. Former House Speaker Thomas "Tip" O'Neill's observation that "all politics is local" is a simple reminder that constituents are ignored at a representative's peril. Even if the member's attentions and interests turn increasingly to becoming a national spokesperson on a significant issue, he or she will rarely feel secure enough to neglect constituents back home. Everything else a member undertakes depends upon the building and mending of bridges to the local community. The methods for doing this involve the prime tools of electoral politics: speeches, letters, press interviews, questionnaires, and appearances at countless meetings. Combined with the use of at least one district office, these tools serve to nurture sufficient local support.

But if members of Congress get to Congress by "retailing" their politics to the average voter, success in influencing the political agenda depends upon mastering the considerable structural and rhetorical demands that exist in the capital city.

Internal Channels: Dealing with the Middle Ring

We have described internal communication in Congress as existing in rings moving out from the member, ranging from an inner circle of colleagues and party leaders to an outer circle of Washington lobbyists and others. This latter group is considered in the next chapter. Our focus here is on the middle ring, an increasingly important bureaucracy represented by the members' own staffs and the staffs of their legislative leaders, the committees, and their own party (see Figure 9.4). These nonelected but ambitious professionals are often identified by their age (generally young), their extensive and advanced training as lawyers and academics, and by the fact that they are notoriously overworked and underpaid. Their power flows from the added complexities of legislating in the information age. Members need better information about the complex businesses and activities affected by legislation. Their importance also flows from the fact that these staffers are the gatekeepers of access to the leadership and to vital information "on the Hill."

About 16,000 people are employed by Congress and its 535 members. Another 10,000 work in research and support services, specifically: the Congressional Research Service, the Congressional Budget Office, the Office of Technology Assessment, and the General Accounting Office. Overall, Congress now spends about $2.3 billion in staff salaries and support ("Staff" 1993, 363).

As David Whiteman has documented in his study of the sources of congressional information, mountains of data now flood the committees of Congress as they draft new legislation and weigh its weaknesses and benefits. How many planes should be able to land in one hour at the nation's busiest airports? Should trucks carrying hazardous wastes be permitted to travel through crowded areas at any time of the day? These are typical of problems in search of legislative remedies that succeed or fail depending on the quality of information available. Such issues nec-

Figure 9.4
***Roll Call's* List of the Hill's "Most Powerful Staffers"**

***Roll Call* is a newspaper published for members of Congress and their staffs. Here is a partial 1996 list of staffers who they described as among the most powerful. Notice the diverse range of staff positions they hold. Some work for members, some for committees, and others for parties.**

***Doug Badger*, Staff Director, Senate Republican Policy Committee**

***Mitch Bainwol*, Chief of Staff, Sen. Connie Mack (R-FL)**

***Tony Blankley*, Press Secretary, Speaker of the House**

***Ed Buckham*, Chief of Staff, House Majority Whip**

***M.D.B. Carlisle*, Chief of Staff, Sen. Thad Cochran (R-MS)**

***Alan Coffey*, Majority General Counsel, Staff Director, House Judiciary Committee**

***James English*, Minority Staff Director, House Appropriations Committee**

***David Hobbs*, Policy Coordinator, Floor Assistant, House Majority Leader**

***Jack Howard*, Assistant to the Speaker, Speaker of the House**

***Michael Kinsella*, Administrative Assistant, Sen. Alfonse D'Amato (R-NY)**

***Monica Maples*, Chief of Staff, Rep. Vic Fazio (D-CA)**

***Bob Stevenson*, Majority Communications Director, Senate Budget Committee**

***Mildred Webber*, Staff Director, House Government Reform, National Economic Growth, Natural Resources, and Regulatory Affairs Subcommittee**

***Don Wolfensberger*, Majority Chief of Staff, House Rules Committee**

Source: "Here They Are . . . The Fab Fifty!" *Roll Call Online*, 16 October 1996.

essarily involve background study and, frequently, recommendations from the staffers, policy analysts, and lawyers spread throughout Congress and its research agencies (Whiteman 1995, 60–67). On issues such as tax and banking reform basic information is vital. The sweeping changes in the tax code that occurred in 1986, for example, were largely governed by numbers passed to the House Ways and Means Committee by its own staff of economic technocrats. President Reagan said that the reforms had to be "budget neutral." They could not be seen as tax increases. That left the committee with constraints set down by a popular president and by staff projections on the effects of tax reform on the national budget.

Given the fact that it has thousands of employees, it comes as no surprise that Congress enjoys a good deal of *internal* reporting about its activities. Arguably few organizations have as many chances to view its work through so many media mirrors that reflect it. There are four news organizations that cover Congress for its members and other Washington insiders, including *The Hill* and *Roll Call*, each published in newspaper format twice a week. In addition, *Congressional Quarterly* provides a range of online and magazine-style services, along with *National Journal*. Stories in the first two publications tend to focus more on what one staffer called "the juicy inside stuff" of the institution, for instance: news in which the chief of staff of a Republican opposed to same-sex marriage announced her resignation in order to work for a gay rights group (Henneberger 1997, D13). The latter two services often track progress on the legislative goals of various factions inside and outside Congress. The effect of all this coverage is to portray the culture and norms of the institution to both elected officials, and the thousands more who work for them.

External Channels: The Battle for National Visibility

Members of Congress usually begin their careers with expectations of having a voice in national affairs. The nature of the office at least theoretically gives members a number of opportunities to influence public discussion on a range of issues, especially on subjects relevant to their committee work. They have free mailing privileges, access to radio and television studios paid for in large part by the taxpaying public, access to impressive policy and economic research services, a wealth of standing invitations to speak, and the opportunity to cross-examine the leaders of countless agencies, businesses, and institutions.

In addition, the press has a long and well-institutionalized presence in both houses. Each side has separate galleries for the daily press, the periodical press, and radio and television. Over $1 million is spent by each house to support the needs of journalists (Elving 1994, 186). And each member assigns at least several staffers to handle press relations, which range from producing press releases to feeding sound bites into a machine that serves them up to radio stations back in the district.

Members of the more exclusive Senate have a greater chance to stand out as a resource or partisan voice in various forums of the national news media (i.e., an Op-Ed page of the *New York Times*, NBC's "Meet the Press," "ABC's "Nightline," or PBS's "Newshour") The reality, however, is that the institution and its members are widely believed to be undercovered, especially in light of the enormous number of reporters and staffers committed to making congressional news.

Just how much coverage the House and Senate get is subject to a lot of variables. But most studies tend to agree that coverage of the institution of Congress is generally low, especially in comparison to the president. Steven Waldman's study of the passage of President Clinton's national service bill—better know as AmeriCorps—is somewhat typical. A reporter himself, he documents the generally poor press coverage of the elaborate lobbying campaign to kill or change this program encouraging community service in exchange for college tuition. The press, he notes, "ought to be watching out for whether the political process is serving the public will." But in this case, it did not.

> Having ignored national service most of the year, reporters became briefly attentive during the [Senate] filibuster—conflict! sports metaphors!—and then lost interest again. Hardly a word was spoken or written about the essential issues that would determine the success or failure of the program. (Waldman 1995, 246)

Moreover, when Congress gets detailed coverage of its actions, the coverage is often negative[3] As Stephen Hess has noted, "at the same time that fewer stories about Congress are getting produced, a larger proportion of them are about activities that cast the institution in an unflattering light" (Hess 1994, 149). Reports of investigations of ethical violations by the Speaker of the House and others are now common, as are reports on procedural moves in the Senate that seem to thwart the will of the majority. In Waldman's view, negative coverage proves that a reporter is not "in the tank," not blindly naive about governmental leaders or processes (Waldman 1995, 72).

At an individual level, coverage is somewhat more positive, but it is also heavily skewed toward the House and Senate leadership. One classic study by Michael Robinson indicated that about 75 percent of the members felt that the national mass media paid no attention to them. "The fact is," Robinson noted, "the nationals ignore members and pick on the institution—unless there is a scandal to cover" (1981, 87). Studies of the Senate by Stephen Hess found a similar pattern. In his estimate, only 20 members of that body received most of the news coverage that focused on individuals (Hess 1986, 10).

In terms of publicity for their views, most members of the House and Senate remain—in the British parliamentary phrase—"backbenchers," destined to play supporting roles to other legislative leaders and the more intensely-covered president. Backbenchers are generally loyal to their party, but are subordinate to their leaders, who literally occupy the front seats of the House of Commons. Only the Senate has such a seating arrangement, but both houses still have their backbenchers, many of whom are rarely sought out by the national press.

Many are quite happy with this arrangement. Especially in the House, a large number of members enjoy the security and prestige of their surroundings, and are usually proud of the casework they carry in behalf of their local constituents. If Washington reminds them of their limits as but one member among many, their role as representatives of their districts gives them a compensating sense of accomplishment. As one member of the House told Richard Fenno:

> My lack of confidence is still a pressure which brings me home. I feel I have to come home to get nourished, to see for myself what's going on. It's my security blanket—coming home. (Fenno 1978, 217–18)

Others in Congress lament the tight competition for attention. In a town where egos are often measured in column inches of newsprint, the power to influence others may be closely tied to the importance the press attaches to a legislator's career (Cook 1989, 119–78).

Who gets the coverage? In the recent past high visibility has come to Senate figures like John Glenn (astronaut/Senator), Bob Dole (former majority leader), Ted Kennedy (heir to the family legacy, and effective liberal activist), and Daniel Patrick Moynihan (Hess 1986, 14). These and a few others can be truly called "national" frontbenchers. They differ from backbenchers in that they usually have an opinion-leading function both within the chamber in which they serve and to special interest constituents well beyond the borders of their own state or district. Publicity powers sufficient to influence national debate on a question (i.e., access to television talk shows such as PBS's "Newshour") are sometimes within their grasp.

Moynihan especially illustrates why some members are "good copy" and why many others are deemed less newsworthy. The colorful Irish "pol," former Harvard professor and cabinet official in the administrations of both parties, has served in the Senate for 20 years. Known as the intellectual father of policymaking on welfare reform, he loves to weigh in on the causes of urban decay and its effects on the lives of ordinary citizens. The sum total of these features is the credibility he has as a commentator on an array of urban issues. It does not hurt that he is from media-centered New York and is also a certified character: full of quotable stories and facts and unpredictable in his ascerbic assessments of popular ideas as well as his own party's president. As one writer put it in a flattering *New York Times* profile, Moynihan relishes the fact that he "has become the Grumpy Mayor of America," a national resource who cannot be dismissed in key debates on social policy issues (Purdum 1994, 26).

The political muscle of other members is more predictably based on formal leadership or chairmanship roles. Committee leadership is perhaps still the most certain road to influence in Congress and grudging acceptance by the national press. In the recent history of the Senate, for example, the names of Hubert Humphrey, Russell Long, Lyndon Johnson, Howard Baker, and Robert Dole have become synonymous with effective leadership. Johnson proved to be a master negotiator in the late 1950s as Senate minority leader, managing an uneasy coalition of southern and liberal Democrats, while maintaining good relations with the popular Eisenhower regime at the other end of Pennsylvania Avenue (Miller 1980, 247–48). And as majority leader, Robert Dole salvaged a number of crucial Reagan administration programs, including its controversial support for the Contra rebels who attempted to overthrow the government of Nicaragua. He would be asked to repeat that process—but with less success—nearly 10 years later, after the House leadership

Figure 9.5
Common Communication Channels in Congress: An Overview

There are many ways to describe networks and channels of congressional communication. The list below offers a simple scheme, beginning with vital internal channels and ending with several common external channels.

Channel	Sample Transaction
Internal Channels	
Member to Member	Request for another member to sign on as a co-sponsor of a new piece of legislation.
Member to Office Staff	Request for suggested questions to be asked in Judiciary Committee Hearing to confirm a nominee to a federal judgeship.
Member to Hill Research Staff	Request for information from the Congressional Research Service for data on handgun deaths.
Member to Lobbyist	Request for information from a lobbyist representing a city in the member's district on how a water-quality bill will affect municipal utility costs.
Member to Political Action Committee	Request to director for "participation" (money) in the member's upcoming reelection campaign.
Member to Reporter (not for attribution)	Description of meeting with a White House official to find a legislative compromise. (Story cannot be attributed to the source.)
External Channels	
Member to Reporter (on the record)	Interview to defend or challenge a legislative initiative. (Cannot be attributed to the source.)
Member to Constituent	Letter, drafted by staff, thanking a voter for her concern about using U.S. troops in peacekeeping missions.
Member to Constituents (via Senate television)	Satellite hookup from Senate television studios to NBC affiliate in district for live interview with the local news anchor.

attempted to force the Clinton administration to buy into a number of conservative legislative initiatives.[4]

Communication in Congress can thus be seen as a web of informational and influence networks that link members to each other, congressional support staffs, and to the public via the mass media (see Figure 9.5). Members with an internal orientation seek power by mastering the institutional processes of Congress and by acquiring leadership roles in their own committees. Members who hope to influence public opinion on legislative issues seek external contacts that reach into their states and districts, and sometimes into the national news media.

CONGRESS ON TELEVISION

Perhaps more than the courts or the presidency, Congress represents an institution that has been in continuing adaptation to its own publicity needs and the needs of the electronic press. C-SPAN now offers full coverage of the Senate and House, with a potential to reach over 50 million cable television subscribers. The press galleries of the Senate and House regularly hum with activity. And the parties have become increasingly saavy in their use of satellite technology to reach local television news programs in their own states, along with web sites to draw in party activists. Yet, as Ronald Elving notes, the results of more television coverage are decidedly mixed. Better media coverage of the body cannot make the process any prettier to watch.

> As it displays itself to the public in the galleries or on C-SPAN and the conventional news media, Congress seems tortured by intentional inactivity and delay, Byzantine procedures, and anachronistic rules. The monotony is broken by intermittent outbreaks of rancor and rhetoric leading to protracted votes on incomprehensible motions. (1994, 187)

The addition of television in legislatures everywhere has had a variety of effects, some intended, some unintended. When the BBC started broadcasting Prime Minister's Questions and other events in Britain's House of Commons, for example, public reaction was dramatic and negative. Britons were genuinely shocked by the "jeers, insults, cat-calls, impromptu witticisms, interruptions, baying, howling, ranting, point-scoring and general nonsense" that they heard from the "mother of parliaments." (Leigh 1978, 2) Reactions in the United States were more muted when television coverage of the House began in 1979. Ten years later J. Bennett Johnston—who originally opposed the cameras—conceded that most early fears about "grandstanding" senators and flamboyant hearings were generally "unfounded." ("Senate Adapts . . ." 1987, 47). On the plus side, television has given millions of television viewers a window on the culture and substance of Congress, if they choose to wade through the hours of unnarrated coverage provided by C-SPAN. It has also increased the length of the legislative day by encouraging more speeches (Frantzich and Sullivan 1996, 263). On the negative side, television has made the leadership more dominant and the intense partisanship of the current Congress a subject of general frustration.

It is possible to see both of these effects in the rise of Newt Gingrich, who became the Speaker of the House of the 104th Congress partly through the skillful use of television. As one of his political biographers notes, "Gingrich moved from being a backbencher despised by Democratic House leaders and mistrusted by Republicans in the executive branch to the guiding if not commanding figure in American politics" (Barone and Ujifusa 1995). His rise was fueled by a single-minded ambition to reform Congress, the political ineptness of the long-serving Democratic majority, the luck of surfacing as a leader at the time when much of the public was tired of the mores of "big government" easily seen in the actions of Congress. As party whip, Gingrich successfully organized backbenchers to carry a common message of complaint against the Democrat-controlled Congress, augmenting their speeches with similar themes communicated to activists through his own political action committee, GOPAC.

In this process television was critical (Frantzich and Sullivan 1996, 274–278). Well before the 1994 congressional elections gave control of Congress to the GOP, Gingrich had mastered the use of "special order" speeches given on any topic at the end of a legislative day to reach out beyond the usually empty House. He and others developed the same themes of corruption and political inertia again and again, creating interest in the relatively small numbers of viewers of C-SPAN and—increasingly—other television news producers looking for colorful video sound bites. The targets of these speeches were nearly always Democrats: for showing unpatriotic sympathy for Nicaragua's Sandinista rebels, for alleged solicitations of sex made by a member to a House page, and for allowing shoddy loan practices to blossom in the House bank. Countless other personal and policy transgressions of the House emerged in these speeches, which became a constant drumbeat for reform and overturning the tired and careless Democratic majority (Clymer 1992, 48).

To be sure, the television persona of anyone engaged in sustained partisan attack finally grows unattractive. As a nation we value the politics of inclusion more than exclusion. By 1996 the medium that helped give Gingrich his power had also defined his limits. Running against the "Dole-Gingrich Congress" was at least partly effective in Clinton's successful bid for a second term.

SUMMARY

As our analysis of Congress indicates, the institution as a setting for communication offers a number of paradoxes. On one hand, the House and the Senate are rich in human resources, including researchers, staffers, press relations specialists, and the enormous talent and energy of many of its members. And yet it struggles as a body to have an identity—a friendly face—that it can offer to the general public. In many ways, public discussion of the great issues of the day ought to be centered in the deliberations and hearings that occur in Congress. But media attention and our need for a single leader gives the presidency the preferred spot for defining and clarifying national issues.

Congress has dealt with the increasing complexity of national issues by fragmenting its decision-making structure into committees and specialized research arms, such as the Congressional Budget Office. Most of the real work in each body is done in committee or in party caucuses. These features have generally made its work even more inaccessible to Americans, who have little time and even less inclination to follow its work. Except for those who keep up with Congress via C-SPAN and a limited number of other outlets, the body makes news only when there is the immediate promise of a showdown between well-defined public enemies.

In addition, the legislative process calls for patience on the part of its observers and practitioners and respect for the rules and procedures of coalition-building and compromise. But respect for these attributes are in short supply, a fact generally reflected in the press coverage of Congress and public attitudes towards its work.

Even given its paradoxes, Congress remains a fascinating setting for political communication. As we have noted, most of its members seek power by mastering its "internal" processes: the "inside game" of the institution. By learning how to work into its committee power structure—and especially its "middle ring" of staffers and professional analysts—members are able to influence legislation within the realm of their specializations. Those who also seek "external" channels to the public via the mass media have a much harder time. Media facilities in Congress are extensive, but media attention to Congress is limited, and heavily weighted toward the House and Senate leadership. Even so, the prize for the member who gains national recognition is the chance to influence colleagues and influence the public discussion of issues at a national level.

NOTES

1. See, for example, Abner J. Mikva and Patti B. Harris, *The American Congress: The First Branch* (New York: Franklin Watts, 1983), pp. 123–54.

2. The "Contract with America" was the 1995 multipolicy initiative of House Republicans to win reforms on a series of conservative issues, including term limits for members of Congress, a balanced budget amendment, a middle-class tax cut, and cuts in taxes and spending. See "Contract Score Card," *Congressional Quarterly Weekly Report*, 9 December 1995, p. 3713.

3. "Network News Underplays House, According to Study" *Broadcasting and Cable*, 24 August 1987, p. 74; Charles Tidmarch and John Pitney, "Covering Congress," *Polity* (Spring 1985): 463–83.

4. Dole arguably faced one of his toughest leadership tasks in his long 30-year Senate career after 1994, when a new group of conservative house freshmen

teamed up with Speaker Newt Gingrich to propose dramatic economic and policy reforms. Dole at times had to arbitrate between the fiery Speaker and the more centrist Clinton administration, a task made even more difficult by the necessity to begin his own presidential campaign. See Bob Woodward, *The Choice* (New York: Simon & Schuster, 1996), pp. 340–43.

REFERENCES

Barone, Michael, and Grant Ujifusa. 1995. *The Almanac of American Politics 1995.* Washington, DC: National Journal.

Clymer, Adam. 1992. "House Revolutionary." *New York Times,* 23 August: 48.

"Contract Score Card." 1995. *Congressional Quarterly Weekly Report,* 9 December: 3713.

Cook, Timothy. 1989. *Making Laws and Making News.* Washington, DC: Brookings Institution.

Elving, Ronald. 1994. "Brighter Lights, Wider Windows." In *Congress, The Press, and the Public,* ed. Thomas Mann and Norman Ornstein. Washington, DC: American Enterprise Institute/Brookings, pp. 171–206.

Fenno, Richard 1978. *Home Style: House Members in Their Districts.* Boston: Little, Brown.

Fox, Harrison W., Jr., and Susan Nebb Hammond. 1977. *Congressional Staffs: The Invisible Force in American Lawmaking.* New York: Free Press.

Frantzich, Stephen, and John Sullivan. 1996. *The C-SPAN Revolution.* Norman: University of Oklahoma Press.

Henneberger, Melinda. 1997. "Seeing Politics, and Mirrors, in the Coverage of Capitol Hill." *New York Times,* 6 October: D1, D13.

"Here They Are . . . The Fab Fifty!" 1996. *Roll Call Online,* 16 October [online].

Hess, Stephen. 1986. *The Ultimate Insiders: U.S. Senators in the National Media.* Washington, DC: Brookings Institution.

———. 1994. "Decline and Fall of Congressional News." In *The New Congress,* 2d ed., ed. Thomas Mann and Norman Ornstein. Washington, DC: American Enterprise Institute, pp. 141–56.

Hilts, Philip. 1994. "Tobacco Chiefs Say Cigarettes Aren't Addictive." *New York Times,* 15 April: A1, A20.

Leigh, David. 1978. "MPs Worried About Radio Image." *The Guardian,* 30 May: 2.

Mikva, Abner, and Patti Harris. 1983. *The American Congress: The First Branch.* New York: Franklin Watts.

Miller, Merle. 1980. *Lyndon: An Oral Biography.* New York: Ballantine.

"Network News Underplays House, According to Study." 1987. *Broadcasting and Cable,* 24 August: 74.

Paletz, David, and Robert Entman. 1981. *Media Power Politics.* New York: Free Press.

Pew Research Center for the People and the Press. 1996. "Democratic Congressional Prospects Improve." 5 April [online].

Price, David E. 1992. *The Congressional Experience.* Boulder, CO: Westview Press.

Purdum, Todd. 1994. "The Newest Moynihan." *New York Times Magazine,* 7 August: 24–29.

Roberts, Steven. 1979. "Slow Pace of Congress." *New York Times*, 5 October: A20.
Robinson, Michael. 1981. "Three Faces of Congressional Media." In *The New Congress*, ed. Thomas Mann and Norman Ornstein. Washington, DC: American Enterprise Institute.
Salant, Jonathan. 1995. "Packwood Hearings up to Panel." *Congressional Quarterly Weekly Report*, 8 July: 1982.
"Senate Adapts to Television." 1987. *Congressional Quarterly Almanac* 43: 42–50.
"Staff." 1993. *Congress A to Z*, 2d ed. Washington, DC: Congressional Quarterly, p. 393.
Tidmarch, Charles, and John Pitney. 1985. "Covering Congress." *Polity* (Spring): 463–483.
Vanderbilt News Archive. 1994. *News Abstracts of the Networks*, 13 April [online].
Waldman, Steven. 1995. *The Bill*. New York: Penguin.
Warren, Sidney, ed. 1967. *The American President*. Englewood Cliffs, NJ: Prentice-Hall.
Whiteman, David. 1995. *Communication in Congress: Members, Staff, and the Search for Information*. Lawrence: University Press of Kansas Press.
Wines, Michael. 1994. "Makers of Laws and Tobacco Joust." *New York Times*, 15 April: A20.
Woodward, Bob. 1996. *The Choice*. New York: Simon & Schuster.

Chapter 10

Unofficial Washington

> Political Washington is a special community with a culture all its own, its own established rituals and folkways, its tokens of status and influence, its rules and conventions, its tribal rivalries and personal animosities. Its stage is large, but its habits are small town.
>
> Hedrick Smith (1988)

It is often said that politics is Washington's only interest and nearly its only industry. The statement is largely true, even though it overlooks the city's thousands of other inhabitants outside the orbit of government. To be sure, governing is the dominant passion inside the beltway. Most of those who populate the region maintain an undiminished interest in the rising or falling fortunes of official Washington: the president, key officials in the federal agencies, parties and leaders in Congress, and the more remote Supreme Court. The city's elite media—especially the *Washington Post* and scores of national news sources—feed this interest continuously, providing a running commentary on the politics of politics.[1]

But beyond official Washington is another political industry with its own objectives and approaches to government. *Unofficial* Washington exists to communicate with those in power, and to interpret events to the rest of the nation beyond the beltway. Spilling into offices from Capitol Hill to the farther suburbs of Maryland and Virginia, countless journalists, lawyers, lobbyists, corporate and trade association representatives, consultants, embassy officials, researchers, and professional thinkers exist in a symbiotic relationship with elected and appointed members of government. Behind them are thousands more secretaries and staffers that keep their offices connected to official Washington. By one estimate those who actually work for the federal government are a smaller part of the population than those in the vast unofficial sector (Smith 1988, 30).

The flow of people and information across the permeable line that separates official and unofficial Washington is constant. In countless ways each side at various times serves as host or client for the other. Segments of the unofficial side provide a steady flow of information and persuasive appeals, often presenting themselves as representatives of important constituencies dispersed across the nation. For their part, members of the Congress and the administration know that they need to gather the information and opinions of organized interest groups represented in Washington. They also know that policymaking in the United States is now closely tied to the work of thousands of former government officials and employees who populate the city's trade associations, law firms and think tanks.

This chapter describes the work of those in Washington who depend on government, but are not on its payroll. Our goal is to offer a brief tour of the side of the Washington power loop that is not seen on any government organization chart. The blocks we focus on include the press, consultants and government contractors, business and social action lobbies, as well as think tanks and foundations. All provide functions that are as much a part of the culture of Washington as the work of the White House and Congress.

We begin with some cases that illustrate how the two sides of Washington are connected.

NETWORKS OF INFLUENCE AND ACCESS

A useful way to see how individuals outside of government have effects on those inside is to look at specific cases. Consider, for example, a few of *National Journal*'s list of people and organizations outside of government "who made a difference" in national politics in the late 1980s. Several sample profiles from this catalogue of scholars, lobbyists, lawyers, and media figures are instructive.

Richard B. Froh, Vice President for government relations, Kaiser Foundation Health Plan Inc.: Is influential not merely in representing Kaiser's interests but also frequently called upon by Republican and Democratic members for advice.

ICF Inc., Consulting Firm: Has offices around the country; known as numbers crunchers; comes up with the numbers that the Environmental Protection Agency uses to base its regulations on.

Pat Choate, Director, policy analysis, TRW Inc.: Serves as a link between Capitol Hill and enlightened business leaders; members of both parties look to him to develop and market ideas.

Peter D. Hart, Chairman, polling firm of Peter D. Hart Research Associates, Inc.: As probably the foremost Washington pollster for the Democratic Party and its centrist candidates, plays a key role in identifying and shaping national trends and political messages.

Robert S. Strauss, Partner, law firm of Akin, Gump, Strauss, Hauer and Feld. Clients: Archer-Daniels-Midland Co., MCA Inc. Lone Start Industries Inc., American Telephone and Telegraph, Southland Corp.: As former U.S. trade representative and chairman of the Democratic National Committee, is widely respected on Capitol Hill . . . is one of the handful of Washington people who can accomplish something dramatic with a phone call.

David Broder, Columnist, reporter, *The Washington Post*: Plays a critical role in identifying the leading national political issues and players.

Jeane J. Kirkpatrick, Senior Fellow, American Enterprise Institution for Public Policy Research; Professor, Georgetown University: Although the Reagan Administration could find no suitable foreign policy role for her after she tired of being United Nations Ambassador, she remains the patron saint of conservative Republican foreign policy. ("Getting on the List," 1986, 1436–74)

These names suggest an essential truth about the federal city; it is a place dominated by personal connections and networks. Froh and Choate have been among scores of articulate and credible figures within corporate America who can influence the decisions of federal administrators and members of Congress. Like others in the country's largest industries, their objective was to explain to legislative members and staffers how pending actions would affect segments of the economy. Hart's and Strauss's connections were somewhat different, but had a similar function. Both have advised presidents and countless members of Congress. And both know who to reach out beyond the party to communicate with members of the press, corporate America, and members of the other party. Hart's access to members of the Democratic Party and the press is derived from his soft-spoken style and the credibility of his poll data. Strauss's power flows from a different vital feature of those in unofficial Washington: an impressive resume that includes both government and private work. His career has become something of a Washington legend.

Like so many insiders, Strauss moved with ease from government positions to private positions where he lobbies government. Now nearly 80, this affable Texan's career has included time with the FBI and the Texas Banking Commission. He was also national chairperson of the Democratic Party, U.S. ambassador to the former Soviet Union, and an official in the Carter administration (Adelman 1995, 27–32). As a lawyer/lobbyist, he represented scores of clients, including Archer-Daniels Midland, a huge agri-business firm that contributed heavily to the Republican Party in 1992 (Makinson and Goldstein 1994, 17). As an official in the Democratic Party and an ambassador, he was a regular on the political talk-show circuit. More recently, he sought to arbitrate legislative compromises between President Clinton and the Republican-led Senate (Woodward 1996, 163). His lifelong bipartisanship is a reminder that in Washington party affiliation does not necessarily dictate friendships.

Strauss represents the web of contacts that individuals in unofficial Washington cultivate in the course of their careers. Like those who spend a professional lifetime in any organizational setting, these accumulated contacts make access to others easier and create goodwill with those who may one day be helpful. Such a folkway comes easily to a city of 40,000 lawyers and nearly 80,000 lobbyists of various types (Birnbaum 1992, 7). It is home to nearly 3,000 trade associations and interest groups housed in sleek offices on K Street and elsewhere around the city. Add in the thousands of members of the press assigned to Capitol Hill, the White House, and other federal beats, and it is easy to see why a fat Roledex is an essential tool of work in the city.

For example, faced with pending legislation deemed harmful to transportation interests, a "government relations" staffer at the American Trucking Association may find it helpful to know the name of a wire-service reporter or news producer at NBC. She may try to plant the seed for a story favorable to the goals of her organization. At the same time she may also seek allies from General Motors, the American Automobile Association and other groups in opposing the legislation.

It would be a mistake, however, to make too much of these networks, particularly to assume that they represent a closed loop of power. Our language is filled with ominous phrases that suggest that Washington is "captive to special interests" and controlled by "power brokers" that leave most Americans unrepresented. No image in American political life is more durable than the view that Congress, the president, or certain agencies like the Department of Defense have been captured by an unelected cadre of powerful elites.

To be sure, figures like Robert Strauss and David Broder certainly have more influence and access than most others. It is equally true that Congress has come to rely more on the information and arguments given to its staffs and members by organizations with specific legislative objectives (Wines 1993, A1, B14). At the same time, Washington is anything but a closed universe. Competition for access to members is enormous, and to some extent subject to the same limitations that affect any community in which many competing voices seek to be heard (i.e., corporations, churches, and institutions).

THE PRESS

The press is the most visible and vocal segment of unofficial Washington. Its importance in fueling the machinery of politics is hard to underestimate. It is reflected in the cliches used to symbolize the institution of Washington-based journalism. Identified as "power brokers," the "fourth branch of government," or—less reverently—as "the beast" that must be continually fed, the political press is the vital communications network of national civic life. And it is treated accordingly. As William Rivers wrote in *The Other Government*,

> Privileged as no other citizens are, the correspondents are listed in the Congressional Directory; they receive advance copies of governmental speeches and announcements; they are frequently shown documents forbidden even to high officials; and they meet and work in special quarters set aside for them in all major government buildings, including the White House. Fantastic quantities of government time and money are devoted to their needs, their desires, and their whims. Some White House correspondents talk with the president more often than his own party leaders in the House and in the Senate, and there are correspondents who see more of the congressional leaders than do most other congressmen. (1982, 10)

No one knows precisely how many journalists are based in Washington. Census data suggests more that than 12,000 live inside the District of Columbia (Smith 1988, 30). The number is considerably larger if producers, editors, and other news personnel are included. Some organizations are based in the Washington area, such as National Public Radio, C-SPAN, and Gannett, the owner of *USA Today* and operator of the largest chain of newspapers in the United States. Other large news organizations from various locations around the country maintain sizable news bureaus in the city. For some like the Associated Press, *The New York Times*, and ABC, staff assignments to Washington are as prestigious as assignments to their New York headquarters. For most other outlets such as the *Wall Street Journal, The Los Angeles Times*, Reuters, and CBS, it would be unthinkable not to have a considerable presence in Washington. NBC and CBS maintain about 13 correspondents each, in addition to large production staffs (Kimball 1994, 23–24).

For most national media outlets, a Washington presence is important and jealously guarded by the reporters assigned to the city. Approximately 60 percent of the networks' news content deals with Washington politics or elections (Graber 1993, 73). And those who deliver it—including the three network news anchors—are familiar and trusted narrators of America's civic culture to millions of viewers. Few candidates for the presidency or nominees to an important federal post can afford to turn down the requests for interviews, especially if they are made by these anchors, *The Post's* David Broder or Bob Woodward, CNN's Larry King, and a cadre of other influential journalists.

All of this attention on Washington has had the effect of hot-wiring the American public to political events in the District of Columbia. When President Truman announced the 1945 dropping of the atomic bomb on Japan, the White House press consisted of about 25 reporters (Graber 1984, 60). Now approximately 2,000 journalists have regular White House press passes. They are joined by thousands more in the congressional press galleries, and key agencies around the city such as the Defense and State Departments. Some of these journalists work for trade publications which keep tabs on Washington news for their professional members around the country (i.e., *Broadcasting and Cable, Automotive News, Journal of the American Medical Association*). Others work for regional papers and magazines. But they all share an awareness that they are an important force in the public discussion of national issues.

The venerable National Press Club is one tangible sign of this power. Many of the city's journalists are members, and scores of newsmakers seek invitations to address the club.[2] It's F Street venue near the White House is an essential stop for a rising political leader and something of a national shrine to the great news men and women who have reported on the historic events of the nation's past. The club represents the growing professionalism of political journalism, and the increased weight the press carries as the institution that mediates and constructs the nation's political life.

For its part, official Washington goes out of its way to accommodate the needs of the press. Congress spends more than $1 million a year to support the seven news galleries within the capitol building (Elving 1994, 186). Its 435 members each dedicate at least one staff member to handle press contacts, with leaders and party organizations using considerably more. Most federal agencies have an assistant secretary for public affairs reporting to the leader of the agency. And the secretaries in agencies such as the State Department and Defense Department have a wealth of subordinates to feed the daily press machine. The Pentagon alone operates its own professional journalism school, with over 2,000 graduates a year (Hess 1986, 8).

The cramped space of the White House's West Wing houses an especially important segment of the press. The presidency is a prestigious assignment for a journalist to win. Gauging an administration's success in managing the flow of information to this elite group which has risen to the top of their own profession is a long-standing beltway pastime.[3] At best the relationship is an uneasy one, a fact that usually results in a White House which is unhappy with the critical coverage it receives and a collection of ambitious reporters with a sense that they are being used.

Perhaps no single group in unofficial Washington gets under a president's skin as much the the national press, especially those covering the White House. Every president decries their cynicism and their lack of sympathy for understanding his ostensibly honorable intentions. After struggling early in his first term to win over the press and the public, Bill Clinton privately noted that presidents routinely "get brutalized" by the media. "You might as well understand that's part of the deal" of winning the office (Woodward 1996, 421).

CONSULTANTS AND CONTRACT "SHOPS"

In their now classic study of how government money is spent, Daniel Guttman and Barry Willner offer a reminder that a "shadow government" exists in Washington to provide services in exchange for lucrative federal contracts. Corporations that "market their expertise" to federal agencies are largely unseen by the American public, but they represent "the largest industry in the nation's capital."

> A recent edition [of the Yellow Pages] lists about 120 "economic and social researchers," 400 "management consultants," 60 "operations researchers," 60 "transportation consultants," and 15 "urban affairs consultants." Some are tiny operations, living on one or two contracts and with histories no longer than the government programs that gave them life. Others are divisions of well-known industrial corporations, such as Westinghouse Electric Corporation or General Electric, the Washington offices of advisers to the corporate world, such as McKinsey & Co. or Price Waterhouse, and "think tanks" that have been publicly associated with defense spending, such as the Institute for Defense Analysis and the Stanford Research Institute. (Guttman and Willner 1976, 4)

Who has contracts with the federal government? Virtually every major American corporation provides products or services to programs administered by scores of federal agencies, ranging from agriculture to urban housing. In the defense area alone the companies with Washington staffers are large and small, well known and obscure: Grumman, GE Aerospace, Rockwell, Boeing, Ford Aerospace, General Dynamics, Fairchild, and the Rand Corporation.

Rand is an especially interesting case. Started in 1946 as a research branch of the Douglas Aircraft Company, it eventually was spun off as a separate research and development organization contracting for work on defense-related issues. Today it bills itself as a nonprofit and nonpartisan corporation supplying detailed analysis and expertise on a the effects of various defense and policy issues. The majority of Rand's funding comes from federal grants and contracts ("About Rand" 1997). It has always had especially close ties to the Air Force (Guttman and Willner

1976, 248). Along with organizations like the Institute for Defense Analysis and the Urban Institute, it has carved out a role as an elite advisory institution bridging the gap between the academic world and the specific agencies responsible for developing and implementing federal policies and programs. Rand has the distinction of being known as the policy analysis firm that developed a significant portion of the American military's cold war strategy against the former Soviet Union.

Most federal contractors provide more specific services than policy analysis. Hundreds of American companies are dependent on federal contracts in return for expertise in software and computing, accounting, manufacturing, technical support, and construction. Sought-after work may include construction contracts from the U.S. Army Corps of Engineers, cleanup systems for the Environmental Protection Agency, program assessment for the Department of Education, or management of facilities owned by Department of Energy (DOE). Just one recent DOE contract up for bids called for a five-year management plan to deal with nuclear waste at the enormous Hanford nuclear materials storage site in Washington state. The contract was expected to be worth about $4.6 billion ("DOE's RFP" 1996, 15).

Not all companies feel a need to nurture hard-won contracts with federal agencies by having a Washington presence. But about 4,000 corporations do (Ricci 1993, 43). Many, like the Bechtel Group—a San Francisco–based construction company of huge projects, including dams and nuclear power plants—maintain "government relations" offices in the District of Columbia to keep channels open to federal administrators and legislators who sit on committees responsible for certain federal projects. Bechtel has not only succeeded in obtaining many lucrative contracts for reactors and dams, it has also seen one of its former executives become a secretary of state and another, secretary of defense.[4]

In addition to employees of corporations doing business with the government, the nation's capital is also populated with a wealth of consultants who offer a range of services to the whole infrastructure of political Washington. An entire class of political consultants sell a range of services to candidates and parties, including polling, campaign management, direct mail, and radio and television advertising.[5] Some, like Robert Squire, have made long careers out of campaign consulting. Squire has helped to elect as much as 20 percent of the Senate, in addition to assisting in Bill Clinton's successful 1996 bid for relection (Woodward 1996, 127–28).

Another class of communications consultants focus on more nonpartisan public relations issues. Their clients are typically trade organizations, states and cities, unions, professional societies, and social action groups. All are intent on influencing political discourse in the nation or the federal bureaucracy, and many use Washington public relations firms in place of establishing a permanent outpost in the capital.

Consider the services of Marlowe and Company, a public relations firm headed up by a former senior staff member to Senator Vance Hartke of Indiana. In its promotional information to potential customers, the company describes itself as "a government relations consulting firm that helps its clients navigate the Washington legislative and regulatory arenas." Specific services offered include "lobbying of Members of Congress and Executive Branch officials, grassroots lobbying, public policy analysis and issue monitoring, as well as public relations." ("Firm Profile" 1996). One of the specialties offered by this Marlowe is representing coastal cities—including San Diego, Sarasota and Venice, Florida, and Huntington Beach, California—on pending legislation and existing federal laws effecting erosion and flood protection. Other clients have included the Brotherhood of Locomotive Engineers, the Connecticut Association of Realtors, Union Carbide, and the Edison Electric Institute.

Typically, public relations consultants cite the former contacts of their employees as evidence of their ability to deliver a message in behalf of a client. And Marlowe identifies how the owner's background includes "established relationships with key members of the Administration, the Departments of Transportation, Defense, Commerce and Energy, as well as officials at independent agencies."

TRADE ASSOCIATIONS AND THE LOBBYING PROCESS

A trade association is an organization of companies and individuals in the same business. Members who are normally in competition with each other come together in these professional groups to deal with problems common to their industries. With the enormous growth of the federal oversight of businesses and the constant prospect of congressional lawmaking that could help or hurt industries, these associations have increasingly established offices or headquarters in Washington to watch out for members' interests. One estimate places the number of trade associations represented in the District of Columbia at about 1,600, employing more than 80,000 people (Ricci 1993, 43). Any random sampling of industry representatives will reveal a virtual who's who of industrial America: for example, the American Public Gas Association, the United States Trademark Association, the Society of Industrial Realtors, the Milk Industry Foundation, the Airline Pilots Association, and the National Association of Broadcasters. Many have big budgets and membership roles. The National Homebuilder's Association boasts 125,000 members around the country; the American Banking Association, 13,000. And both have multimillion dollar budgets (Birnbaum 1992, 7). They are joined by 100 labor unions and perhaps as many as 1,000 other social or political action groups, such as the Sierra Club and the National Organization for Women. When one figures in the number of others in the capital representing particular firms, it becomes evident how much corporate America monitors the pulse of the administrative and legislative process.

The National Association of Broadcasters (NAB), for example, has had an enormous stake in recent decisions by the Federal Communications Commission (FCC) effecting new media technologies such as standards for digital "high definition" television. It has also traditionally fought to preserve broadcast access to the American public in the face of stiff competition from the cable and direct-satellite television industries. The fact that cable systems must carry local broadcast television stations is largely because of the efforts of the NAB in Congress and before the FCC, the Patent and Trademark Office, and the Justice Department. The association is supported by member radio and television stations around the country, along with their staffers and related suppliers of equipment and programming. Its recently renovated headquarters near DuPont Circle houses approximately 185 full-time staffers[6] and is responsible for continually monitoring and representing the legislative and administrative interests of station owners. For the first six months of 1996 the NAB spent over $2.3 million on lobbying. Among their expenses were $40,000 paid to the Davidson Colling Group, a lobbying firm, to represent the association on tax and budget issues (Fleming 1996, 18).

THE LOBBYING PROCESS

When most Americans think of trade associations and specific industries doing business with the government, the process of "lobbying" is probably never far from their thoughts. And for good reason. Individual companies and trade associations do seek to gain access to the legislative process directly or indirectly by communicating their positions to elected officials or the directors of federal agencies. Almost any piece of legislation can be assessed in terms of how it may change the fortunes of an industry or tip the balance toward one kind of service and away from another. Railroads will typically oppose laws that favor trucking. Automakers dislike taxes dedicated to mass transit rather than roads. Builders oppose legislation that increases the price of individual homes. And manufacturers object to bills that favor the ability of a competitor to import inexpensive parts from overseas. As a result, it is a fixed American commonplace to assume that lobbyists have enormous clout.[7] Countless examples are retold in the media to keep the view alive (Wines 1993, A1, B14).

THE LIMITS OF LOBBYING

Lobbyists are perhaps the most discussed and distrusted professionals in unofficial Washington, even though their activities are clearly protected by the First Amendment.[8] They represent virtually every institution, social cause and profession in American society. Their power, however, is easily overestimated. In the prolonged congressional battle to deregulate the communications industry, for example, virtually every major segment sought to have its interests served. Phone and broadcasting interests contributed more than $13 million to congressional campaigns. Long distance carriers, AT&T, local phone systems like Bell Atlantic, cable companies, and networks all had their lobbyists. And many included former government officials, such as Marlin Fitzwater, who was the White House press secretary for President Bush, Howard Baker, Jr., the former Senate Republican leader, and Ray Marshall, the secretary of labor under Jimmy Carter (Andrews 1995, D1, D6). But in this long legislative battle, as in many others, the interests tended to cancel each other out. Each of the lobbyists was involved partially as a defensive move, hoping to at least not lose business opportunities at the expense of their competition. The net effect on the lawmakers, as one observer put it, was the desire to "tune out the noise" and get on with the legislative negotiation (Andrews 1995, D6).

Jeffrey Birnbaum's exhaustive 1992 study of a handful of effective lobbyists presents a similar picture of lobbying's limits. The prize for many of his subjects was valuable corporate tax breaks or subsidies to be won from the 101st Congress. Some succeeded in their objectives, but, he noted, engaged in a good deal of ineffective "wheel spinning."

> Lobbyists and the deficit were always clashing. Every time a lobbyist wanted to get some goodie for a client, whether it was a tax break, a federal grant, or a deferred regulation, lawmakers demanded to know, "How are you going to pay for it?" And that was one question that most lobbyists were reluctant to answer, since it usually meant taking money away from somebody else's client. That made a lobbyist's job a hard sell, even under the best of circumstances. (17)

In fact, Birnbaum documented what is frequently the case with lobbying undertaken by industries and trade associations. It rarely occurs in a vacuum, and thus falls victim to the nulification of its potential benefits at the hands of opponents. Those opponents may be other lobbyists, legislators, congressional staff, or the president.

In sum, lobbying as practiced by trade associations and others can be as effective as the popular image suggests. But it is subject to the same limitations any group encounters when it attempts to win adherents for its cherished positions. There is nothing extraordinary or necessarily sinister about the process of seeking to win the support of those who govern. And, as we have seen, resistance frequently triumphs over persuasion in the lobbying process.

THINK TANKS AND FOUNDATIONS

By the standards of businesses or institutions of higher learning, foundations and so-called think tanks are not large. But because they frequently support research into how political and economic theories can be applied to legislation, they have become increasingly important in the charged partisan atmosphere of Washington. It is increasingly the case that many foundations and think tanks now supply the critical ideas and philosophical justifications that underpin arguments by those in the thick of America's ongoing culture wars.

Foundations are nonprofit organizations given funds from donors or industries which are then dispursed to recipients. In the United States some carry the names of well-known industrialists, such as the Ford Foundation, the Rockefeller Foundation, and the Carnegie Endowment for International Peace. Others are smaller, and more focused. Washington's Benton Foundation, for example, works with a relatively modest focus on the use of media to "promote communications tools, applications, and policies in the public interest." Among other things, it sponsors publications on the operations of Congress and meetings of professionals on emerging media technologies ("About the Benton Foundation" 1997).

In the United States many foundations stay clear of direct political advocacy. But some newer philanthropies have become supporters of writers and thinkers on both the political left and right. The John M. Olin Foundation, for example, was created by the Olin Corporation, the maker of munitions and Winchester rifles. In 1993 it issued over $14 million in grants ("Conservative Coalition" 1996). Over the years it has funded a number of Washington-based groups, including the Institute on Religion and Democracy, a group generally opposed to the progressive politics of the National and World Council of Churches (Howell 1995, 702).

Think tanks are gathering places for scholars, recent or future government officials, and others interested in promoting more thorough discussion of public policy issues. An appointment to serve in a think tank is likely to bring an economist or political theorist in closer contact with those who write or administer laws than would be the case if the researcher was teaching and writing at a university. Sometimes called "research brokers," think tank scholars usually describe social and economic problems and their remedies in more detail than elected leaders involved in the daily crush of politics. They are often invited to testify during congressional hearings, and they usually have a network of beltway friends that include politicians, agency directors, and journalists.

The two most visible Washington think tanks are the Brookings Insitution and its more conservative and newer counterpart, the American Enterprise Institute (AEI). Brookings was established in the 1920s by a

St. Louis businessman and has become the model for most of Washington's newer think tanks. Researchers and fellows at the institution focus primarily on foreign, domestic, and economic issues, with the goal of bringing "knowledge to bear on the current and emerging public policy problems facing the American people" (Brookings 1995, 4). After receiving big grants from the Ford and Rockefeller Foundations in the 1950s and 1960s, it moved into its own office on Massachusetts Avenue, providing an intellectual home for various Democratic administrations and political liberals (Ricci 1993, 152–53). Brookings fellows have included Charles Schultze, chairman of the Council of Economic Advisers in the Carter administration, and Alice Rivlin, who joined the Clinton administration as assistant director of the Office of Management and Budget.

The newer American Enterprise Institute is home to a number of former members of the Bush and Reagan administrations. Along with the Heritage Foundation, it was established in part by wealthy business groups concerned about an alleged liberal tilt of university researchers and the national political media (Ricci 1993, 160–62). Both have received substantial support from a collection of conservative foundations, including the Bradley, Olin, and Scaife foundations (Howell 1995, 701). Heritage's budget in 1994 was $25 million, part of the rapid growth in conservative think tanks that began in the Reagan era of antigovernment politics.[9]

Though their ideological differences are evident, most think tanks have similar goals: to support a range of scholars and political thinkers in their work as speakers at seminars and as authors and researchers of books and opinion articles for newspapers. In recent years a number of writers seeking to influence public debate on a range of issues have been nurtured by think tanks, among them Brookings' Gary Orfield on school integration (*Must We Bus?* 1978) and AEI's Dinesh D'Souza on higher education (*Illiberal Education: the Politics of Race and Sex on Campus* 1991).

Increasingly, as well, these institutions seek clout by supplying television news producers with expert sources capable of explaining the intricacies of everything from trade policy to the funding of Social Security. Within hours of the Iraqi invasion of Kuwait, for example, Brookings was flooded with media requests for experts who could explain what it meant in terms of American policy (Smith 1991, 131–34). Some think tank scholars may spend nearly half of their time handling media queries, using the press to feed ideas to the public and into the mix of lobbyists, federal bureaucracies, and members of Congress.

SUMMARY

Biologists talk about organisms that enter into mutually beneficial relationships. Among others, mammals often act as hosts to other animals (bacteria and much more), providing protection and food in exchange for the benefits the guest provides. The same kind of symbiotic relationship exists in the nation's capital, where thousands of nongovernmental professionals engage in the processes of monitoring, informing, and influencing government. Some—such as corporate lobbyists and journalists—act as early warning systems for constituencies they represent outside the beltway. Others—such as those in consulting and think tank positions—act as service providers, offering expertise or specific functions that government is not equipped to supply itself.

The crossover of talent and work between "official" Washington and "unofficial" Washington is so extensive that they seem at times to blend together. For every bureaucrat, governmental staffer and elected official, there seems to be an equal number of consultants, "hired gun" lobbyists, and corporate government relations representatives who seek influence by offering warnings or support.

In one sense the presence of a huge extragovernmental apparatus should come as no surprise. Virtually any complex organization has similar if smaller relationships with its own constituents, consultants, and media monitors. What the existence of unofficial Washington does imply, however, is that we may need to rethink what we mean when we talk about "government." In one sense, at least, the line between government and other powerful corporations and institutions of American life is quite blurred. The links between the two are numerous. For example, there is no ambiguity in the observation that what goes on in Congress or the presidency is "political communication." But how should we label the cautious concern of a CBS television network president in response to presidential proposals that mandate a certain number of programming hours to children (McConnell 1996, 4–10)? CBS is both a corporation and a government-regulated industry. In making its business decisions it will consider the needs of its private stockholders and its viewers. But it must consider its privileged access to the American public and, hence, its place in the political world. It is—along with the rest of the communications industry—part of the political debate about what kind of communication is in the "public interest."

In a sense, the entwined communities of official and unofficial Washington represent in concentrated form what exists everywhere in organizational fabric of the United States: networks of cooperative and competitive relations between governments and all of those other institutions affected by its decisions.

NOTES

1. In addition to the *Post*, any sampling of other sources constantly observant of political Washington would probably include the *Washington Times*, the *New*

York Times, *Washington Monthy*, *Time*, *Newsweek*, *The Atlantic*, *The New Yorker*, *The New Republic*, *National Journal*, CNN's daily "Inside Politics," C-SPAN, and "All Politics" [online].

2. The nation's last 15 presidents have spoken at the Press Club, along with many thousands of politicos and celebrities. "History of the National Press Club," *National Press Club*, 23 July 1996 [online].

3. For samples from a journalism critic, a presidential aide, and a reporter see Mark Hertsgaard, *On Bended Knee: The Press and the Reagan Presidency* (New York: Schocken, 1989), pp. 54–76; Jody Powell, *The Other Side of the Story* (New York: Morrow, 1984), pp. 11–53; Sam Donaldson, *Hold On, Mr. President* (New York: Random House, 1987), pp. 90–108, 129–52.

4. The two cabinet officials were Secretary of State George Shultz and Secretary of Defense Caspar Weinberger. See Laton McCartney, *Friends in High Places* (New York: Simon & Schuster, 1988), pp. 197–228.

5. For a comprehensive overview of consulting, see Larry Sabato, *The Rise of Political Consultants* (New York: Basic Books, 1981), pp. 3–67.

6. Private communication with John Merli, the NAB, 26 July 1996.

7. For a detailed review of lobbying techniques see Bruce C. Wolpe, *Lobbying the Congress: How the System Works* (Washington, DC: Congressional Quarterly, 1990).

8. The relevant clause of the amendment is that "Congress shall make no law . . . abridging . . . the right of the people peaceably to assemble, and to petition the Government for a redress of grievance."

9. See, for example, John Hood, "Send in the Tanks," *National Review*, 11 December 1995: 80–81.

REFERENCES

"About the Benton Foundation." 1997. *Benton Foundation*, 2 October [online].

"About Rand." 1997. *The Rand Corporation*, 3 October [online].

Adelman, Kenneth. 1995. "It Ain't Bragging." *Washingtonian* (February): 27–32.

Andrews, Edmund. 1995. "Phone-Bill Lobbyists Wear Out Welcome." *New York Times*, 20 March: D1, D6.

Birnbaum, Jeffrey. 1992. *The Lobbyists*. New York: Times Books.

Brookings Media Guide: 1995–1996. 1995. Washington: Brookings Institution.

"Conservative Coaltion Targets the Food and Drug Administration in Push for Deregulation." 1996. *Philanthropy News Digest*, 30 July [online].

"DOE's RFP for Hanford Covers $4.6 Billion Over Five Year Period." 1996. *ENR*, 15 January: 15.

Donaldson, Sam. 1987. *Hold On, Mr. President*. New York: Random House.

Elving, Ronald. 1994. "Brighter Lights, Wider Windows: Presenting Congress in the 1990s." In *Congress, The Press, and the Public*, ed. Thomas Mann and Norman Ornstein. Washington, DC: Brookings/AEI.

"Firm Profile." 1996. *Marlowe & Company*, 22 July [online].

Fleming, Heather. 1996. "Tallying the Price of Persuasion." *Broadcasting and Cable*, 16 August: 18.

"Getting on the List: 150 Who Make a Difference." 1986. *National Journal*, 14 June: 1436–74.

Graber, Doris. 1984. *Processing the News*. New York: Longman.

———. 1993. *Processing the News*, 2d ed. Lanham, MD: University Press of America.

Guttman, Daniel, and Barry Willner. 1976. *The Shadow Government*. New York: Pantheon Books.

Hertsgaard, Mark. 1989. *On Bended Knee: The Press and the Reagan Presidency*. New York: Schocken.

Hess, Stephen. 1986. *The Ultimate Insiders: U.S. Senators in the National Media*. Washington, DC: Brookings Institution.

"History of the National Press Club." 1996. *National Press Club*, 23 July [online].

Hood, John. 1995. "Send in the Tanks." *National Review*, 11 December: 80–81.

Howell, Leon. 1995. "Funding the War of Ideas." *Christian Century*, 19–26 July: 702.

Kimball, Penn. 1994. *Downsizing the News*. Baltimore: Johns Hopkins/Woodrow Wilson Center.

Makinson, Larry, and Joshua Goldstein. 1994. *Open Secrets*, 3d ed. Washington, DC: Congressional Quarterly.

McCartney, Laton. 1988. *Friends in High Places*. New York: Simon & Schuster.

McConnell, Chris. 1996. "It's Unanimous." *Broadcasting and Cable*, 17 June: 4–11.

Powell, Jody. 1984. *The Other Side of the Story*. New York: Morrow.

Ricci, David. 1993. *The Transformation of American Politics*. New Haven, CT: Yale University Press.

Rivers, William. 1982. *The Other Government: Power and the Washington Media*. New York: Universe.

Sabato, Larry. 1981. *The Rise of Political Consultants*. New York: Basic Books.

Smith, Hedrick. 1988. *The Power Game: How Washington Works*. New York: Random House.

Smith, James. 1991. *Brookings at Seventy-Five*. Washington, DC: Brookings Institution.

Wines, Michael. 1993. "A New Maxim for Lobbyists: What You Know, Not Whom." *New York Times*, 3 November: A1, B14.

Wolpe, Bruce C. 1990. *Lobbying Congress: How the System Works*. Washington, DC: Congressional Quarterly.

Woodward, Bob. 1996. *The Choice*. New York: Simon & Schuster.

Part IV

Meta-Politics

Chapter 11

Litigation, Crime, and the Courts

> The judicial organization of the United States is the hardest thing there for a foreigner to understand. He finds judicial authority invoked in almost every political context, and from that he naturally concludes that the judge is one of the most important political powers in the United States.
>
> Alexis de Tocqueville (1969)

At first glance the various local, state, and federal courts of the United States would seem to be largely outside of the rest of the political system. It was clearly the intent of the writers of the Constitution to give the courts the status of impartial arbiters and fact finders insulated from the influences of individual factions. Federal judges and many of their counterparts in the states are appointed for life, immune from the more obvious pressures of public opinion. Such permanent tenure, Alexander Hamilton noted in *The Federalist Papers,* is an "excellent barrier to the encroachments and oppressions" of Congress and the best way to assure "steady, upright, and impartial administration of laws" (Hamilton et al, 1961, 465).

The idea of justice is synonymous with fairness and impartiality. In theory at least, the courts are not agents for any one faction, but guarantors of justice and fairness for all parties involved. The obvious symbolism of the traditional courtroom communicates this ideal. The judge is the beneficiary of what Jerome Frank has called "the cult of the robe." Special black garments make a symbolic plea to view the men and women of the judiciary as a "priestly tribe" removed from the rest of government (Frank 1950, 256–57). All seating within the court gives the litigants equal distance and equal access to the judicial arbiter, who sits on an elevated dias. Juries are literally and figuratively held apart from the proceedings by a barrier that defines their status as close observers, but also suggests their separation from the maneuvers of defendants, prosecutors, and other agents of the court.

To be sure, most judicial business in the United States occurs in conference rooms designed to bypass the rituals of a trial. Private bargaining for quicker resolution of cases is the norm rather than the exception in both civil and criminal sides of the law. Currently, nearly 90 percent of criminal defendants in the United States negotiate a guilty plea rather than go to trial, where sentences could be even stiffer (Church 1995, 132). Even so, the nation's courts are the primary settings for narratives about the resolution of conflict or the establishment of guilt.

The political consequences of the nation's increasing interest in issues of crime and justice is the subject of this chapter. Courts have a significant effect on the political communication process in the United States.

THE SPECIAL FUNCTIONS OF THE COURTS

As agencies of the state, courts perform three general functions. Most obviously, they exist in large measure to settle disputes, including conflicts that arise between individuals, corporations, municipalities, and states. When cases involve single individuals, this spectrum can extend from family and divorce courts, where the fallout of domestic crises are resolved in relative privacy, to much more complex cases where courts are asked to determine if certain contracts are enforceable. Nearly all disputes in the business community follow a relatively predictable pattern: a settlement is either worked out prior to the start of a court trial or a trial takes place that results in a decision about whether one of the parties has satisfied the conditions of a contract. Occasionally these commercial and domestic forms of conflict resolution meet, as in the widely reported "Baby M" case involving the custody of a child as part of an adoption arrangement. After a pregnancy that began when Mary Beth Whitehead was artificially inseminated with sperm donated by William Stern, and after making a contract with the Sterns to give them the child, Ms. Whitehead decided to keep the baby. In 1986 the nation read daily accounts of the New Jersey trial that would determine if a surrogate mother who underwent a change of heart could break a $10,000 contract with an adopting couple. The Sterns eventually won the right to raise the child, but not until after this court case created a good deal of national soul-searching.[1]

A second important function of the courts is to determine whether individuals or groups have violated laws, and, if so, to define appropriate punishments. This is the familiar territory of the criminal trial, the kind of judicial action that is for many Americans the essence of the legal system. In both fictional and news forms, the details of crime and punishment provide a continuing and vital form of public theater. The courtroom drama remains as much a staple of popular entertainment as an enduring form of journalism.[2] Most major newspapers devote copious amounts of space to crime and criminal justice processes, leading many of their readers to overestimate the actual number of instances of crime in their communities (Jaehing, Weaver, and Fico 1981, 88–96).

With its riveting details of character and conflict and its almost certain all-or-nothing resolution, the criminal trial plays out a range of class frictions and social fantasies that can be given satisfying closure in the form of a verdict. When Bernard Goetz went on trial in 1987 for shooting four young men who demanded that he give them money, he was alternatively seen by various Americans as a hero or a villain. The case gained its national notoriety in part because of its racial angle. Goetz was a white New Yorker who claimed that he had been threatened by the black youths on a subway, one of whom he permanently paralyzed with a bullet from his .38 revolver. The young men argued that they had only been panhandling. The familiarity of the circumstances hit a raw nerve, turning the brief episode into a story New York City's tabloids and the nation's television news programs would not allow to fade away.[3]

In some ways its twin was the case involving the arrest of a black motorist Rodney King and the resulting 1993 federal case against the four white Los Angeles police officers who were videotaped in the act of beating him (Noble 1996, p. D5). Like the Goetz trial, extensive coverage grew out of simmering distrust between the races. King was a victim of the institutional racism of the Los Angeles police. Goetz represented a very different narrative; in his view he was guilty of nothing more than standing up to a parasitic band of misfits who happened to be black. In each case estimations of whether "justice" would be served were measured in opposing white and black perceptions in these two racially polarized cities.

The third function of the justice system in the United States is as much a consequence as a formal goal. A whole range of high state and federal courts increasingly share the function of policymaking and policy implementation with the legislative and executive branches. This rulemaking process comes in sharp focus periodically when Senate hearings are held to confirm federal judges. Conservatives routinely decry "activist" judges who "legislate" social policy without the accountability that goes with elective office. Progressives often welcome court mandates that force state and federal agencies to provide protections or services, usually by invoking state obligations linked to constitutional guarantees.

School integration cases in the 1970s are among the clearest cases of so-called judicial policymaking. In a significant number of instances federal judges ruled that individual districts needed to take specific steps—including busing—to racially integrate schools in their districts. Lower courts increasingly built on the Supreme Court's landmark 1954 ruling in *Brown v. Board of Education* and other subsequent cases that have been used to prod school boards into equalizing the educational resources available to white and black families. In one 1970 case, the Court agonized over whether to uphold a U.S. district court judge's decision to enforce a desegregation plan for a North Carolina school district. The plan called for the busing of 13,000 students to achieve a racial mix in each of the district's schools. Characteristically, the Court ended up endorsing the principle of mandating racial balance, but it gave no conclusive support to any specific busing plan. That fell to a lower court to decide (Woodward and Armstrong 1979, 95–112).

This pattern of creating a decision that has the effect of policy is a common occurrence. As Donald Horowitz has noted,

> Federal courts have laid down elaborate standards for food handling, hospital operations, recreation facilities, inmate employment and education, sanitation, and laundry, painting, lighting, plumbing, and renovation in some prisons; they have ordered other prisons closed. Courts have established equally comprehensive programs of care and treatment for the mentally ill confined in hospitals. They have ordered the equalization of school expenditures on teachers' salaries, established hearing procedures for public school discipline cases, decided that bilingual educations must be provided for Mexican-American children, and suspended the use by school boards of the National Teacher Examination and comparable tests for school supervisors. . . . They have told the Farmers Home Administration to restore a disaster loan program, the Forest Service to stop the clear-cutting of timber, and the Corps of Engineers to maintain the nation's nonnavigable waterways. (1977, 4–5)

All of these examples are a reminder that the legal system travels down the same political tracks that have been well worn by leaders in the executive and legislative branches. Cases like those involving surrogate parenting or school desegregation and prayer are vivid evidence that the courts must deal with problems that have not been disposed of by legislative or administrative action. The remainder of this chapter focuses especially on the communication dimensions that exist when such cases emerge as part of the nation's political consciousness.

THE COURTS IN A POLITICAL WORLD

In some ways the diffuse American legal system provides ideal ground to nurture political debate. Because the trial process has the effect of personalizing the consequences of laws in ways that other political institutions such as legislatures might not, courts provide a ready source of social details from which to construct popular narratives of tension and change. Although it is a by-product rather than a purpose of its structure, the trial elicits for the public record the uniquely private features of personal and social conflict. Other institutions like Congress and its agencies may reduce issues to generic principles and abstract "what ifs"; the courts deal in the personal details of ordinary lives. The common law tradition is to build judgmental principles based on the particulars of individual cases. The insanity defense, for example, is almost always discussed in the popular media in the context of a specific instance rather than through the abstract discussions of psychiatrists and legal scholars who focus on the underlying principles. For example, most Americans heard and judged arguments about the insanity pleas of John Hinkley and John Salvi. Hinkley searched for a strange kind of fame by attempting to take the life of Ronald Reagan in 1981;[4] Salvi used an insanity defense after murdering two receptionists at a Massachusetts abortion clinic in 1994 (Butterfield 1996, A10). But fewer Americans have probably ever encountered the bitter academic debate between legal and mental health professionals over the legitimacy of basic psychiatric categories routinely used in the construction of legal defenses.[5] In the public mind there may be a vague sense in which "the law" is understood as a body of abstract codes, but for most Americans the legal system exists at any time in the dramatic events that have surfaced in the national news agenda.

In addition to becoming the arena of justice for segments of society and their representatives, the nation's courts are also overtly political in several other ways. Judicial selection procedures themselves may be political. Forty-one states choose some of their judges in partisan elections or provide mechanisms for rejecting a sitting judge (Blum 1995, 19). In New York, for example, party dominance is so strong in various regions that the power of local political bosses to choose a candidate for a judgeship is tantamount to the power to appoint. As New Yorker and former Secretary of State Cyrus Vance has noted, in many instances "judges are selected for their political service rather than their judicial ability. Far too often judges chosen by the bosses have been lazy, incompetent or, worse, corrupt" (1988, E30).

The other common route for selection of judges is by executive appointment. All 740 members of the federal judiciary are assigned in this way. Ronald Reagan and George Bush, for example, appointed 579 judges—including four to the Supreme Court—in their combined three terms (Hickok and McDowell 1993, 160).

Appointments made ostensibly on merit would seem to have some advantages over popular elections, since it is easy to imagine that many voters may not know the qualifications of candidates seeking a judgeship. But appointments can have their own problems. The principle of "senatorial courtesy" makes the candidate for any judgeship the subject of considerable political maneuvering between the president and the senators from the district of the vacancy. By tradition, senators expect to be consulted about nominees, especially if they have established a positive relationship with the White House. A long-standing custom obliges other members to seriously consider that objection by denying confirmation ("Senatorial Courtesy" 1993, 350–51).

And, of course, Supreme Court nominees are closely scrutinized by legislators and interest groups for indications of how they may rule in future high-profile cases. The Senate defeat of Reagan nominee Robert Bork and the stormy confirmation of Clarence Thomas in 1991 have demonstrated how high the political stakes have become. Bork was eventually defeated by a Senate that viewed his record as too conservative and too inflexible in adapting the Constitution to present needs. Thomas barely overcame questions about his judicial philosophy and stunning last-minute charges of sexual harassment raised by Anita Hill. But the effects of both rounds of confirmation hearings was clear. Few high-level appointees will escape the political minefields of Senate and presidential politics in the future.

Neither election or appointment processes guarantee good judges, but they serve as a reminder that access to the third branch of government is frequently gained by winning the favor of leaders from the two elective branches.

Further evidence of the implicit link between the political world and the judiciary has steadily accumulated over the years in memoirs, speeches and articles that have generally served to demystify courts and the legal system. What Thurman Arnold did to the "mysteries of jurisprudence" in a book written before he became Franklin Roosevelt's attorney general, countless others have done more recently in unmasking the operations and private tensions that play out in some court rulings. In *The Symbols of Government* Arnold took a fresh look at the "fictions" and "myths" in the legal system. "Here is a subject," he noted, "which not even lawyers read." To the extent legal philosophy is discussed in public, its purpose is largely symbolic and reassuring. "Without a science of jurisprudence, law might be considered a collection of man-made rules for practical situations. With it the Law becomes the cornerstone of government" (1962, 46).

The tendency to unmask the special status of the courts probably reached its highest point in 1979 with the publication of *The Brethren* by Bob Woodward and Scott Armstrong. This hugely popular book gave the impression that a large number of former Supreme Court law clerks and perhaps several associate justices abandoned their pledges to secrecy about the inner workings of the nine-person tribunal. No book had ever attempted to describe the peculiar proclivities and working habits of members of the court. It provided riveting accounts of vote swapping, pettiness, and earthiness that made the justices all too familiar. Members were variously portrayed as devoted, often diligent, sometimes lazy and confused, and usually careful to withhold opinions until others had committed themselves to an emerging point of view. Woodward and Armstrong's insider style made the book a stunning revelation, if only because it portrayed the ordinariness of the Court's routine. In one case a justice is said to have "seethed" at having been assigned the task of writing up the majority opinion on a "chickenshit" case (1979, 359). So much for the dignity of the institution.

Such reporting is now a routine part of popular writing about the nation's highest court, aided in part by more open tensions between some of its members, and by "insider" journalism that seeks to expose and reconstruct moments from the Supreme Court's back regions. A 1996 *New York Times* profile of Chief Justice William Rehnquist, for example, uses sources "close to" him and other associate justices to construct the tensions and working styles of the current court. Among the observations are estimates of the effects of Antonin Scalia's sometimes caustic dissents from majority opinions, especially those that have "deeply wounded" other justices such as Sandra Day O'Connor.

> A former Scalia clerk acknowledges that Scalia "completely alienated" O'Connor and "lost her forever," and a former Rehnquist clerk notes how O'Connor's "personality is in many ways just the opposite of Justice Scalia's. She's very willing to build (a) consensus on opinions." But Scalia, says another ex-clerk, is not only "in love with his own language," he also believes that "what he's doing is a matter of principle. He knows how right he is." (Garrow 1996, 69)

Many Court followers wonder how the traditionally shrouded Court has suddenly become so transparent to journalists. Whatever their doubts, however, there is little reason to question the conclusion that the most prestigious court is now at least partly understood in terms of its bureaucratic and political style.

THE PUBLICITY FUNCTIONS OF LITIGATION

The vast majority of the nation's courts go about their work without the attention of the mass media and general public. But the exceptions are important to consider. Even routine court cases, ranging from the divorce of a celebrity to a suit brought by one large corporation against another, may become news. The higher the visibility of a case, the greater the likelihood that its details will seem to raise questions or doubts about public policy. Conflicts that go to trial under the scrutiny of the press usually touch on issues of class, status, or policy. This section explores several kinds of trial settings that illustrate these connections.

The Politics of Prosecution

The process of determining who will become a defendant in a criminal or civil trial is partly selective, as it is in every complex society. Justice in the United States is frequently pursued at the discretion of the police, prosecutors, judges, regulators, and victims. At various times all of these interested parties may function as gatekeepers in the application of justice. Using a wide variety of crime reports and general population surveys, for instance, criminal justice experts estimate that over half of all assaults and rapes go unreported by their victims; most burglaries go unsolved; and the vast majority of "victimless crimes" such as gambling and prostitution remain concealed (Davis 1969, 17; Davis 1976, 1–2).

In his own account as a fledgling assistant district attorney in Manhattan, David Heilbroner describes the power he and his newer colleagues had in attempting to arrive at decisions that would have enormous effects on all of those affected by crime: those who allegedly committed it and those who were its victims. That task of being a DA involved using "discretion wisely, looking for cases worth fighting for."

> I supposed the power we wielded over other people's lives made us feel as if we were the executors of morality. A word from us and a person goes free; another word and he is whisked away to the pens by court officers. We were judges of sorts, but also advocates—roles that were in some sense incompatible. And we had been handed power at an age when we were not likely to understand how to use it wisely. I still heard too much "lock up the sleaze" talk from rookies, and not enough worry over race relations, poverty, or rehabilitation. (1990, 284)

"No government has ever been a government of laws and not of men in the sense of eliminating all discretionary power," notes Kenneth Davis (1969, 17). This is especially true in the prosecution of cases involving antitrust violations or tax evasion, where the decision to go forward is largely up to the investigators involved.

Among the factors that weigh in the decision to prosecute higher level cases are political and public relations considerations. Prosecutors must regularly navigate through the traffic of political issues and media agendas that regularly cross through their jurisdictions. Because prosecutors often use their offices to launch themselves deeper into the political world, they are likely to be very responsive to the exigencies of public opinion.

One case study of the pragmatic and political factors that figured into decisions to prosecute in the Seattle area points out a number of deciding variables that can be worded as questions. How much public exposure will a prosecutor have in the courtroom for going forward? Could a case put him or her in an embarrassing situation; for instance, by forcing a confrontation with a popular leader or party ally? And are seemingly "victimless" crimes worth the effort and the use of limited court resources (Cole 1978, 100)? In some cases the decision to go forward with cases involving prostitutes or adult bookstore owners may have more to do with the public relations needs of a county or district attorney, than the protection of the relatively contented "victims" of these crimes (Zelensny 1997, 454).

A high position in the criminal justice system can provide a fast track to someone with an eye on a political career. Theodore Roosevelt was hardly the first to discover that being a flamboyant enemy of crime—as New York City's police commissioner—could pay enormous political dividends. Large numbers of state and federal legislators have followed similar paths, using highly visible careers as prosecutors as springboards into politics. Senator Arlen Specter of Pennsylvania, for example, first became a district attorney in Philadelphia, specializing in the prosecution of sensational cases, ranging from widely reported rapes to the structural failure of the roof of a newly constructed sports arena. As one observer of his career noted, "Hardly a day went by during Specter's stint in which he didn't hold a news conference, announce some new investigation, or release a statement to the press" (Waas 1985, 13–15). New York City Mayor Rudolph Giuliani followed a similar route. He first gained national notoriety some years earlier as an associate attorney general in the Reagan administration, changing the focus of what that office had done. Under the Carter administration a "white collar crime" unit was established within the FBI to gather evidence about illegal business practices and corruption within federal contractors. McDonnell Douglas, among other firms, was nearly in the net of Justice Department prosecution at the time. But over the strenuous objections of many professionals who had been working on these cases, Giuliani dropped or settled them, favoring instead a more publicized $130 million enlargement of federal drug enforcement efforts (Winerip 1985, 37).

The Politics of Litigation

Another important way the courts function as extensions of the political process is in the way civil litigation can be used to generate favorable publicity. Many groups use legal action as a way to activate public opinion. Civil suits may manifestly seek financial damages, changes in the conduct of one of the parties, or a combination of both. But they also function to raise concerns or orchestrate general public opinion for the future.

Among the most specific rhetorical objectives of litigation is the chance to shape public opinion against a defendant, frequently a scenario that gives the upper hand to those who take on corporate Goliaths. Litigation attracts attention and sometimes taps into considerable public sympathy for the victims portrayed in widely reported news stories. For instance, the decision by an environmental group to seek damages in behalf of the residents near a corporation's factory can carry a credibility that simple charges of pollution might not have. The filing of a suit binds the corporation to respond, a scene graphically portrayed in films and popular nonfiction, such as Jonathan Harr's best-selling book about industrial pollution in a New England community. In *A Civil Action*, defendants charged with contributing to the cancer-related deaths of five children included major national companies who saw media coverage of the case as an "especially frightening specter" (1995, 95). "Everyone understands that the deck is stacked," noted one of the company's lawyers. "Somebody who's been hurt has the sympathy of the jury. Big companies don't get that sympathy" (96).

Once the threat of a public trial has been made, the prime objective of the plaintiff has sometimes been achieved. Both parties to the conflict may find that the uncertainty of a verdict is less desirable than an out-of-court settlement that allows each side to save face.

Among the many private groups that use litigation as a form of publicity is the Public Citizen Litigation Group, and the Center for Science in the Public Interest (CSPI). Both organizations were founded by lawyers and activists associated with consumer activist Ralph Nader and his Center for the Study of Responsive Law. The Public Interest Litigation Group is a ten-lawyer public interest law firm with self-stated goals of "serving as a watchdog to make sure that the government enforces the laws that are designed to protect the public" and "combating the use of corporate power that jeopardizes the rights and well-being of the American consumer" ("Government and Corporate Responsibility" 1996). Objects of suits range from General Motors over allegedly unsafe fuel systems in trucks to the now bankrupt Dow-Corning corporation over the use of silicone-gel breast implants. Similarly, the Center for Science in the Public Interest has focused on consumer issues, mostly relating to food. The work of this organization was largely responsible for passage of the landmark Nutrition Labeling and Education Act of 1990, which mandates nutritional labeling on nearly all food labels. More recently, the group has taken on ethnic restaurants for their high fat menus, movie theaters because of their saturated fat popcorn oils, and Proctor and Gamble over the side effects of their controversial fat substitute, Olestra. CSPI only rarely engages in litigation as part of its efforts to reform the

American diet. But powerful food interests ranging from the Food and Drug Administration to individual corporations remain as potential targets of unwanted attention and litigation ("A Brief History" 1996).

Legal Action on Status Issues: Race and Affirmative Action in California

One of the notable ironies of modern political life is that the same legal institutions charged with guaranteeing "equal protection under the law" have unintentionally become agents for conferring legitimacy to factions locked in volatile status disputes. Political issues become status issues when activists representing gender, ethnic, or lifestyle concerns come to believe that a pending decision will have the effect of affirming or denying the political legitimacy of their group. They come to see a decision as a test of their group's "place" in American life. Any governmental decision on the issue has the effect of making one side in a status conflict feel like its in-group honor has been either reinforced or rebuffed. The suffrage and civil rights movements, the temperance movement, and efforts to pass an equal rights amendment all clearly involved such stakes.[6] In contemporary politics issues of status have laid near the surface of debates about the rights of homosexuals in the military and as marriage partners, access to upper-management positions by women and minorities, the place of recent immigrants to the United States, and access of African Americans to full legal protection in the criminal justice system.

For many Americans the beating of Rodney King by the members of the Los Angeles police involved status issues. The vindication of the police in an earlier trial had produced widespread anger and urban rioting. King had become an unwilling symbol, a surrogate for the city's underclass in a case that would test the depths of institutionalized racism. Would King, a black motorist, see justice served in a second trial that accused his white assailants of violating his civil rights? When the guilty verdict of the federal case against several of the officers was announced, many residents of the city breathed a sigh of relief, noting that the polarized community would probably be spared further riots and racial rage.[7]

The presence of status issues accounts for much of the public and press attention that court cases receive. Nowhere has this been more apparent than in recent court cases in California that paved the way in the 1970s for large-scale affirmative action programs and contributed to a surprising backlash from residents against such programs in 1996.

Affirmative action programs provide institutional safeguards that seek to assure that minorities which have historically been deprived of equal access to education or jobs are given full consideration. Especially in education and job placement, affirmative action is easily portrayed in polar terms that translate into status. Such programs are seen either as necessary efforts to redress decades of discrimination against blacks and women or as intrusive forms of social engineering that "discriminate in reverse" by denying access to the best prepared or most talented. The decision of a majority of California's voters to end such programs in 1996 in the form of a proposition that would prohibit "preferential treatment to any individual or group on the basis of race [or] sex" was largely the product of years of white resentment, triggered in part by high-visibility court cases (Pear 1996, B7).

Arguably the most visible affirmative action case in California was one that ended up in the Supreme Court in 1978. The details of *Regents of the University of California v. Bakke* were quite simple. In 1972 Allen Bakke applied to and was turned down by the University of California for admission to its new medical school in Davis. He was not admitted in part, he later discovered, because a certain number of positions at the university were held for candidates in the affirmative action program intended for minority candidates. It was true, he was told, that his high "B" average was better than those of some of the affirmative action candidates, but the university remained committed to hold some spaces for minority students who had suffered from years of racial prejudice and second-rate schooling in the United States.

Bakke's suit brought little national attention when it was raised in the quiet Sacramento Valley town of Woodland. But the decision to appeal to the California Supreme Court brought quick responses from a number of groups and their constituencies. There was deep irony in this case; a white middle-class man charged that his civil rights had been violated by the admissions personnel at the university. In some ways his complaint was a mirror image of desegregation cases in the 1960s and early 1970s that were brought against colleges in Mississippi, Alabama and, later, against schools in many northern states as well. The difference, of course, was that Bakke's suit opposing the university split apart two civil rights principles that had usually been aligned. His attorneys raised the issue of whether protections against discrimination weren't by themselves discriminatory. Was Bakke the victim of reverse discrimination, or a dangerous threat to hard-won programs to finally redress the imbalance in educational opportunity within the United States? The Anti-Defamation League and the American Federation of Teachers spoke out in his defense and attacked race "quotas" that, they argued, unfairly excluded Bakke. On the other side of the issue the NAACP and various university associations supported the university's affirmative action plan.[8]

News accounts of Bakke's complaint provided tangible proof to large numbers of Americans that civil rights cases had "gone too far." And eventually the Supreme Court ruled that rigid quotas for minorities applying for admission to these kinds of programs were unconstitutional. However, the justices were careful not to overturn the ideal of affirmative action. But the die had been cast. In 1995 the University of California ended affirmative action programs, and the state's governor ran on the issue in the early months of the 1996 presidential campaign. In the fall of the same year a plurality of the state's residents voted in favor of Proposition 209, which mandated an end to all preferential programs across the state. The Bakke case and several decades of public debate about racial quotas and affirmative action had left Californians and many Americans with very different views of how far the United States had come in addressing issues of racial justice. Cases such as those involving King and Bakke will continue to serve as dramatic representations of the social tensions and resentments in American life.

TELEVISED TRIALS AND THE POLITICAL AGENDA

The large majority of those who administer the courts in the United States view the publicity value of mass media coverage with skepticism and occasional hostility. Former Supreme Court Chief Justice Warren Burger's legendary contempt for television journalism became one of the most identifiable features of his tenure before he retired. He repeatedly cautioned clerks and staff in the Court to avoid talking to the press. It was not unusual for Burger to specify to a group that he would speak before them only if broadcasters were excluded (Rivers 1982, 95–96). His reactions were extreme, but they reflect what have been the feelings of many who control the judiciary—that publicity is not a constructive force in the administration of justice.

The clearest evidence of this wary relationship is in continuing concerns about the effect that extensive press coverage of crime has on potential jurors and witnesses. Widespread coverage of crime pits two important constitutional principles against each other. On one hand, the First Amendment protects the rights of journalists, but at the same time the Sixth Amendment promises defendants a fair and impartial trial (Zelensny 1997, 231–33). Extensive coverage of arrests and pretrial proceedings have sometimes made it difficult to find jurors who have not already formed opinions about a defendant's guilt based on what has been reported.

The issue may be further complicated when a trial actually begins; judges and journalists then must deal with very specific questions of privacy. For example, to what extent should the victims of crimes and their families have the protection of the courts to keep their names and faces from public view? And are witnesses to be given any protection if their testimony could place them in possible danger? It is easy for most people to accept a judge's decision to restrict the reporting of the names of children and other vulnerable victims. But members of the press are understandably hostile to any court proceedings that give weight to "gag rules" issued from the bench which restrict reporting. And, in general, court cases that have challenged the concept of the open courtroom have resulted in decisions that favor journalistic access. In the words of Thomas Tedford,

> The U.S. Supreme Court has determined that America's courtrooms are presumed open to the public and the press unless the trial judge presents convincing evidence to prove that closure is essential to a fair trial. (1993, 244)

But for many jurists and observers there is a qualitative difference between access for the print media and access for cameras. The immediacy and sometimes intense visibility of video coverage is often questioned, primarily on the grounds that it may change the process and put unreasonable pressures on the participants.

The nearly year-long trial of sports celebrity O. J. Simpson presented such a case and produced scores of legal and media experts who worried about the effects of its high visibility. The Los Angeles proceedings were awash in coverage from the Court Channel, CNN, E-Entertainment Television, and the traditional networks. Many of the network affiliates even dumped their popular afternoon soap operas in favor of extensive coverage and commentary. Prior to the 1995 trial, judges and many states had cautiously opened their proceedings to more coverage. By 1994 forty-seven states allowed some form of video reporting in certain courts (Thaler 1994, 23). Federal courts have remained far more reluctant to grant video access, and experiments with cameras in federal courts have left most courts closed to cameras and observers deeply divided ("Progress on Courtroom Cameras" 1996, A22).

But the media circus of the Simpson trial created its own backlash against coverage at all levels. Some, like legal affairs professor Susan Estrich and *New York Times* senior editor Max Frankel, argued that cameras in the courtroom corrupted and prolonged the trial by months, leaving a trail of misinformation and cynicism rather than enlightenment about the American judicial system (Estrich 1995, 19; Frankel 1995, B27). Others including *60 Minutes* producer Don Hewitt argued that the coverage "overpowered" the audience and distorted the process (Goodman 1995, Sec. 2, 27).

In the immediate aftermath of the trial, journalists, who found some judges and prosecutors much more wary, decided against camera coverage. In the case of Susan Smith, a mother charged in the drowning death of her two children, cameras were removed from the court after pretrial hearings. The request was made by the defense attorney who noted that "the moment the cameras were turned off it was as though someone had pumped the air back in the courtroom" ("Simpson Case" 1995, 35). In another California murder trial a judge greatly restricted coverage of television and placed a partial gag order on reporters, warning that "nothing like the O. J. Simpson case is going to happen in my courtroom" (Smolowe 1995, 38). Even the second civil trial of Simpson (for violating the civil rights of those he allegedly murdered) proceeded without cameras.[9]

Many critics point to an increasing trend by television to focus on only more sensational cases, and recent history prior to the Simpson trial is not very encouraging. Rape and murder rank high as likely candidates for sustained coverage of television (Kaplan 1988, 37; Henry 1984, 64). And the coverage is often highly selective. While some observers agree with First Amendment lawyer Floyd Abrams that "the more exposure the public has to the judicial process, the better we'll be as a society and the better our courts will become," others note that cameras only offer "out of context untruths" (Volk 1989, 24–25).

In the immediate future it is evident that state courts will continue to take the lead in the use of cameras. What is interesting about this difference is how it probably distorts perceptions of the legal process. The reason is that federal cases are often about "paper" rather than "physical" crimes. Cases involving bribery, fraud, espionage, obstruction of justice, and civil rights violations are typical. Defendants tend to be corporations and their officers, heads of institutions, or major political officials. The net effect of this unequal access is that public attitudes are more susceptible to the voyeuristic pleasures of trials dealing with physical crimes than to the less photogenic instances of lawbreaking that occur in the bureaucratic layers of institutions. If those who administer the federal courts continue to hold out against the presence of cameras, the effect will probably be to heighten the national tendency to view crime in its stereotypical forms: largely in terms of grizzly assaults. While Americans were pulled into days of continuous coverage of the Simpson trial, for example, federal attempts to come to terms with widespread Medicare fraud received scant coverage. By one estimate, well over 120 hospitals nationwide had submitted false Medicare billing claims (MCarthy 1995, 564). In one case alone a Philadelphia hospital agreed to pay $30 million in penalties (Johnston 1995, A18). Network evening news reports on the subject added up to less than 30 minutes for the entire year, a tiny fraction of the time devoted to the Simpson trial.[10]

If this differential between federal and criminal courts remains, the American perceptions of the legal process will continue to be distorted. The main reason is that television transforms almost any subject that it covers. Because its content always comes through someone, it invites the emotions to actively participate in the mapping of responses and attitudes. As Joshua Meyrowitz has pointed out, television content creates a kind of visceral contact between its subjects and viewers that is quite unlike more discursive forms of communication (1985, 94–114). It can make outrage an instant pleasure available to everyone, a response that does not have to be confirmed by the disembodied facts of a written narrative. It also allows us to be "present" at an event, even while it sometimes keeps us from understanding its limitations.

SUMMARY

In this chapter we have argued that the courts need to be considered as a major agent in the influence of public discourse about American politics. The conventional view that the courts are apolitical because they exist outside the administrative and legislative institutions of government does not hold up under close scrutiny. In many ways the judiciary contributes to political debate and public discussion. Some judges and prosecutors are elected. Some courts issue decisions that make policy. And trials have a natural dramatic structure that can make them ideal settings for distilling larger cultural conflicts. They can focus attention on the effects of controversial policies. Trials personalize issues in ways that make it easy to attract media attention. They sometimes focus attention on tensions in the society that flow from group feelings of social alienation or rejection. And trials that include television coverage carry the special opportunity to emerge as major events, especially when celebrities or high-visibility crimes are involved. The televised trial can make outrage and vindication instant pleasures available to everyone, visceral responses that do not have to be confirmed by the disembodied facts of a second-hand narrative.

In these pages we have also argued that litigation frequently has a political effect, and sometimes a political purpose. Prosecutors may make calculations about the nature of public opinion and how it squares with the need to pursue or ignore certain kinds of "victimless" or white-collar crimes. And organizations with public policy objectives may make the same calculations, knowing that the publicity value of a lawsuit against a key institution can energize supporters and focus public attention.

NOTES

1. Articles in popular media such as *Time* magazine reflected the power of a court case to raise larger political considerations. See, for example, Richard Lacayo. "Is This Womb a Rented Space?" *Time*, 22 September 1986, p. 36.

2. The novelist John Grisham and the film director Sidney Lumet have both made successful careers using the courtroom as a setting. See, for example, Grisham's novel and film, "A Time to Kill," and Lumet's 1982 drama, "The Verdict."

See Doreen Weisenhaus, "A Crowded Docket for Courtroom Addicts," *New York Times*, 24 November 1996, p. H38.

3. For background on this case see Pete Axthelm and David L. Gonsalez, "A Death Wish Vigilante," *Newsweek*, 7 January 1985, pp. 10–11.

4. See, for example, "It's a Mad Mad Verdict," *The New Republic*, 12 July 1982, pp. 13–18; and Lincoln Caplan, "Annals of Law," *The New Yorker*, 2 July 1984, pp. 46–78.

5. For representations of this debate, see Michael S. Moore, *Law and Psychiatry: Rethinking the Relationship* (New York: Cambridge University Press, 1984); and Thomas S. Szasz, *The Myth of Mental Illness* (New York: Hoeber-Harper, 1961).

6. For background on status issues see Joseph R. Gusfield, *Symbolic Crusade: Status Politics and the American Temperance Movement* (Urbana: University of Illinois, 1963), p. 22.

7. See, for example, Tom Mathews, "Looking Past the Verdict," *Newsweek*, 26 April 1993, pp. 20–24.

8. Our summary of the case is drawn from Joel Dreyfuss and Charles Lawrence's *The Bakke Case: The Politics of Inequality* (New York: Harcourt Brace Jovanovich, 1979).

9. The second Simpson judge was certain that he did not want a repeat of the first televised trial. He banned cameras. But one network, E-Entertainment Television, took the unusual step of using each day's transcript as a basis for recreating courtroom events with actors and an official narrator. See Caryn James, "No Cameras in Court? No Problem," *New York Times*, 2 December 1996, p. C14.

10. A search of the Vanderbilt University News Archives for all of 1995 yielded only 6 stories running for an average of just over 2 minutes on the three network newscasts (Abstracts, Vanderbilt News Archives, 11 November 1996 [online]).

REFERENCES

Abstracts. 1996. Vanderbilt News Archives, 11 November [online].

Arnold, Thurman. 1962. *The Symbols of Government*. New York: Harcourt, Brace and World.

Axthelm, Pete, and David Gonsalez. 1985. "A Death Wish Vigilante." *Newsweek*, 7 January: 10–11.

Blum, Lawrence. 1995. "Electing Judges." In *Contemplating Courts*, ed. Lee Epstein. Washington, DC: Congressional Quarterly Press, pp. 18–43.

"A Brief History." 1996. Center for Science in the Public Interest. 11 November [online].

Butterfield, Fox. 1996. "Dispute Over Insanity Defense Is Revived in Murder Trial." *New York Times*, 4 March: A10.

Caplan, Lincoln. 1984. "Annals of Law." *The New Yorker*, 2 July: 46–78.

Church, Thomas W. 1995. "Plea Bargaining and Local Legal Culture." In *Contemplating Courts*, ed. Lee Epstein. Washington, DC: Congressional Quarterly, pp. 132–54.

Cole, George. 1978. "The Decision to Prosecute." In *American Court Systems*, ed.

Sheldon Goldman and Austin Sarat. San Francisco: W. H. Freeman, pp. 97–102.

Davis, Kenneth. 1969. *Discretionary Justice: A Preliminary Inquiry*. Baton Rouge: Louisiana State University.

———. 1976. *Discretionary Justice in Europe and America*. Urbana: University of Illinois.

Dreyfuss, Joel, and Charles Lawrence. 1979. *The Bakke Case: The Politics of Inequality*. New York: Harcourt, Brace, Javonovich.

Estrich, Susan. 1995. "Playing to the Cameras." *New York Times*, 3 June: 19.

Frank, Jerome. 1950. *Courts on Trial: Myth and Reality in American Justice*. Princeton, NJ: Princeton University Press.

Frankel, Max. 1995. "Out of Focus." *New York Times*, 5 November: 26.

Garrow, David. 1996. "One Angry Man." *New York Times Magazine*, 6 October: 68–69.

Goodman, Walter. 1995. "The Camera as Culprit? Look Again." *New York Times*, 17 September: B27.

"Government and Corporate Responsibility." 1996. *Public Citizen*, 9 November [online].

Gusfield, Joseph. 1963. *Symbolic Crusade: Status Politics and the American Temperance Movement*. Urbana: University of Illinois.

Hamilton, Alexander et al. 1961. *The Federalist Papers*. New York: Mentor.

Harr, Jonathan. 1995. *A Civil Action*. New York: Vintage.

Heilbroner, David. 1990. *Rough Justice, Days and Nights of a Young D.A.* New York: Pantheon.

Henry, William III. 1984. "When News Becomes Voyeurism." *Time*, 26 March: 64.

Hickok, Eugene, and Gary McDowell. 1993. *Justice vs. Law: Courts and Politics in American Society*. New York: Free Press.

Horowitz, David. 1977. *The Courts and Social Policy*. Washington, DC: Brookings Institution.

"It's a Mad Mad Verdict." 1982. *The New Republic*, 12 July: 13–18.

Jaehing, Walter, David Weaver, and Frederick Fico. 1981. "Reporting Crime and Fearing Crime in Three Communities." *Journal of Communication* (Winter): 88–96.

James, Caryn. 1996. "No Cameras in Court? No Problem." *New York Times*, 2 December: C14.

Johnston, David. 1995. "University Agrees to Pay in Settlement on Medicare." *New York Times*, 13 December: A18.

Kaplan, David. 1988. "The Camera Is Proving Its Case in the Courtroom." *New York Times*, 18 December: 37.

Lacayo, Richard. 1986. "Is This Womb a Rented Space?" *Time*, 22 September: 36.

Mathews, Tom. 1993. "Looking Past the Verdict." *Newsweek*, 26 April: 20–24.

McCarthy, Michael. 1995. "Major US Hospitals Named in Fraud Suit." *Lancet*, 26 August: 564.

Meyrowitz, Joshua. 1985. *No Sense of Place*. New York: Oxford University Press.

Moore, Michael. 1984. *Law and Psychiatry: Rethinking the Relationship*. New York: Cambridge University Press.

Noble, Kenneth. 1996. "The Endless Rodney King Case." *New York Times*, 4 February: D5.

Pear, Robert. 1996. "In California, Foes of Affirmative Action See a New Day." *New York Times*, 7 November: B7.

"Progress on Courtroom Cameras." 1996. *New York Times*, 23 July: A22.

Rivers, William. 1982. *The Other Government: Power and the Washington Media*. New York: Universe.

"Senatorial Courtesy." 1993. *Congress A to Z*, 2d ed. Washington, DC: Congressional Quarterly, pp. 350–351.

"Simpson Case Backlash Keeps Cameras Out of Other Courtrooms." 1995. *New York Times*, 17 September: 35.

Smolowe, Jill. 1995. "TV Cameras on Trial." *Time*, 24 July: 38.

Szasz, Thomas. 1961. *The Myth of Mental Illness*. New York: Hoeber-Harper.

Tedford, Thomas. 1993. *Freedom of Speech in the United States*, 2d ed. New York: McGraw-Hill.

Thaler, Paul. 1994. *The Watchful Eye: American Justice in the Age of the Television Trial*. New York: Praeger.

Tocqueville, Alexis de. 1969. *Democracy in America*, ed. J. P. Mayer, trans. George Lawrence. New York: Doubleday.

Vance, Cyrus. 1988. "Now, Party Bosses Decide the 'Elections.'" *New York Times*, 22 May: E30.

Volk, Patricia. 1989. "The Steinberg Trial: Scenes from a Tragedy." *New York Times Magazine*, 15 January: 20–25.

Waas, Murray. 1985. "Media Specter." *The New Republic*, 30 September: 13–15.

Weisenhaus, Doreen. 1996. "A Crowded Docket for Courtroom Addicts." *New York Times*, 24 December: H38.

Winerip, Michael. 1985: "High Profile Prosecutor." *New York Times Magazine*, 9 June: 37–52.

Woodward, Bob, and Scott Armstrong. 1979. *The Brethren: Inside the Supreme Court*. New York: Simon & Schuster.

Zelensny, John. 1997. *Communications Law*, 2d ed. Belmont, CA: Wadsworth.

Chapter 12

Politics and Popular Culture

All art is propaganda; the only difference is the kind of propaganda.
Diego Rivera (1988)[1]

One of Ronald Reagan's biographers noted that the former film actor only played a villain once, in what was by his own admission a forgettable film called *The Killers*. He preferred to play heroes, as he did in two of his favorites, *Kings Row* and *Knute Rockne, All American* (Von Damm 1980, 18). That the former president would have rather enacted such roles cannot come as a surprise. In his preferences there is a lesson about the importance of entertainment as a shaper of political attitudes. More than most presidents, Reagan's rhetoric was always heavily laced with graphic images of personal courage and selfless sacrifice. Depictions of heroism, on film or in speeches, dramatized an essential premise of Reagan's brand of political conservatism—that the individual is fundamentally responsible for his own circumstances.[2]

From the abstract to the representational, the arts cannot help but serve as vehicles of explicit or implicit political commentary. Virtually everything from the largest grand operas to the humblest television situation comedies convey attitudes about values, organizations, and social relations: ranging from Verdi's nineteenth-century themes of political repression to a 1997 situation comedy that takes the "risk" of making its primary character a lesbian. Only a small percentage of commercial television time is devoted to national public issues. But it would be a mistake to assume that the rest of the remaining space does not contribute to political perceptions in both planned and accidental ways.

In this chapter we briefly explore the communication of political themes in entertainment. Our belief is that civil discourse has partly merged into the language and forums of public amusement. News is now marketed as entertainment (or "info-tainment"), merging the lines between journalism and ratings-driven programming. "NBC's "Dateline" and CBS's venerable "60 Minutes" successfully employ the same story formulas used by the entertainment shows they compete against. Narratives of all forms are sometimes designed as "consciousness raising" exercises by their designers. Metro Goldwyn Mayer's famous motto, "Ars Gratia Artis" (Art for Art's Sake), hardly accounts for the fact that there are many politically relevant messages conveyed in our popular entertainment. In films, as in other media, these messages may be contained in reconstructions of historical settings (*The Longest Day, All the President's Men, Silkwood, The Crying Game, Evita*), portrayals of political conflict (*Mr. Smith Goes to Washington, Z, The China Syndrome, The Milagro Beanfield War, The Crucible*), the contested status of particular groups (*Whose Life Is It Anyway?, Philadelphia, Do the Right Thing*) or important power relationships, such as those between men and women (*My Brilliant Career, Thelma and Louise, Waiting to Exhale, The Joy Luck Club*).[3] In general, the products of popular culture leave their unique imprints on our collective consciousness. They define our status and relevance by telling us how we fit into the mythic America they so persuasively represent (Nimmo and Combs 1990, 110).

Our overview is in three parts, beginning with a look at political subtexts in popular narration or artistic presentation. It proceeds with a brief discussion of the nature of political celebrity. And the chapter closes with an overview of two recurring themes in assessing how political values are imposed on the products of popular culture.

TEXT AND SUBTEXT OF POLITICAL STORYTELLING

Portrayals of the nation's civil life have always been a feature of our public media. D. W. Griffith's spectacular silent 1915 epic, *Birth of a Nation* is an early landmark in film history. Woodrow Wilson is alleged to have said that it was "like history written by lightning" (Williams 1980, 74). It not only refined many of the current conventions of narrative film (i.e., the fade to black at the end of a scene), it also stirred controversy for its positive treatment of the Ku Klux Klan and its overt racism (Sklar 1975, 58–61). In World War I, government use of film as a suasive tool was augmented by all forms of media, including hundreds of popular recordings glorifying American honor. These recordings and the Victrolas to play them were routinely issued to troops in the field. By the time World War II began, the popular media of most nations was awash with themes intended to enshrine the civil affairs of the state. German films such as *Triumph of the Will* and American efforts like Frank Capra's *Why We Fight* series were vivid attempts to meld entertainment and political advocacy. Ronald Reagan's own war service was confined to this kind of work. He was assigned to a Hollywood production unit responsible for instructional and propaganda films. And his screen presence gave him a political persona that fit well with the untamed heroes he had sought to play earlier in his career. Years later it was used to good effect. If Hollywood frequently thwarted his attempts to play the avenging sheriff, he could at least use his post as president of the Screen Actor's Guild to guard again a Communist takeover of the studios.[4]

In some ways drama is the perfect vehicle for mass-oriented political discussion. It comes to the receiver in an attractive context (as entertainment) and in a perfect persuasive environment (when the viewer's defenses against persuasion are reduced). Dramatists routinely function as messengers to the society about its successes and failures. In Hugh Dalziel Duncan's apt phrase, theater is "the means by which we become objects to ourselves" (1968, 79). Plays and novels have "historically something of the same importance as journalism has for our own day" (80). They allow us to see our counterparts respond to shifting situations, many of which are personal, but also play out against the panorama of our times. Even seemingly innocuous fare can have direct political connotations, such as George Gershwin's *Strike Up the Band,* and the children's story, *The Wizard of Oz.* The first was a subtle but thorough send-up of presidential corruption and military spending (Rosenberg 1984, H4, H13). The second was originally written in book form as a populist diatribe against the presidential lethargy of William McKinley (Nimmo and Combs 1980, 146).

Popular melodramas and comedies are suited to conveying the ironies and hypocrisies built into institutions. Some, like *Wall Street, The Firm,* and *Jerry Maguire* unmask the venality of wealth or power in ways that have struck a responsive chord with audiences. Others (*To Kill a Mockingbird, Gandhi, Schindler's List*), have taken on legal or moral issues with the same populist fervor. And more recently, films have begun to reflect the growing public distrust of national leaders (*Primary Colors, Nixon*), political movements (*Bob Roberts, Michael Collins, Citizen Ruth*), and the media that cover them (*Network, Broadcast News, The Paper*).

Even forms of mass media with ostensibly nonpolitical objectives frequently contain at least an implicit political subtext or motivation. An exhibit, film, or television program that may have the manifest goal of simple entertainment can itself be the direct outcome of an intensely political agenda or a sustained power struggle. Consider the following cases:

- In 1987 the United States Information Agency was forced to cancel a planned exhibition of American portraits in Beijing. The reason: Chinese officials objected to the inclusion of paintings of General Douglas MacArthur and former Israeli Prime Minister, Golda Meir. MacArthur's likeness offended the Chinese, who recalled his involvement in the Korean War. They apparently also feared that a painting of Meir displayed in a Chinese exhibition hall would offend Arab allies (Molotsky 1987, C19).
- The armed services often assist filmmakers in stories about the military—if the stories are complimentary. *The Hunt for Red October, Top Gun, Patriot Games,* and *Air Force One* are among those that were made with the assistance and advice of military officials (Shenon 1997, D2). Films that reflect poorly on the armed services are discouraged. For the 1997 film, *G.I. Jane,* which portrays Demi Moore as a woman undergoing brutal training and rampant sexism to become a Navy Seal, there was no help. The treatment of women in the Navy has been an especially sensitive issue in recent years. The Navy wanted no part of the movie.
- A planned 1995 Smithsonian Institution exhibit entitled "The Last Act: The Atomic Bomb and the end of World War II" became embroiled in controversy over how the the dropping of the bomb would be portrayed. Veterans and conservative groups had come to believe that the exhibit would be "pro-Japanese," suggesting that the United States' decision to use the atomic bomb against two Japanese cities was undertaken for self-serving, racist reasons. Groups, including a writer in *Air Force Magazine,* called the museum "unpatriotic" for planning the exhibit, which was to feature the Enola Gay, the first and only plane that has dropped an atomic bomb on a foreign target. Eventually the museum cancelled the original exhibit, much to the frustration of historians who argued that sanitized popular memory had gotten in the way of historical truth (Sherwin 1995, 692–694).
- In the 1990–91 television season, Ted Turner's WTBS "superstation" carried over 360 hours of programming devoted to the environment, a reflection of Turner's interest in promoting ecological issues. At the same time, CNN increased its coverage of foreign affairs, reflecting another passion of its owner: a belief in the value of neutral "one-world" programming. CNN International was started. Non-Americans were hired as reporters. And journalists in the company were warned that they would be fined $100 if they used the word "foreign" in their reporting (Goldberg and Goldberg 1995, 423). In 1997, to further dramatize his internationalism, Turner pledged to give $1 billion to the United Nations—perhaps the largest gift ever offered by a philanthropist.
- One of the most-discussed films of 1996 was *The First Wives Club,* a comedy about three middle-aged women who seek revenge on former husbands who left them for younger "trophy" wives. One of the characters is a Hollywood star (Goldie Hawn), who laments that producers now only want her for "mother" roles. "Sean Connery," she notes, "is over 300 and he's still a stud." For *Time Magazine,* which gave the film a coveted cover, the story represented at least a momentary return to the powerful women that used to frequent the nation's movie screens. "It says women can thrive in the good old '30s way:

by being smart, sexy, human" (Corliss, 1996). For others such as the *Washington Post's* Rita Kemply, the film was "a bit of stale feminist fluff," a "femme empowerment fantasy" that unintentionally made its villains the younger and inarticulate women courted by the lead characters' former husbands (Kempley 1996). One suspects that the film's makers did not see themselves as promoters of a political statement. But it was partly "read" that way, fueling already charged feelings of about gender and power in American life.

- Herbert Mitgang and others have uncovered evidence that the Federal Bureau of Investigation and other agencies have long collected files on writers and entertainers, presumably to track their political views. Mitgang was able to gain access to dossiers on a number of major figures in American literature, including Ernest Hemingway, Pearl S. Buck, Sinclair Lewis, William Faulkner, W. H. Auden, Tennessee Williams, Thomas Wolfe, and Thorton Wilder (Mitgang 1987, 47–90). After a 20-year battle, a California historian also forced the agency to release a 300-page dossier on John Lennon. The former Beatle was under surveillance supposedly because of his antiwar activities in the early 1970s (Smith 1997, El).
- In 1996 the Chinese government warned the Walt Disney Company that the release of "*Kundun*," Martin Scorsese's sympathetic film about the Dalai Lama, would injure the company's efforts to expand China. The film tells the story of the Tibetan leader's exile after China extended its control over Tibet. The threat of economic repercussions against Disney was clearly intended to serve as a warning against media companies who might produce programming questioning China's control of Tibet, as well as its human rights record. Several years earlier the same government required the News Corporation to drop the BBC World Service from its satellite television feeds to Asia. Although it is perhaps the most admired broadcast news organization in the world, the BBC—like Disney—had apparently offended Chinese officials (Weinraub 1996, C11–12).

These examples are quite diverse. But they collectively suggest that the content of much of popular culture is touched by political intentions, or by messages that define important themes.

All of this suggests that media content overtly communicates attitudes and values. But it is also important to note that the *absence* of content can have significance, though it is admittedly harder to measure. Sometimes what is missing in reconstructions of events communicates its own message. What might be called "arguments by omission" include subjects and issues that *could be but are not* represented in a specific plot line or character choice. The consistently omitted perspective or image can carry its own weight in shaping public perceptions. Thoughtful observers often ask questions about the features of ordinary life that are sometimes missing in popular entertainment. Are black males in prime time overrepresented as sports figures and underrepresented as professionals? Where in popular entertainment are there models of young men engaged in peaceful resolution of conflict? In contrast to the rest of the world, why are America's networks and television stations so reluctant to purchase programming from foreign producers? All of these questions suggest that public opinion is *not* tempered by forces that could be constructive and socially useful. We do not usually know what the media's gatekeepers have omitted, but those omissions frequently form patterns that have their own effects.

THE PERSONAL AS POLITICAL

In both fictional and news forms of media, the formulas of narration require a strong focus on the individual. Television almost always illuminates policy through the solitary actions of specific characters.

One feature of narration is that the individual typically is represented as a free agent responsible for his or her own salvation. Institutional solutions to complex problems tend to be ignored or underplayed. Where social scientists talk of the fragmentation of American life, our dream factories suggest a rich pluralism. Where economists and critics find systemic national problems, our popular drama usually suggests that we—as individuals—have become what we chose to be. The political or governmental solution to a personal trauma is not the stuff of great art.

Audiences would feel cheated if a victim of social injustice were saved by a slow-working agency carrying out the mandates of a new state law. Such is reality. But melodramatic fantasy calls for something more sweeping and catalytic, for the victim to become the agent of his own redemption: for a person who seems like the rest of us—a rape victim, Clark Kent, or Bruce Wayne—to be transformed into an idealization of heroism.

Even though we often name eras after leaders (i.e., the Victorian age, the era of Jacksonian democracy), single figures rarely have the clout that has sometimes been assigned to them. Modern historical methods generally shun the "great leader" model. Even so, it is hard to ignore the power of narrative visual media like television and film to personalize a movement or issue in a single leader. This process is evident in struggles that have been intensified in the public memory through their associations with key actors: Harvey Milk and the activist gay agenda in San Francisco, Martin Luther King, Jr., and the early Civil Rights Movement, Sarah and Jim Brady on gun control, Jesse Jackson and the fight to maintain the social activism of the Democratic Party's left wing, and so on. Each has benefited from the tendency of the visual media to let them stand in for the views they expressed. Each has served as a condensation of their much more complex ideological commitments. Leaders seeking to capture public attention are well-advised to heed the dramatic imperative for the personal. Even those least interested in popular culture know that the pathway to shaping policy in the United States often requires sidetracks through the nation's vital media/celebrity circuits: TV talks shows, "life-style" interviews, even sitcoms, like the episode of *Seinfeld* featuring New York Mayor Giuliani.

Garry Wills's recent analysis of the legacy of film actor John Wayne carries this idea even further. As Wills describes him, Wayne had few concrete political ideas. But his lifelong reconstruction of the myth of the cowboy became its own symbol of rugged individualism. *Stagecoach, Red River, Fort Apache, The Alamo,* and *True Grit* were only a few of the films that contributed to the legend of a man whose public persona merged with the American myth of the frontier. His acting cumulatively suggested a recurring American fantasy that strong inner direction provides its own moral compass. It is a theme of autonomy and personal accountability that resonates through contemporary conservative thought (Dionne 1991, 62–63). The actor, Wills writes, embodied "a politics of large meanings, not of little policies—a politics of gender (masculine), ideology (patriotism), character (self-reliance), and responsibility" (Wills 1997, 29).

> Naturally, so political an art caused political resistance from those who disagreed with or feared its meaning—women, for instance, opposing the ethos of masculine supremacy. But the Wayne idea drew so deeply upon the largest mythos of our past—of the frontier, of a purifying landscape, of American exceptionalism, of discipline as the condition of rule—that some had trouble resisting the idea even when they renounced its consequences. (30)

Wayne's support of a pro-Vietnam film, *The Green Berets,* at a time when the war was becoming unpopular also cemented his traditionalist ethos. Though he had avoided military service himself, he had become a potent condensation symbol of aggressive American imperialism: General MacArthur's idea of the "model American soldier" (Wills 1997, 12).

Our point here is that popular political thought is sometimes interlaced with an awareness of public figures who have come to be identified with certain sensibilities. These individuals may be as diverse as Hillary Clinton, Pat Robertson, Karen Finley, or Camille Paglia. What they share is a tendency to be a "lightning rod" on a particular issue at a particular time.

TWO RECURRING THEMES IN THE ANALYSIS OF POPULAR ENTERTAINMENT

Two frames of reference are often used in assessing the political side effects of a society awash in the products of popular entertainment. Each is very different, but shares the same function of serving as a starting-point for deeper excursions into the analysis of political messages in "non-political" media. The first is the idea that the media extend experience to realms far beyond localized values and knowledge, thereby resituating us into less parochial and more global frames of reference. The second deals with those who hold the power to control media content.

Theory of Liberalizing Influence

Part of the conventional wisdom that comes with the study of the pluralistic mass media in Western nations is that they create "a window on the world" that has unprecedented breadth. Mass media within the reach of nearly everyone provide a wealth of new experiences that expand horizons and widen perspectives. When measured against the limited experiences of any one individual, the opportunities made possible by television alone represent a vast increase in a person's range of cultural consciousness. Marshall McLuhan's pivotal notion that we now live in a "global village" carries the implication that distance is no longer an impediment in gaining access to a diversity of human actions, attitudes, and tragedies. We can now extend ourselves into the lives of others in ways that were not possible a generation ago.[5] The foreign settings to which we are exposed are as obvious and pervasive: viewing the funeral of a foreign leader, witnessing the final moments of a soldier shot down in a Bosnian village, eavesdropping on a confession of sexual transgressions by a member of Britain's royal family. To be sure, this reality is distinctly secondhand. But its limits do not override the fact that the experience it offers is not of our own making. Media exposure is liberalizing because it places us in frames of reference beyond our own provincial concerns. At the same time, it raises problems about the effects of extending the outward margins of our own experience. We are sometimes the reluctant beneficiaries of scenes and events created dramatically which illuminate features of racism, social custom, religious practice, and cultural tradition.

There is no shortage of analysts who have expressed frustration over "watered down" attempts by the popular media to treat significant social issues, such as various forms of racism (Farley 1996, 66–68). But even commercial television's strongest critics have found examples of entertainment programming that discuss issues that might never surface on the consciousness of some. Writing originally in the *Socialist Review*, Douglas Kellner noted:

Miniseries like *Roots, Holocaust, Captains and Kings, Second Avenue, The Money Changers,* and *Wheels* have dealt with class conflict, racism and anti-Semitism, imperialism, and the oppression of the working class and blacks. They have often sympathetically portrayed the oppressed, poor, minorities, and workers, and presented capitalists and right-wingers as oppressors and exploiters. Docudramas like *Tailgunner Joe, Fear on Trial,* and *King* have criticized Joe McCarthy, J. Edgar Hoover, and the FBI, and vindicated Martin Luther King as well as victims of McCarthyism and FBI persecution in the entertainment industry. (1982, 412)

In the contemporary media climate it would be difficult to avoid exposure to the lives and values of other classes and groups in the United States. Even some of the most innocuous entertainment in the United States tends to be racially and ethnically inclusive, expansive rather than narrow in representations of class, tolerant of political and cultural differences, and optimistic about the young. Arguably, the contact that millions of white Americans have with their African American counterparts is not a result of interactions that occur in their largely segregated suburbs but in their exposure to television's much richer racial mix. Committed nativists who fear or revile this pluralism sometimes retreat to remote corners of America in the apparent hope of escaping it's effects.[6] Most other Americans embrace this diversity, or at least make accommodations to it.

For some—usually on the political right—there is a dark side to the liberalizing influence of pluralistic media. The very pluralism that defines the culture can also appear to undermine it. A common fear expressed by many observers is that the sacred canon of American principles and values has been eroded by an acceptance of ideas foreign to the nation's character. Those responsible for the content of popular culture have been challenged by a newly vibrant right wing of American politics to defend their output in terms of its ostensibly exotic themes: film violence, angry rap music, sympathetic portrayals of gays, hostile portrayals of the police, revisionist views of the life of Christ, attacks on "traditional" gender roles, funding of controversial art, the teaching of afro-centric history, and so on. Writer Allan Bloom (*The Closing of the American Mind* 1988), the American Family Association, former Education Secretary William Bennett (*The Book of Virtues* 1993) and many others have fed an increasingly potent backlash against art and culture that offends because it is appears to be closer to the margins than the center. Never mind that, as Robert Hughes notes, art has always had a valuable tradition of challenging sacred cows (1993, 155–203). For a large cadre of traditionalists, American culture has abandoned its sturdy Judeo-Christian anchors, falling into pit of moral relativism. What progressives observe as multiculturalism, those with more orthodox views see as a collapse of moral authority: a decline in the idea of American exceptionalism (Hunter 1991, 42–44).

Theory of Elite Control

Another important assessment applied to the most pervasive elements of entertainment and popular culture is that they reflect the values and economic interests of an elite power structure, notably a homogeneous alliance of media owners, advertisers, and tastemakers centered on the east and west coasts. In contrast to the traditionalist's fear that these owners have alien agendas, elite theorists (usually but not always on the political left) hold that media content reflects the ideas of a mostly white, male, and affluent class driven by the search for profits.[7] The "domination of our media by corporate profiteers" notes Mark Miller, threatens democracy and the pluralism of media voices that has made the United States the home of a broad "marketplace of ideas" (1996, 10). Fewer owners means fewer real choices, decreasing the chances that unpopular ideas will be expressed. For Miller, the fact that General Electric owns NBC decreases the chances that Tom Brokaw will do stories about the dangers of nuclear power, or that ABC—which is now owned by Disney—will ever do an expose of the entertainment conglomerate's practices (9).

In addition to concerns about corporate size and power, arguments about elite control also note that corporate owners have an inherent bias against raising questions about larger issues or fundamental problems that persist in society. The content they inevitably produce is hegemonic, favoring fantasized remedies to problems rather than political solutions.

This hegemony argument generally runs along the following lines: Most of the nation's media are in the business of selling audiences to advertisers. Media content is constructed as a way to "hook" the attention and interest of audiences. That hook needs to be sufficiently deep to keep restless consumers attentive long enough to see the advertising that is interlaced into media content. Two separate clients thus need to be satisfied. Audiences have to be entertained or informed in a nonthreatening way. And advertisers need to be convinced that the media they are purchasing time or space within fits their corporate objectives. As an ABC vice president put it,

> Program makers are supposed to devise and produce shows that will attract mass audiences without unduly offending these audiences or too deeply moving them emotionally. Such ruffling, it is thought, will interfere with their ability to receive, recall, and respond to the commercial message." (Barnouw 1975, 114)

Since politics involves controversy, and controversy intensifies anxieties, the most stable entertainment—especially on television—is that which is apolitical. But "apolitical" does not mean nonpolitical. Even though most popular entertainment avoids controversial issues and unpopular ideas, that process itself is a political option. The world of prime time opts for what amounts to a subtle deference to most of the segments of the established economic and social order. With some exceptions, this results in depictions of a world where individuals know their place, where order triumphs over disruption and dispute, and "the system" and its subsystems such as the courts, the health care system, schools, and businesses generally work. As David Paletz and Robert Entman note:

> Advertisements and entertainment programs lead viewers away from political awareness. When television characters do exhibit imperfections or experience problems, their misfortunes are linked to bad luck, laziness, ineptitude. The structure of power rarely obtrudes into their lives: economic justice, class, race, or age discrimination, illness caused by the workplace, injuries or industrial pollution—these dilemmas are absent. . . . The implicit lesson is that people are not constrained by the social order. (1981, 182)

With the exception of police dramas, hour-long programs that could deal with socially significant topics are rare.[8] Harmless family and workplace sitcoms tend to dominate prime time. Sitcoms depend on a durable formula of trivial plots and characters who have been depoliticized of everything except a veneer of political correctness. It would be unusual for a continuing series of any type to focus on the grinding effects of poverty on its victims, the severe lifelong struggles of trauma victims, or the discrimination experienced by an immigrant family living in a major city. Films, novels, and occasional television dramas may present such unpleasant images without the closure of a happy ending, but television programs depending on a loyal audience week in and week out generally do not. The popular NBC comedy, "Seinfeld," is perhaps the ultimate apolitical vehicle for advertising. It is "about" virtually nothing. Instead, it stays safely in the realm of a comedy of manners, avoiding plots that would bind its characters to choices with lifelong consequences. Like another favored form of entertainment—professional football—sitcom programming rarely puts itself in competition with its corporate underwriters. Television football interrupts its incessant commercials long enough to squeeze in 10 minutes of actual play on the field (Real 1977, 94–95). The sitcom similarly keeps its fictional world far away from issues that could provoke or alienate.

Elite theory thus flows out of an old view of how the powerful in a society seek to maintain their place within it. Those who have succeeded and been rewarded by the society are naturally going to see little need to change it. In this perspective, elite control of the mass media and its content depends on creating widespread public *quiescence* through programming that entertains and reassures.[9] Harmless and politically neutral content guarantees return visitors to a medium. This same content also increases the likelihood that relatively contented audiences will be delivered to the advertising messages of corporate advertisers.

SUMMARY

In several ways we have been exploring the same essential feature of popular entertainment: the power of the media to offer fantasies that build or sometimes challenge cherished national myths. Films and other forms of narration have political significance by reconstructing important historical settings, political battles, the status of particular groups, and power relationships. These reconstructions often have the effect of deconstructing politics, replacing policies and ideas with exaggerated attention on their advocates.

The fantasy drama—as in Michael Douglas's portrayal of *The American President*, or *Primary Colors'* Governor Jack Stanton—lets us idealize or revise features of our national character. Douglas as President Andrew Shepherd pits his basic decency against the jaded kingpins of Congress and the White House, unlike John Travolta's governor (modeled by author Joe Klien on Bill Clinton), who reflects a competing national fantasy of political expediency behind a thin veneer of idealism.

Themes of honor and dishonor are communicated in museum exhibitions, films, paintings, novels, and prime-time television. Most often these are eulogistic reconstructions of scenes from our civil life. At other times omissions may communicate their own messages, as when a television sitcom implies a political choice by *avoiding* certain topics. In prime time, for example, young women simply do not end unwanted pregnancies through abortion. The avoidance of that subject in our most popular media is itself a reflection of the politicized nature of that decision.

Beyond specific themes in content, two larger forces that influence our popular culture work in different directions. One force is the growing presence of a mediated world that is far more inclusive and cosmopolitan than our individual lives. Print, broadcasting, and their many allied forms serve as a liberalizing force in the consciousness of their consumers. They minimize the possibilities for social and cultural isolation. Even the most commercial of Hollywood's films today effectively undermine racial and ethnic stereotypes that thrived only a generation ago.

The effects of the second force, the media-industry power structure, are less positive. "Elites" that control the nation's major media corporations have the power to control their content. A fear of that power is the basis of elite theory, which triggers worries about how the commercial imperative to avoid alienating audiences may weaken portrayals of the nation's problems.

NOTES

1. Diego Rivera quoted in David E. Pitt, "Retracing Diego Rivera's American Odyssey," *New York Times*, 28 August 1988, p. 29.

2. See, for example, Reagan's flattering comments to the director of the film, "Patton," in Helene Von Damm, *Sincerely, Ronald Regan* (New York: Berkley Books 1980), pp. 19–20.

3. The authors are indebted to the Internet Movie Database [online] for providing background on the films mentioned in this chapter.

4. Reagan's excessive fears are expressed in an early autobiography, *Where's the Rest of Me?* (New York: Karz, 1981), pp. 159–75.

5. See, for example, Joshua Meyrowitz's discussion of this phenomenon in *No Sense of Place* (New York: Oxford University Press, 1985), pp. 35–51.

6. For an interesting study of the rebellion against an increasingly pluralist nation see Philip Weiss, "Off the Grid," *New York Times Magazine*, 8 January 1995, pp. 24–33.

7. For a representative survey of entertainment media from this perspective, see Michael Parenti, *Inventing Reality: The Politics of the Mass Media* (New York: St. Martin's Press, 1986).

8. Most network dramas focus on either police or hospital settings. In recent years police work as portrayed in programs like "N.Y.P.D. Blue" has perhaps been more accurately and continuously portrayed than any other area of American life.

9. The word is drawn from Murray Edelman's landmark analysis of modern political discourse in *The Symbolic Uses of Politics* (Urbana: University of Illinois, 1964), pp. 22–43.

REFERENCES

Barnouw, Erik. 1975. *Tube of Plenty: The Evolution of American Television*. New York: Oxford University Press.

Corliss, Richard. 1996. "The Ladies Who Lunge" [online]. *Time*, 7 October: 1–3.

Dionne, E. J. 1991. *Why Americans Hate Politics*. New York: Simon & Schuster.

Duncan, Hugh D. 1968. *Communication and Social Order*. New York: Oxford University Press.

Edelman, Murray. 1964. *The Symbolic Uses of Politics*. Urbana: University of Illinois.

Farley, Christopher. 1996. "TV's Black Flight." *Time*, 3 June: 66–68.

Goldberg, Robert, and Gerald Goldberg. 1995. *Citizen Turner*. New York: Harcourt Brace.

Hughes, Robert. 1993. *Culture of Complaint: The Frying of America*. New York: Oxford University Press.

Hunter, James D. 1991. *Culture Wars: the Struggle to Define America*. New York: Basic Books.

Kellner, Douglas. 1992. "TV, Ideology, and Emancipatory Popular Culture." In *Television: the Critical View*, 3d ed., ed. Horace Newcomb. New York: Oxford, pp. 386–421.

Kempley, Rita. 1996. " 'First Wives Club:' Out With the Old" [online]. *Washington Post,* 20 September.

Meyrowitz, Joshua. 1985. *No Sense of Place.* New York: Oxford University Press.

Miller, Mark. 1996. "Free the Media." *The Nation,* 3 June: 9–15.

Mitgang, Herbert. 1987. "Annals of Government: Investigating Writers." *The New Yorker,* 5 October: 47–90.

Molotsky, Irvin. 1987. "U.S. Cancels Show in Beijing Over China's Demand to Cut It." *New York Times,* 16 July: C19.

Nimmo, Dan, and James Combs. 1980. *Subliminal Politics: Myths and Mythmakers in America.* Englewood Cliffs, NJ: Prentice-Hall.

———. 1990. *Mediated Political Realities,* 2d ed. New York: Longman.

Paletz, David, and Robert Entman. 1981. *Media Power Politics.* New York: Free Press.

Parenti, Michael. 1986. *Inventing Reality: The Politics of the Mass Media.* New York: St. Martin's Press.

Pitt, David. 1988. "Retracing Diego Rivera's American Odyssey." *New York Times,* 28 August: 29.

Reagan, Ronald. 1981. *Where's the Rest of Me?* New York: Karz.

Real, Michael. 1977. *Mass Mediated Culture.* Englewood Cliffs, NJ: Prentice-Hall.

Rosenberg, Deena. 1984. "A Lost Musical by the Gershwins Makes a Comeback." *New York Times,* 24 June: H4, H13.

Shenon, Philip. 1997. "What's Wrong With this Picture of Women in the Military?" *New York Times,* 31 August: D2.

Sherwin, Martin. 1995. "The Assault on History." *The Nation,* 15 May: 692–94.

Sklar, Robert. 1975. *Movie Made America.* New York: Vintage.

Smith, Dinitia. 1997. "F.B.I. Reveal Little. . . ." *New York Times,* 25 September: E1, E7.

Von Damn, Helene, ed. 1980. *Sincerely, Ronald Reagan.* New York: Berkley Books.

Weinraub, Bernard. 1996. "Hollywood Feels Chill of Chinese Warning to Disney." *New York Times,* 9 December: C11–12.

Weiss, Philip. 1995. "Off the Grid." *New York Times Magazine,* 8 January: 24–33.

Williams, Martin. 1980. *Griffith: First Artist of the Movies.* New York: Oxford University Press.

Wills, Garry. 1997. *John Wayne's America: The Politics of Celebrity.* New York: Simon & Schuster.

Selected Bibliography

Ansolabehere, Stephen et al. 1993. *The Media Game*. New York: Macmillan.

Ansolabehere, Stephen, and Shanto Iyengar. 1995. *Going Negative*. New York: Free Press.

Aristotle. 1954. *Rhetoric*, trans. W. Rhys Roberts. New York: The Modern Library.

Armstrong, Richard. 1988. *The Next Hurrah*. New York: William Morrow.

Arnold, Thurman. 1962. *The Symbols of Government*. New York: Harcourt, Brace and World.

Arterton, F. Christopher. 1978. "Campaign Organizations Confront the Media-Political Environment." In *Race for the Presidency*, ed. James D. Barber. New York: Prentice-Hall, pp. 3–24.

Asher, Herbert. 1980. *Presidential Elections and American Politics*, rev. ed. Homewood, IL: Dorsey Press.

Barber, James David. 1980. *The Pulse of Politics*. New York: Norton.

Barilleaux, Ryan. 1988. *The Post-Modern Presidency*. New York: Praeger.

Barnouw, Erik. 1975. *Tube of Plenty: The Evolution of American Television*. New York: Oxford University Press.

Bartels, Larry. 1989. *Presidential Primaries and the Dynamics of Public Choice*. Princeton, NJ: Princeton University Press.

Baskerville, Barnet. 1979. *The People's Voice*. Lexington: University of Kentucky Press.

Bellah, Robert N., Richard Madsden, William Sullivan, Ann Swidler, and Steven Tipton. 1985. *Habits of the Heart: Individualism and Commitment in American Life*. Berkeley: University of California Press.

Bennett, W. Lance. 1988. *News: The Politics of Illusion*, 2d ed. New York: Longman.

———. 1996. *The Governing Crisis*, 2d ed. New York: St. Martin's Press.

Birnbaum, Jeffrey. 1992. *The Lobbyists*. New York: Times Books.

Bitzer, Lloyd. 1981. "Political Rhetoric." In *Handbook of Political Communication*, ed. Dan D. Nimmo and Keith R. Sanders. Beverly Hills, CA: Sage, pp. 225–48.

Blumenthal, Sidney. 1982. *The Permanent Campaign*, 2d ed. New York: Touchstone Books.

Bormann, Ernest, and Nancy Bormann. 1977. *Speech Communication: A Comprehensive Approach*. New York: Harper & Row.

Boynton, G. R. 1996. "Our Conversations about Governing." In *Political Communication Research*, ed. David Palez. Norwood, NJ: Ablex Publishing, pp. 91–109.

Buchanan, Bruce. 1978. *The Presidential Experience*. Englewood Cliffs, NJ: Prentice-Hall.

Bunzel, John H. 1970. *Anti-Politics in America*. New York: Vintage.

Burke, Kenneth. 1953. *A Rhetoric of Motives*. New York: Prentice-Hall.

———. 1966. *Language as Symbolic Action*. Berkeley: University of California Press.

———. 1967. "Dramatism." In *Communication Concepts and Perspectives*, ed. Lee Thayer. Rochelle Park, NJ: Hayden, pp. 322–55.

Cappella, Joseph N., and Kathleen Hall Jamieson. 1997. *Spiral of Cynicism: The Press and the Public Good*. New York: Oxford University Press.

Cathcart, Robert, and Gary Gumpert. 1986. "Mediated Interpersonal Communication: Toward a New Typology." *Quarterly Journal of Speech* 69: 267–77.

Ceaser, James et al. 1983. "The Rise of the Rhetorical Presidency." In *Essays in Presidential Rhetoric*, ed. Theodore Windt. Dubuque, IA: Kendall/Hunt.

Chagall, David. 1981. *The New King-Makers*. New York: Harcourt Brace Jovanovich.

Charon, Joel. 1979. *Symbolic Interactionism: An Introduction, an Interpretation, an Integration*. Englewood Cliffs, NJ: Prentice-Hall.

Cobb, Roger, and Charles Elder. 1972. "Individual Orientations in the Study of Political Symbolism." *Social Science Quarterly* 53: 82–86.

Collins, Ronald, and David Skover. 1996. *The Death of Discourse*. Boulder, CO: Westview Press.

Combs, James. 1980. *Dimensions of Political Drama*. Santa Monica, CA: Goodyear.

Cook, Timothy. 1989. *Making Laws and Making News*. Washington, DC: Brookings Institution.

Corcoran, Paul E. 1979. *Political Language and Rhetoric*. Austin: University of Texas Press.

———. 1990. "Language and Politics." In *New Directions in Political Communication: A Resource Book*, ed. David Swanson and Dan Nimmo. Newbury Park, CA: Sage pp. 51–85.

Corrado, Anthony. 1997. "Financing the 1996 Elections." In *The Election of 1996*, ed. Gerald Pomper et al. Chatham, NJ: Chatham House, pp. 135–71.

Corwin, Edward S. 1948. *The President: Office and Powers*, 3d ed. New York: New York University Press.

Craig, Stephen C. 1996. *Broken Contract? Changing Relationships between Americans and Their Governments*. Boulder, CO: Westview Press.

Cronin, Thomas. 1975. *The State of the Presidency*. Boston: Little, Brown.

Crouse, Timothy. 1972. *The Boys on the Bus*. New York: Ballantine.

DeFleur, Melvin, and Everette Dennis. 1996. *Understanding Mass Communication*, 1996 ed. Boston: Houghton Mifflin.

Denton, Robert E., Jr. 1988. *The Primetime Presidency of Ronald Reagan*. New York: Praeger.

———. 1982. *The Symbolic Dimensions of the American Presidency*. Prospect Heights, IL: Waveland Press.

Denton, Robert E., Jr., and Rachel L. Holloway. 1995. "Presidential Communication as Mediated Conversation." In *Research in Political Sociology*, vol. 7. New York: JAI Press, pp. 91–115.

———. 1996. "Clinton and the Town Hall Meetings: Mediated Conversation and the Risk of Being 'In Touch.' " In *The Clinton Presidency: Images, Issues, and Communication Strategies*, ed. Robert E. Denton, Jr., and Rachel L. Holloway. Wesport, CT: Praeger, pp. 17–41.

Devlin, Patrick. 1986. "An Analysis of Presidential Television Commercials: 1952–1984." In *New Perspectives on Political Advertising*, ed. Lynda Kaid, Dan Nimmo, and Keith Sanders. Carbondale: Southern Illinois University Press, pp. 21–54.

———. 1997. "Contrast in Presidential Campaign Commercials of 1996." *American Behavioral Scientist* 40(8): 1058–84.

Dewey, John. 1954. *The Public and Its Problems*. Chicago: Swallow Press.

Diamond, Edward, and Kathleen Friery. 1987. "Media Coverage of Presidential Debates." In *Presidential Debates*, ed. Joel Swerdlow. Washington, DC: Congressional Quarterly Press, pp. 43–51.

Diamond, Edwin. 1995. *Behind the Times*. Chicago: University of Chicago Press.

Diamond, Edwin, and Stephen Bates. 1984. *The Spot*. Cambridge, MA: MIT Press.

DiClerico, Robert E., and Eric Uslaner. 1984. *Few Are Chosen: Problems in Presidential Selection*. New York: McGraw-Hill.

Dionne, E. J. 1991. *Why Americans Hate Politics*. New York: Simon & Schuster.

Duncan, Hugh D. 1968. *Communication and Social Order*. New York: Oxford University Press.

———. 1968. *Symbols in Society*. New York: Oxford University Press.

Easton, David. 1965. *A Systems Analysis of Political Life*. New York: John Wiley and Sons.

Edelman, Murray. 1964. *The Symbolic Uses of Politics*. Urbana: University of Illinois Press.

———. 1971. *Politics as Symbolic Action*. Chicago: Markham Publishing.

Edwards, George. 1983. *The Public Presidency*. New York: St. Martin's Press.

Edwards, George C., and Stephen Wayne. 1990. *Presidential Leadership: Politics and Policy Making*, 2d ed. New York: St. Martin's Press.

Elshtain, Jean. 1989. "Issues and Themes in the 1988 Campaign." *In The Elections of 1988*, ed. Michael Nelson. Washington, DC: Congressional Quarterly Press, pp. 111–26.

Entman, Robert M. 1989. *Democracy without Citizens*. New York: Oxford University Press.

Epstein, Edward. 1974. *News from Nowhere*. New York: Vintage.

Epstein, Lee. 1995. *Contemplating Courts*. Washington, DC: Congressional Quarterly Press.

Fallows, James. 1996. *Breaking the News*. New York: Pantheon.

Faules, Don, and Dennis Alexander. 1979. *Communication and Social Behavior*. Boston: Addison-Wesley.

Felton, Keith S. 1995. *Warrior's Words: A Consideration of Language and Leadership*. Westport, CT: Praeger.

Fenno, Richard. 1978. *Home Style: House Members in Their Districts*. Boston: Little, Brown.

Ferrarotti, Franco. 1988. *The End of Conversation*. Westport, CT: Greenwood Press.

Fisher, Walter. 1982. "Romantic Democracy, Ronald Reagan, and Presidential Heroes." *The Western Journal of Speech Communication* 46 (Summer): 299–310.

Fox, Harrison W., Jr., and Susan Webb Hammond. 1977. *Congressional Staffs: The Invisible Force in American Lawmaking*. New York: Free Press.

Friedenberg, Robert. 1994. "The 1992 Presidential Debates." In *The 1992 Presidential Campaign: From a Communication Perspective*, ed. Robert E. Denton, Jr. Westport, CT: Praeger, pp. 89–110.

———. 1997. *Communication Consultants in Political Campaigns*. Westport, CT: Praeger.

———. 1998. "The 1996 Presidential Debates." In *The 1996 Presidential Campaign: From a Communication Perspective*, ed. Robert E. Denton, Jr. Westport, CT: Praeger, pp. 101–22.

Fukuyama, Francis. 1995. *Trust: The Social Virtues and the Creation of Prosperity*. New York: Free Press.

Gans, Herbert. 1980. *Deciding What's News*. New York: Vintage.

Garment, Leonard. 1997. *Crazy Rhythm*. New York: Times Books.

Ginsberg, Benjamin. 1986. *The Captive Public*. New York: Basic Books.

Gitlin, Todd. 1980. *The Whole World Is Watching*. Berkeley: University of California Press.

———. 1995. *The Twilight of Common Dreams*. New York: Metropolitan Books.

Goldberg, Robert, and Gerald Goldberg. 1995. *Citizen Turner*. New York: Harcourt Brace.

Goldenberg, Edie, and Michael Traugott. 1984. *Campaigning for Congress*. Washington, DC: Congressional Quarterly Press.

Graber, Doris. 1981. "Political Languages." In *Handbook of Political Communication*, ed. Dan D. Nimmo and Keith R. Sanders. Beverly Hills, CA: Sage, pp. 195–224.

———. 1984. *Processing the News*. New York: Longman.

———. 1993. *Mass Media and American Politics*, 4th ed. Washington, DC: Congressional Quarterly Press.

Gronbeck, Bruce. 1986. "Ronald Reagan's Enactment of the Presidency in His 1981 Inaugural Address." In *Form, Genre and the Study of Political Discourse*, ed. Herbert Simons and Aron Aghazarion. Columbia: University of South Carolina Press, pp. 226–45.

Grossman, Michael, and Martha Kumar. 1981. *Portraying the President: The White House and the News Media*. Baltimore: Johns Hopkins University Press.

Hacker, Kenneth. 1995. *Candidate Images in Presidential Elections*. Westport, CT: Praeger.

———. 1996. "Political Linguistic Discourse Analysis." In *The Theory and Practice of Political Communication Research*, ed. Mary Stuckey. Albany: State University of New York Press, pp. 28–55.

Hall, Peter. 1972. "A Symbolic Interactionist Analysis of Politics." *Sociological Inquiry* 42: 35–73.

Harr, Jonathan. 1995. *A Civil Action*. New York: Vintage.

Hart, Roderick. 1984. *Verbal Style and the Presidency*. New York: Academic Press.

———. 1987. *Sounds of Leadership*. Chicago: University of Chicago Press.

———. 1994. *Seducing America*. New York: Oxford University Press.

Hellweg, Susan et al. 1992. *Televised Presidential Debates*. Westport, CT: Praeger.

Herrnson, Paul S. 1998. *Congressional Elections*, 2d ed. Washington, DC: Congressional Quarterly Press.

Hertsgaard, Mark. 1989. *On Bended Knee: The Press and the Reagan Presidency*. New York: Shocken.

Herzik, Eric. 1985. "The President, Governors and Mayors: A Framework for Comparative Analysis." *Presidential Studies Quarterly* 15(2): 354.

Hess, Stephen. 1986. *The Ultimate Insiders: U.S. Senators in the National Media*. Washington, DC: Brookings Institution.

Hickok, Eugene, and Gary McDowell. 1993. *Justice vs. Law: Courts and Politics in American Society*. New York: Free Press.

Hodgson, Godfrey. 1980. *All Things to All Men*. New York: Touchstone Books.

Holloway, Rachel. 1998. "Clinton's Rhetoric of Conjoined Values." In *The 1996 Presidential Campaign: A Communication Perspective*, ed., Robert E. Denton, Jr. Westport, CT: Praeger, pp. 123–41.

Hughes, Emmet J. 1972. *The Living Presidency*. New York: Penguin Books.

Hughes, Robert. 1993. *Culture of Complaint: The Fraying of America*. New York: Oxford University Press.

Hunter, James D. 1991. *Culture Wars: The Struggle to Define America*. New York: Basic Books.

Iyengar, Shanto, and Donald R. Kinder. 1987. *News That Matters*. Chicago: University of Chicago Press.

Jamieson, Kathleen H. 1988. *Eloquence in an Electronic Age*. New York: Oxford University Press.

Jamieson, Kathleen Hall, and David Birdsell. 1988. *Presidential Debates*. New York: Oxford University Press.

Johnson-Cartee, Karen, and Gary Copeland. 1997. *Inside Political Campaigns*. Westport, CT: Praeger.

Just, Marion. 1996. "Candidate Strategies and the Media Campaign." In *The Election of 1996*, ed. Gerald Pomper. Chatham, NJ: Chatham House, pp. 77–106.

Kaid, Lynda. 1998. "Videostyle and the Effects of the 1996 Presidential Campaign Advertising." In *The 1996 Presidential Campaign: A Communication Perspective*, ed. Robert E. Denton, Jr. Westport, CT: Praeger, pp. 143–60.

Kaid, Lynda, and Dorothy Davidson. 1986. "Elements of Videostyle." *In New Perspectives on Political Advertising*, ed. Lynda Kaid, Dan Nimmo, and Keith Sanders. Carbondale: Southern Illinois University Press, pp. 184–209.

Keeter, Scott, and Cliff Zukin. 1983. *Uninformed Choice*. New York: Praeger.

Kellerman, Barbara. 1984. *The Political Presidency*. New York: Oxford University Press.

Kerbel, Matthew. 1994. *Edited for Television*. Boulder, CO: Westview Press.

Kernell, Samuel. 1985. *Going Public: New Strategies of Presidential Leadership*. Washington, DC: Congressional Quarterly Press.

Kessel, John. 1988. *Presidential Campaign Politics: Coalition Strategies and Citizen Response*. Chicago: Dorsey.

Kimball, Penn. 1994. *Downsizing the News*. Baltimore: Johns Hopkins/Woodrow Wilson Center Press.

Klapp, Orrin. 1964. *Symbolic Leaders*. Chicago: Aldine Publishing.

Klein, Joe. 1992. "The Bill Clinton Show." *Newsweek*, 26 October: 35.

Ladd, Everett, and John Benson. 1992. "The Growth of News Polls in American Politics." In *Media Polls in American Politics*, ed. Thomas Mann and Gary Orren. Washington, DC: Brookings Institution, pp. 19–31.

Lasswell, Harold. 1930. *Psychopathology and Politics*. Chicago: University of Chicago Press.

———. 1962. *Power and Personality*. New York: Viking.

Lewis-Beck, Michael, and Tom Rice. 1992. *Forecasting Elections*. Washington, DC: Congressional Quarterly Press.

Lichter, S. Robert et al. 1988. *The Video Campaign: Network Coverage of the 1988 Primaries*. Lanham, MD: American Enterprise Institute.

Lippmann, Walter. 1930. *Public Opinion*. New York: Macmillan.

Lorenzo, David. 1996. "Political Communication and the Study of Rhetoric." In *The Theory and Practice of Political Communication Research*, ed. Mary Stuckey. Albany: State University of New York Press, pp. 1–27.

Lowi, Theodore. J. 1985. *The Personal President: Power Invested, Promise Unfulfilled*. Ithaca, NY: Cornell University Press.

MacNeil, Robert. 1968. *The People Machine*. New York: Harper and Row.

Makinson, Larry, and Joshua Goldstein. 1994. *Open Secrets*, 3d ed. Washington, DC: Congressional Quarterly.

Maltese, John. 1992. *Spin Control*. Chapel Hill: University of North Carolina Press.

Mann, Thomas, and Norman Ornstein. 1994. *Congress, the Press, and the Public*. Washington, DC: American Enterprise Institute/Brookings.

Maraniss, David. 1995. *First in His Class*. New York: Touchstone Books.

Martel, Myles. 1983. *Political Campaign Debates*. New York: Longman.

Matalin, Mary, and James Carville. 1994. *All's Fair*. New York: Random House/Touchstone.

Mauser, Gary. 1983. *Political Marketing: An Approach to Campaign Strategy*. New York: Praeger.

McCartney, Laton. 1988. *Friends in High Places*. New York: Simon & Schuster.

McConnell, Grant. 1976. *The Modern Presidency*. New York: St. Martin's Press.

McDonald, Forrest. 1975. *The Presidency of George Washington*. New York: Norton.

McGinniss, Joe. 1969. *The Selling of the President: 1968*. New York: Trident Press.

McGraw, Kathleen, and Milton Lodge. 1996. "Political Information Processing: A Review Essay." *Political Communication* 13: 131–42.

McNair, Brian. 1995. *An Introduction to Political Communication*. London: Rutledge.

Mead, George H. 1972. *Mind, Self, and Society*. Chicago: University of Chicago Press.

Merton, Robert. 1968. *Social Theory and Social Structure*. New York: Free Press, pp. 73–138.

Meyrowitz, Joshua. 1985. *No Sense of Place*. New York: Oxford University Press.

Mikva, Abner, and Patti Harris. 1983. *The American Congress: The First Branch*. New York: Franklin Watts.

Morris, Dick. 1997. *Behind the Oval Office*. New York: Random House.

Mueller, Claus. 1973. *The Politics of Communication*. New York: Oxford University Press.

Mullen, William. 1976. *Presidential Power and Politics*. New York: St. Martin's Press.

Newman, Bruce. 1994. *Marketing of the President*. Thousand Oaks, CA: Sage.

Nimmo, Dan. 1970. *The Political Persuaders*. Englewood Cliffs, NJ: Spectrum Books.

———. 1978. *Political Communication and Public Opinion in America*. Palo Alto, CA: Goodyear.

Nimmo, Dan, and James Combs. 1980. *Subliminal Politics: Myths and Mythmakers in America*. Englewood Cliffs, NJ: Prentice-Hall.

Nimmo, Dan, and James Combs. 1990. *Mediated Political Realities*, 2d ed. New York: Longman.

Nimmo, Dan, and Keith Sanders. 1981. *Handbook of Political Communication*. Beverly Hills, CA: Sage.

Novak, Michael. 1974. *Choosing Our King*. New York: Macmillan.

Osborn, Michael. 1986. "Rhetorical Depiction." In *Form Genre and the Study of Political Discourse*, ed. Herbert Simons and Aron Aghazarion. Columbia: University of South Carolina Press, pp. 79–107.

Owen, Diana. 1991. *Media Messages in American Presidential Campaigns*. Westport, CT: Greenwood Press.

———. 1997. "The Press' Performance." In *Toward the Millennium: The Elections of 1996*, ed. Larry Sabato. Boston: Allyn and Bacon, pp. 205–21.

Paletz, David, and Robert Entman. 1981. *Media Power Politics*. New York: Free Press.

Parenti, Michael. 1986. *Inventing Reality: The Politics of the Mass Media*. New York: St. Martin's Press.

Patterson, Thomas. 1994. *Out of Order*. New York: Vintage.

Perelman, Chaim, and L. Olbrechts-Tyteca. 1969. *The New Rhetoric*, trans. John Wilkinson and Purcell Weaver. Notre Dame, IN: University of Notre Dame Press.

Perloff, Richard. 1998. *Political Communication*. Mahwah, NJ: Lawrence Earlbaum.

Pfau, Michael, and Henry Kenski. 1990. *Attack Politics: Strategy and Defense*. Westport, CT: Praeger.

Pfau, Michael, and Jong Kang. 1991. "The Impact of Relational Messages on Candidate Influence in Televised Political Debates." *Communication Studies* 42(2): 114–28.

Phillips, Kevin. 1979. *Mediacracy*. New York: Doubleday.

Pious, Richard. 1979. *The American Presidency*. New York: Basic Books.

Polsby, Nelson W., and Aaron Wildavsky. 1980. *Presidential Elections: Contemporary Strategies of American Electoral Politics*, 7th ed. New York: Free Press.

Postman, Neil. 1985. *Amusing Ourselves to Death: Public Discourse in the Age of Show Business*. New York: Penguin.

Powell, Jody. 1984. *The Other Side of the Story*. New York: Morrow.

Price, David. 1992. *The Congressional Experience*. Boulder, CO: Westview Press.

Ratzan, Scott. 1989. "The Real Agenda Setters." *American Behavioral Scientist* 37(2) (November/December): 451–63.

Reedy, George. 1970. *The Twilight of the Presidency*. New York: World.

Ricci, David. 1993. *The Transformation of American Politics*. New Haven, CT: Yale University Press.

Richards, I. A. 1965. *Philosophy of Rhetoric*. New York: Oxford University Press.

Rivers, William. 1982. *The Other Government: Power and the Washington Media*. New York: Universe.

Rockman, Bert. 1984. *The Leadership Question*. New York: Praeger.

Rose, Richard. 1970. *People in Politics: Observations Across the Atlantic*. New York: Basic Books.

Rosenstiel, Tom. 1993. *Strange Bedfellows*. New York: Hyperion.

Rossiter, Clinton. 1962. *The American Presidency*. New York: Mentor Books.

Sabato, Larry. 1981. *The Rise of Political Consultants*. New York: Basic Books.

———. 1993. *Feeding Frenzy*. New York: Free Press.

Schram, Martin. 1987. *The Great American Video Game*. New York: William Morrow & Co.

Schram, Sanford. 1991. "The Post-Modern Presidency and the Grammar of Electronic Engineering." *Critical Studies in Mass Communication* 8: 210–16.

Schudson, Michael. 1995. *The Power of News*. Cambridge, MA: Harvard University Press.

Selnow, Gary. 1991. "Polls and Computer Technologies: Ethical Considerations." In *Ethical Dimensions of Political Communication*, ed. Robert E. Denton, Jr. New York: Praeger, pp. 171–98.

Sennett, Richard. 1978. *The Fall of Public Man*. New York: Vintage.

Shea, Daniel. 1996. *Campaign Craft: The Strategies, Tactics, and Art of Campaign Management*. Westport, CT: Praeger.

Sklar, Robert. 1975. *Movie Made America*. New York: Vintage.

Smith, Carolyn. 1990. *Presidential Press Conferences*. Westport, CT: Praeger.

Smith, Craig Allen. 1990. *Political Communication*. San Diego: Harcourt Brace Jovanovich.

Smith, Craig A., and Kathy Smith. 1994. *The White House Speaks*. Westport, CT: Praeger.

Smith, Hedrick. 1988. *The Power Game: How Washington Works*. New York: Random House.

Smoller, Fredric. 1990. *The Six O'Clock Presidency*. New York: Praeger.

Stoler, Peter. 1986. *The War Against the Press*. New York: Dodd and Mead.

Swanson, David, and Dan Nimmo, eds. 1990. *New Directions in Political Communication: A Resource Book*. Newbury Park, CA: Sage.

Tedford, Thomas. 1993. *Freedom of Speech in the United States*, 2d ed. New York: McGraw-Hill.

Thaler, Paul. 1994. *The Watchful Eye: American Justice in the Age of the Television Trial*. New York: Praeger.

Tolchin, Susan. 1996. *The Angry American*. Boulder, CO: Westview Press.

Traugott, Michael. 1992. "The Impact of Media Polls on the Public." In *Media Polls in American Politics*, ed. Thomas Mann and Gary Orren. Washington, DC: Brookings Institution, pp. 125–49.

Trent, Judith. 1978. "Presidential Surfacing: The Ritualistic and Crucial First Act." *Communication Monographs* 45: 281–92.

Trent, Judith, and Robert Friedenberg. 1995. *Political Campaign Communication*, 3d ed. New York: Praeger.

Waldman, Steven. 1995. *The Bill*, rev. and updated ed. New York: Penguin.

Walsh, Edward. 1992. "The More Seed Money, the Better the Harvest." In *The Quest for National Office*, ed. Stephen Wayne and Clyde Wilcox. New York: St. Martin's Press, pp. 50–56.

Wayne, Stephen. 1992. *The Road to the White House 1992*. New York: St. Martin's Press.

Weaver, Richard. 1953. *The Ethics of Rhetoric*. Chicago: Henry Regnery.

White, Theodore. 1973. *The Making of the President, 1972*. New York: Atheneum.

Whiteman, David. 1995. *Communication in Congress: Members, Staff, and the Search for Information*. Lawrence: University of Kansas Press.

Wills, Garry. 1997. *John Wayne's America: The Politics of Celebrity*. New York: Simon & Schuster.

Wolpe, Bruce C. 1990. *Lobbying Congress: How the System Works*. Washington, DC: Congressional Quarterly.

Woodward, Bob. 1996. *The Choice*. New York: Simon & Schuster.

Woodward, Bob, and Carl Bernstein. 1974. *All the President's Men*. New York: Simon & Schuster.

Woodward, Bob, and Scott Armstrong. 1979. *The Brethren: Inside the Supreme Court*. New York: Simon & Schuster.

Woodward, Gary. 1990. *Persuasive Encounters: Case Studies in Constructive Confrontation*. New York: Praeger.

———. 1997. *Perspectives on American Political Media*. Boston: Allyn and Bacon.

Zelensny, John. 1997. *Communications Law*, 2d ed. Belmont, CA: Wadsworth.

Index

About the Authors

ROBERT E. DENTON, JR. holds the W. Thomas Rice Chair of Leadership Studies and serves as Director of the Virginia Tech Corps of Cadets Center for Leader Development at Virginia Polytechnic Institute and State University. He has degrees in political science and communication studies from Wake Forest University and Purdue University. In addition to numerous articles, he is author, co-author, or editor of eleven books. Recent works include *Studies in Media and the Gulf War* (Praeger), *The Clinton Presidency: Images, Issues, and Communication Strategies* (with Rachel Holloway) (Praeger) and *The 1996 Presidential Campaign: A Communication Perspective* (Praeger). Denton serves as editor for the Praeger Series in Political Communication and Presidential Studies.

GARY C. WOODWARD is a Professor in the Department of Communication Studies at the College of New Jersey. He has degrees in communication and rhetorical theory from California State University at Sacramento and the University of Pittsburgh. Woodward is the author of *Persuasive Encounters* (Praeger) and *Perspectives on American Political Media* and is co-author of *Persuasion and Influence in American Life*. In addition, Woodward has published numerous articles and book chapters in the areas of communication and rhetorical theory.

ISBN 0-275-95782-9
90000>
EAN
9 780275 957827
HARDCOVER BAR CODE